COOL

MUSIC VIDEOS FROM SOUNDIES TO CELLPHONES

Roger Beebe and Jason Middleton, editors

© 2007 Duke University Press
All rights reserved
Printed in the United States of America on acid-free paper ⊗
Designed by Jennifer Hill
Typeset in Chaparral Pro by Tseng Information Systems, Inc.
Library of Congress Cataloging-in-Publication Data
appear on the last printed page of this book.

CONTENTS

Jason Middleton and Roger Beebe

n recent years it has become common to lament the disappearance
of music videos from MTV. Over a decade ago Andrew Goodwin had
already noted in his *Dancing in the Distraction Factory* that MTV was
increasingly moving toward familiar televisual programming schedules and further from a simple "radio with images," the twenty-four-hour
flow of videos that it seemed at first to be. In the decade since Goodwin's
landmark text, MTV has only moved further in the direction that Goodwin describes, thereby confining (or condemning) music video to very
specific programming slots, often in the "dead" parts of the daily schedule. In fact, by 2004 MTV even finally acknowledged its abandonment of
music video. That year saw the release of a series of ads for MTV2, one of
the Viacom-owned sister networks of the music television pioneer, that
proclaimed "MTV2: Where the music's at," thus conceding implicitly that
MTV was no longer *music* television.[1] Ironically enough, within months
of this ad campaign, MTV2 itself abandoned its all-video format, instead
opting to devote a substantial portion of its daily schedule to rerunning
programs from MTV.

Faced with such evidence of the disappearance of music video from
the regular line-up of MTV, it would at first glance seem strange to foist
on the world a new collection of writing about music video. If music video
is indeed disappearing from M[usic]T[ele]V[ision], then why turn our attention to it once again?

Simply put, music video has in no way disappeared. While MTV has
increasingly focused on the TV over the M, music video has in actual-
ity concurrently enjoyed a major renaissance by circulating in a number
of other places and other media. While MTV may not program twenty-
four hours of video a day, when we look at the amount of music video on

all television stations — MTV, MTV2, Video Hits 1 (VH1), Fuse (formerly MuchMusic USA), Black Entertainment Television (BET), Country Music Television (CMT), not to mention the Digital Suite, a package of thirteen digital channels from MTV Networks including MTV Hits, MTV Jams, MTV Español, VH1 Classic, VH1 Hits, VH1 Soul, and VH1 Country — we cannot avoid the conclusion that there are, in fact, many, many more hours of music television available now than ever before, even if MTV itself has moved away from video as the staple of its programming. And while we might be encouraged by MTV to confuse MTV and "music television," it seems that such confusion is no longer justified, if indeed it ever was. In fact, the separation of MTV from music television is one of the primary goals of this collection. While previous music video scholarship has always conflated the network with the format, this collection insists on the difference between MTV and the broader array of music television(s).

We might also note that this lament about the "death of music video" centered on the United States is further undermined by taking even a quick glance around the world at the various music televisions springing up in almost every corner of the globe. In Italy, for example, a similar proliferation of music television channels can be seen; Italian viewers can get their video fix on MTV Italia, MTV Brand New, MTV Hits Italia, Match Music TV, Deejay TV, Music Box Italia, Video Italia, and Rock TV through Rupert Murdoch's SKY satellite television service as well as on other channels delivered through local providers like Napoli Music, IMC (the Italian Music Channel), and Hit Channel. Faced with such observations (which could easily be repeated from country to country and continent to continent), the claim that music television has come and gone seems even more untenable.

But this is only part of the picture, as we want also to insist on the perhaps even more neglected difference between music television and music video as a form that can be disseminated through media other than television. As important as the proliferation of channels that devote a substantial part of their programming days to music video may be, equally important is the proliferation of other media venues for watching music video. Music videos have started showing up in forms that belie the confusion of music video (as a form) and music television (as a delivery technology for that form): music videos now come to us on DVDs and enhanced CDs; on PDAs, cell phones, and other wireless communication

JASON MIDDLETON AND ROGER BEEBE

devices; and, perhaps most importantly, on the Internet. In this new millennium nearly every band seems to have a Web site, and vast numbers of these sites are home to music videos. Every record label—from indies like K Records and Matador to the music arms of multinational corporations like Arista—features videos on its site, where they almost always are promoted on the front pages. And MTV has gotten into the act, too, with its high-traffic Web site featuring literally thousands of video clips. There are dozens upon dozens of other sites— including Launch.com (now part of Yahoo!), sonicnet.com (now owned by Viacom and branded by VH1), and Rollingstone.com—that offer access to music videos in which a model is used similar to the MTV online model with videos as part of a broad array of music information. The increasing availability of broadband coupled with the difficulty of streaming longer videos through the current Internet technology has been a real boon for short films and videos generally, and the vast storehouse of music video has frequently been called upon to provide content for streaming or quick downloads. Given the rapid development of technology, music video has seen a tremendous explosion beyond the narrow limits of "music television."

These three changes—the proliferation of multiple niche-based cable and satellite channels showing music videos, the explosion of music video production and programming globally, and the advent of alternative technologies for the dissemination of music video—set the stage for this collection. Together these changes demonstrate a significant transformation in the culture of music video from that in which the extant body of scholarship on the form emerged.

This collection's title is, of course, derived from the title of Haskell Wexler's 1969 film, which is itself derived from concepts elaborated in Marshall McLuhan's famous essay "Media Hot and Cold." The phrase carries a deliberately polysemic quality when recontextualized as the title for a new collection on music video. It points to the "cooling," described above, of the relationship between music video and television as video has proliferated into other exhibition and display formats. Music video itself would have been considered by McLuhan a very "cool" media form, in that its generally fragmentary and incomplete narrative structures compel the viewer toward a greater interaction with the text, filling in the gaps him or herself. But its current dissemination on the Web takes us even further in this direction of interactivity, suggesting that a media form which has always positioned itself as "cool" in the terms of the popular vernacular, that is, at the forefront of youth-cultural trends, is also ideally suited to the overall "cooling" effect of the contemporary digital mediascape.

So what, then, do we as the authors of this collection take as our task in this historical and cultural moment? To begin, we revisit, revise, and sometimes reimagine the existing scholarship on music video (most of which is more than a decade old now) by providing both historically and theoretically expansive perspectives on our understanding of music video as a cultural form. Over the past decade, the first wave of writing on music video from the late 1980s and early 1990s has transformed into a canon for teaching and scholarship. This canon includes Andrew Goodwin's *Dancing in the Distraction Factory*; the collection *Sound and Vision: The Music Video Reader* edited by Goodwin along with Simon Frith and Lawrence Grossberg; E. Ann Kaplan's *Rocking around the Clock*; and Lisa Lewis's *Gender Politics and MTV*. Kaplan's book sought to demarcate the specificities of the forms of spectatorship constructed by music video and the televisual apparatus that it embodies, casting MTV as an almost pure realization of Raymond Williams's notion of television as "total flow" that decenters and fragments the subject position of the viewer. The other works in this group attempted to rethink Kaplan's earlier study by looking more closely at the programming structure, textual strategies, and historical context of MTV, but they remained largely within the boundaries of debate established by Kaplan's book.

This volume works in several ways toward expanding both the theoretical scope and the range of objects addressed by the canonical works as noted above. Most of the essays in the collection address in some way this earlier work—pointing to what we may still find valuable, demarcating its limitations, and proposing new theoretical models. Several of the essays specifically seek to provide new frameworks for understanding the problematics of the music video *form*, a challenging endeavor that has caused many previous scholars to resort to models of narrative derived from film and television studies. The authors in this collection seek not only to be theoretically expansive but also to develop a broader historical perspective that accounts for both the current state of music video production and dissemination (with the proliferation of music video channels and the abandonment of music video by some of the traditional outlets noted above) and the neglected prehistory of music video (that is, articulations of "music" and "video"—as well as "music" and "television"—prior to the advent both of MTV and of the modern music video clip). Through this renewed attention to the form and the cultural situation of music video, we hope to reinvigorate the earlier lively debates that developed during the first wave of writing on music video and to demonstrate that it remains a germane and largely unexplored terrain for further investigation.

The study of music video, even during the initial period of relative productivity on the part of scholars, has remained a marginal subfield within television studies. In its efforts to demarcate itself from the study of cinema, television studies has developed rich theoretical tools and paradigms specific to the medium. But much of this rigorous theorization has been lost on the music video form. One difficulty in music video studies in relation to television studies is the fact that theorists of the visual are often not trained in musical analysis and perhaps are not even particularly familiar with or interested in popular music itself. Music video has been approached by scholars working within the loosely defined field of "popular music studies,"[2] but this work has also foundered on the lack of theoretical frameworks adequate to an accounting of the (tele)visual. At the moments when music video is discussed in the field of popular music studies, it is generally addressed within the frameworks of the British cultural studies tradition and of audience-oriented reception theories. Such work, focused overwhelmingly on the oeuvre of Madonna, has tended primarily to explore questions of identification and resistance among music video fans.

Despite the intersections with the field of television studies, then, popular music studies has tended to operate according to fairly different, more sociological, models, including industry practice analysis and star studies along with those mentioned above. Television studies has, on the contrary, broadly engaged with major theoretical frameworks that initially were oriented toward literary and film studies. This engagement is attested to by the collection *Channels of Discourse* (and its more recent update, *Channels of Discourse, Reassembled*), a teaching-oriented volume that brings in prominent scholars to provide overviews of the bodies of scholarship on Marxism, feminism, psychoanalysis, postmodernism, and so on as they relate to television. An equivalent theoretical primer that would substitute "popular music" for "television" would be difficult to imagine based upon the extant scholarship. And, as Lawrence Grossberg has argued, popular music studies has yet to develop its own particular theoretical tools and concepts in the way that film studies, and subsequently television studies, have done.[3]

It should also be noted that the major collections on sound such as Rick Altman's *Sound Theory/Sound Practice* neglect television and the televisual, while, conversely, the major collections on television such as *Channels of Discourse*, Horace Newcomb's *Television: The Critical View*, and Patricia Mellencamp's *Logics of Television* contain no articles focused on sound. Altman's important essay "Television/Sound" is perhaps an exception to this rule, but the essay itself is focused on the way sound works to lure the viewer to the image in domestic television reception rather than on a specific analysis of the way sound and image interact when the viewer is already focused on the screen.[4] The very idea of theorizing the sound/image relation seems at this point largely to have been the province of film studies and of the small body of scholarship outlined above on music video.

Although this first wave of writings on music video is important, it has also proven to be both limited and limiting for those who wish to continue to explore music video's form and the evolving formats of its presentation. One problem with the current canonicity of this work is that the small amount of subsequent scholarship on music video that has emerged has relied upon these initial models by picking and choosing theoretical bases from among the established positions rather than developing new theories, or, perhaps more importantly, constructing challenges to and disruptions of the existing ones. Thus, while Kaplan in her book draws extensively from major theorists such as Fredric Jameson, Jacques Lacan, and Jean Baudrillard, subsequent considerations of music video in relation to questions of postmodernism or psychoanalytic accounts of spectatorship have often been of a second order; that is, interpreting videos through (or against) Kaplan's interpretation of these theorists.

This book seeks to redress this apparent standstill in the theorization of music video by offering new and innovative models for analysis. Many of the essays in the collection engage with the extant body of music video scholarship, but rather than simply using this scholarship as a framework for their discussions, the authors are concerned with identifying and working through its limitations in order to break new ground. Kay Dickinson's essay, "Music Video and Synaesthetic Possibility," takes as a point of departure the Kaplan/Goodwin debates and attempts to break the theoretical deadlock based in each theorist's respective emphasis on either the visuals or the music. In elaborating upon definitions of synaesthesia in neuropsychology (via a detour through the work of theorists such as Jacques Derrida and Gilles Deleuze and Félix Guattari), Dickinson proposes this concept as a means of tracking down the points where meanings cross over from music to image and how they might open up (or close down) certain political possibilities.

Other essays in this collection also present innovative attempts to theorize the sound/image relation and to develop new models of reception that rework the visually circumscribed concept of the "spectator." Michel Chion's book *Audio-Vision* has offered some compelling leads toward such efforts — leads that seem to have been somewhat ignored prior to this collection. Amy Herzog's contribution, "Illustrating Music: The Impossible Embodiments of the Jukebox Film," examines two types of short musical films viewed in "musical jukeboxes" of the 1940s and 1960s in order to reconsider contemporary understandings of the televisual apparatus. By developing the theoretical concepts established by Chion, Herzog explores the ways in which these forms indicate the potential for a new kind of musical image, one that is distinct from the musical images of the big screen of their day and that seems driven by a purely musical logic. Jason Middleton's essay, "The Audio-Vision of Found-Footage Film and Video," examines Bruce Conner's 1969 experimental film *Permian Strata* alongside the cultural practice of the substitution of Pink Floyd's 1973 album *The Dark Side of the Moon* for the soundtrack of *The Wizard of Oz* (1939). In so doing Middleton argues that these audiovisual objects allow us to theorize a dialectical sound-image relation that is not adequately accounted for in the existing scholarship on film music and music video, one that perhaps more fully realizes Chion's concept of "audio-vision" than either of these forms. The analysis of this form of audio-vision leads him to a new theorization of the sound-image relation in music videos that are characterized by a linear narrative structure.

While most of the essays in the collection involve a formal analysis of music video styles and structures, two essays in particular are concerned with exploring the issues related to video form. Maureen Turim's essay, "Art/Music/Video.com," considers videos that reference twentieth-century art movements such as Dadaism, surrealism, and video performance art in an effort to break away from established music video norms in the relationship between sound and image. The essay develops a reading of the complex borrowings of music video from these traditions to develop an understanding of music video that moves beyond, and indeed largely sidesteps, the terms of debate set by Kaplan and Goodwin. Carol Vernallis's contribution, "Strange People, Weird Objects: The Nature of Narrativity, Character, and Editing in Music Videos," takes as a point of departure the ways in which some theorists (e.g., John Fiske) have analyzed videos as mininarratives, whereas others (Kaplan, for example) have argued for their fundamentally anti-narrative qualities. In attempting to break this deadlock Vernallis provides a number of avenues for nuancing what we mean by "narrative" in music video, and she points to the ways in which the images perform functions such as underscoring the music, highlighting the lyrics, and showcasing the star. Vernallis examines a range of videos along the narrative to nonnarrative continuum and proposes new models for understanding specific nonnarrative modes such as what she terms the "process video" and the "catalogue."

In going beyond the expansion of the theoretical tools of the first wave of music video scholarship, this collection also represents an intervention in a historical and industrial climate that has changed significantly. In the extant scholarship, there has been an implicit equation of MTV with music television, as if an analysis of MTV could stand in for an analysis of all other marginal stations and programs that show music videos.[5] Just as Herzog and Middleton's essays disarticulate music video from music television by exploring nontelevised uses of the sound-image nexus, we hope also to break the implicit equation between music television and MTV. As the very notion of "music television" has gradually become less critical to MTV's self-presentation (a source of constant reproach from fans and critics alike),[6] and as other competing and contrasting channels have occupied the music televisual terrain, this use of MTV as a stand-in for music video has become increasingly problematic. The drastically transformed media landscape outlined in the first pages of this introduction has simply made apparent the limitations in this regard that were built into the earlier scholarship. In an era characterized by a splintered and proliferating market for all genres of music video, the current inattention to networks such as CMT, BET, Fuse, VH1, and the Box (now subsumed by MTV2), each of which reaches more than thirty million households in the United States alone, represents a significant gap in the extant writing on the form. And with literally dozens of other channels blooming on the digital delivery horizon (including special-

JASON MIDDLETON AND ROGER BEEBE

ized scions from the older networks such as BET Jazz or MTV Jams) this omission becomes even more problematic. Further, despite MTV's massive global footprint (with regional networks in most parts of the globe reaching an estimated five hundred million households), we can also no longer ignore the dozens of regional networks and programs around the globe and the music videos that they feature.

While no single collection could pretend to exhaust this unexplored territory, we attempt here to make a first gesture toward exploration. Several essays in this book attempt to expand the MTV-centric perspective of music video studies, primarily by exploring forms of music video production and dissemination outside of the United States. Philip Hayward's "Dancing to a Pacific Beat: Music Video in Papua New Guinea" explores the relatively recent emergence of indigenous music video production in this culturally and linguistically diverse nation. Taking great pains to avoid a simple celebration of the local as opposed to the forces of U.S.-led globalization, Hayward details the many negotiations and struggles of local directors and musical acts as they attempt to marry tradition to a markedly modern form that they wish to differentiate not only from the U.S. product but also from that of other Pacific islands.

From the opposite side of the globe, Antti-Ville Kärjä documents the development of a music video industry in Finland that entails its own uniquely telling set of national and international issues. He locates a tension in contemporary Finnish culture between the traditional ethnonationalist conceptions of the "Finnish character" and the efforts to acknowledge the presence of new ethnicities and hybrid cultural identities. Kärjä argues that many elements in Finnish music video often interpreted within nationalist frameworks can be better understood in terms of generic determinations and intertextual references that disrupt the stability of an imagined "Finnish-ness." Karen Pegley's contribution, "'Coming to You Wherever You Are': Exploring the Imagined Communities of MuchMusic (Canada) and MTV (United States)," examines the Canadian channel (which, we should note, should not be confused with the now-defunct Much Music USA) as a point of resistance to MTV's assumed hegemonic status in the global music video programming marketplace. Pegley compares the two networks' extramusical content, televisual flows, and video repertoires in order to develop an understanding of the role of nationalism in the construction of MuchMusic as a specifically "Canadian" cultural form.

Just as soon as we have disarticulated MTV from its former equation with music television, another problem in the first wave of music video scholarship becomes evident: namely, the existence of forms of music television *before* the advent of MTV. If, in fact, music video is not coterminous with MTV, then we should expect to be able to discover significant and interesting articulations of music and television before 1981. The myopia of the extant scholarship in this regard not only ignores other outlets for music video that preceded MTV such as the USA cable network's program *Night Flight*, but it also significantly shuts down the possibilities for thinking about music television in a broader historical sense.

While many of the essays in the collection are historically expansive—the essay by Herzog in particular represents an exploration of a certain prehistory of the music video form—two essays address earlier kinds of music television as their central problematic. Fittingly, both works reference the rock icon Elvis Presley, who passed away before the advent of MTV but was instrumental in establishing the centrality of the performer's visual image in rock and pop music culture. Norma Coates's contribution, "Elvis from the Waist Up and Other Myths: 1950s Music Television and the Gendering of Rock Discourse," examines 1950s music television programs such as *American Bandstand* and *The Ed Sullivan Show*, their reception in the trade press, and the construction of teenage female fans in that discourse. Coates argues that this historical conjuncture of music and television provided the "discursive conditioning" for rock criticism (as well as for other discourses of rock culture that would emerge more fully in the 1960s) to entrench the marginalization of women in this culture and maintain stereotypical 1950s gender roles. Lisa Parks and Melissa McCartney's essay, "Elvis Goes Global: Aloha! Elvis Live via Satellite and Music/Tourism/Television" examines Elvis's internationally broadcast *Aloha from Hawaii* concert in the context of discourses surrounding tourism and music in Hawaii during the 1970s. Parks and McCartney explore questions of authenticity as well as the local and the global in popular music culture in relation to this widely viewed televisual event that showcased the possibilities of the emergent satellite technology.

The three final essays in the collection combine and expand upon the issues and insights of the other contributors by addressing, in particular, questions of authenticity and cultural identification in music video culture. Warren Zanes's piece, "Video and the Theater of Purity," picks

JASON MIDDLETON AND ROGER BEEBE

up Parks and McCartney's interest in the issue of authenticity, this time exploring it in the context of its more familiar home of rock discourse — specifically dealing with the question of the underground versus the commercial. Zanes examines the role of music video within the debates concerning commercialization, developing, as does Norma Coates in her essay, a historically grounded theorization of the troubled relation between the visual and the concept of the "authentic" in rock culture. Through his productive suggestions about the legacy of Napster in these issues, Zane also allows us to consider the impact of the Internet on music video formats. Cyndi Fuchs, too, takes an interest in authenticity and commercialization in her essay "'I'm from Rags to Riches': The Death of Jay-Z." Fuchs tracks the complex forces that shaped the evolution of the rapper Shawn Carter through his various personas, then she turns to his music videos as the primary site where these identities are performed, solidified, and, at times, terminated (as in the case of his "final" video for "99 Problems," where he stages his own death). Closing out the collection, Roger Beebe's contribution, "Paradoxes of Pastiche: Spike Jonze, Hype Williams, and the Race of the Postmodern Auteur," provides innovative new perspectives on many of the concerns raised in the other essays, such as retheorizing music video in relation to the concept of postmodernism; examining the tensions and negotiations in music video between high-art influences and ideals and mass cultural appeal(s); and considering the different modes of address among different videos and video formats, particularly as these modes of address are articulated through race. In his essay Beebe ultimately demonstrates the racial biases of both music video culture and postmodern theory, and he proposes that we must come to imagine a cultural logic that can accommodate other visions — an imagining that might begin by attempts such as those offered in this collection to explore other music televisions.

NOTES

1 These ads were meant to prompt cable and satellite television subscribers to contact their providers in order to declare, once again, "I want my MTV[2]."

2 This field finds its institutional form in the International Association for the Study of Popular Music (IASPM).

3 Lawrence Grossberg, plenary panel discussion, IASPM conference, Murfreesboro, TN, September 1999.

4 Rick Altman, "Television/Sound," in *Studies in Entertainment: Critical Approaches to Mass Culture*, ed. Tania Modleski (Bloomington: Indiana University Press, 1986).
5 One significant exception is Mark Fenster's excellent essay "Genre and Form: The Development of the Country Music Video," in *Sound and Vision: The Music Video Reader*, ed. Simon Frith, Andrew Goodwin, and Lawrence Grossberg (New York: Routledge, 1993).
6 For just one of literally hundreds of such public upbraidings of MTV for its abandonment of music video, see Joy Press, "Reality Killed the Video Star: The Music TV Wars," *Village Voice*, July 23–29, 2003, 52.

Kay Dickinson

T
he study of music video has provoked various territorial skirmishes between university disciplines, precisely because music videos are media hybrids. Being both visual and musical, videos lie not so much in a no-man's land but rather in a space that overlaps various scholarly (as well as sensorial and semantic) domains. The two major books on the topic—E. Ann Kaplan's *Rocking around the Clock* and Andrew Goodwin's *Dancing in the Distraction Factory*—each take one of two often very contrary positions, with Kaplan drawing upon postmodernism and film theory (particularly feminist film theory and its obsession with "the gaze") and with Goodwin self-defined as rock sociologist.[1] Ostensibly, one habitually privileges the visual, while the other compensates by placing the sonic on a pedestal. In response to Kaplan's overindulgence of the visual dimension, *Rocking around the Clock*'s critical nemesis, *Dancing in the Distraction Factory*, retaliates with the insistence that music video's visual aspects are secondary to "the music itself." In contradiction to the film theory trajectory, Goodwin's book, along with the anthology *Sound and Vision: The Music Video Reader*, herald a more exactingly music-centered methodology.

Although both the image and music figure in Goodwin's argument, he is so eager to stress the importance of the latter and to oppose Kaplan, that, again, the intrigue of music video's specific *union* of sound and image suffers shorter shrift than it deserves. Goodwin's response to Kaplan's earlier work is presented in the form of a conscious, self-imposed polarity, one whose bias toward one media industry edges toward the factionalism that marks Kaplan's neglect of music. While it definitely seems more sensible to understand videos as promotional devices created by the music industry, their birth out of and continual clinging to the moving-image arts should not be undermined. In this essay my objective is to insist that we investigate *how* these two registers interact, rather than simply picking what we consider to be the most robust opponent in a largely fantastical battle for authority.

What is lacking in much of this side-taking work is the recognition of music video's central paradox—that the various components of these synergistic arrangements waver opportunistically between states of separation and attachment. Their composite parts are compatible yet incompatible and the "dominance" of any given element is constantly under negotiation. With the help of Busta Rhymes's "Gimme Some Mo'" (1998) as my chosen example, I intend to rummage around in the writhing hermeneutic melee that is music video. In doing this, I am keen to draw upon the energy mustered by these configurations in order to fluctuate between singular and joint identities and to assess whether this dynamism can be harnessed and used to power certain liberating gestures within the politics of representation. To help me in this endeavor, I enlist a concept that Goodwin also finds useful—synaesthesia—although my understanding of it is not quite the same as his.

SYNAESTHESIA AND THE MERGING OF THE SENSES

In its literal sense, synaesthesia can be defined as the transposition of sensory images or attributes from one modality into another. Synaesthetes claim the ability, for example, to see music (usually in terms of color) or to taste shapes, with the former being the most common of its manifestations and the most pertinent to the study of music video. In addition to being a recurrent trope in various forms of artistic expression,[2] synaesthesia has been well documented by scientific investigation, particularly in neuropsychology.[3]

What all of these diverse studies of synaesthesia argue is that we very rarely use any sense (as it is presently socially circumscribed) on its own—and music video "viewing" is blatantly one such case. The senses inform each other, cross each other's tracks, and, most importantly, embody both a singularity and the potential to merge. With such ideas at the fore, analyses of audio-visual art forms that lavish attention so unreservedly on one sense in isolation seem doubly aberrant, and this shadow even looms in the background of Goodwin's cross-modal aspirations. The conclusion to his deployment of synaesthesia is telling, especially in its

KAY DICKINSON

use of italics: "I have tried to show, with some textual detail, exactly how we might invert the position of film studies, by demonstrating exactly how the visuals *support* the sound track."[4] The image, it would appear, is now the compliant factor, the reacting and molded feature buckling under the weight of music's importance. Furthermore, the assertion of synaesthesia's existence and its support of such an argument against film studies is pretty much an end point for Goodwin, who does little to deconstruct his own disciplinary hegemony.

It is a shame that, in so doggedly striving to show how image follows music in videos, Goodwin fails to value the haphazard, perhaps more involuntary realignments of meanings that happen when audio-visual formats are thought of not as a parade with one leader, but as a thoroughfare with two-way traffic. As has already been suggested, synaesthesia helps dissolve sensory boundaries as they are currently socially delineated; it is a physical, perceptual experience that, as I demonstrate below, seems to overlap with cultural inscription. This coalescence also lends resonance to a theoretical skipping between the representational and the corporeal. And the implications of this mutability become extremely poignant when the body is being portrayed and discussed in these visual and musical encounters. For instance, when a human body is represented in an audio-visual manner, the implications of the sonic components may radically contradict how we are socially educated to interpret the image. Therefore the obligatory reunion of any such multisensory expressions into a single music video confuses patterns of depiction that may seem fairly stable within, say, a song or an image on its own. Synaesthesia, in its blurring of the distinctions between bodily experience and cultural convention, coaxes out our curiosity about how the senses interact and influence each other and the extent to which any of our understanding of this is "natural." What lies behind our present and seemingly so arbitrary subdivision of the senses? And what, moreover, does this schism support? Together with a multiplicity of other phenomena, synaesthesia may help to chip away the political ordering of perception. With this in mind, the metaphorical notion of synaesthesia that I intend to improvise upon becomes a possible strategy for unsteadying so fixed and blinkered a view; for defying segregations of the senses and for exposing the extent to which these are socially interpellated.[5]

What I propose in this essay — in contradiction to theoretical assumptions that tend only to recognize unitary, fenced-in modalities — is that we not only acknowledge this conjoining of the two senses (and many of their objects) but also that we search out methods for probing the political impact of these (re)constituting movements. Of prime concern here is the fact that the performing body is differently regulated by the codes of both musical and visual representation: it is perceived differently by the ear and by the eye, and our responses are enormously reliant on our notions of such things as format and genre. Yet in music video these representations are forced to coalesce in a very specific manner. While this evidently leads to various forms of exclusion, it also opens up opportunities for various 'synaesthetic' transferences, or loopholes of representation and perception. What any theorist of music video should take into account is how some of our standard devices of sensorial encoding might be at odds with one another. The question, then, is what this might entail for a depicted presence—for example, a body—that is more often than not asked to function as some sort of constant, unified identity (although I would consider this a misguided request).

THEORETICAL DISCOURSE AND
SYNAESTHESIA AS METAPHOR

At this point, I want to stress that the overlapping of sensory experience is not simply some sort of fortuitous confusion, but instead is an integral part of the way humans consciously and strategically build up language, understanding, and political regulation—and that the manufacture of music video is as much a part of this process as anything else. While synaesthetic sympathies allow us to fantasize about a less rigid perceptual world, they also enable us to take on board how each sense's phasing into and out of the other is neither accidental nor uncontrollable.

Here I want to draw upon the rhetorical power of figural, even poetic language—and in particular the functioning of metaphor—to argue for a notion of language and sensory perception that has a greater amount of such malleability. As Lawrence Marks suggests: "Synaesthesia is fundamentally illogical, improper, a violation of common sense . . . Perhaps the character of synaesthesia is a microcosm of metaphor itself, going as it does beyond ordinary meaning to new meanings."[6] Before exploring this parity, however, I am eager to scrutinize how language itself works synaesthetically in its creation of metaphors, after which I intend to examine the opportunities that a metaphorical exchange between the visual and the sonic (as often happens within music video) can offer us.

According to Joseph William, when the sense of an image or sound lies beyond our linguistic grasp, attainable words belonging to other senses are borrowed to fill in the gaps. For example, "a loud shirt" is not actually a noisy garment but one colored in such a way that it startles us like a blast of high volume. Here the instantly evocative experience shares its impact with another sensory domain. For William, the synaesthetic exchange is "so regular, so enduring, and so inclusive that its description may be the strongest generalisation in diachronic semantics reported for English or any other language."[7] This is such a commonplace descriptive process that it has become almost unnoticeable—we would rarely stop to think back to the derivation of "the loud shirt" because it has become naturalized as a mode of description. Yet in these very familiar means of figural expression lie the potential for new articulations, even new consciousnesses, precisely because they draw upon sensory perception.

It does not seem unreasonable, then, to promote the ability of metaphor to expand, rather than to capture or explain—and by metaphor I here refer to both the way "synaesthesia" might work figuratively and the manner in which music and image "act out" each other's parts within videos. While metaphors are essentially epistemologically unreliable (they are productive rather than reproductive; facilitators rather than translators), their talents dwell in their flexibility and in their incitement of new consciousnesses. This capacity has not escaped the attention of several twentieth-century philosophers,[8] whose excitement about metaphor I now wish to briefly feed upon. Richard Rorty clarifies the critical difference between metaphors as describers of alien outside worlds (which he undermines) and metaphors as "causes of changing beliefs and desires . . . [making] possible novel scientific theories as causes of our ability to know more about the world, rather than expressions of such knowledge."[9] In the face of a ravine in meaning, metaphor obliges semantically (as we have seen in synaesthetic adjectives) not with a translation of the intangible but through references to altogether different objects or sensations.

The implied sliding between the material and the immaterial, language and object, and imagination and manifestation is an angle that fascinates another theorist, Paul Ricoeur: "By displaying a flow of images, discourse initiates changes of logical distance, generates *rapprochement*. Imaging and imagining, thus, is the concrete milieu in which and through which we see similarities. To imagine, then, is not to have a mental picture of something but to display relations in a depicting mode."[10] Later he expands this idea: "One of the functions of imagination is to give a concrete dimension to the suspension or *epoche* proper to split reference. Imagination does not merely schematize the predicative assimilation between terms by its synthetic insight into similarities nor does it merely picture the sense thanks to the display of images aroused and controlled by the cognitive process. Rather, it contributes concretely to the *epoche* of ordinary reference and to the projection of new possibilities of redescribing the world."[11]

Ricoeur places great emphasis on imagination as the key to the fetters of everyday life and its truth values, the key that opens doors onto different perceptual planes. From this perspective, imagination can be used to transfigure the literal—it conveniently speaks the same language yet is distanced enough not to be swamped by it: "What is given to thought in this way . . . [is the] most hidden dialectic—the dialectic that reigns between the experience of belonging as a whole and the power of distanciation that opens up the space of speculative thought."[12]

Such thinking diverges dramatically from that of Goodwin, who is eager to "prove" a synaesthetic allegiance while writers like Ricoeur argue persuasively for the facility and *potential* of metaphor rather than its mere existence. In fact, it is perhaps more useful to conceive of metaphor itself not as a static object but as an action or interaction—that is, more like a verb, a refusal of semantic stasis. Ricoeur associates the position of metaphor with "neither the name, nor the sentence, nor even discourse, but the copula of the verb to be. The metaphorical 'is' at once signifies both 'is not' and 'is like.'"[13] The separation and similarity that I consider to be so central to unlocking the political potential of media synergy is supported by arguments like these. Moreover, as Ricoeur continues, metaphor reintroduces an important factor into ontology: the concept of "as" to evoke action and liveliness. And it is this dynamism embodied in the union of various art forms that carries promises of movement and change.

Such a preoccupation with energy is also urgently expressed in Gilles Deleuze and Félix Guattari's sense of metaphor, which similarly favors an instigation of proliferating rather than destructive forces. Communication between previously unaffiliated meanings and their realignment into new "assemblages" (their term for configurations of what seem to have been previously discrete entities)—which is exactly what metaphor achieves—evades the restrictive impulses of established modes of consciousness.[14] Assemblages not only function to mutual benefit, they also create lines along which power can flow, and it is this second quality of assemblages which has been so sorely neglected in the study of music video. Syntheses and interactions of these kinds are politically determined for Deleuze and Guattari and cannot be consigned purely to the realm of thought. Synaesthetic metaphor should no longer be considered disinterested play because it can be employed to smuggle advantageous though previously unsanctioned plots into hostile territory. In many ways this notion resembles two children in a large coat passing themselves off as a giant or conjoined twins, or the liminal being dragged into the mainstream by its more acceptable partner—something that will become increasingly more believable when music video examples are singled out for investigation.

Using this kind of thinking, a space for potentially less-constrained writings and readings may be found (if enough people look, and if their actions are repetitively reaffirmed and acted upon)—even in so highly regulated a zone as music video. Such spaces, I would argue, open up most readily when the primary art form of one sense is less restrictive than the one to which it is linked through video. In making these suggestions, then, I want synaesthesia to stretch far beyond Goodwin's rhetorical use of it as evidence for the importance of studying image and music synchronously. In the following analysis, "synaesthesia" will be thought of not only as an intrinsic property, but also as a political tool at work within both the object of analysis itself and its audience's active perception.

SYNAESTHETIC POSSIBILITY IN PRACTICE: AN ANALYSIS OF BUSTA RHYMES'S "GIMME SOME MO'"

An obvious historical period offering rich pickings for synaesthetic allegiances would be the first half of the 1980s, when there was an accelerated airing of pop promos on television. It was at this point that music video not only came into its own by becoming pretty much essential in the promotion of a mainstream hit, but also was in the process of working out its stylistic conventions. Of course this latter factor was largely determined by the constraints of what was considered to "work" as televisual material, which often was a set of concepts entirely different from what was appropriate musically. For example, the MTV schedulers deemed fit for consumption a new wave of challengingly androgynous *music* by bands such as Culture Club, Duran Duran, the Human League, and the Eurythmics (who were largely British and of European descent), largely because its performers were, in their eyes, commendably visually seductive. On the other side of the coin, however, it has been noted that there was a great resistance to showing work by African American artists.[15] Television's widespread underrepresentation of this section of the population is the issue I address below, but with reference to a more recent video.

The exclusion of African Americans from so much television programming was, of course, merely a fragment of their consistent, ongoing, and only slowly eroding banishment from the narratives of visual mass communications (including film, television, and even theater). Obviously this blockage supports and is supported by something larger: namely, a history of socioeconomically driven racial prejudice that uses, among other methods, the politics of visual appearance as a category through which to instigate discrimination. While this has been and continues to be the case in the worlds of film and television, African American performers have been allowed to flourish somewhat more freely within the realm of music production, perhaps partially because racism is so concerned with what people look like.[16] Although it would be entirely foolish to claim that the story of African Americans in music has been one of success and free from abuse, corruption, prejudice, and exploitation, it is safe to say that there have been many more African Americans who have triumphed as musicians than those who have made a living in front of or behind the camera. This unevenness of production and representation tells us much about how the achievements of "minorities" are regulated. But the presence of this stronger factor and its joining of forces with a more marginalized mode of expression does, however, allow for some extremely useful synaesthetic opportunism. The very fact of a profitable *audio* product needing also to be aired in a visual format necessarily brings about a certain change in programming policy. In the mid-1980s, this led to African American performers being increasingly allowed to invade tele*visual* spaces, precisely because their (more) condoned musical popularity demanded a visual counterpart at that historical moment. Michael Jackson is the obvious figure here in terms of early MTV, and there is a strong argument for the proposition that his market position (and thus the clout that his work carried) brought about significant change in the way MTV thought about presenting African Americans visually. Yet, regardless of Jackson's breakthrough success, the absence of people of non-European descent within other spheres of audio-visual media — such as cinema and nonmusical television — is still a major political issue and one that music video is constantly using its synergistic power to address. Music video is perhaps still the key mainstream audio-visual art form where we get to *see* African Americans most frequently, and as such the synaesthetic possibilities it offers place its makers in an enormously tactical position.

The video that Hype Williams directed to accompany Busta Rhymes's "Gimme Some Mo'" exemplifies how synaesthetic power ascribed through the market forces of African American music allows for a commentary upon the injustice of the ideologically loaded notion of spectacle that is rife within the filmic and televisual establishments. What follows is merely a suggestive inquiry into how this sense of synaesthesia might work; one that, unfortunately, has little time to delve into the career details of either Busta Rhymes or the groundbreaking director Hype Williams (a man who works almost exclusively with a roster of A-list African American performers such as TLC, R. Kelly, Will Smith, and Wu-Tang Clan). While a breakdown of how the more specific formal qualities of the song and the video interact would be an equally rewarding task, here I want to focus, for the most part, on how the space that music has created for African Americans on television (which is something of a synaesthetic by-product) can be used to critique that very terrain and, with it, the film industry as well.

The video for "Gimme Some Mo'" is riddled with film and television references, several of which derive from the song itself. After Busta Rhymes's own voice, the song's most prominent musical feature is a sample from Bernard Herrmann's score for *Psycho*, and this idea is synaesthetically picked up in certain characters' swirling black-and-white eyeballs which bring to mind the art work in the opening titles of another Hitchcock film (*Vertigo*). Film's creative playing field, from which African Americans are so often barred, is casually trespassed upon in both the song and its video — an action that synaesthesia helps make possible. However, the image of addled eyeballs is a double quotation, and its second source —

animation—is more central to the video's semantic content. The video's relentlessly bright colors are cartoonlike, as are the bulging perspectives created through unusual camera angles, fish-eye lenses, and a medley of post-production effects. At various points Rhymes is dressed up as a Yosemite Sam–type figure, but the most pointed and satirical recollection of cartoon themes figures in the first section of the video. Here a child version of Busta Rhymes and his doting homemaker mother are located in the garden of a suburban home, replete with a white picket fence. These are not only the symbols of the classic cartoon world, but also those of a post–World War II and pre–civil rights era America in which the only place for an African American woman was, for the most part, as domestic labor. These ideas echoed through the cartoons of the time, especially *Tom and Jerry*, and they were forcefully hammered "home" as a preferred American way of life in contemporary films and TV programs (which, interestingly, now form the scheduling backbone of several American "nostalgia" channels). Rhymes's presence in such a world, then, is a simultaneous infiltration and a mockery of both this idea's representational centrality and its position as a desirable reality. The video draws on the fact that the cartoons of the time often parodied this lifestyle, but not at the level of who was free to live it and who was not. In this sense, the video works on several planes: by lambasting the exclusivity of a supposed "everyday life" and also by pointing out how such ostracism was supported through media practices, regardless of how irreverent toward authority they otherwise were.

"Gimme Some Mo'" not only uses its air-play power to attack such politics, but also it does its best to stretch out beyond the designated confines of the promo format. The video is framed at the start by a title card bearing the legend "Flipmode Cartoons" in the graphic style of Warner Brothers' *Looney Tunes* a sequence that features its own theme tune, which is distinct from the track itself. Here the video strains at the leash that keeps it to certain restrictive boundaries (namely the duration and the conventions of the format). It is as if it were trying to make itself into not (just) a promo but a whole show or a short film—a luxury that traditionally has too often been denied to African Americans. Hype Williams's extension of narrow and debilitating borderlines does not stop here. With this move he is not only insinuating something beyond the scope of music video, but through his power as auteur within this mode he also managed to land the directorship of the feature film *Belly* (1998)—at the time still a shockingly rare accomplishment/allowance for an African American.

Something that *Belly* achieves and shares with both "Gimme Some Mo'" and Williams's other work is that its means of representation and commentary are deliberately antirealist, as if to pour scorn on the project of realism ever being able to portray African American experience, and to rescue them from the often blunt unimaginativeness to which realism often adds up. Hype Williams's videos seem to campaign for the freedom to not be tied down to "keeping it real"; for the dual privileges of fantasy and wealth, neither of which are self-deprecatingly effaced in the way he puts digital technologies to use. Williams repeatedly transforms musicians into bulbous, pulsating incarnations of themselves who bulge out of a screen that can only just contain them. At some level this is a synaesthetic extension of certain ideas that are presented musically within hip hop,[17] a genre where instrument use and voices are warped and stretched, with the notes punching all the way through their passage until they exit via the mouth or hands. Here the power of a musical tradition is synaesthetically drawn upon in order to innovate within the visual and narrative spheres, which is further buoyed along by music video's indulgence of fantasy and the self-aggrandisement of its stars. Listening to "Gimme Some Mo'" is as exhilarating an experience as is watching its video, in which the vocal phrasing seems almost supra-human in its dexterity. This kind of impossibly fast delivery was employed, to give just one example, in the 1950s by singers like Little Richard in their desperate attempts to outfox contemporary white copyists like Pat Boone. Its history of political maneuvering, as well as its breathtaking double-jointedness, is something that the video welcomes into visual communication.

In achieving all this, Hype Williams wields a previously unobtainable power specific to his place within a history of technological development and the relative freedom and wealth of the music video format. In much of his work he not only depicts African American bodies without circumscribing them in the ways in which the film and TV industries have helped to pin in place, but he also extends them prosthetically. There's a hydralike quality to, for instance, Missy Elliot in her Hype Williams–directed video "Get Ur Freak On"—that is, you get the feeling that if you cut off her head at its limber, Tenniel-style neck, at least one more would grow back. Similarly, in the "Gimme Some Mo'" video, Rhymes morphs into a monster in a use of technological shape-shifting that sees its visual precedent in the special effects in Michael Jackson's videos (particularly "Black and White") and in its immediate musical forefather in early hip hop—electronica and techno (to name but a few genres).

While they present a staggering ability to defy bodily limitations and to metamorphosize, these audio-visual ideas still maintain an aloofness within and cynicism about designated physical identity (something that becomes evident in Rhymes's incarnation in the video as a comical posturing and obviously artificially padded muscle man). However, these figures also manage to acquire extra attributes (as they do in the CGI work associated with Hype Williams), which, when knitted into the fantastical license allowed to music video, can propel the surface of the human body somewhere else, somewhere, hopefully, beyond the confines of these pre– and post–civil rights imprisonments of African American physicality. Such limitations have been challenged for many years within African American music; namely, the ecstatic and temporary unfettering to be heard in, say, the voices of Mahalia Jackson or Aretha Franklin. However, it is doubtful that such ideas would make it onto the television screen with as much frequency were it not for the previously established power of African American music whose coattails directors like Williams catch hold of, use to ride into the visual mainstream, and then weave into innovative new patterns. Deriving from technological addition rather than narrative limitation, these televisual moments are part of a surprisingly beneficial synaesthetic strategy that is catapulting African American representation off into new and hopefully less constricted spaces—ones where more advantageous relationships between finance, music, and the moving image might possibly be achieved.

Yet what does it mean to convey these ideas through references to the cartoon; to aspire, by and large, to a sort of "novelty" status that has cordoned off the efficacy of so many African American performers? Rhymes is, after all, a bit of a joke figure in the video, which is not the sense that comes across when one hears his track in isolation. On one level, this status may mean that a lot of barbed commentary can pass through unchecked because it is seemingly harmless (or just harmless enough). In such instances, the focus has to be on whether being childlike and comedic is necessarily totally regressive. Is there something profitable in a cartoon that has come to life—a cartoon on the loose, and, most importantly, one that is just as uncanny as the surging string section dynamics and harmonic chordal unease of the *Psycho* sample?

Part of this uncanny quality derives from the sexuality expressed within the video—the coupling of the squidgy, lolloping cartoon world with the more "adult" nature of the women in bikinis grinding suggestively in close up. This is just one nexus point where the dilemma of exactly how to render music visual becomes a political sticking point, where it might fall back on a tired and oppressive history of representation in which (African American) women might be seen to have drawn a rather short straw. A similar but perhaps more complicated argument could be leveled at the song's major preoccupation—money. Lyrically "Gimme Some Mo'" demands social ascendancy and increased power, but it does so for the most part through insatiable lust and the personal acquisition of money. Along with its cartoon reference points, the video is littered with boardrooms, business suits, and flashy cars. This may be an invasion and a subversion, but it is one that buys into a conservative capitalist aesthetic based around individual gain ("Gim*me* Some Mo'") rather than any suggestion of change at the level of community or governmental policy. It is at points like these that the strictures of synaesthetic possibility have to be outlined: when dealing with music videos we are, by and large, working within and not outside everything that big business capitalism stands for (such as the championing of personal liberty as expressed through consumption), and it is vital to see what can be done within that space without getting ridiculously idealistic.

SYNAESTHESIA'S POLITICAL LIMITATIONS . . . AND ITS POTENTIAL

In almost any textual analysis, then, the inevitable has to be faced: music video (like so many other synergistic enterprises) functions within the promotional machinery of global corporate business, with all the protocol and political injustice that such a framework embodies and endorses. Likewise, because of (and even in spite of) this setting, synaesthesia and its metaphorical trappings also abide by certain regulations. Despite the occurrence of many cross-modal analogies, the senses do not, as yet, exhibit the ability to completely transcend their present ontological isolation.

A synaesthetic perspective cannot overthrow the old order for a new one, nor should it aspire to such autocracy. Instead there should perhaps be a more modest understanding of the alternations at work and how they profit not only the analysis of audio-visual media and its political aspirations, but also the healthy functioning of an often less egalitarian capitalism. Evidently, the overlapping of the old and the new in synaesthetic metaphor also shares ground with the production of consumer goods. Within music video, the trace of the old (the song) is never erased—primarily because it needs to be recognized as a commodity in its own right. Consequently, a video points not only to itself in these terms, but also to a piece of recorded music and a wealth of more visually evocative consumer goods such as films, TV shows, posters, book, and T-shirts, thus using synaesthesia to entice the audience back to previously singular elements and to increase the quantity of available products. Such items are able to waver between multisensory union (for the purposes of cheaper promotion) and singularity (for the multiplication of identifiable potential consumer goods). Segregating the senses establishes more single entities within the market, more points of divergence for potential profit.[18] Here we glimpse the less idealistic use of metaphor yet, under its cloak, many other implications for change may travel. Like metaphor, music video creates a surplus profit (often in the loosest sense of the word) through its by-products. And, as with any creation of economic surplus value, attainment depends upon the effacement of human toil—in a way almost a parallel to metaphor's supposed "naturalness" despite the contrivance involved in setting it up.

And yet surely there are still benefits to the suppleness of the synaesthetic metaphor with its prolongation of an object's semantic content—something that, as has become clear, is rarely exploited by academics analyzing music video. The generative capacities of metaphor hint not only at infinite (although not all-embracing) polysemy, but also at the implausibility of retracing points of linguistic origin. Admittedly, plasticity is neither unbounded nor wholly liberating, but the synaesthetic metaphor (among many others) divulges an apt strategy for reasonable change—although certain rules cannot, at the moment, be conceivably violated.

Certainly, as "Gimme Some Mo'" exemplifies, there are vacillating, marginal, and peripheral modes of perception that may help liberate certain social groupings, and these feature more commonly than we might suppose. There is flexibility rather than free play, and scouting out such pliancy is one of the things that theorists of media convergence should perhaps be trying to do. Obviously, amid these sensorial frameworks sit more commercial and ideological factors that discourage, if we pay them

KAY DICKINSON

heed, a solely utopian belief in the metaphorical functioning of music video. The marriage of the televisual and the sonic in music video comes not, after all, from some grand plan for social liberty, but from historically specific commercial avarice (again, the Busta Rhymes video articulates this very knowingly).

Yet, as with all new alliances, inert components may suddenly become catalysts in the most surprising ways. The inevitable repercussion of metaphor—the old object gaining additional meanings by proxy—may perhaps wear down each sense's traditional cultural compliance and limitations. The divorced image and sound in music video will never add up to a whole equal and stable meaning; because each aspect has cumulative effects on the other, new relationships are sometimes created. In this sense, synaesthetic inquiry delivers more than just a critique of certain dominant power structures; indeed, it also suggests not only that fixed sensory experiences can be perceived in this more fluid manner but also that they are knowingly constructed in this way, even in something as "mainstream" as music video.

Ultimately, the synaesthetic metaphor bridges the murky unreconciled areas that we perceive as the internal and the external, the physical and the intellectual, the body and the mind, and their relatives, fact and fiction, figural and literal. The link between conscience and consciousness—feeling—and its political and commercial circumscription becomes more tangible under these terms. Although these seem to be abstract essences, they are constantly being crystallized into specific visual and musical entities (within music video and well beyond it). Most pressing is the fact that such actions have a material effect upon their performers and audiences and it is vital to break down how the dislocation, followed by the reunion, of music and image reflects and affects these subjects. Above all else, there needs to be an exploration of how the body and its citizenship is outlined, colored in, and erased in media mergings. Physicality is always suggested, if not implicated, in signification of this kind (or, indeed, signification at large) and, of course, signification also depends on whatever the material body might be. Work has to be done on exposing the porous division between the material/corporeal and the cultural, which is why my central metaphor has been synaesthesia. In the wider political scheme of things, the body is where power and harm are exacted and often where subordination is naturalized through various complex cultural processes (prejudice toward African Americans in terms of "color" is one such mechanism). Perception, as well as representation (how we experience as well as what we are given to experience), can be aggressive, power hungry, even violent. How the media industry convergence embodied in music video might figure in this (in terms of both the consumer and the consumed) is of prime importance—not only in order that we are wary of its machinations but also that we might realize its latent and surprising political possibilities.

NOTES

1 E. Ann Kaplan, *Rocking around the Clock: Music, Television and Consumer Culture* (New York: Methuen, 1987); Andrew Goodwin, *Dancing in the Distraction Factory: Music Television and Popular Culture*. London: Routledge, 1992.

2 Synaesthesia was, for example, a favored trope of French writers such as Stéphane Mallarmé, Joris Karl Huysmans, and Charles Baudelaire, and it also informed the musical compositions of Alexander Scriabin and Olivier Messiaen, as well as the paintings of Wassily Kandinsky.

3 See, for instance, the works of Lawrence Marks, such as *The Unity of the Senses: Interrelations among the Modalities* (New York: Academic Press, 1978), "Bright Sneezes and Dark Coughs, Loud Sunlight and Soft Moonlight," *Journal of Experimental Psychology: Human Perception and Performance* 8.2 (1982): 177–93; and "On Cross-Modal Similarity: Audio-Visual Interactions in Speeded Discriminations," *Journal of Experimental Psychology: Human Perception and Performance* 13.3 (1987): 384–94. In *The Unity of the Senses*, Marks claims that "the domain of each sense is limited, but not wholly distinct: sensory domains overlap, for the world about which the senses inform us is, in itself, a unitary one, and so usually is our conception of it" (185).

4 Goodwin, *Dancing in the Distraction Factory*, 70.

5 Obviously a change in the meaning of "synaesthesia" begs an explanation, not least in ethical terms. The use of the term may seem to warrant authorization because of its association with abnormal brain functioning. However, the word has been commonly exploited to imply imaginative rather than believed perception; appreciation of shared qualities rather than confusion over sense data; correlation rather than inability to distinguish. Ultimately, this is not a real bewilderment of the senses, but a correspondence and deliberate interchange between what each sense stands for and its concomitant prohibitions. This reinterpretation moves slightly further away from actual bodily experiences and is instead located within a long chain of language and meaning that, although unfettered, is neither limitless nor latched to a "real" that is anything but a set of positions in this grid. It is not experience, but it evokes the feelings and responses stimulated by experience. As such, my particular definition of synaesthesia is more a trope than a neurologi-

KAY DICKINSON

cal condition, its correct meaning is not so much divested from it but con-spicuously added to and reproportioned. While I will elaborate upon a more tactile bodily synaesthesia, the "synaesthetic" qualities of music video (its visual casting of the music, and its sonic echoing of the image) work with a less restricted interpretation of the word.

6 Marks, *The Unity of the Senses*, 222.

7 Joseph William, "Synaesthetic Adjectives: A Possible Law of Semantic Change," *Language* 52 (1976): 461.

8 Unfortunately, here space constraints inhibit an extended examination of the history of philosophy's engagement with the metaphorical, as well as an examination of perhaps the most eloquent writer on metaphor, Friedrich Nietzsche (see, for example, his "On Truth and Falsity in Their Ultramoral Sense," in *The Complete Works of Friedrich Nietzsche*, vol. 2, ed. Oscar Levy; trans. Maximilian Mugge [London: George Allen and Unwin, 1924]).

9 Richard Rorty, *Objectivity, Relativism and Truth: Philosophical Papers*, vol. 1 (Cambridge: Cambridge University Press, 1991), 163.

10 Paul Ricoeur, "The Metaphorical Process as Cognition, Imagination and Feeling," in *Philosophical Perspectives on Metaphor*, ed. Mark Johnson (Ann Arbor, Mich.: University Microfilms International, 1994), 236.

11 Ibid., 241.

12 Paul Ricoeur, *The Rule of Metaphor: Multi-Disciplinary Studies of the Creation of Meaning in Language*, trans. Robert Czerny (Toronto: University of Toronto Press, 1977), 313.

13 Ibid., 7.

14 See, for example, Gilles Deleuze and Félix Guattari, "1837: Of the Refrain," in *A Thousand Plateaus: Capitalism and Schizophrenia*, trans. Brian Massumi (London: Athlone Press, 1996).

15 For more on African American music in this period, see Russell Sanjek, *American Popular Music and Its Business: The First 400 Years* (New York: Oxford University Press, 1988).

16 There are, however, many other reasons why African American music was al-lowed its success, some of which actually work to the detriment of the fight against racism.

17 The ideas are also presented in hip hop graffiti.

18 The commodification of the senses is delineated more expertly in Karl Marx's "Private Property and Communism. Various Stages of Development of Communist Views: Crude, Equalitarian Communism and Communism as Socialism Coinciding with Humaneness," in *Economic and Philosophic Manuscripts of 1844*, trans. Martin Milligan (New York: International Publishers, 1971), 89–114.

Amy Herzog

ichel Chion, writing on the distinction between film and television, argues that "the difference . . . lies not so much in the
visual specificity of their images, as in the different roles of
sound in each."[1] Referring to television as "illustrated radio,"
Chion describes the medium as driven by sound, speech, and music. The
image in television and video serves to supplement the sound, which
bears the primary burden of conveying meaning. The examples that Chion
draws upon (televised sporting events, video art, and the music video) all
share this quality; the soundtrack tells us what is happening while the
images are "added on." The specific nature of this addition is, of course,
vastly different—ranging from the illustrative images cut into a news-
caster's report to the "visual fluttering" of a music video or video game.[2]
Yet whether these images are synchronous, explanatory, harmonious, or
discordant, each must move through sound in order to be understood—a
movement that inverts the cinematic image-sound hierarchy.

What is perhaps most provocative about Chion's analysis, however, is
the implication that the technological medium alone does not determine
what constitutes the televisual. Instead, transformations in audiovisual
regimes can be mapped through shifting relations among images, sounds,
and their temporal and spatial affectivity. These knotted evolutions are
sparked on multiple fronts and invariably involve overlapping technologies, texts, and ideas. As such, we might best approach the music video
by exploring the configurations of music and image that compose its modality. To understand its emergence would require mapping these configurations as they occur in other technological contexts. Devices such as
the cinematic jukebox offer glimpses of music-image combinations that,

although markedly different from the music video, reveal much about the video's underlying logic.

The cinematic jukebox's two most successful manifestations—the Panoram Soundie of the 1940s and the Scopitone of the 1960s— surfaced long before the music video. Soundies and Scopitones were short-format musical films viewed in jukeboxes outfitted with 16mm projectors and ground-glass screens. Located in bars, hotels, clubs, and bus stations, these hybrid devices occupied a curious cultural and aesthetic position. This position had as much to do with the peculiarity of the films' visualizations as it did with the unusual format; the images that accompanied each song were crafted with an excessive literalness that was distinct from other contemporaneous musical films, often resulting in stilted and disquieting combinations. Although these experiments were relatively short-lived (and financially unsuccessful), they nevertheless indicated the potential for a new kind of image, one that was distinct from feature-length works and that seemed to be driven by a purely musical logic.

Cinematic jukeboxes generated limited press during their lifetime, and the coverage that does exist focuses almost exclusively on the question of novelty, a trend that has remained intact in contemporary scholarly work. Largely critically ignored, Soundies and Scopitones are only occasionally cited as records of rare performances or as failed precursors to the music video, fleeting anomalies not substantial enough to maintain more than a passing interest.[3] Hovering outside the realms of film and television, and featuring material that is often obscure and unsophisticated, jukebox films might be easily dismissed as historical curiosities. Yet I would argue that jukebox films provide a significant field for research into the relations between popular music and image precisely because of their anomalous nature. Ungainly and disjointed, jukebox films nevertheless maintain a deeply affecting presence. Their impact, in fact, seems to emanate directly from those moments of stuttering. Although the woodenness of many of these productions might thwart the intentions of their creators, the films' awkward gestures highlight the mechanisms by which they operate—structures that would be much less obvious yet no less prevalent in more sophisticated works.

My interest in cinematic jukeboxes centers on several key issues. The first is the unique experience of viewing jukebox films. As a format founded on sound, musical shorts may have more in common with other aurally based media than with more traditional filmic or televisual works. The jukebox as an apparatus underscores the links between the jukebox film and the record album—Soundies and Scopitones are, in effect, illustrated songs following similar paths of distribution and consumption as recorded music. These material circulations greatly influenced the films' visual construction, as did the location, size, and operation of the jukebox.

Second, in focusing on the relations between popular music and image, jukebox films provide a particularly salient example because they are entirely music based. Much of the literature on film music looks either at music's role as a supplement to the image or, in the case of musicals, at the interactions between musical numbers and narrative. Similarly, although music video scholarship has paid critical attention to the enmeshed interests of the video and recording industries, closer examinations of music video texts often disproportionately center on their imagery or lyrics.[4] Freestanding musical shorts, because they contain no overarching narrative framework, allow us to more fully explore the function of music in its own right. The jukebox film must be considered as part of a regime in which the preexisting song takes precedence over the image.

Finally, the circuits of movement of Soundies and Scopitones are incredibly complex, profuse, and at times contradictory. These flows include not only the films' material circulations (in terms of both distribution and presentation), but also the reproduction of familiar songs and the recycling of culturally coded images and modes of representation— all factors contributing to the mobile ways in which the films construct meaning. The seemingly obvious or literal nature of the images chosen to accompany songs becomes complicated when we consider the functions that jukebox films performed and the snared collisions between their various aesthetic and social elements. Soundies and Scopitones are therefore best understood not as individual, fixed texts but through an examination of the larger tensions between these shifting elements. Even the most cliché-ridden musical short can tell us vital information about its aspirations (however unsuccessfully it meets them)—goals that are invariably more complex than the film's means of expression.

Jody Berland suggests that an understanding of the music video must entail "a retrospective summary of the economic, iconographic, and structural issues relevant to the continuous integration of pop music with the powerful visual media." These interlaced interests work through

AMY HERZOG

audiovisual technologies to create new spaces, conceptions of community, and sets of practices. The most significant issue, she writes, is "the technological mediation of sound in relation to that of images, and the need to understand such mediation as a productive process that constitutes or changes our relations to each other in spatial and temporal as well as symbolic terms."[5] Though music television's apparatus is different from that of the cinematic jukebox, the process that Berland points to highlights the degree to which all audiovisual technologies are multifaceted, interdependent, and nested within larger cultural modes of seeing, hearing, and communicating. This framework guides my approach to cinematic jukeboxes by providing a means of understanding these devices' cultural positions and the modes of viewing and listening they might have engendered. Given the limited scope of this essay, however, and the dearth of available data regarding the production, distribution, and reception of Scopitones and Soundies, I am less interested here in the commercial and economic development of these mediums. Instead, I focus on the general structure of these films by examining their music-image combinations as a means of grasping the affective responses they attempted to produce. There are, of course, vast differences between Soundies and Scopitones: their precise format, their countries of origin (Scopitones were invented in France; Soundies in the United States), their aesthetics, and their historical occurrence. The particularities of each technology thus provide the foundation for my inquiry.

THE SOUNDIE

In September 1940, the Mills Novelty Company premiered its Panoram "movie machine" in Hollywood: a large cabinet with a screen on which patrons could watch three-minute musical films, one number for every ten cents deposited.[6] Soundies, as these films came to be known, were distributed to Panoram jukeboxes in bars, restaurants, transit stations, and hotels throughout the United States. As one of several coin-operated image and sound devices being developed in the early 1940s, the Panoram's success, while limited, far exceeded that of its competitors.[7] The Soundies catalogue featured a range of musical styles: big-band swing, country and western and "hillbilly" acts, romantic ballads, and "exotic" Hawaiian and Latin numbers. Perhaps most significantly, a large number of African American artists and jazz orchestras created Soundies at a time when the circulation of these performances on film was exceedingly rare. The distribution of film reels for the Panoram was exclusive to the Soundies Distributing Corporation of America, which released nearly two thousand Soundies during the company's seven years of operation.

Yet even early press lauding the Panoram as the next sure thing expressed some reservations about the quality of the product. "If early 'soundies' are on the monotonous side," *Look* magazine commented, "they will probably get by on their novelty."[8] Indeed, novelty and topicality were the primary operatives of the Soundie, with vaudeville-style acts, burlesque numbers such as Sally Rand's "The Bubble Dance," a flurry of numbers related to World War II, and comedy titles such as "Who Threw the Turtle in Mrs. Murphy's Girdle?" Certainly the fusion of image and popular music was not what made the Soundie new. Musical features dominated the box office in the 1940s, and there was a tradition of musical shorts dating back at least to the Vitaphone. The visual aesthetics of the films were also far from innovative. Limited by extremely small budgets and resistance from both the film and recording industries, the producers of Soundies created shorts that were often formulaic, stilted, and riddled with clichés. Despite attempts to engage viewers with comedic acts and even sexually suggestive material, the Soundies Distributing Corporation was never able to build or sustain a consistent audience.

The novelty of the Soundies, therefore, appears to be tied to the unusual format of the medium: the integration of moving images with musical jukeboxes, the location of the machines in nontheatrical public spaces, the reliance on exclusively musical subject matter, and the visual documentation of artists outside the Hollywood studio system. These material conditions resulted in image-sound combinations that did, in fact, differ significantly from more traditional musical films. Soundies were never intended to be miniature musicals. Experienced by audiences of the 1940s as a phenomenon that closely echoed that of popular recorded music, the Soundie required a new kind of image, one not dictated by narrative but by the affectivity of song. Unlike feature-length musical films, Soundies contain no surrounding narrative. The visual structure of the jukebox film is set by the music, and the emotions expressed are native to the song alone; even in those Soundies with a rough story line, there is no true character development. Although some shorts might mimic the tropes of Hollywood production numbers, they share little else in common.

The development of the Soundies' display and distribution system was influenced by a combination of technical, economic, and social concerns. Unlike traditional jukeboxes, the design of the Panoram did not allow listeners to choose individual songs. The cabinet contained a 16mm projector holding an 800-foot loop of film. The film was projected onto a mirror, which in turn reflected the image onto an 18 by 22 inch ground-glass screen.[9] Because the loop was continuous, patrons could only watch and listen to whichever song was next on the reel. Producers were therefore anxious to include a range of musical genres to attract as many customers as possible. Each week, the Soundies Distributing Corporation provided Panoram owners with a new reel of films. According to Soundies expert Mark Cantor, these eight-song preassembled reels adhered to a loose formula that included a variety of set genres. It became common practice, for example, to include an African American number in the eighth position on the reel. Although the Soundies catalogue offered the option of customized reels, they provided a "general outline of what a reel should look like (one vocalist, one novelty number, one ethnic number, one dance number, etc.)." Renters certainly could, however, choose to tailor their reels according to more specific demographic tastes. That shorts by African American artists were listed in a separate "Negro" section suggests that racial divisions might have affected the distribution of these Soundies, although little data regarding the actual distribution patterns has survived.[10]

Many Soundies were set in barrooms and addressed their audiences in ways that suggested a continuity between the diegetic space and the space of the viewer—with an invitation to sing along or even to make a request.[11] Others relied on the premise of a nightclub performance or the barest sketch of a narrative based on the song's lyrics. The stars of Soundies shorts covered a broad spectrum, from well-known artists such as Louis Armstrong and Hoagy Carmichael to unknowns who went on to greater fame: Gale Storm, Cyd Charisse, Nat "King" Cole, and Liberace. The location of the Panoram machines seems to have had some bearing on the selection of images: many, like Spike Jones's "Clink! Clink! Another Drink," featured drinking as an explicit theme. Soundies also contained an inordinate amount of "cheesecake"—nearly every number, regardless of genre or lyrical content, included a parade of pretty girls (often the same six pretty girls) in revealing outfits vaguely related to the song's theme.

Like many Soundies, "Clink! Clink! Another Drink" (1942), by Spike Jones and His City Slickers, features drinking as an explicit theme. The Panoram machine makes an appearance in the film, inviting patrons to sing (and drink) along.

Soundies, by definition, take music as their primary element. The sound was recorded prior to filming, and the performers would lip-synch to the song as it was played back. As a result, the music does not become folded into the visual narrative that it accompanies, but rather the visuals are conceived of as a complement to the preexisting sound. This hierarchy becomes painfully obvious the more Soundies one views. Filmed at breakneck speed and on a shoestring budget, most performances were starkly set and costumed, and it was not uncommon for the performers to occasionally stumble out of sync.

In many ways, the Soundie can be likened to the record album. The two industries were closely linked, and their products moved along similar paths of distribution and consumption. Critical to an understanding of both the cinematic jukebox film and the musical jukebox is the experience of time that each evokes. Popular recorded music has a unique and multifaceted temporality. The record is portable, reproducible, and can be played repeatedly at will. Yet pressed into its grooves is the indexical mark of the voice and the strains of the instruments—an indelible reference to a particular instant. Murmurs of that irretrievable past reemerge, anachronistically, in the present of each listening. In addition to its temporal manipulations, the recorded popular song unleashes new configurations of space. There is a continual pull between proximity and distance, the closeness of the recorded performance belying, or at times highlighting, the remoteness of its point of origin. These temporal and spatial relations become even more involved when music is paired with the filmed image. Film is similarly imprinted with the mark of the past

AMY HERZOG

and is experienced in the ephemeral, temporal, and repeatable duration of the projection. Both mediums bear a distinct emotive force that circulates beyond the moments they capture.

Like the record player or sound-only jukebox, the Panoram affords the viewer a strange amalgam of intimacy and longing in a public setting. The prurient nature of some of the images might lend an intimate tone, but the size of the screen would as well, since it required that viewers stand in close proximity to see the image. The familiarity of many of the artists and tunes could only heighten the sensation of proximity, as would the individual control over repeatability that the jukebox provided (though one would have to spend eight dimes and a good portion of time waiting for the desired number to work its way around the reel). The limitations of recording and playback technology, however, only serve to reassert the remoteness of the originary performance. The affectivity of the Soundie seems to arise from this incongruity: the continued rehearsal of an instant that can never be fully grasped.

The images of the Soundie, even at their most uninventive, appear tailored toward this somewhat conflicted viewing experience. Despite the range of musical genres and shooting styles embodied by the Soundie, several common tensions persist. One of the most obvious exists between the prerecorded soundtrack and attempts to visually mime a live rendition. Soundies commonly act as a document of a singular performance, especially in the case of well-known, more expensive performers such as Cab Callaway, Duke Ellington, or Stan Kenton. The scenarios for these Soundies are extremely simple and straightforward. Positioned on decorative stages before audiences in a club, the musicians are the primary focus of the camera. More often than not, these films contain no narrative elements and are accentuated only by occasional shots of dancing couples or chorines. In these performance-based Soundies, the viewer is aware of the artists in an intimate, bodily sense. Removed from the inaccessible sheen of the glitzy, big-budget numbers found in the typical feature-length musical, these performances seem more spontaneous and sincere. Since many of these musicians had not been filmed previously, the impact of such Soundies, displayed in a small format and controlled by the viewer, cannot be overestimated. Yet, at the same time, the clumsiness of the production, the clear distance between the poorly synched and separately recorded tracks, opens a fissure that makes the viewer's distance from the performance painfully felt. Moreover, these glitches throw into question the authenticity of that performance itself; faced with the evidence of its existence, the performance remains uncannily detached.

A second tension emerges between the nonrepresentational status of music and the fumbling attempts to represent it quite literally. Soundies functioned not only as documents, but also as enhanced visual illustrations. This role is most evident in comedy numbers or lower-budget filler numbers, which impart a cute visual twist on what would otherwise be an uneventful rendition. Whereas more established or dynamic musicians were able to hold the viewer's attention within the simplest of scenarios, lesser-known performers needed additional visual emphasis. Stock musicians and comedic vaudeville acts were employed to fill out the shooting schedule during extended periods of union dispute between Soundies producers and musicians' unions.[12] Many of these songs relied on humorous lyrical content or generic themes (wartime propaganda, traditional Irish songs, etc.) rather than on inherent musical interest. The directors faced the challenge of translating these often mediocre numbers into a visual format as quickly and inexpensively as possible.

The solutions to this challenge range from the mundane to the utterly bizarre. The images in these films frequently correspond directly to the lyrics. In "The Wise Old Owl," Sylvia Froos's straight rendition of the swing ballad is punctuated by the hoots of a stuffed owl jerking back and forth on a branch over her head. Comedy numbers usually consist of rough narrative reenactments. Cindy Walker's "Seven Beers with the Wrong Man" depicts Walker in an Old West–style jail cell, intercutting slapstick scenes of her seduction. Soundies that fall within distinct musical subgenres employ the most obvious locations and tropes as a backdrop. Countless country and western shorts, for instance, take place in barnyard settings. Other Soundies use the visual component of the medium as fodder for one-liners. "The Biggest Aspidistra in the World" depicts singers with the Johnny Mercer Orchestra lauding the features of their aspidistra plant. As they emphasize the first syllable of the word, however, the camera pans to a row of girls with watering cans, who bend over to reveal their ruffled panties. Such scenarios encapsulate the often dissonant humor of the Soundie, which results from the desire to interpret the song absolutely literally, and excessively so. The image becomes a comic, or perhaps even a monstrous, illustration of the lyric.

Chion, in his writings on film and sound, develops the idea of "added

"The Biggest Aspidastra in the World" (1942), by Johnny Messner and His Orchestra, makes use of a crude visual-sonic pun.

value" to describe "the expressive and informative value with which a sound enriches a given image so as to create the definite impression . . . that this information or expression 'naturally' comes from what is seen, and is already contained in the image itself."[13] Although the concept of added value is useful in exploring the function of music in narrative film, it is a relation that does not exist in musically based visual formats. Discussing the music video, Chion writes: "This is yet another way in which the music video leads us back to the silent cinema—seemingly a paradox, since we're talking about a form constructed on music. But it is precisely insofar as music does form its basis, and none of the narration is propelled by *dialogue*, that the music video's image is fully liberated from the linearity normally imposed by sound."[14]

Charges of musical cliché are levied against narrative film when sound and image exist in a direct and obvious relation to each other. Abstraction and autonomy are cited as the best means of complicating these relations. Yet as both Chion and Claudia Gorbman suggest, in musically based works all visual movements are in a sense abstractions in that they are dictated by the logic and temporality of music rather than narrative. The elements within the film frame, set in motion by the music, become mobile and thus are freed, at least to a certain degree, from the burdens of signification, motivation, and logical development.[15]

The musical logic that Chion and Gorbman point to, I would argue, dictates the Soundie's visual construction. Instead of reading Soundies as linear constructions, it may be more productive to view them as constellations of images. The Soundie's images in fact obtain their emotive affectivity through the tensions between their irrational and anachronistic juxtapositions. The images, melodies, and ideas that constitute meaning within Soundies circulate in ways that are always fluid and multifaceted. Each element within the Soundie works as part of this mobile assemblage, but the overall effect is rarely one of harmonious synthesis. Instead, each component (the culturally charged scenario, the poorly timed performance, the familiar tune) seems to reverberate disparately, leaving the impression of discordant refrains that are always somehow out of time.

Although the producers of Soundies might have designed imagery in a literal and linear manner, the overall effect of the Soundie's sonic and visual couplings is a viewing and listening experience that is hardly straightforward. Indeed it is the very failure of the Soundie to re-create an integrated, convincing illustration of a performance that exposes the conflicts at the core of that project. Moreover, the often politically troubling imagery of the Soundie, which seems to stoop to the most obvious and stereotypical portrayals of gender, race, and ethnicity at every opportunity, points to the prevalence of such representations within the twentieth-century cultural imagination. The glaringness of such depictions, surely amplified by historical distance, suggests the possibility that these perspectives are more subtly embedded in the songs themselves. The uncomfortable melding of abstract and representational elements in the Soundie opens the musical-image to multiple, critical interpretations—readings that perhaps would be foreclosed by more slickly produced or narrative-based works.

The Mills Brothers's Soundie for their hit "Paper Doll," for example, opens with the brothers seated in a garden set. Three of the brothers have smiling women seated on their knees, while the brother singing lead cuts out a picture of Dorothy Dandridge with a pair of scissors. He sings of a paper doll "to call his own," wishing for her affections rather than "a fickle-minded, real-life girl." As he places the cutout paper Dandridge on the ground, however, she dissolves into a live image and begins to dance energetically in a short, frilled, girlish dress. The brothers look down as they sing over her miniature, ghostly figure superimposed before them.

"Paper Doll" is composed of two distinct sections. In the first half, the camera's attention is divided between documenting the singers' performance and enacting the song's lyrics. Though adequate attention is paid to the real "dolls" adorning the brothers' laps and the cutting of the photograph, the center of action is each singer's face: the "column of air" leaving the mouth that constitutes, for Chion, the visual essence of the

AMY HERZOG

The Mills Brothers's "Paper Doll" (1942), featuring a silent Dorothy Dandridge.
(left to right, top to bottom)

vocal performance.[16] Both the imagery and the musical rhythm shift dramatically, however, when Dorothy Dandridge's paper cutout comes to life. The focus, too, shifts from an enhanced documentation of the Mills Brothers's performance to a surreal visualization removed from the actions of the singers. The relationship between image and sound at this point is significantly transformed. Our perspective on the singers is now the back of their heads looming over Dandridge — an uninviting composition lacking a clear visual reference to the sound source. Dandridge's spastic movements have little relation to what is happening musically, or perhaps only seem out of time because her tapping feet are silent. In combination with her girlish frock, Dandridge's choreography seems to reflect less the delicate steps of a breathing paper doll and more the gesticulations of an invention gone awry.

To say that Dandridge appears as a projection of the Mills Brothers's fantasy of femininity is nearly beside the point. Although such a reading would correctly highlight the problematic, sexist premise of the song and film, it leaves unexamined the uneasy excessiveness of Dandridge's pasted-on figure, a presence that resists any obvious critique. The image is in fact so literal that it exceeds or even defies the meaning of the original lyric. Dandridge's disquieting presence, however spectral, makes the desire for "the truest doll in all this world" too palpable, too real. And this, to me, is where the discomfort lies. The stolid framework of the scenario gives rise to an image that is surprising and unsettling, for it confronts us with an impossible embodiment. What we see laid bare is the very structure of the fantasy.

Music, as a nonrepresentational medium, is itself visually unrepresentable. Chion compares attempts to film an instrumental performance with pornography's attempt to capture the sexual act: no matter where you train the camera, what you are looking for always seems to be elsewhere.[17] Soundies do not succeed in this impossible task. Yet where these representations falter, a different framework becomes apparent, one that imbues these images with their haunting affectivity. This is where the primacy of music, and a musical logic, is essential. What would otherwise remain a stereotypical or prosaic image becomes abstracted, exaggerated, immoderate. That which is threatening need not be resolved or punished as it often is in narrative forms. Soundies may make use of oppressive images, but they also in many ways interrogate them. Within Soundies there is room for irrationality, transformation, eruption—even a joy in difference. Surely the threat of the irrational never exceeds its containment within the song, but its mere existence hints at a nascent potential.

OVERLAPPING TECHNOLOGIES

The Soundies Distributing Corporation ceased its distribution of films in 1947. Conflicts with the musicians' unions, competition with other entertainment industries, and the pressures of wartime manufacturing had plagued the enterprise throughout its lifetime. The shorts enjoyed a comparatively long run on the home movie market, however, as the films

AMY HERZOG

were purchased by several corporations (namely Castle and Official) and spliced onto "thematic" reels for mail order distribution.[18] Another series of musical films emerged shortly after the Soundies; although similar in structure, they differered in terms of their marketing and distribution. Two companies, Snader Telescriptions and Studio Telescriptions, began producing musical shorts exclusively for television in the early 1950s.

Sold primarily to local stations and commercial enterprises, telescriptions could be used to fill broadcasting gaps or be edited into pseudo variety shows interspersed with sponsored messages. Some of these shorts are indistinguishable from Soundies in terms of their props, costuming, and lyric-based scenarios. Many telescriptions, however, filmed and recorded sound simultaneously in simple studio settings, resulting in significant shifts in tone and address. "Home," a Snader Telescription by Nat "King" Cole feels markedly more intimate than some of his more elaborate Soundies; the tracks appear to be recorded directly, and the bare set and close camera work resemble a live televised performance. In the end the telescription market proved to be limited, and it became outmoded after only a few years of production. *Bandstand*, the Philadelphia television program that evolved into *American Bandstand*, was introduced as a telescription-deejay show in 1952. Audiences disliked the format, however, and it was quickly reformulated into a performance showcase with a teen studio audience.[19]

Television was indeed beginning to assert its presence during the Panoram's brief lifetime, yet the transition between the cinematic jukebox and television might not be as straightforward as this history implies. There are ways in which jukebox technology, in fact, may have influenced early perceptions of television's position within public spaces. Although much attention has been paid to the cultural impact of television in the home, Anna McCarthy points to the integral role that TV plays in nondomestic environs. In her study of television in 1940s taverns, McCarthy discusses the early use of coin-operated devices to regulate relations between spectators, customers, and the television monitor. In an attempt to maintain beverage sales and dissuade those seeking a free show, television jukeboxes were marketed to bar owners, providing an allotment of viewing time for each coin deposited.[20] The Panoram and television were each seen as a challenge to the social atmosphere of the bar and to preexisting forms of entertainment. When placed in taverns or clubs, both formats faced regulation and fierce opposition from theater owners and other media interests.[21] It is clear that each technology occupied a contested and often undefined space within the shifting terrains of the entertainment industry and the public sphere.

There are crucial differences, however, between the manipulations of space and time produced by the film jukebox and early television. The use of a coin-operated interface represented an ill-fated attempt to harness TV's continuity and immediacy, arguably the most characteristic aspects of the medium. The film jukebox, however, is structured around the fixed, encapsulated time frame of each three-minute song. Soundies, for example, began and ended with titles and credits or visual devices such as opening and closing curtains. The coin-op interface of the film jukebox also lent intimacy and control to the viewer rather than an unwelcome intrusion. The brevity of each song, coupled with the cost of feeding the machine, prevented the film jukebox from providing the kind of ambient presence that McCarthy argues television provides.

The transition between the Panoram Soundie and television is thus extraordinarily tangled. Like television, the Panoram was a sound-based format and had closer ties to the radio and music industries than to the film industry. Yet the Panoram offered an affective experience markedly distinct from that of television, even in instances where the placement and operation of the device was relatively similar. Soundies set a precedent that clearly influenced later televisual manifestations, yet at the same time they were incapable of capitalizing on the simultaneity of the video medium. The tensions between these two formats had much to do with their status as emergent technologies in the 1940s. In the 1960s, however, when a second incarnation of the cinematic jukebox was released, television held a more established position within the public and private spheres. Popular music, too, underwent significant transformations in terms of marketing, audience, and style. The Scopitone jukebox thus differed from the Panoram in terms of format, aesthetics, and social function. At the same time, the Scopitone producers were careful to distinguish their films from televised musical programming.

THE SCOPITONE

In "Notes on Camp" Susan Sontag places Scopitone films third on her list of "random examples of items which are part of the canon of Camp." Though she does not describe Scopitones in detail, they seem to epitomize her definition of "pure" or "naïve Camp"; Scopitones don't intend to be funny, yet humor emerges precisely from the failure of their earnestness.[22] Released in the early 1960s, Scopitone jukeboxes offered a selection of hip-shimmying bubblegum pop. Shot with very small budgets, Scopitone films featured a catalogue of performers and songs that, even at the time, were decidedly square. Given the complex evolution of the term, however, I would hesitate to identify Scopitones as "camp." Many critics have thoroughly countered Sontag's assertion that "the Camp sensibility is disengaged, depoliticized—or at least apolitical" through theorizations of the practices of performance and political critique associated with camp.[23] Given camp's centrality to queer theory and to gay culture in general, it seems inappropriate to apply the term to cultural artifacts that lack a critical rhetorical stance, let alone any shreds of self-awareness or irony.

Yet, at the same time, the multifaceted nature of the term *camp* may suggest a useful means of approaching Scopitones. Despite the debates that surround camp and the somewhat related categories of kitsch and cheese (also common descriptors for Scopitones), each term is interchangeably applied to objects, events, and strategies of interpretation.[24] Meaning, this slippage implies, resides neither with the object or the subject who perceives it, but in the collapsed space of their interaction. Labeling Scopitones campy or cheesy may reveal little about these films, yet it is critical to understand that these texts are inseparable from the act of reading them. Responses to anomalous material such as jukebox films are almost entirely determined by one's cultural and historical position. This is perhaps the most prominent tension contained within the reading of kitsch, camp, or cheese: the temporal and spatial distance of the audience from the artifact's place of origin.[25]

Sontag does in fact see this temporal displacement as essential to a camp sensibility. "The process of aging or deterioration," she writes, "provides the necessary detachment—or arouses the necessary sympathy. . . . Time contracts the sphere of banality. (Banality is, strictly speaking, always a category of the contemporary.) What was banal can, with the passage of time, become fantastic. . . . Thus, things are campy, not when they become old—but when we become less involved in them, and can enjoy, instead of be frustrated by, the failure of the attempt."[26] It is somewhat curious, then, that Scopitone films should take such a prominent position in Sontag's camp catalogue in 1964, the year they were first

Jody Miller is upstaged by the dancing "ponies" in "The Race Is On."

released in the United States. Perhaps this can be attributed to a geographic displacement. Scopitones were a French invention, and though many shorts were produced in the United States, the earliest titles were predominantly European. The production standards for French Scopitones were generally low, and they frequently depicted artists unknown to North American viewers, who sang popular English-language songs in French.[27] There are other ways in which Scopitones distanced themselves from certain audiences. Even English-language Scopitones favored older, established performers, singing bouncy pop standards, over more youth-oriented rock groups. The most immediately obvious feature of Scopitones is their shameless, clumsy reliance on sexploitative visual material, regardless of the subject matter or tempo of the song. It would be difficult to argue that even a viewer in 1965 could watch a Scopitone such as Jody Miller's "The Race Is On"—which depicts four female dancers in bikinis and feathered tails prancing like horses around a race track—without experiencing some form of disconnection.

Scopitones represent a departure from Soundies in a number of ways. Scopitone jukeboxes were selectable, presenting viewers with a choice of up to thirty-six separate titles. The visual composition of Scopitones is completely dissimilar to that of earlier jukebox films; they were shot on color stock and filmed either on location or on highly stylized sets. Scopitone films contained a magnetic soundtrack, which provided a vast improvement on the quality of the Panoram's optical soundtrack. Compared to Soundies the subjects of Scopitones were more stylistically limited, mainly consisting of upbeat standards. As in Soundies, in Scopitones the preexisting, prerecorded song dictates the structure of its visualization. And here again there is a marked disjunction between the sound and its image, a faltering that feels at once intimate and remote. The Scopitone's disorienting effect is distinct from that of the Soundie, however. Certainly both formats suffer from low production values, a factor that contributes to the failed synthesis of the tracks and the unsuccessful engagement of the viewer. But whereas the distancing tension between image and music in the Soundie has much to do with the novelty of the format, the primary tension in the Scopitone seems to lie elsewhere. Instead, the disconnection between sound and image may arise from the Scopitone's idiosyncratic attempts to be both an innovative and a staid form of entertainment. The contradictory nature of the Scopitone is linked to this pull between the new and the outmoded and the various pleasures and discomforts to which it gives rise.

Unlike Soundies, Scopitones emerged at a moment when the televisual apparatus had achieved a highly developed state. There is even evidence to suggest that Scopitone technology was envisioned as a competitor to television. In a release promoting the Scopitone's potential for "'theme' and 'mood' advertising," *Billboard* predicted that the Scopitone would replace "television sets in some cafes and bars, and if the insertion of advertising is successful it promises to replace TV altogether because of its revenue-generating advantage."[28]

Yet the Scopitone jukebox did not follow through on this threat, and in fact it enjoyed only a limited presence in the United States. In many ways this failure was caused by the lack of integration of the recording and jukebox film industries—a shortcoming that music video producers were careful to avoid. Whereas music videos were considered one of the most potent tools for advertising popular music at the height of the MTV era, the music industry in the 1960s viewed jukebox films as ineffective at best and a liability at worst. Reporting on the lack of British-produced Scopitones circulating in the United Kingdom, *Billboard* attributed the problem to the uncooperative nature of the British record industry. "Record firms generally feel that the cinema juke box is a good medium for standards, but they have reservations about the use of the unit for current hit material."[29] Though French "diskeries" allowed for the simultaneous production and release of Scopitones and record singles, the industries in the United States and Britain did not follow suit. Caught somewhere between television, the recording industries, and the coin-op jukebox distribution networks, the Scopitone represented a failed synthesis of interests.

The Scopitone jukebox was developed in France from surplus military equipment in the late 1950s. The first model was released in 1960 by the Compagnie d'Applications Méchaniques à l'Electronique au Cinéma et à l'Atomistique (CAMECA) to be distributed throughout Europe.[30] The Scopitone machine featured a complex loading mechanism: up to thirty-six films were held on a rotating drum that could play and rewind each individual selection. In 1963 the Scopitone was brought to test markets in the United States, and in 1964 Scopitone Inc., a subsidiary of the Chicago Tel-A-Sign manufacturing company, introduced an updated model of the jukebox for nationwide distribution.

Initially, U.S. Scopitone machines were stocked with French and European titles licensed from CAMECA. The French Scopitones were shot on extremely low budgets, often outdoors, using available light and Eastman Color stock. French-produced Scopitones featured performers such as Françoise Hardy, Vince Taylor, Serge Gainsbourg and Brigitte Bardot, and lesser known artists such as Les Surfs, Aimable et Zappy Max, and Les Soeurs Kessler.[31] These performers had limited appeal outside France, however, and by late 1964 Harman-ee Productions (a branch of the Hollywood company Harman Enterprises, owned by Debbie Reynolds and Irving Briskin) was enlisted as the principal producer of Scopitone films in the United States. The production values were significantly increased for these shorts. Shot in Technicolor, the United States films were vibrant and less susceptible to fading. They also made greater use of sets, props, and scenarios loosely inspired by song lyrics. The catalogue of U.S. Scopitones was far smaller than that of the French; artists included Debbie Reynolds, Nancy Sinatra, Neil Sedaka, Lou Rawls, Della Reese, January Jones, and the Hondells.

The industry response to Scopitones, as to Soundies, often contained thinly veiled skepticism. A *Billboard* article titled "Cinema Juke Box: Just a Novelty?" reports decidedly mixed predictions from coin-op industry representatives.[32] In an explicit attempt not to challenge the domain of the music-only jukebox, Scopitone avoided appeals to the burgeoning youth market. As *Billboard* assessed Harman-ee's strategy:

> Programming is based on the theory that the machines will be placed in adult locations and that grown-ups want to hear familiar artists singing familiar songs.
>
> If Scopitone becomes established in teen-age locations, the program-

AMY HERZOG

ming will have to be supplemented with films made by some of the newer pop artists. In that case, the film producer would have to gamble. The current material is primarily library stuff. It's not calculated to die quickly. And as making a film entails a lot more expense than cutting a single, its [sic] unlikely that the emphasis will shift too much from bread-and-butter artists to new chart entries.[33]

Many of the problems cited in trade publications seem to anticipate the successful strategies of the music video industry: close ties between the video and recording industries; the cooperation of artist trade unions; and shared systems of marketing, research, and distribution. One anonymous industry executive "noted for progressive business practices" stated that "after close acquaintance with the music-film trend he has become convinced that the audio-visual concept is here to stay—but not in its present form."[34]

Scopitones represent more, however, than just a failure on the road to the music video. Like Soundies, they draw on different manipulations of space and time, modes of address, and visual and sonic relations. After viewing any number of Scopitones, one quickly surmises that their primary objective is to display as much scantily clad female flesh as possible. Certainly Soundies had relied on similar appeals to audiences, but shifts in musical style and thresholds of permissiveness rendered the Scopitones far more explicit. Shooting styles were also greatly transformed by the 1960s; mobile cameras, zooms, extreme close-ups, and fast edits allowed for the inclusion of more gratuitous footage.

The use of such material in Scopitones is frequently incongruous. There is no question that the preponderance of bikinis and up-the-skirt camera angles is blatantly sexist and exploitative. Yet the producers miscalculate the timing and impact of this imagery on every level, nearly to the point of desexualization. It is impossible to measure, of course, the degree to which this retrospective response is a result of historical distance. We can nevertheless with some certainty point to empirical elements in the films that demonstrate attempts to incorporate disparate interests. Many of the vocalists selected to appeal to the adult market were themselves middle aged. Singers like Kay Starr appeared in modest attire, yet they were always surrounded by a chorus of Scopitone "beauties." In "Wheel of Fortune," Starr sings on a casino-styled set, begging the wheels of fate to grant her love. The lilting tempo of the song, how-

Brook Benton's Scopitone for "Mother Nature, Father Time" includes some jarring juxtapositions.

ever, is undermined by the undulations of young dancers in spangled showgirl skivvies; in attempting to match their gyrations to the song's slow rhythm, their legs visibly shake as they spin on roulette tables. It is in fact quite typical for the movements of Scopitone dancers to exist completely outside the temporality of the song. The frenetic bouncing of the bikini-clad women in most of the films suggests that, for the producers, eroticism is equated with jumping up and down as quickly as possible while completely ignoring the accompanying music. This results in many baffling juxtapositions, such as in Brook Benton's "Mother Nature, Father Time." While Benton soulfully coos his warning, "If Mother Nature don't stop you, Father Time sure will," his image is intercut with that of a nearly naked woman in a bonnet and a bearded man in a loin cloth flailing against each other in a most alarming manner.

Other unbalanced combinations are surely amplified through hindsight yet nevertheless seem hopelessly mismatched. Lesley Gore, who was later to become a celebrated lesbian icon, gives an incredible performance in "Wonder Boy," asking the bookish, male object of her affections, "if you're so smart, how come you don't know I adore you?" This viewer found it simultaneously delightful and tragic (perhaps truly campy?) to watch Gore moon over the oblivious boy while a bevy of girls in miniskirts and well-exposed white panties do the twist behind her. Line Renaud, in "Le Hully Gully," sings while strolling around a swimming pool, seemingly unaware of the homoeroticism generated by her male back-up dancers, clad in tiny, tight swimsuit briefs, who kick and dive in line formation. Not all of the Scopitone's visual contradictions are so pleasant, however. Dick and Dee Dee's "Where Have All the Good Times Gone,"

Line Renaud's "Le Hully Gully" is one of the few Scopitones to
feature a chorus of male dancers, to delightful effect.

features the couple wandering around a semi-deserted amusement park.
Given the haphazard nature of this scenario, it seems likely that most
of the visual compositions were created on the spot and with little plan-
ning or foresight. The bizarre and disturbing decision to include a woman
dancing in front of a rifle in a target-shooting game, however, registers
as a needless shock, casting a violent, misogynist pallor over the entire
film.

Like Soundies, Scopitones demonstrate a staunch reliance on the literal. Joi Lansing's "Web of Love" is exemplary in this regard. The song's
sequences escalate in their preposterous illustration of the lyrics. Lansing compares love to a witch doctor while sitting in a frothy cauldron
surrounded by unconvincing "natives"; when she describes herself as a
bird in a cage, she stands in a birdcage, flapping feathered arms across
her cleavage. The next verse calls love "a big black cobra," at which point
a man clad in a patterned body suit attempts to slither across Lansing's
lap. Though Lansing's body remains well exposed throughout, the ridicu-
lousness of these images, clearly comic yet not ironic or self-conscious,
drastically undermines the potential eroticism of the scene.

We cannot determine retrospectively whether the majority of the Scopitone's contemporary viewers found its films to be as campy or kitschy
as Sontag did. Nevertheless, Scopitones addressed that audience in a
manner that was simultaneously earnest, humorous, racy, and square,
indicating at the very least a multiplicity of intentions from the outset.
Scopitones neither possessed the spontaneity of televised performance
programs such as *Shindig, Hullabaloo,* and *American Bandstand* (although
there is a great deal of similarity between the imagery used in Scopitones

Dick and Dee Dee engage in a disturbing game of target practice in "Where Have All the Good Times Gone."

and in the prerecorded musical performances sometimes aired on these shows) nor were they remotely similar to feature-length rock and roll films. While not exactly a fusion of either of these formats, the Scopitone fell somewhere between them, forging an entirely distinct, more intimate mode of address. Unlike either the television music show or the rock film, the images of the Scopitone figure the individual viewer solidly within the space of the song—not as an anonymous audience member but through the personalized nature of the images and projection apparatus. Scopitone users selected tracks individually and would need to stand near the machine to enjoy their purchase. The cinematography imagines a singular viewer as well, since performers always address the camera directly (not to mention the direct address of the up-the-skirt shot). Though this experience takes place, paradoxically, in a public space, the individualized fantasy that the Scopitone encourages seems not unlike the interpellation of viewers by the music video. Though vastly different in their imageries and market appeals, both the Scopitone and the music video position the viewer as the sole recipient of the performance.

This manner of addressing the audience is perhaps where the hints of a televisual mode surface most clearly. Steve Wurtzler characterizes various sound "events" according to a spatial/temporal schema of absence and presence, simultaneity and anteriority.[35] Recorded events, through their spatial and temporal remove, are thus experienced differently than are live performances. Yet as Wurtzler is quick to point out, there are numerous events that confuse and collapse these binaries: telephone conversations, live television and radio broadcasts, and lip-synching. Moreover, the discursive address of a particular medium may further obscure

AMY HERZOG

Joi Lansing meets a witch doctor before being literally trapped in a "Web of Love."

distinctions between the original and the represented. Television in particular constructs itself according to the parameters of the simultaneous, such that even prerecorded material may be experienced as somehow live.[36]

Scopitones do not purport to be live, but they do position themselves at the interstices of the temporal and spatial axes Wurtzler identifies. In this way the address of the Scopitone correlates to that of the music video. Scopitones and music videos both strive to overcome the repeatability of the reproduction and the public format of the presentation to elicit an intimate and direct connection. The proximity of the microphone to the performer during sound recording works to generate what Rick Altman calls a "for-me-ness" quality, whereby the sound remains direct, close, and at a consistent volume even when the images show the sound source at a distance. The effect is that the sound has been created specifically for the listener, "lending a discursive 'feel' to images that seem to deny discursivity."[37] Whereas in film this recording practice is often used to increase the legibility of dialogue (although it is by no means limited to this purpose), in the freestanding musical short the consistency and closeness of the music ensure a personal connection with the viewer. At the same time, the stability of the music allows the image to veer into fragmentation and irrationality. As Berland observes about the contemporary music video, "However bizarre or disruptive videos appear, they never challenge or emancipate themselves from their musical foundation, without which their charismatic indulgences would never reach our eyes."[38] Thus while the images of the Scopitone visualize the music with little spatial or temporal consistency, the music itself works to collapse the distance between listener and event. The Scopitone's visualizations are neither as free nor as seamless as the music video, yet they do rely on this same commingling of abstraction and intimacy. Rather than flights into utter irrationality, however, the misguided contradictions contained within the Scopitone expose the viewer's conflicted position. The seduction of the personalized appeal is undermined by the failure of its realization, thereby forcing each component (images, music, film, viewer, etc.) into an uneasy confrontation.

IMPOSSIBLE EMBODIMENTS

We cannot trace a simple historical trajectory from film jukeboxes to the music video. Nevertheless there are critical connections among each of the formats I have discussed here in terms of the manner in which they portray popular music. The discomfort elicited by Soundies and Scopitones seems to emerge from their spatial and temporal dislocations. Yet these disorienting qualities point to the very thing that the films seek to accomplish—to achieve presence. With the ubiquity and simultaneity of television and video, the music video does this work in radically different, more effective ways. This shift represents more than an advancement in sophistication, however; it is the evolution of a mode of listening, seeing, and communicating that developed with and through earlier technologies.

Perhaps this is a movement that is specific to the combination of popular music and moving images, one enacted through the process of playback. "In playback," Chion writes, "there is someone before us whose entire effort is to attach his face and body to the voice we hear. We're witnessing a performance whose risks and failures become inscribed on the film. . . . Playback is a source of direct, even *physical* emotion. . . . Playback marshals the image in the effort to embody."[39] Unlike dubbing, where the labor of melding voice and body remains unseen, playback, for Chion, palpably enacts the longing for a union that is always revealed to be impossible.

This impossibility lies at the heart of the work that jukebox films perform. The moment at which the union between sound and image is proved false is the point at which these films, intentionally or not, are

AMY HERZOG

the most affecting. The impossibility of the combination, however, extends beyond the rift between body and voice. The social and political implications of each embodiment are also hyperexaggerated, depicting a confluence of elements that feels decidedly false. These representations demand critique, but I would argue that at the same time they contain a highly productive tension. The labor of their aspirations is also palpable, and their falterings, even when funny or endearing, are overwhelmingly uncanny. The failures of these performances, and our failed affective involvement with them, expose a rift in our system of representation, revealing the desires and discomforts of our fantasies as equally impossible to represent or to obtain.

NOTES

I would like to thank Ed Stratman and the George Eastman House for granting me access to their archive; and Fred MacDonald for film transfers from the MacDonald and Associates archive. I am further indebted to the insights provided by Claudia Gorbman, Gillian Anderson, and the participants at the Music / Image in Film and Multimedia conference at New York University, June 2001, where a version of this paper was first presented.

1 Michel Chion, *Audio-Vision: Sound on Screen*, ed. and trans. Claudia Gorbman (New York: Columbia University Press, 1994), 157.

2 Ibid., 158, 163.

3 There are several notable exceptions to this trend. Jeff Smith gives an excellent account of the development of the Scopitone and its impact on narrative film music in *The Sounds of Commerce: Marketing Popular Film Music* (New York: Columbia University Press, 1998). Gregory Lukow also presents a well-researched discussion of both formats in his essay "The Antecedents of MTV: Soundies, Scopitones and Snaders, and the History of an Ahistorical Form," in *The Art of Music Video: Ten Years After*, ed. Michael Nash (Long Beach, Calif.: Long Beach Museum of Art, 1991), 6–9. John Mundy links Soundies to other film and television formats in *Popular Music on Screen: From Hollywood Musical to Music Video* (Manchester: Manchester University Press, 1999), 93–95. For discussions of Soundies in relation to the history of jazz and jazz on film, see Klaus Stratemann, *Duke Ellington Day by Day and Film by Film* (Copenhagen: Jazz Media, 1992); and Krin Gabbard, *Jammin' at the Margins: Jazz and the American Cinema* (Chicago: University of Chicago Press, 1996).

4 While this was the overwhelming case with early work on music videos, subsequent criticism has moved in new directions. For critical correctives, see Andrew Goodwin, *Dancing in the Distraction Factory: Music Television and*

Popular Culture (Minneapolis: University of Minnesota Press, 1992); and Will Straw, "Popular Music and Post-Modernism in the 1980s," in *Sound and Vision: The Music Video Reader*, ed. Simon Frith, Andrew Goodwin, and Lawrence Grossberg (New York: Routledge, 1993), 3–21.

5 Jody Berland, "Sound, Image and Social Space: Music Video and Media Reconstruction," in *Sound and Vision: The Music Video Reader*, ed. Simon Frith, Andrew Goodwin, and Lawrence Grossberg (New York: Routledge, 1993), 30.

6 "Personal Report on Movie Premiere," *Billboard*, October 5, 1940, 34. For the corporate history and complete Soundies filmography, I am indebted to Maurice Terenzio, Scott MacGillivray, and Ted Okuda, *The Soundies Distributing Corporation of America: A History and Filmography* (Jefferson, N.C.: McFarland, 1991).

7 Other companies promoting cinematic jukeboxes included Vis-o-Graph, Featurettes, Phonovision, Tonovision, Metermovies, Phonofilm, and Talkavision. See Terenzio, MacGillivray and Okuda, *The Soundies Distributing Corporation of America*, 4–5; and "The Buyers Guide," *Billboard*, January 18, 1941, 80. In addition to the official "Soundies" films, I will also be considering shorts produced by rival companies during the same period. For the most part, these films do not differ widely in terms of their structure, tone, or execution, and I will group them under the general name of "Soundies" (a practice that has become commonplace among collectors and other Soundies enthusiasts).

8 "Jimmy's Got It Again," *Look*, November 19, 1940, 14. The "Jimmy" in question is James Roosevelt (son of Franklin D. Roosevelt), one of the partners and principal promoters of the enterprise.

9 The reflected nature of the Panoram mechanism causes the image to be reversed from left to right. Thus original Soundies reels, when projected normally, are flipped, including all titles and credits. After the Panoram became defunct, several companies purchased the rights to distribute existing Soundies for the home market. Often the backwards titles were snipped from the originals, and either replaced by new titles or left out altogether. This presents great problems for researchers and collectors attempting to identify obscure artists and songs.

10 Mark Cantor, e-mail correspondence with author, October 22, 2002. See also Terenzio, MacGillivray, and Okuda, *The Soundies Distributing Corporation of America*, 15.

11 Terenzio, MacGillivray, and Okuda, *The Soundies Distributing Corporation of America*, 10.

12 On the conflict between the Soundies Distributing Corporation and the American Federation of Musicians, see ibid., 12–13.

13 Chion, *Audio-Vision*, 5.

14 Ibid., 167.

15 See Claudia Gorbman's discussion of "orchestration" in a scene from *Nights*

of *Cabiria* in her *Unheard Melodies: Narrative Film Music* (Bloomington: Indiana University Press, 1987), 24–25.

16 Michel Chion, *Le Son au Cinema* (Paris: Cahiers du Cinema / Editions de l'Etoile, 1985), 183–84.

17 Ibid., 191.

18 Terenzio, MacGillivray, and Okuda, *The Soundies Distributing Corporation of America*, 17–24.

19 Lukow, "The Antecedents of MTV," 9.

20 Anna McCarthy, *Ambient Television: Visual Culture and Public Space* (Durham, N.C.: Duke University Press, 2001), 45.

21 See ibid., 29–62; and Terenzio, MacGillivray, and Okuda, *The Soundies Distributing Corporation of America*, 1–16, for outlines of the conflicts each technology faced in the public market.

22 Susan Sontag, "Notes on 'Camp'" (1964), in *Against Interpretation and Other Essays* (New York: Farrar, Straus and Giroux, 1966), 277; 282–84.

23 Ibid., 277. For anthologies providing an introduction to the debates surrounding camp, see Moe Meyer, ed., *The Politics and Poetics of Camp* (New York: Routledge, 1994); and Fabio Cleto, ed., *Camp: Queer Aesthetics and the Performing Subject, a Reader* (Ann Arbor: University of Michigan Press, 1999).

24 For a discussion of kitsch and cheese in relation to camp, see Annalee Newitz, "What Makes Things Cheesy? Satire, Multinationalism, and B-Movies," *Social Text* 18.2 (summer 2000): 59–82.

25 Although somewhat beyond the scope of this essay, it is interesting to consider the contemporary status of Scopitones (and Soundies) as highly collectible, almost fetishized objects of curiosity. This status, along with a more generalized historical distance, has inevitably influenced my own reading of these formats.

26 Sontag, "Notes on 'Camp,'" 285.

27 Among the numerous titles in this vein are Sylvie Vartan, "Locomotion"; Les Surfs, "Si J'Avais Un Marteau"; Les Chats Sauvages, "Sherry Baby"; Les Baronets, "Twiste et Chante"; and Richard Anthony "Itsi Bitsi Petit Bikini."

28 "Ad Tests for French Movie Juke," *Billboard*, September 11, 1961, 66.

29 Andre De Vekey, "Scopitone Seeking British Cooperation," *Billboard*, January 2, 1965, 32.

30 See Smith, *The Sounds of Commerce*, 141–46. Alternate histories are available on several Web sites. While their accuracy is sometimes questionable, given the lack of academic work on the medium, they provide a considerable amount of information. For a well-researched historical overview, see Jack Stevenson, "The Jukebox That Ate the Cocktail Lounge—The Story of the Scopitone," 1999, http://hjem.get2net.dk/jack_stevenson/scopi.htm. Another valuable resource is Bob Orlowsky's "Scopitone Archive," http://scopitone.tripod.com, which provides the most complete Scopitone filmography available.

31 French Scopitones did feature a limited number of artists from the United States and Britain, such as Paul Anka, Dion, Dionne Warwick, and Petula Clark. Germany also produced a number of titles, as did Britain.

32 Ray Brack, "Cinema Juke Box: Just a Novelty?" *Billboard*, July 10, 1965, 45.

33 "Scopitone Puts Out Pics by Disk Artists," *Billboard*, July 10, 1965, 46.

34 Brack, "Cinema Juke Box," 48.

35 Steve Wurtzler, "'She Sang Live, but the Microphone Was Turned Off': The Live, the Recorded and the *Subject* of Representation," in *Sound Theory / Sound Practice*, ed. Rick Altman (New York: Routledge, 1992), 89.

36 Ibid., 91.

37 Summary taken from Rick Altman, "Afterword: A Baker's Dozen Terms for Sound Analysis," in *Sound Theory / Sound Practice*, ed. Rick Altman (New York: Routledge, 1992), 250.

38 Berland, "Sound, Image and Social Space," 25.

39 Michel Chion, *The Voice in Cinema*, trans. Claudia Gorbman (New York: Columbia University Press, 1999), 156.

Jason Middleton

n this essay I explore a form of what Michel Chion terms "audio-vision"; that is, a "specific perceptual mode of reception" in which the auditory and visual perceptions influence and transform one another in a mutual fashion.[1] In the process of exploring this idea, I examine the mythical audiovisual unity produced when Pink Floyd's 1973 album *The Dark Side of the Moon* is substituted for the soundtrack of Victor Fleming's *The Wizard of Oz* (1939), and I suggest that an analysis of the resultant audiovisual text might add some insight to theories of the sound-image relation. The particular sort of audio-vision that is constructed by this text is based upon the pairing of familiar music—the pop or rock song—and familiar found footage. This unique conjunction, I argue, allows us to theorize a dialectical sound-image relation not fully accounted for in the existing scholarship on film music and music video. The effectiveness of a successful pairing of music with found footage depends upon the extent to which the viewer/listener is able to simultaneously perceive two incongruous interpretations of the same scene. More specifically, the viewer must be able to recall or sense the way in which the scene was inflected by its original soundtrack at the same time that he or she is perceiving the different inflections created by the new soundtrack. This mode of dual perception is most enabled when the sound-image relation is structurally similar between the two versions, and when the two possible meanings are associatively linked with one another. In addition to examining the Floyd-Oz pairing, I establish my theoretical framework through an analysis of another pairing of popular music and found footage—namely, Bruce Conner's experimental short film *Permian Strata* (1969). Finally, I examine two music videos, one by Radiohead and another by Tori Amos, that can be understood and perhaps generically classified in terms of the analytical framework I develop in relation to the conjunction of music and found footage.

In *Dancing in the Distraction Factory*, Andrew Goodwin addresses one of the most frequently voiced concerns about the sound-image relation produced in the music video form. Since the popularization of music video with the advent of MTV in 1981, critics of all stripes have frequently suggested that music video images create *limitations* upon the range of possible meanings and emotions allowed for by songs on their own. Goodwin responds by arguing that: "The debate about whether or not the video image triumphs over the song itself needs to take account of *where the emphasis lies in the visualization* (lyrics, music, or performance iconography) and surely then must engage with the question of whether or not it illustrates, amplifies, or contradicts the meaning of the song."[2]

Focusing on the lyric-image relation, Goodwin cites examples of each of the three possible modes of representation. The first of these modes — illustration — refers to music videos that attempt a fairly straightforward visualization of the song's lyrics. As Goodwin points out, the danger with this form of music video is the issue of the "making too literal of metaphors and tropes," whereby layers of meaning implicit in the song's lyrics are foreclosed.[3] Goodwin cites as an example the video for Elvis Costello's song "Shipbuilding," which reduces metaphorical lyrics about preparations for war to the simple image of constructing boats. A second mode, which Goodwin discusses third, is contradictio, referring to videos in which there is an apparent disjuncture between lyrics and image. Here Goodwin cites videos by Depeche Mode that contain very oblique lyric-image relations, and he also makes note of Michael Jackson's "Man in the Mirror" video, in which the images seem to "unintentionally undermine" the lyrics (in other words, the video represents on at least one level an aesthetic failure).

I am most interested here in the second of Goodwin's possibilities, amplification. In this case the images do not contradict the lyrics, but they do add additional meanings not explicitly manifest in the original song. One of Goodwin's examples is the video for Culture Club's "Do You Really Want to Hurt Me?" Following Graeme Turner's reading of this video, Goodwin argues that the lyrics, which seem to concern a troubled relationship, take on a more politicized meaning in the video. The singer Boy George, whose gender-bending image was the band's trademark, sings the lyrics to a courtroom judge, thus making the song take on the connotation of a plea against homophobic discrimination. As Goodwin points out, however, this additional layer of meaning is not simply arbitrarily imposed. Rather, it represents the "teas[ing] out" of a potential reading of the song that is based upon visual codes that are already in play through Boy George's star image.[4] Thus, rather than creating a *lack* in the possible meanings of the song, the video produces an *excess* of signification.

Jeff Smith, in his excellent essay "Popular Songs and Comic Allusion in Contemporary Cinema, "analyzes a related manner in which images can add an excess of signification to the lyrics of a song. Smith argues that pop songs have been increasingly used in film soundtracks to "comment . . . on the situations depicted either through [their] lyrical content or through an extramusical system of pop culture references."[5] Smith refers to the placement of familiar songs in narrative contexts, such as in the movie *The Big Chill* when Marvin Gaye's "I Heard It Through the Grapevine" aurally describes the spreading news that the characters' mutual friend has died. He points to the way that the narrative context splits the song's referent into both the familiar, original signification, and the new signification occasioned by its placement in the film. Goodwin's and Smith's analyses of semiotic excess in these sound-image relations provide a starting point for my study. But what distinguishes the audiovisual objects I will be examining from those analyzed by Goodwin and Smith is that the excess of meaning (or multiple layers of signification) is produced in the *images as well as* in the songs. What we will find is a sound-image relation that allows for a fuller realization of Chion's ideal of "audio-vision" than do most examples of film music or music video.

The pairing of *Dark Side of the Moon* with *The Wizard of Oz* must be regarded simultaneously as an audiovisual object and as a cultural practice. It has been presented as an artist's video by Julie Becker under the title *Suburban Legend*, but as a cultural practice it can simply be termed *The Dark Side of Oz* following the terminology of various Web sites devoted to the phenomenon. Depending upon context, then, it can on the one hand be situated, like the Conner film, in the domain of experimental film and video (in this case, installation art). On the other hand, understood as cultural practice, it is not simply an object that can be analyzed on its own terms but it also raises questions of audiences and reception contexts — questions to which I will return at greater length.

Watching *The Dark Side of Oz* alongside films like Conner's *Permian*

Strata led me to question exactly what it is about these sound-image pairings that offers a form of audiovisual pleasure (and in the case of *The Dark Side of Oz*, elevating the practice to something like cult status). The standard description given by Web sites devoted to *The Dark Side of Oz*; by people with whom I spoke at a public screening; or by my students after watching Conner's film is that the pleasure comes from how successfully the sound-image pairing seems to work, despite the fact that each comes from a separate, unrelated source. The classical film score is (generally) composed so as to function in a very specific relation with the image track, and music video images are shot and edited in relation to the song. But here we have two sources, apparently not intended for an audiovisual union, brought together in a way that seems to meet the criteria established by film soundtracks and music videos.

My argument is that the basis for this sense that these audiovisual pairings "work," and the source of the pleasure they seem to give people, can be understood through Noël Carroll's analysis of the logic of the "sight gag." Carroll argues that the source of humor in the sight gag is *incongruity*: two simultaneous yet incompatible interpretations are put into play visually by the image. Carroll distinguishes the sight gag from the verbal joke in that the verbal joke initially presents an incongruity, but this incongruity is retroactively resolved through the joke's punchline, which makes the joke comprehensible. With the sight gag, the play between competing interpretations is available to the audience throughout the gag. As viewers we see things one way; a character sees things another way; *and* we see that the character sees things this other way.[6] As Carroll writes, "the pleasure comes of a visually motivated conflict of interpretations over the nature of the scene."[7] The crucial detail about this experience of pleasure is that all possible interpretations, however incongruous, are available to the viewer simultaneously, despite their being unavailable to individual characters. The sight gag thus depends upon the film employing an unrestricted form of narration.

Conner's *Permian Strata* depends for its effect on a structural logic akin to the sight gag as analyzed by Carroll. The spectator is simultaneously aware of different and incongruous meanings in the film, meanings that are, however, associatively and metaphorically linked with one another. The source for the visual footage is a black-and-white Hollywood biblical film. The scenes Conner selects from the film depict a despotic ruler cruelly overseeing the stoning of a prisoner; the same ruler being visited in his chambers by a hooded figure who is visually coded as a "wise man"; and the ruler finally being subject to a message from God in the form of a blinding white light from the sky. The soundtrack for the film is provided by Bob Dylan's song "Rainy Day Women no. 12 and 35," famous for the double entendre of its chorus—"Everybody must get stoned."

Conner sets up two main forms of correspondence between the music and the images. The first is parallel editing that matches the lyrics of the Bob Dylan song and the action on the screen, thereby creating a series of visual puns. The second form involves synchronization between the tempo, rhythm, and other qualities of the music with the movement of characters in the film, as well as with the film's editing and scene-to-scene transitions. I should note again here, in relation to the subject of visual puns, that Jeff Smith's article "Popular Songs and Comic Allusion" demonstrates how the placement of familiar pop songs in contemporary films often functions to create additional meanings for the song lyrics based upon the narrative situations in the films. In what follows I suggest that the punning functions a bit differently in *Permian Strata*. The dual meaning *inherent to* the song adds a secondary level of meaning to the *images*, each playing off the other in a dialectical fashion.

The overriding pun in the film is based on the correspondence between the central lyrical refrain in the Dylan song—"Everybody must get stoned"—and the action in the film clips, which literalize Dylan's words by depicting the stoning of a prisoner. This visual literalization is in effect a natural extension of the double entendre at the heart of the song. In the verses, Dylan describes a series of situations in which one will "get stoned": "They'll stone you when you're at the breakfast table," etc. In the context of Dylan's songwriting oeuvre and the 1960s U.S. social context within which the song was released, we can understand the lyrics on one level to be a description of the persecution of the individual, possibly by authoritarian figures of "the establishment": government, organized religion, and so on. The song's chorus, however, puns on this theme established by the verses: "But I would not feel so all alone," Dylan sings, "Everybody must get stoned." Thus, the chorus can be interpreted to mean that all individuals share in the persecution described in the verses. But the chorus' phrasing also indicates that Dylan is suggesting that everyone should respond to this social pressure by "getting stoned," that is, smoking marijuana. The film footage, then, represents the song's theme of the persecution of the individual by authority figures but visually depicts the song's most overtly literal referent—the "stoning" of an individual—rather than the "covert" yet obvious exhortation to smoke marijuana. In this sense, the Conner footage could be said to de-metaphorize the song lyrics.

At the same time, however, Conner's editing creates correspondences that allow the image track to also take on the second level of meaning expressed in the song. Certain moments in the film are matched with the song's chorus in a manner that codes the characters' behavior according to conventional visual signs of the influence of marijuana on an individual. In the scene in the film in which the despot is visited by a wise man, a shot of the wise man standing with his hand on the despot's shoulder is matched with the third verse of the song. As Dylan again iterates a number of different instances in which they will "stone you," we see the wise man standing in the same position, with the despot unmoving as well. Close attention to the image reveals that the wise man appears to be talking, but, without the original soundtrack, we cannot hear his words and instead are presented with a virtually unchanging image. Then, gradually, the camera begins to dolly forward very slowly. Given the conventional use of a dolly-in to emphasize dramatic moments in a film's narrative action, the viewer is given a sense of expectation about an imminent action that will disrupt the inaction in the visual field. This sense of expectation is further increased by the cadence of the music. Just as the dolly shot pulls in tighter on the two men, we shift to the chorus, and a change from the three-chord progression of the verse, as Dylan sings "but I would not feel so all alone." The cadence of the song thus leads us to expect a moment of harmonic and lyrical resolution, and this is provided by Dylan's singing the refrain "Everybody must get stoned" followed by a return to the root chord of the verses.

The slow dolly-in, in turn, cues us to expect resolution of the dramatic action of the scene. The image track does not disappoint, but, given that we have been unable to hear any of the dialogue spoken by the wise man, the despot's reaction at this moment appears particularly inscrutable. Just as Dylan sings "Everybody must get stoned," the despot rapidly and repeatedly blinks his eyes. Then, widening his eyes to the point where he appears bug-eyed, he slowly turns his head to look up at the wise man, his expression indicating the awakening from a trance and a sense of confusion and disbelief at the man's presence. Matched with the Dylan lyric, of course, his expression and actions fit perfectly with conventional representations of the behavior of people who have "gotten stoned" by smoking marijuana. The visual puns thus function to represent both the song's overt and covert levels of meaning.

Even as it produces these puns the music maintains its overall function of providing a sense of *unity* in the image track. As Michel Chion writes: "The most widespread function of film sound consists of unifying or binding the flow of images."[8] In analyses of the classical film score, such as Kathryn Kalinak's comprehensive *Settling the Score*, music is described as functioning to emphasize and fill in information that is conveyed through the image track and dialogue. It is introduced at key moments within the film to fulfill particular functions. Such functions include smoothing over transitions between scenes and moments of spatial and temporal disjunction (such as montage sequences), compensating for a lack of diegetic sound, emphasizing narrative action through parallelism or counterpoint, creating mood and emotion, and signaling the presence of major characters or themes (the leitmotif).[9] The music, then, could be said to compensate for any perceived *lack* in the image and dialogue. As Jeff Smith and others have noted, popular music has often been employed for many of the same functions.[10]

The nondiegetic music in *Permian Strata*, however, both conforms to this unifying function and at the same time exceeds it. Connor's editing of the image track sets it up so that we generally experience a close parallelism between the rhythm and tempo of the music and the movement of characters on the screen, at times approaching what animators derogatively term "mickey mousing" (an excessive, slavish correlation between sound and image). Transitions between scenes are matched with transitions between verses and choruses, and actions that resolve a given scene are matched up with the harmonic resolution of the song's chorus when we return to the root of the chord progression. The music thus binds the images together according to many of the conventional principles of film scoring, while at the same time splitting the images into two levels of meaning. Rather than simply serving as the unobtrusive glue that fills in for the *lack* in the image track, the sound produces an *excess* in the image track. Returning to our framework from Carroll, then, the pleasurable incongruity here lies not only in the dual layers of meaning in both sound and image track produced through Conner's vertical montage, but also in how effectively these two incongruous sources are held together according to conventional principles of film scoring. The sound-image relation

is at once totally wrong and yet exactly right. We are able to simultaneously conceive of how the footage would have functioned in its original
narrative context and perceive it working but reconfigured by the new
audio track.

This simultaneous coexistence of two incongruous forms of perception is the starting point for a discussion of the effectivity of *The Dark
Side of Oz*. But this audiovisual text moves us beyond the parameters of
the logic of the sight gag. Where Conner's film produces a humorous reaction to the juxtaposition of the ostensibly serious, dramatic film footage with the Dylan song, *The Dark Side of Oz* allows for different affective
dimensions to the viewing experience, including, but not limited to, humor. I suggest below that it even allows for some rather significant thematic rereadings of the film. The suggestiveness of Julie Becker's phrase
Suburban Legend as the title of her video points to the object as representing a shared idea or experience among a particular socio-cultural
group; in this case, middle-class suburban youth. The media texts—the
film and the album—that combine to produce the audio-visual object can
both be characterized by their extreme familiarity to large sections of
this socio-cultural group. *The Wizard of Oz* was the first feature film to be
broadcast on television during prime time, on November 3, 1956. It also
holds the record for the longest-running annual television broadcast of a
feature film, from November 3, 1956, through May 8, 1998.[11] Since then,
it has been broadcast on the Turner cable stations, Turner Classic Movies
(TCM) and Turner Broadcasting Station (TBS). Particularly in the period
prior to the proliferation of VCRs in the home, this broadcast practice
constructed a common experience of spectatorship: a highly ritual form
of sharing an annual event with family, like the group spectatorship of
It's a Wonderful Life during the Christmas holidays.[12]

Pink Floyd's album *The Dark Side of the Moon* in turn has a great deal
of familiarity for certain audiences based upon a similar cultural longev-
ity. First released in March 1973, *The Dark Side of the Moon* holds the record for the longest run—724 straight weeks—on the *Billboard* top 200
albums chart.[13] Although it never had the sort of overwhelming sales
during a brief period of time enjoyed by albums like Michael Jackson's
Thriller, the Pink Floyd album has maintained a constant presence as a
staple album of rock music since its release, steadily selling copies year
after year, supported by the continual playing of key tracks on so-called
classic rock radio stations.

     JASON MIDDLETON

The familiarity of both the film and the album are attested to in an article by *New York Daily* staff writer Helen Kennedy examining *The Dark Side of Oz*: "When deejay George Taylor Morris at WZLX-FM in Boston first mentioned the phenom on the air six weeks ago, he touched off a frenzy. 'The phones just blew off the wall. It started on a Friday, and that first weekend you couldn't get a copy of "The Wizard of Oz" anywhere in Boston,' he said. 'People were staying home to check it out.' It's fun, he said, because everyone knows the movie, and the album which spent a record-busting 591 straight weeks on the Billboard [top 100] charts can be found in practically every record collection. Dave Herman at WNEW-FM in New York mentioned the buzz a few weeks ago. The response of more than 2,000 letters was the biggest ever in the deejay's 25-year on-air career."[14]

Such reports point to the aptness of the phrase "suburban legend" to describe this phenomenon. *The Dark Side of Oz* is a fairly widely shared part of the oral culture of a particular socio-cultural group—suburban youth who have come of age in the period of the 1970s through the present, intimately familiar with both the film and the album. Another testament to the pervasiveness of this "legend" is its incorporation into the ritual of the annual broadcasts of *The Wizard of Oz*, now taking place no longer on CBS but on cable through TCM. During one airing, *The Dark Side of the Moon* was made available through the Second Audio Program for DirecTV subscribers. Additionally, when the show returned to network television on the WB (Warner Brothers) network, promo spots for the airing featured scenes from the film matched with music evoking *The Dark Side of the Moon* (to the exclusion of the original soundtrack).

In using the term "familiarity" I want to take into account a specific connotation of the word as it pertains to intimate relationships, particularly the family. As I have suggested, the film is widely known and is associated with childhood and the ritual of familial group spectatorship. *The Dark Side of Oz*, in turn, represents a form of group spectatorship. As Christopher Eamon, curator for the Whitney exhibit featuring Becker's *Suburban Legend*, puts it: "In recreation rooms across America, teenagers have watched the film for decades with the sound turned off while playing the Pink Floyd album." While the exact origins for the practice and the length of its history are difficult to establish (and Eamon probably overestimates the length of its history), one thing is certain: the proliferation of the World Wide Web in the 1990s has greatly contributed to the development of a community of viewer/listeners. Web sites and message boards devoted to the phenomenon feature extensive discussion of the various sync points, debate on whether or not the synchronization was intended by the band, analysis of the concept of "synchronicity" itself, and proliferating examples of other possible synchronizations between popular films and rock albums.[15]

Certain themes become apparent from examining such sites. One is the generic consistency among the sorts of films and albums that are presented as examples of synchronization. The films tend to be science fiction and fantasy, including, along with *The Wizard of Oz, Fantasia, Blade Runner, 2001: A Space Odyssey, The Lord of the Rings* (both the 1978 Ralph Bakshi animated version and the contemporary Peter Jackson films), *Yellow Submarine*, and *The Matrix*. Other films frequently cited may not strictly fall into these generic categories but certainly intersect with them, such as *The Truman Show* and *Pi*. Albums that are frequently cited can be generically situated in the category of "progressive rock," a category characterized by epic song lengths, complex instrumentation, and "concept albums" that link their songs through the development of a narrative or thematic thread. Thus, we find not only the expected examples of progressive rock from the 1960s and 1970s, with frequent references to most of the Pink Floyd albums as well as certain albums by Led Zeppelin and the (later) Beatles, but also more contemporary examples of bands that tend to (reluctantly or not) bear the "prog rock" mantle, such as Radiohead and Tool. Additionally sometimes techno albums are cited, such as works by the Prodigy and the Dust Brothers. Both the film selections and the musical selections are generally associated with mind- or sensory-altering experiences. More specifically, many are associated with the use of hallucinogenic drugs, often in conjunction with the experience of group spectatorship or listening. This association with "mind-altering" experiences would seem to be the common denominator linking music as otherwise diverse as Led Zeppelin and the Prodigy. The connection is attested to in articles about *The Dark Side of Oz* by comments suggesting that drug use is a common part of the experience.[16] The discussion on message boards such as the one on "The Synchronicity Arkive" often lapses into a debate about the pros and cons of drugs themselves, above and beyond any discussion of synchronicity. Additionally, the logo of the same Web site prominently features a colorful mushroom that evokes psychedelic-style artwork of the 1960s.

JASON MIDDLETON

The Dark Side of Oz can thus be seen to represent the passage from one form of group spectatorship, the familial, to another, the social. In turn, this passage from the company of one's parents and siblings to the company of one's peers is figured through the recontextualization of "the most beloved family film of all time" into a very different text from the original. The familiarity of both sound and image tracks is crucial to the effectivity of the pairing of these two incongruous elements. As I argue below, the original soundtrack maintains its presence in our perception as a sort of trace left after its removal and replacement by the new soundtrack. This process of reinscription produces a new, *darker* text, in which many of the implicit themes of the original film may become more pronounced, or read in new and different ways.

In *The Dark Side of Oz*, the lyrics of the Pink Floyd songs will often create audiovisual puns, adding additional layers of meaning to or commentary upon the narrative action seen on the image track. For example, the song "Brain Damage" commences with the lyrics, "The lunatic is on the grass/The lunatic is on the grass/Remembering games and daisy chains and laughs/Got to keep the loonies on the path." Matched with this section of the song, we first see Dorothy and the scarecrow lying in the grass beside the yellow brick road, with the scarecrow gesticulating in an animated fashion. Then the scarecrow gets up and begins flailing about in a wild jig on the road, until he falls over. Finally, just as Pink Floyd sings the last line in the stanza, we see Dorothy rush over to him and reassuringly pat his back, stuff some straw back into his shirt, and straighten his clothing. The scarecrow's behavior is thus figured as a form of lunacy, while Dorothy's assistance to him is a matter of safely containing this lunacy. Many such audiovisual puns emerge throughout the duration of the album. When Dorothy is in Munchkin City with the Good Witch Glinda, the Wicked Witch of the West suddenly appears, and Dorothy looks back and forth in confusion between the two witches. At this moment on the soundtrack, the lyrics from the song "Us and Them" ask: "And who knows which is which, and who is who," thus describing Dorothy's quandary through a verbal punning (which/witch). As the witches seem to argue, while the Good Witch holds on to Dorothy protectively, the song continues with the line, "Haven't you heard, it's a battle of words."

Because of the familiarity of *The Wizard of Oz*, however, while watching *The Dark Side of Oz* the viewer is continually aware of the *absence* of the original soundtrack. This differs from the experience of watching the

Conner film. Although we are aware in principle of the absence of the biblical film's original soundtrack, the relative obscurity of the source material, coupled with Conner's editing that selects scenes with little visibly spoken dialogue, reduces our sense of lack in the audiovisual text. In watching *The Dark Side of Oz* this lack is apparent in the most obvious sense when we see the characters speaking or singing but cannot hear their words. Thus, we have a fairly apparent disjunction between the image track as we remember it working with its original soundtrack, and the image track as it is working, or not working, with the substituted soundtrack. At moments such as these, to return to our theoretical framework derived from Carroll, the two simultaneous ways of viewing the film are too incongruous, or even incompatible. We cannot reconcile our sense of the original audiovisual text, based upon its familiarity, with this second version.

At other times, however, notably when the dialogue and singing are visibly absent, our perception of the absence of the original soundtrack fades somewhat, and the music is better able to take on the characteristics conventionally associated with the nondiegetic soundtrack, namely, providing an emotional tenor for the action and sustaining continuity. At these points the two possible ways of viewing the film can exist simultaneously. The original soundtrack remains somewhat perceptible in its absence, as a trace left on the narrative situations represented in the image track and in our memory of them, but its absence is not obtrusive to the new soundtrack. Our pleasure, then, results from the semiotic play between an original text that is placed under erasure and a new text that is being written over it, in the manner of a palimpsest. The secondary text derives its meanings from its inscription upon the primary text.

One particularly effective sequence that matches this description takes place through the duration of "The Great Gig in the Sky," the fourth song on the album. As is frequently the case in *The Dark Side of Oz*, one song on the album ends at the close of a scene, and a new one commences along with a new scene. In this case, the song "Time" has segued into the "Breathe Reprise" as Dorothy sits with Professor Marvel and he pretends to tell her fortune from what he sees in his crystal ball (though he actually bases the fortune upon a quick peek at a photo in Dorothy's bag of her and Aunt Em). One of the many audiovisual puns closes out the scene, as Pink Floyd sings the final line of the song, "To hear the softly spoken magic spells," just as Dorothy, in rapt attention to the words of the fortune teller, gets up to return home. The song gently fades out as Dorothy leaves Marvel's caravan, and then segues directly into the soft opening piano line of "The Great Gig in the Sky." Here we cut to a series of shots depicting Dorothy running away toward home, the Professor packing up the caravan in anticipation of the storm, and an extreme long shot showing the family farm with a tornado rapidly approaching in the distance.

For those familiar with the album, the connection is apparent between the song's title and the repeated shots of the sky as Dorothy's family prepares the farm for the oncoming tornado. The music begins gently, but as the family's preparations become more frantic the intensity and tempo of the music build in a steady crescendo. The film begins crosscutting shots of the family with shots of Dorothy trying to make it home, even as tree branches and tumbleweeds fly all around her and the front screen door to the house is blown away as she tries to open it. During this sequence, increasingly intense wailing female vocals seem to express Dorothy's fear and distress. Failing to get into the cellar storm shelter where her family is hidden, Dorothy returns to the house where she is hit in the head by a window. After she is hit, Dorothy falls down on the bed, apparently knocked unconscious, and a superimposition of multiple images of her face suggests she is entering a dream state. Just as Dorothy is hit, the musical crescendo reaches its peak, and the song slows down again. The singer's final wails come out in an exhausted manner, sounding more like moans, which seem to express Dorothy's pain upon being knocked unconscious. The gentle piano line with which the song begins is reintroduced, and the vocals then become much softer and more melodic. This dreamlike music seems to perfectly match Dorothy's slipping into another state of consciousness and the ensuing shot of the house slowly rising from the ground and up into the tornado.

The music continues through this scene, in which the house sails through the tornado, as Dorothy, looking out the window, sees first her Aunt Em, then the two farmhands, then Miss Gulch, who, before Dorothy's eyes, turns into the Wicked Witch. As the scene progresses, the music becomes more dramatic, with minor chords played on the piano and the vocals again building up somewhat in intensity. On the film's original soundtrack, up until the point where Dorothy is hit in the head by the window the sound is entirely diegetic, comprised mainly of the wailing winds and objects banging around in the storm, and Dorothy's occasional cries out to Aunt Em. When Dorothy enters her dream state, a shift in the soundtrack takes place, as it does in *The Dark Side of Oz*. Here, however, we find an introduction of nondiegetic music, rather than a shift in the feeling of the music. In its initial introduction, the music features a slow-tempo melody played by a woodwind, punctuated by quick staccato horn bursts and other instruments arranged in a cacophonous fashion that give the moment a chaotic and surreal feeling. As the house rises into the tornado, the music shifts to a quick, jaunty tempo, filled with horns in marching-band style. This music gives Dorothy's trip through the cyclone a carnivalesque, even comic feel. Diegetic sounds are included, such as the clucking of chickens as they blow past the window, and Dorothy saying to Toto, "We must be up in the cyclone!" As farm animals blow past the window, followed by Aunt Em in her rocking chair, who smiles and waves to Dorothy, the scene takes on an increasingly comic quality.

In *The Dark Side of Oz*, on the other hand, there is an absence of these diegetic sounds (we cannot hear Dorothy speak her one line to Toto, or even see her mouth the words because her back is turned to the camera). Where the sound in *The Wizard of Oz* functions to defuse the potential scariness of this first surreal scene of the film, here the absence of diegetic sound, coupled with the minor piano chords and moaning vocals of the Pink Floyd song, foreground the scene's frightening quality. The figures passing by the window evoke the memories of a dying person, with the important figures from Dorothy's life literally passing in front of her eyes. The theme of passage from one world into another, whether from waking to sleeping or life to afterlife is much more strongly emphasized by this soundtrack, which takes on the quality of a dirge. By the time Miss Gulch appears outside the window, and then is transformed into the Wicked Witch of the West, Dorothy's fear as she buries her face in the bed to hide from this vision is palpable.

Unlike the moments in the film where there is an apparent disjunction between the way the Pink Floyd soundtrack functions and the traces of the original soundtrack (in our memory or through our perception of the characters' mouths moving as they speak), here the present soundtrack and the soundtrack under erasure are able to coexist simultaneously in our perception. This depends in part upon substitutions of associatively linked elements between the two. For example, in the opening section of the scene, when Dorothy is trying to find her family while the storm rages all around her, the wailing vocals on the Pink Floyd song substitute for the diegetic wailing winds on the original soundtrack. After this, the structurally identical placement of the nondiegetic music as Dorothy is hit in the head by the window and commences her ride into the sky allows for an easy substitution. This alignment of the image track and the new soundtrack are additionally enhanced by the absence of visual signifiers of diegetic sound (moving mouths, etc.); the absence of lyrics that would give the song a specific and potentially disjunctive meaning from the narrative action; and the semiotic play between the narrative action and the title of the song ("The Great Gig in the Sky"). The palimpsestic inscription of the new soundtrack over the old soundtrack, then, allows for a rewriting of the scene, a bringing forth of different narrative subtexts and the creation of a new emotional tenor from those constructed by the original soundtrack. Here the surreal and frightening qualities of the scene, and the theme of a passage from reality—or perhaps one stage of life or of self-perception to another—are foregrounded in a significantly different manner from the original film. If we understand the passage from Kansas to Oz in terms of the passage from childhood to adolescence (as have many critics), this passage is here figured as a source of anxiety, even trauma.

Perhaps one of the most widely discussed moments from *The Dark Side of Oz* comes at the end of the scene in the tornado. As "The Great Gig in the Sky" slowly winds down, with the vocal and piano lines gradually becoming slower and more gentle, we see a shot of the house slowly descending back down to earth. The song ends just as the house touches the ground and Dorothy, looking stunned and clutching onto Toto, gets up off of the bed. Dorothy walks through the house with an expression of apprehensive curiosity, while there is a brief stretch of silence on the soundtrack. Dorothy reaches the front door, and just as she turns the handle and pulls back the door to reveal the technicolor landscape of Oz, we hear the percussive, repeated sounds of a cash register followed by the walking bass line that together signal the start of "Money," one of the better-known songs from *Dark Side of the Moon*. The music seems to work in perfect synchronization with the action here. First, as Dorothy looks around herself in awe, the movements of her head match with the percussive sound of the cash register. Then, the walking bass line kicks in just as Dorothy begins walking forward into the landscape and the camera slowly yet steadily tracks sideways to reveal the sumptuously colored flowers and plants of Oz.

For those fans of *The Dark Side of Oz* who design Web sites and discuss the synchronization in chat rooms, this moment has great significance to the oft-made argument that Pink Floyd deliberately recorded the album as an alternative soundtrack for the film. The crux of this argument is that the first side of the (vinyl) album is exactly the same length as the black-and-white portion of the film that precedes Dorothy's entrance to Oz. The transition into Oz and the technicolor portion of the film syncs up perfectly with the transition to the second side of the album and the start of the song "Money." Proponents of this theory also point to the album cover, which depicts a prism splitting a beam of light into the multiple colors of the rainbow as an additional clue to this intentional synchronization. The cover supposedly plays upon the transition between the two sections of the film, and the iconic status of the "rainbow" from the film's most well-known song. I am less interested here in the question of intentionality than in why moments such as this in *The Dark Side of Oz* seem to resonate so strongly with viewers. But I would certainly acknowledge the point that these factors all contribute in some way to the viewer's sense that the sound-image pairing here "works." The absence of the original soundtrack does not prevent us from maintaining an engagement with the images and perceiving a coherent narrative and thematic thread.

As I argued in relation to the placement of the music during the tornado scene, the music-image relation during the sequence from the landing of the house to Dorothy's emergence into Oz is structurally quite similar between the original film and *The Dark Side of Oz*. On the original soundtrack, the nondiegetic music also ends just as the house touches down in Oz and we see Dorothy make a somewhat bumpy landing while lying on the bed. She gets up and walks through the house, with no musical accompaniment. At first, we hear diegetic sound when she picks up her basket and opens a door, but then, notably, even the diegetic sound drops out altogether. We do not hear her footsteps as she makes her way through the house, nor is there any Foley sound added to the image (framed in a medium shot) of her opening the front door of the house. This transitional moment, virtually identical in both soundtracks, thus takes on a rather eerie quality. The eeriness is quickly dissipated by the film's original soundtrack, however, when Dorothy opens the door and the string symphony begins playing the leitmotif from the film's most prominent song, "Over the Rainbow." The song, matched with a medium shot of Dorothy depicting her expression of wonder, helps to construct the moment as one of magical wish fulfillment. Any apprehension that Dorothy might have had about this strange journey is dissolved in her sense of awe and pleasure at this colorful new world, with all of its contrasts to the barren landscape of her home in Kansas.

The viewer's dual mode of perception is thus enabled in this sequence because the sound-image relation is structurally similar between the two versions of the film, and the original and revised meanings are associatively linked with one another. The sound in this sequence is structurally identical in both versions of the film, functioning to provide an emotional tenor, sustain continuity, and bridge the transitions between different scenes. The thematically associative links between the two are based upon a chain of signifiers starting with the "Over the Rainbow" leitmotif that is brought in on the original soundtrack just as Dorothy emerges in Oz. The association connects the "Over the Rainbow" theme to the object that is conventionally situated over the rainbow, a "pot of gold." The association between the image of a pot of gold and the Pink Floyd song "Money," which commences with the jingling sounds of a cash register, is clear. The figure of the pot of gold thus serves as an associative link between the two different songs on each soundtrack.

This associative substitution allows for a rereading of the scene, in which, as with "The Great Gig in the Sky," a different yet related narrative subtext and emotional tenor emerge. In the original film, Dorothy's reaction to the sight of Oz, while represented as the fulfillment of a desire, is coded in the most positive sense of a "dream come true." With the Pink Floyd song as the substituted soundtrack, Dorothy's response takes on a less innocent quality. The narrative subtext of her dissatisfaction with her simple life at home in Kansas is brought to the foreground, and her pleasure at the sight of Oz takes on an almost avaricious quality. *The Dark Side of Oz* thus functions specifically as re-vision. The effectivity of its sound-image relation is based upon a structural similarity to the original text, and, through a semiotic play between trace and inscription, new connotations are brought out in familiar narrative elements.

These examples of the audio-vision of found-footage video point to the possibilities of a dialectical sound-image relation that allows for the production of semiotic excess in both sound and image. This production of semiotic excess, or the adding of multiple layers of meaning, is, as Goodwin notes in the section of his book that I cited at the start of this essay, the mark for many critics of a "good" music video.[17] I would argue that music videos that perform this function (what Goodwin terms the "amplification" of the meaning of the song) tend to feature a more linear narrative than do most other videos. This sort of video also tends to be made for musicians situated in the category of "alternative rock," whose images are constructed so as to confer upon them the title of "artist," not simply rock star. Examples include videos by Tori Amos ("Past the Mission," "Spark"), Radiohead ("Karma Police," "Just"), R.E.M. ("Everybody Hurts"), the Beastie Boys ("Sabotage," "Body Movin'"), and Elastica ("Car Song"). These videos depict stories that unfold in a linear manner, construct scenarios not explicitly described by the song lyrics, and tend to feature few to no images of the band performing in the manner typical of music videos.

At the same time, however, these videos generally manage to avoid the trap outlined by Goodwin wherein videos present overly literal representations of metaphors (as in Elvis Costello's "Shipbuilding"). When a metaphor is represented through an overly literal image, then the video seems to "fix," or impose a limitation upon, the meaning of the song. Another example that Goodwin provides of this semiotic "fixing" is the video for the Cars's song "Drive." The lyrics of the song seem to be simply about a lost love, without presenting very specific scenarios or imagery in relation to this theme. In the video, the woman to whom the song is addressed (particularly in its central refrain, "Who's gonna drive you home?") has been placed in a mental institution. In presenting this fact, the video provides a scenario that literalizes and concretizes a metaphorical image that could otherwise be open to multiple interpretations.

In the videos by Tori Amos and Radiohead mentioned above, a different sort of sound-image relation is constructed. Rather than the concrete literalization of metaphorical lyrics, there is a much looser relation between sound and image, but not so loose that it would fall into Goodwin's third category of videos that "contradict" the lyrics of a song. The image tracks of these videos present what could for the most part be regarded as short films, in relation to which the music plays an important role—though compared with other videos it is not an essential one. The image track would for the most part be coherent without its soundtrack, except for the inclusion of the performer lip-synching the song lyrics while also acting in a role in the narrative.[18] These videos' linear narrative structure would seem to undermine the aesthetic convention of music video wherein the video follows a song's cyclical structure, preventing us from becoming overinvested in a narrative that might distract our attention from the song and its performer. Here the music takes on more of the quality of film music, sometimes receding into the background during points of narrative interest.

These videos tend to function according to two main logics: first, the scenarios reflect an overall mood or atmosphere expressed in the song; second, particular images or metaphors described in the lyrics are given visual correlates. Radiohead's song "Karma Police," while characterized by typically elliptical lyrics, could be said to metaphorically describe the desire to see unpleasant people get their comeuppance, and then possibly implicates the narrator in his own trap (of bad karma) for wishing such a fate on others. The video is comprised mainly of a single take, shot by a mobile camera mounted at the position of the driver's seat in a large sedan. The camera pans back and forth between the backseat of the car, where Radiohead singer Thom Yorke sits and (occasionally) lip-synchs to the lyrics, and a view through the front windshield, as the car pursues a man who seems to be running away in terror. There is thus a loose relation between the song lyrics, taken at a superficial level, and the scenario of the video, which could be seen to represent an arrest situation. Lyrics such as "Karma Police, arrest this man," are associatively linked with the image of the car pursuing a man who becomes potentially coded as a "suspect."

In terms of the second of my two logics, there are several moments in the video where individual lyrical phrases seem to correspond to the action depicted by the images. Most notably, the music shifts to a third and new section of the song when Yorke sings the line (which is then repeated for the remainder of the song), "And for a minute there, I lost myself." Just as the song moves into this section we see the first cut in the video, to a frontal medium close-up shot of the pursued man running from the car. At this moment, because of the highly subjectivizing qualities of the framing and the man's panicked expression, Yorke's lyrics seem to correspond to his thoughts. There is the implication that he has, at this moment, lost himself in terror, or perhaps that he thinks back on a poor decision that got him into this mess in the first place. These implications are reinforced by the video's editing. The repeated phrase "I lost myself" is matched first with the close-up frontal view of the man running, which then cuts back to the view from the driver's seat of the car. The phrase is repeated several more times as the man slows down, in apparent exhaustion. Just as Yorke finishes singing the initial repetitions of the phrase, which trails off with him moaning expressively, the man falls to his knees on the road.

Both the overall scenario presented by the video and the specific moments such as the way this phrase is matched with particular shots and cuts create associative links between sound and image. These links allow for moments of resonance between the two, without being literal or specific enough for the image to seem to fix or constrain the meaning of the song, as in the examples discussed by Goodwin. A specific image is not presented to represent or correspond to each and every lyrical phrase, nor does the shot selection and editing consistently seem to operate in synchronization with the music. Rather, the relation is somewhat loose, with passing moments of synchronization at both the level of lyric-image matches and at the level of how the editing corresponds to the music.

In these respects, I would argue that videos like this one construct a similar sound-image relation to what we find in *The Dark Side of Oz*. Because the relation is more loosely constructed, the viewer is allowed the "dual perception" of two different elements created by *Oz*. We are able to perceive the song and the video as separate entities, while at the same time the occasional lyric-image matches or moments of correspondence between transitions in the narrative and transitions in the song function as something like a fleeting version of Lacanian "quilting points." They briefly bind free-floating signifiers in both sound and image into a unified concept. But then this concept quickly dissipates in the ongoing flow of signifiers, rather than becoming a fixed reference point upon which the subsequent meaning of the video depends.

Other examples of this type of sound-image relation can be found in videos by Tori Amos. Tori Amos's song "Spark" describes a woman's struggle with addiction and anxiety, possibly also mental illness. The video represents a story not suggested by the song. A woman, played by Amos, lies in the woods blindfolded and with her hands tied behind her back. Next to her is an expensive black car (a Jaguar) that has apparently crashed into a tree. Its doors and trunk are flung open, and the implication is that Amos's character was being abducted but was flung from, or escaped from, the trunk following the collision. She gets to her feet and runs through the woods, pursued by a man dressed in a black suit, whose face we do not see.

Here, the first of my two conditions for the sound-image relation in this type of video is met. The general mood of the song is one of loneliness, instability, and fear (the opening lyrics, for example, are "She's addicted to nicotine patches/she's addicted to nicotine patches/she's afraid of a light in the dark). The images of Amos playing a character trapped in a dire situation are associatively linked with these lyrics, even if we do not see the direct visual correlates to the situation described in the song. The second condition for the sound-image relation is also met: Amos's fairly oblique metaphors for anxiety and mental instability are at several points matched with images that momentarily seem to be described by the lyrics. For example, when Amos sings the line, "Trusting my soul to the ice cream assassin," the video cuts right on the word "assassin" to a shot of the arm of the man in black grabbing hold of a tree as he relentlessly makes his way through the woods in pursuit of her. Later in the video, Amos's character manages to elude her pursuer by swimming across a river in the woods, with her hands still bound behind her back. As she launches forward into the water, Amos sings the line, "How many fates turn around in the overtime/ballerinas that have fins that you'll never find." Again, we have an associative match between lyrics and image, not only because the character manages to swim without the use of her arms, but also because the gauzy dress she wears somewhat resembles a ballerina's outfit. There is also a sense here of synchronization between the music and the narrative action. As Amos's character launches herself into the water, she also frees herself of her blindfold, and that moment is represented as liberation for the character. Just at this point, the bridge of the song begins. The other instruments initially drop out, and an up-tempo piano line, accented by quick drumrolls, kicks in, underscoring the increased freedom of motion.

These two moments of lyric-image correspondence, however, do not cause the video to fully "fix" the meaning of the song. In part this is because of what I have described as the "looseness" of the sound-image relation in this sort of video. For one thing, moments of correspondence are occasional rather than perpetual. Many of the situations and metaphors in the song's lyrics find no visual correlates in the video images. Second, when moments of correspondence like the two I describe above do occur, neither sound nor image seems to fully account for the other, thus avoiding the sort of "fixing" of meaning that Goodwin describes in relation to the Elvis Costello and Cars videos. In the Cars's "Drive," the question of the song's refrain, "Who's gonna drive you home," can be understood as the speaker wondering what has become of his lost love, whereas the video (with the woman in a mental institution) attaches a single and specific meaning to the question.

In the moments from the Amos video, the images cannot fully account for the possible implications of the lyrical metaphors. Rather, they seem to provide visual correlates that *partially* correspond to the lyrics, matching up with a single word or phrase (in "Spark," for example, simply the word "assassin") rather than attempting to fully account for the general concept expressed by a lyrical metaphor. Or, in a slightly different but related manner, they represent a situation that might be described by the lyrics, yet one that is related loosely enough that it must be regarded as one possible scenario among many. The section from "Karma Police" matched with the lyric "And for a minute there, I lost myself" would fall into this category. Thus, because of the linear narrative structure of the videos and the manner in which the sound-image relation is constructed, the song and the visual story maintain a relative autonomy from one another. At the same time, they are linked through the similarities in their general mood and atmosphere and through occasional points of synchronization.

This process closely resembles the way the lyric-image matches function in *The Dark Side of Oz*, such as the moment when Dorothy stands, confused, between the two witches while Pink Floyd sings, "And who knows which is which, and who is who." Many other moments of lyric-image synchronization in *The Dark Side of Oz* could be characterized by the "looseness" of the relation I outline above in the Radiohead and Tori Amos videos. During the song "Breathe," for example, Pink Floyd sings the line "Look around and choose your own ground" just after Dorothy appears to plead her case about something with Uncle Henry and Aunt Em. Busy with their farm work, they dismiss her, and she walks away, pausing to look back at them with an expression that might signal frustration. She thus appears to in effect choose her own ground. The line "Don't be afraid to care," from the same song, is delivered just as Dorothy is anxiously holding a baby chick in her hands. Later in the song, the line "For long you live and high you fly" is sung as Dorothy balances on a fence, holding out her arms as if they were wings.

But for every moment like these, and every synchronization between scene-to-scene transitions and transitions between songs or sections of songs, there are stretches of *The Dark Side of Oz* during which there is little correspondence between sound and image. This looseness of the relation, anchored by periodic moments of synchronization, aids in constructing the form of dual perception for the listener/viewer that I outline above.

It is not my goal here to simply support the view of the critics alluded to by Goodwin, for whom a music video that "amplifies" the meaning of the song is a "good" video. Rather, I have attempted to "amplify" Goodwin's category, via a (lengthy) detour through the unique relation between music and found images. The music videos I outline above function similarly to the found-footage films, but only at the level of the soundtrack. They do not allow for a palimpsestic reinscription of a second layer of meaning on the image track, but we do get a form of dual perception in relation to the song. We are able to simultaneously perceive the song's possible meanings both in conjunction with the images and independently of them. Rather than closing down on the possible meanings of the song, the video allows for a proliferation of meaning. Whether or not this makes a video "better" than one that seems to "fix" the meaning of a song is perhaps not so relevant as is simply the demarcation of a primary, even defining, characteristic of what might be regarded as a subgenre of the music video form.

NOTES

1 Michel Chion, *Audio-Vision: Sound on Screen*, ed. and trans. Claudia Gorbman (New York: Columbia University Press, 1994), xxv–xxvi.

2 Andrew Goodwin, *Dancing in the Distraction Factory* (Minneapolis: University of Minnesota Press, 1992), 86.

3 Ibid., 87

4 Ibid., 10–11.

5 Jeff Smith, "Popular Songs and Comic Allusion in Contemporary Cinema," in *Soundtrack Available: Essays on Film and Popular Music*, ed. Pamela Robertson Wojcik and Arthur Knight (Durham, N.C.: Duke University Press, 2001), 408.

6 One of several examples Carroll provides is the scene in Hitchcock's *The 39 Steps* when the character played by Robert Donat is handcuffed to a woman who hates him. They are trying to check into an inn, where the landlady mistakes them for affectionate newlyweds because of their physical proximity. As Donat tries to get the woman under control, their gestures are further misinterpreted as signs of their mutual infatuation. The way the scene is

blocked allows us not only to see what is really going on between the two characters, but also to see things from the landlady's point of view, such that her misinterpretation is perfectly understandable from our perspective. See Noël Carroll, "Notes on the Sight Gag," in *Comedy/Cinema/Theory*, ed. Andrew Horton (Berkeley: University of California Press, 1991), 26.

7 Ibid., 30.

8 Chion, *Audio-Vision*, 47.

9 Kathryn Kalinak, *Settling the Score: Music and the Classical Hollywood Film* (Madison: University of Wisconsin Press, 1992), 78–110.

10 Smith, "Popular Songs and Comic Allusion in Contemporary Cinema," 414.

11 This data is from http://www.filmsite.org/50sintro.html.

12 As one individual posted on a newsgroup, in response to a CNN headline stating that *The Wizard of Oz* would return to broadcast television on the WB (Warner Brothers) network: "This headline on CNN's website made my jaw drop and my heart jump for joy! It certainly brought back memories of the annual network telecasts of "Oz" on CBS. This time the WB will be airing the classic film during the upcoming holiday season. We should all be happy that EVERYONE with a television set will once again be able to watch Dorothy and her friends journey down the most famous road in movie history!" (http://www.beyondtherainbow2oz.com/wwwboard/messages/1256.html). Another indication of the film's overwhelming familiarity to viewers comes from an instructional Web site for synching up the film and album. Step five, the author writes, is "Turn the volume on the TV off. You know the story (you've probably seen the Wizard of Oz at least 50 times!). Think of the music as the movie and the picture as the soundtrack, as if they have switched places" (http://www.dsom.com/features/features.html). Interestingly, the author's last instruction also suggests the way in which this audiovisual object reconfigures the conventional image-music hierarchy in films.

13 The information here is from http://ask.yahoo.com/ask/20011130.html.

14 This is reproduced at http://www.geocities.com/SunsetStrip/Studio/8571/darksiderainbow.html.

15 See, for example, http://www.synchronicityarkive.com.

16 For example, "The lyrics and music join in cosmic synch with the action, forming dozens upon dozens of startling coincidences the kind that make you go 'Oh wow, man' even if you haven't been near a bong in 20 years" (Helen Kennedy, "Follow the Yellow Brick Road," http://www.geocities.com/SunsetStrip/Studio/8571/darksiderainbow.html).

17 Goodwin, *Dancing in the Distraction Factory*, 87.

18 This applies to Radiohead's "Karma Police" and Amos's "Past the Mission" and "Spark," though in these videos the lip-synching is inconsistent and often deliberately undermines lip-synching conventions. In Radiohead's "Right," the narrative is crosscut with shots of the band performing the song, but, again, at points they stop performing while the music continues.

Maureen Turim

I begin with a parable from history: In belle époque France (1881 through the beginning of the twentieth century) Monmartre and its café concerts became the place of an intermingling of classes. The celebration of popular song appealed to an audience that could come and go, talk and drink, flirt and be seen; an audience that included in its variety artists and intellectuals. From this milieu would come an avant-garde influenced by the music hall, the visual evidence of which is seen in the paintings of Manet and the posters of Toulouse-Lautrec. We are familiar with the music hall as an influence in the visual arts, but less well acknowledged is its influence on the avant-garde musicians such as Eric Satie. Likewise, the composers of popular song such as Van Parys (whose first film score was for *Le Million* of René Clair) would bring to their popular music the influences of Poulenc, Debussy, and Ravel. The model addressed here clearly is not one of hierarchy but of give and take. The avant-gardes that defined the arts from 1880 to 1930 were clearly a distinct force, yet the cross-fertilization between these avant-gardes and the popular art forms was significant.

We are familiar with this give and take between popular and avant-garde music in the United States as a story told primarily about dixieland, blues, and jazz, and thus as a story conditioned by racial barriers and the crossings of those barriers, particularly by immigrant composers and performers. We perhaps miss, however, the parallel to a generalized give and take during the same period between the popular and the high arts, especially the avant-garde sector of high art. By the time we reach the jazz-influenced orchestral compositions of George Gershwin or Leonard Bernstein, it is often Broadway that is seen as the mediating force between Tin Pan Alley and the symphony hall. Give and take, intersection and fusion, is thus the model I use in examining the current moment. Interaction and combustive reenergizing happens today between the popular and the avant-garde in most artistic realms, including echoing instances within contemporary video and music television.

It has become common, following Fredric Jameson, to view pastiche as a prime characteristic of the postmodern.[1] By replacing citation, homage, and intertextuality, pastiche in this sense denigrates the work said to be performing the pastiche. Whereas other terms for textual interaction are less directly negative in their judgment, to say that a text is a pastiche implies the addition of "merely" preceding the term. This assumed qualification speaks to a lack of creative ingenuity and integrity, and in Jameson's theory it corresponds to a flattening out of the entire process of historical causality and interpretation. Sometimes we use pastiche to refer to a satiric send-up, but Jameson holds to a distinction between parody and pastiche. Pastiches, as the very etymology of the term indicates, are replicas taken craftily from an original, and Jameson's concern stems from the way pastiche may be experienced by new audiences without any sense of the context and history that brought about the original formation. He also bemoans the loss of an authentic language that could frame pastiche as a satiric citation.

Popular culture has always been fed by references (sometimes satiric, but as often elegiac or mimetic). It is not surprising that we can find correlations between past art movements and what is after all a form of commercial art. Equally, high art has collapsed upon popular culture, with pop art and hyperrealism finding their inspiration in the commercial commonplace. Preceding the music video works I will discuss in this essay, the Velvet Underground found their visual correlate in the sly graphics of their friend Andy Warhol, assuming for all alternative music to follow an inspiration in art movements that express a fringe outlook while eyeing mainstream culture.

In fact it is tempting to consider music video as an outgrowth of a present moment that the Japanese artist-curator-scholar Takashi Murakami calls "the superflat."[2] The superflat has as its very program the collapse of distinctions, a uniform culture in which the avant-garde and high art have ended and have been subsumed in a popular commercial culture of great vigor. Murakami uses his notion of the superflat as a very clever curatorial parti pris, in which he assembles a wide range of works linked to manga (Japanese comics), anime, and fashion, thereby mixing

MAUREEN TURIM

the commercial and experimental fine arts at will. Yet despite Muraka-mi's cleverness as a curator, and his highlighting of the omnipresence of the popular, the problem with the notion of the superflat is that it has ruled out a priori any process of naming difference. We can no longer recognize differential praxes in any creative activities.

My proposal here is to maintain differentiation without a blinding assumption of hierarchies. In what follows, I analyze music video works that propose references to the manifestations of past artistic avant-gardes. They may do so as strategic placement. If such references do not place them outside the mainstream of music television's flow, they are often in quest of a deviation or a fringe. Theoretically, I hold that reference here may perform an intertextuality that in its most discerning inscriptions compels spectators to think about the histories of art and music, sound and image, poetry and performance.

I want to hold on to the notion of multiple countercultures and microcultures, many of which ascribe to some kind of "keeping it real" slogan in the face of forces of homogenization and commercialization. Some of these impulses are ethnic, some local, some ideological, and some a mixture of all three. Pressed, artists might acknowledge that their Promethean struggles for an essence they name reality evaporates by their very formation in a mediated, commercialized culture. Some might even mount a deconstruction of such essentialist goals. Still, the quest for identity, self-determination, and a nourishment from the roots of one's metaphoric "hood," precursors, or heritage becomes the mantra of many musicians and artists, trying to stay more real than at least the obviously manufactured and marketing-controlled pop groups.

The widespread use of avant-garde, experimental, progressive, and fringe as categories in music reviews and marketing signals much awareness, and much ambiguity, surrounding these terms, which carries over into any investigation of their relevance in speaking of music video. From a marketing perspective they indicate a niche market. The liner notes to her CD-ROM *Puppet Motel* describe Laurie Anderson as the greatest "avant-garde diva." Silke Tudor offers in the *SF Weekly* a genealogy of Gogol Bordello, linking the band to a mixture of gypsy music, *klezmer*, avant-garde taste, and post-punk echoes:

> Originally from Kiev, where his father played guitar in one of that country's first rock bands, Huetz developed avant-garde tastes at an early age, visiting

the black market to buy tapes by Einstuerzende Neubauten, Suicide, Iggy Pop, and the Birthday Party. After the nuclear accident at Chernobyl in 1986, the Huetz family fled to the isolated climes of rural western Ukraine, where violins were still made from trees struck by lightning, and folk music and mysticism twirled hand in hand. There, Huetz discovered the musical richness of the Gypsy Diaspora, and followed its long, winding path through the refugee camps of Poland, Hungary, Austria, and Italy in which the Huetz family was interned. Eventually, Huetz made it to the United States and plunged into his lifelong dream of playing in a punk rock band. But while performing at a Russian wedding, he realized something was missing. After moving to New York, Huetz hooked up with two Russians, two Israelis, and an American with aural wanderlust, and formed Gogol Bordello. Together, the musicians raised a raucous whirlwind of sound that spanned centuries of tradition with post-punk sensibilities and nomadic ferocity.[3]

David Sinclair in the London *Times* laments that Radiohead has abandoned popular "good tunes" in favor of avant-garde esoterica:

> The most fervent British pop music has always drawn much of its impetus from kicking against the musical conventions of its day. Everything from punk to rave culture has evolved through a succession of musical and philosophical stand-offs between those who get it and those who don't.
>
> But Radiohead have taken the outsider concept to new extremes with *Hail to the Thief*, an album of dark, existential laments which draws the starkest of battle lines. Ranged on one side of the divide is a gaggle of high-minded alt.rock musicians, critics, students, their lecturers, the progressive art elite, media sophisticates and dabblers in the avant-garde.
>
> On the other side stands anyone who simply wants to hear a good tune.[4]

Taken together, these three journalistic uses of the word avant-garde to describe contemporary performers indicate a wide range of issues surrounding such categorizations. On one hand is the appeal to a particular audience already identified with the fringe; on the other hand is a disdain for leaving the accessibility of the popular; and in between is a linking of avant-garde aspirations to a historical research into authentic and politically inflected ethnic cultures.

When we turn to the making of images to accompany the presentation of music, all of these issues remain and are perhaps heightened. Music videos function largely as advertisements for a double-sided product: the artist as product through the sale of CDs and the concert tickets that fans will be lured to purchase. They also function to create the identity of a network through the accrual of a certain attitude or appeal; viewers tune in to VH1, MTV, MTV2, and BET with some rather set expectations: pop videos from the biggest pop stars, accompanied by a large amount of sexuality displayed in the narrative stagings and/or the dancers who accompany the act. Pop video staples are tropes drawn from action films and soft-core pornography, where soft sex is crosscut with the band's performance or with sexually suggestive gestures from the performers themselves. Cars, action adventures, and chases may also be crosscut. The industry calls this type of work narrative or performance video, but this one-pony show is better called the "soft sex–action crosscut tease."

Still, for some, these venues are not "pop" enough. The music video networks have embraced other programming to the detriment of what the British industry calls "promos." In Britain, "The Hits," from *Emap*, offers music "from the top 40 with a smattering of older, well-loved videos." Its director, Simon Sadler, has been quoted as saying he requires "simple promos, because of the way people view music television these days. We tell record companies that videos will perform a lot better if they're not complicated. I want something relatively straightforward that's nice and colourful and looks sexy. I'm looking for videos that our viewers will find instantly attractive the minute they switch over. These days people just sit and flick, so you have to catch them."[5]

Another industry response is to create venues for what they view as a niche market for alternative music videos. The network MTV2 promotes itself as "the home of new music" and as a place to support artists who "haven't yet made a big name for themselves." On its Web site, blurbs such as the following are offered that treat mass-marketed groups as "alternative" fare:

Chemical Brothers Video Fantasy—Combat corporate drudgery with a trip down the 'The Golden Path'

Wake Up to New Radiohead—Take a walk with a digitized Thom Yorke in "Go To Sleep"

All Hail the Kings of Leon!—Southern garage rock rules in the "Molly's Chambers" video

What is Ima Robot?—In a word, this California new wave quintet is: "Dynomite"

Expect "Nothin' But a Good Time"—When you watch classic Poison videos right here

Within this directed marketing the network narrows further to specific programs such as *Subterranean on* MTV2, which offers viewer/listeners a chance to "every Friday night at midnight go underground with new and emerging artists."

As an alternative to serving as a niche market within a mass cultural media conglomerate network, those interested in the more experimental parameters of both musical and imagistic expression find themselves turning to the Internet. Sites such as Mssvision.com, world art media television, and the Moment Factory offer venues for videos of performing artists that wouldn't otherwise be shown. Some bands such as They Might Be Giants have started their own sites, an outgrowth of their earlier innovative alternative "dial-a-song" that captured the imagination of a wide fan base after their advertisements of a phone number in the *Village Voice*.

David Kleiler and Robert Moses, in *You Stand There: Making Music Video*, also treat alternative music/imaging aspirations as just another way to appeal to audiences, and they subordinate any relation to historical avant-gardes to a larger category they call "appropriation." Thus the director Mary Lambert appropriates Howard Hawks's *Gentlemen Prefer Blondes* to stage Madonna in "Material Girl," and the directors Jonathan Dayton and Valerie Fariss appropriate Méliès's *Trip to the Moon* (1902) to stage the Smashing Pumpkins' "Tonight, Tonight"—or as the authors put it in an amusing anachronism that itself displays postmodern ahistoricism: "Appropriating not only [Méliès's] whimsical surrealism, but specific images."[6]

Kleiler and Mose see appropriation as a defining characteristic of music videos, and in terms that seem to imply a certain familiarity with theories of postmodernism: "Appropriation renders all genre discussion pointless. There's no such thing as a 'Western' music video, or a 'film noir' music video: Music videos put genres in quotes." Of course there are genres of video apart from those of film, but I cite this rather silly quote to emphasize how the authors' attitude here conforms to Jameson's fear of a leveling of history, reference, and specificity. They welcome these acts of theft that they take to be removed from referential citations. "If television programs and commercials reference movies, theater, litera-

MAUREEN TURIM

ture, opera, history, art, photography and current events, music videos reference all of the above—and other music videos. Music videos rip off any recognizable art/pop cultural movement that gains more than a moment of the public's attention."[7]

These pronouncements aside, Kleiler and Mose speak elsewhere in the volume of various genres of music video: "Over the last 15 years, music videos developed their own aesthetics, genres and visual language."[8] Cinematic versus photographic videos becomes their main genre distinction, which ends up boiling down to a contrast between narrative and nonnarrative music videos.[9] They claim that narrative videos are characteristic of the 1980s and now are superannuated, yet they still group within narrative videos many directors they laud at other moments, such as Adam Bernstein, Spike Jonze, Jesse Peretz, and Sophie Mueller; consistency of argument is perhaps also superannuated. Kleiler and Mose use the term "progressive" to describe what we might call a stream-of-consciousness tone poem video. Further, they sometimes use "concept" video as a term seemingly standing for the Hollywood/Madison Avenue term "high concept," meaning a hook or gimmick. In other words, despite its assertion that "classic videos are one big exercise in the Kuleshov effect," and along with its brief homage to Sergei Eisenstein, the manual has trouble taking music video seriously enough to analyze its relationship to other art forms historically and critically.

In contrast, I want to suggest that many of the most intriguing music videos acknowledge a grand debt to historical avant-garde and progressive (in the usual sense of this term) art movements in all media. This debt is often acknowledged through citation. In other words, the past of the creative arts is not just "appropriated" but also is reworked, and often it is clearly marked as intertextual reference, thus inviting viewers to make connections between the art making at present and its history.

Much of this work issues from musicians deemed "alternative." The directors of many music videos either have parallel pursuits as film and video artists, or once or future aspirations to the same. Like ad making, music video production attracts those we train in our art and film departments and schools, so that odd mixtures of purpose and pretense, and inspiration and calculated lifting abound. Some music video surrealism may be closer to Busby Berkeley than to Max Ernst. Striving to delineate a clear lineage back to the high arts' eroticism of an uncensored unconscious, rather than popular-culture naughty symbolic sexuality would not only be futile but also involve aesthetic assumptions of art history contrary to the often playful mixing that gives life to new forms. Ranging from seamless integration to studied homage, the intertextuality I analyze here may sometimes seem to be postmodern pastiche, but I argue for its historical and theoretical reconceptualization. My working assumption is that it may be hard to tell the difference and is important always to theorize one's motivations for any such judgments.

As Greil Marcus has argued in *Lipstick Traces*, Dada serves as a background set through which to view the punk, garage band, and techno movements, although in what follows I draw the terms of the comparison somewhat differently than he does.[10] Screaming noise as music recalls the Dada poetry of Hugo Ball by imitating industrial cacophony and war and by expressing rage. For all their excess of volume and anger, punks pursued a performance style that had an aesthetic that was rough and therefore in a certain sense pared down. A common spatial trope in punk videos consists of a marginality suggested by concerts in abandoned warehouse spaces. Similarly, some videos suggest apocalyptic narratives through their images of the collapse of surrounding architectures. In borrowing from the Dada ready-made, punk-inspired videos utilize found footage and collage imagery, though it should be noted that these two techniques have remained mainstays of experimental filmmaking and animation throughout a nearly hundred-year history.

Consider Tristan Tzara's intensity of spirit in his "Dada Manifesto" of 1918, in which he calls for a creativity that abandons any pretense at mass appeal, and where he mocks literary value in favor of a highly individualized, ritualized, and ultimately percussive refusal of meaning:

> There is a literature that does not reach the voracious mass. It is the work of creators, issued from a real necessity in the author, produced for himself. It expresses the knowledge of a supreme egoism, in which laws wither away. Every page must explode, either by profound heavy seriousness, the whirlwind, poetic frenzy, the new, the eternal, the crushing joke, enthusiasm for principles, or by the way in which it is printed. . . . Behind them a crippled world and literary quacks with a mania for improvement.
>
> If I cry out:
> Ideal, ideal, ideal,*
> Knowledge, knowledge, knowledge,*
> Boomboom, boomboom, boomboom,

MAUREEN TURIM

I have given a pretty faithful version of progress, law, morality and all other fine qualities that various highly intelligent men have discussed in so many books, only to conclude that after all everyone dances to his own personal boomboom, and that the writer is entitled to his boomboom.[11]

Tzara's social protest introduces contradictions and entertains an entirely personalized rebellion. The crushing joke of that moment belied any faith in a more organized movement, favoring instead a poetic nihilism.

Cabaret Voltaire's name pays homage to the famous Dada meeting place founded by Hugo Ball. Unlike other punk groups, such as the Sex Pistols and The Clash whose presence on film or tape remains limited to stage performance and television interviews, Cabaret Voltaire's Dada citation becomes imagistic as well as musical. At first Cabaret Voltaire experimented not only with sound sampling but with the graphic characteristics of Dada typography in their cover designs. The recordings of their first collection of songs were, according to band members, "done in an attic 10 feet by 6 feet on a domestic reel to reel tape recorder in 1976 including the homage The Dada Man and Ooraseal." The band member Richard H. Kirk notes that the Dada aesthetic emerged even earlier at the Edinburgh Festival in 1975: "We prepared a tape and a flysheet handout. It was produced in the best Dadaist fashion and was played twice we were told, and then removed from the venue."[12]

Yet by the early 1980s the group started producing videos under the label Doublevision; this effort included a ninety-minute video of a multimedia Cabaret Voltaire performance. Another commercial work was a long video piece released in 1985 called "Gasoline in Your Eye." The group continued to use visuals for the live performances, and much of their visual imagery was only seen at the concerts. In a 1986 interview, Kirk remarked: "Nothing's been made available for people to buy."[13] Cabaret Voltaire also worked on a video companion to the *Plasticity* album, and the remnants of their various video works have been collected on *Photophobia—Kirlian Photography*. Other groups also seem to be seeking a similar poetics; the Cocteau Twins, for example, cite Jean Cocteau, the poet-filmmaker-artist whose imagery remained apart from the movements that characterized his moment, even as he would borrow elements of surrealism.

In order to contemplate the full measure of music video's debt to Dada, we should consider more indirect notions of how Dada's collages of letters, words, and images were meant to disturb sanguine readers as well as those who would approach art from a traditionalist aesthetic. First, we should acknowledge that Dada has had a broad influence on many art movements that followed it; this lineage includes lettrist and situationist art. Alan Williams has performed a part of this genealogy in tracing the lettrist and situationist impulses in the films of Jean-Luc Godard.[14] Dada is indeed an acknowledged predecessor of conceptual art; the relay to music video may come from these more recent branchings and their influences on advertising and the culture at large. For music video, the connection between Godard and the American artists Barbara Kruger, Laurie Anderson, and Jenny Holzer would help us continue along the lines of this branching.

If so, what is helpful about retracing the garage band movement's debt to Dada? Consider Hannah Höch, speaking about Dada photomontages: "Our whole purpose was to integrate objects from the world of machines and industry in the world of art. Our typographical collages or montages set out to achieve this by imposing, on something which could only be produced by hand, the appearances of something that had been entirely composed by a machine; in an imaginative composition, we used to bring together elements borrowed from books, newspapers, posters, or leaflets, in an arrangement that no machine could yet compose."[15] In other words, Dada (along with other movements such as constructivism) has at its foundation a redefinition of art in the age of mechanical reproduction. Dada has the distinction of coloring with a decidedly human inflection its assessment of the machine aesthetics. Our attention is drawn to Höch's telling phrasing, "an arrangement that no machine could yet compose." Since her writing, the ability of machines to engender compositions has so grown that at present the struggle of artists to define music or visual composition beyond the limits of mechanical creation proposes new challenges. Hence the attempt to return to more primal and expressionist forms; forms that by their very outrageous denial of orderly rules of composition invite an identification of human hands, minds, and vocal organs emitting these sounds and images directly.

In "Radiohead's Antivideos: Works of Art in the Age of Electronic Reproduction," Joseph Tate credits Radiohead's work with undercutting the commodification inherent in the music video marketplace.[16] Citing Walter Benjamin and Slavoj Žižek, Tate argues that Radiohead succeeds

MAUREEN TURIM

in a neo-Dadaist project. A check on such arguments, however, remains the art historical assessment that Dada could never really escape commodification the first time around. The found object and the antipoem have, of course, found their ways into the museums and canons, just as Radiohead's videos are cablecast and reissued. In fact the marketing of Radiohead took an intriguing corporate swerve when the video "I Might Be Wrong" was released exclusively on the Internet in QuickTime. The group's producer Nigel Godrich then took part in an Apple advertising venture disguised as a news story written by Stephanie Jorgl, in which he was quoted as saying, "We used a multitude of Macs for audio editing, manipulation and sequencing on pretty much all the tracks on 'Kid A' and 'Amnesiac.'"[17]

Adam Bernstein's early work for They Might Be Giants seems to be a more contemporary way to pursue the antivideo, though perhaps its success is augmented by the framework of the famous anti-industry challenge by They Might Be Giants in their dial-a-song counterculture venture. That this rawly styled rendition of a day in Brooklyn recalled the Beatles' romps in *A Hard Day's Night* might force us to admit that even the most spontaneous and street-styled footage may be quite studied when it documents the frolics of emerging rock groups.

Dada visual collage is, however, more often read by current sensibilities as surrealism, which leads us to the consideration of music video's proper debt to the historical surrealist movement. In music video any grotesque or demonic (as in anti-Christian) imagery may also evoke from both critics and the public the label "surreal." Given that the paintings of Salvador Dali remain the popular image of surrealism, this tendency becomes understandable. Consider Joan Lynch's "Music Videos: From Performance to Dada-Surrealism," which is an attempt largely to evaluate music video as a form and to legitimize those efforts she deems superior.[18] Because she is naive as to what constitutes "Dada-Surrealism," Lynch actually addresses under this rubric any creative flows of images that she takes to be nonnarrative. She champions the poetic-symbolic use of imagery yet bemoans the random.

Here I wish to be far more specific about surrealism as a theory and a method of image creation. Much surrealism seeks uncanny images of displaced desire. It aims at unleashing an unrestricted unconscious. Consequently it often performs corollary attacks on institutions of repression. In undercutting Christian imagery, it highlights the erotics of that religion so often denied in Christianity's role as censor. If the surrealists were fascinated with inner organs, death, and the body turned inside-out, they also explored half-beast representations of human beings, thereby melding predatory and victimization roles to uncanny crossings between the natural world and that of society. Surrealism explores the liminal states between life and death, dreaming and waking.

The cult of the demonic in goth, punk, and hard rock may seemingly present some of the same obsessions as those of surrealism. Yet the demon quest is less for an exploration of the poetry of the unconscious than it is for a bold violation of decorum and rectitude through embracing emblems of evil powers. Similarly Marilyn Manson's imagery of martyrdom, filled as it is with masochistic religious imagery in which he commits the sacrilege of substitution (the self for Christ and for John Fitzgerald Kennedy), uses such imagery, without much ironic distance, as pure wish embodiment.

Even if the obvious signifiers seem too direct and lacking in irony to be taken as surrealism, the case of the director Floria Sigismondi represents a challenge to those of us who would otherwise try to delineate the gulfs separating goth from surrealism. Raised in Canada by Italian parents whose career in opera led to her own early devotion to the arts, Sigismondi's photographs stage the goth scene yet also recall the ethereal, haunted, yet threatening women of such female surrealists as Leonore Fini, Leonora Carrington, and Dorothea Tanning. Her Web page borrows contructivist graphics, but the bandaged Ophelia-like subjects of her art work contrast with this background. Insect-like, her subjects also seem to inhabit hospital corridors in a medical imagery that provides a hint of institutional oppression evoking the dissipated and distressed poses she prefers. Sigismondi's two videos for Marilyn Manson have been described as "dark, surrealistic, fantastically costumed."[19] Her most effective imagery is perhaps the dental brace that both fills and imprisons Manson's mouth in "Tourniquet." The Museum of Contemporary Canadian Art presented Sigismondi's first major solo exhibition in Canada, titled "COME PART MENTAL," in September 2001. Sculptures and installation works use manikin-like female figures often bearing strange animal-claw genitalia, nipples, or simply dragon-like protrusions. Minerva, Rome's multibreasted goddess, figures here as well in a slightly transformed incarnation. As a tag for the exhibit the museum offered this quote by the artist: "In order to find ourselves we must destroy ourselves. The human race craves the experience."

It may be hard for rock stars to clothe themselves in the direct exposure of the unconscious coupled with the ironic distance that is a necessary element of the best historical surrealism, such as that of Luis Buñuel, Max Ernst, and Leonare Fini. The structures of the video music industry overlay with a too palpable aura of studied pretension the forceful honesty and self-exposure associated with such historical artists. In undercutting by its commercial exhibition the tone fundamental to surrealism, the music video form remains weakest when it strives for the revelation of the collaborating artists' depth. As Lisa Zeidner puts it in her essay "No Mo Po Mo, Or: I Had a Dream":

> Tex-Mex dim sum. Bacon ice cream. Black bean soup with chocolate croutons. For some time, I have wanted to disgorge myself of a piece of criticism called "No Mo Po-Mo," in which I deride the pathetic state of what passes for postmodernism in contemporary culture. The typical pomo gesture now consists merely of shoveling together two seeming absurd, mismatched, contradictory entities. It is the impulse mocked in the pitches in Robert Altman's *The Player* (the Bride of Frankenstein meets Pretty Woman). . . .
>
> Meaninglessness is not clever. Arbitrariness is not clever. Dreams—which seem, at first glance to be arbitrary—turn out to be deeply moored. And art should be more artful than your average slapdash dream. Compare the shocking but deeply revealing juxtapositions in a Buñuel film with MTV.
>
> Art requires commitment.[20]

Some videos come closer to a certain surrealist spirit simply because they acknowledge in multiple ways their pop culture play, just as Zeidner chastises the pop juxtaposition of pomo while she herself is clearly a self-conscious postmodernist—blending high and low, fiction and non-fiction, with the best of them. Through a humorous engagement with all that undercuts the earnest, even while maintaining at another level direct access to teenage angst, such works constitute what I would call pop surrealism—actually a blending of surrealism and pop art. This may sound like one of Zeidner's absurd, mismatched, contradictory entities, but the movements do conjoin through their twin interests in performing a good joke.

This sort of pop surrealism emerged in some of the videos done for

The "pop surrealism" of the video for Tom Petty and the Heartbreakers' "Don't Come around Here No More"

Tom Petty and the Heartbreakers. Petty offers a humorous take on the legacy of Bob Dylan's symbolist poetics lyrics and on the Beatles of the Sergeant Pepper album. Jeff Stein, in directing the 1985 video "Don't Come around Here No More," drew on Petty's penchant for hats to transform his end-of-relationship-lyrics into the classic misogynist tea party scene between Lewis Carroll's Mad Hatter and Alice. Petty, whose greatest charm remains his roots-rock acknowledgment of influences without any concomitant anxiety, can pull off both a lyric and a video filled with homages. The opening of the video bows to Jefferson Airplane's "White Rabbit" by offering a pictorial interpretation of "a hookah smokin' caterpillar tells you where is at," which is of course itself an interpretation of Carroll. Petty's lyrics replay the same terrain as Bob Dylan's "It Ain't Me, Babe" ("Go away from my window, leave at your own chosen speed") with the irony of the internal name rhymes of Paul Simon's "Fifty Ways to Leave Your Lover" ("Get a new plan Sam, set yourself free"). Petty and Stein use humor to pursue the altered-consciousness scale shifts, as saucers in the shot/reverse shot pattern range from too large to too small, then large enough to become a pool in which Alice struggles to sail afloat, assailed by the bombardment of a giant sugar cube. The humor ironically situates the misogyny, culminating in the moment when Alice looks on in amazement as her body, transformed into a themed birthday cake, is sliced up by Petty and served for tea.

A similar surrealist play with the female body as eroticized corpse

MAUREEN TURIM

Kim Basinger as the eroticized corpse in the video for "Mary Jane's Last Dance."

occurs in Petty's video "Mary Jane's Last Dance." The lyrics alone suggest a struggle with marijuana addiction, but the video literalizes the last dance with a seductive woman. Opening in a morgue, a man (Petty) steals away the corpse of his beautiful girlfriend for a last dance in a gothic castle. The necrophilia inherent in this action is consumated only through a dance draped with the ambiance of a dark fairy tale. Our hero then buries his love at sea in his own private ritual by hurling her off a gothic cliff. Borrowing eroticism here from the obsessional Edgar Allan Poe of "Evangeline," Petty still manages to retell his lyrics as an allegorized prom night disaster story, evoking the sort of surrealist eroticism that revisits the gothic illustration and symbolist poetry, while amplifying the force of unconscious desire.

Petty's videos cultivate a tongue-in-cheek approach to such loaded imagery. "Runnin Down a Dream" (1989), for example, retraces the free-floating imagination of early black-and-white line cartoon films in its "Little Nemo" homage. In this universe, Petty becomes a cartoon character bemused by Nemo's lead through sprouting buildings, transforming landscapes, and the fluid changing sets of a world subject to constant reinvention. Here a popular art form that prefigured surrealism offers the music video its access in the same way that others have cited Méliès and Busby Berkeley. These citations reveal the historical give and take between popular and high culture, especially as various forms address such basic attributes as desire and imagination, and as the historical con-

Spike Jonze's natural treatment of a surreal element (a man with a dog's face wandering the streets) in the video for Daft Punk's "Da Funk."

ditions governing popular cultural production for one reason or another open to a freedom of symbolic representation.

Makers of rock videos often cite surrealism when they are asked about their inspirations or when they describe their own works, and it sometimes signifies any introduction of the bizarre into the everyday. It is in this sense that Spike Jonze uses the term to describe his Daft Punk video "Da Funk," in which a man with a dog's face and a broken leg wanders through a New York neighborhood, echoing, in slower pace, John Travolta's neighborhood jaunt in *Saturday Night Fever*. Jonze says the video was inspired by his desire to present a "surrealistic element and treating it very naturally."[21] Jonze's videos cull ideas both from the art world and from Hollywood. "California" shows in slow motion a man on fire running down a street in L.A. The result evokes video artist Bill Viola's elemental imagery of slow motion transformations, as well as a send-up qua homage to Hollywood special effects. Jonze also flirts with surrealism in his video for Fatboy Slim's pulsing "Weapon of Choice" by staging the gravity-free dancing of a sternly unflappable Christopher Walken dressed in a business suit. It is the deadpan acting here that introduces the ironic commentary on the hotel environment.

More blatant surrealist bows are made in Chris Cunningham's digitally altered images that depict bearded and buxom bathing-suit models in his "Windowlicker" video for Aphex Twin (1998). Special effects video editing, as well as masks, makeup, and prosthetic devices characterize Cunningham's work. There is often a tension between figurative bodies and narratives on one hand, and abstract visual impulses on the other.

MAUREEN TURIM

Blending Bill Viola and Hollywood special effects in Spike Jonze's video for "California."

Cunningham's treatment for "Afrika Shox" indicates the narrative lines and suggested interpretations that underlie that video:

> Suddenly out of nowhere a city-type carrying a briefcase bumps hard into him (the black man who has been wandering, alone) and his arm is knocked clean off at the elbow. We see it hit the floor and shatter in slow motion.
>
> It gives us the impression that this strange crumbling disease is a voodoo curse of some kind.[22]

Thus the shots of a body breaking apart that resonate so strongly with surrealism, and are presented in a stunning black-and-white image tinged with just elements of color, are edited to accentuate the shock and fascination with this extraordinary treatment of the body in the city. It is debatable whether this narrative (as well as other images of blacks by Cunningham) reiterates a stereotype without much consciousness of its social implications or rather strives for a symbolic reading of urban racial relations. Clearly, any such interpretations seem somewhat secondary to the effects fetish that Cunningham has with dispersed body parts as well as his striving for grotesque humor: by the end of the video the lead character has lost all of his appendages, only to be asked "Do you need a hand?" Similarly, in "Frozen" (1998) Cunningham morphs an image of Madonna falling apart into dozens of flying ravens upon her impact with the ground.

Chris Cunningham's bearded and buxom bathing suit models (surrounding Aphex Twin's Richard D. James) in his video for "Windowlicker."

The tendency toward abstraction informs several videos, but it foregrounds the 2002 remix of Autechre's "Second Bad Vilbel." Having removed the elements of an earlier narrative involving an alien, the only clearly representational image is one of a robot insect that is always filmed in such a way as to emphasize its abstract qualities. Still, it is possible to interpret the montage of abstract images corresponding to the beats of the techno music either as close-ups of certain elements of the creature or as the world seen through its eyes.

Flex, a seventeen-minute piece set to music of Aphex Twin, was commissioned by the Anthony d'Offay Gallery in 2000 as part of a month-long exhibition with the sculptor Ron Mueck. The piece was subsequently shown later in 2000 as part of "Apocalypse: Beauty and Horror in Contemporary Art," an exhibition by the Royal Academy of Arts. Naked bodies figure in abstract patterns, often reduplicated as overall image patterns or stretched to distortion by image manipulation. At other points the bodies are quite discernible in highly suggestive poses and positions, and a narrative emerges about an abused woman's fear of rape. If abstraction struggles with the symbolically loaded surreal in Cunningham's work, in its movement from music video commissions to the fine arts world it revives surrealism's taste for controversy and ability to shock in both contexts.

When the singers themselves are artists, the relationship between their lyrics and artwork can stimulate an imagistic encounter of neosurrealist dimensions. The Incubus singer Brandon Boyd and drummer Jose Pasillas were responsible for the cels in the animated sections of their video "Drive." Floria Sigismondi's direction of a new video for Incubus

MAUREEN TURIM

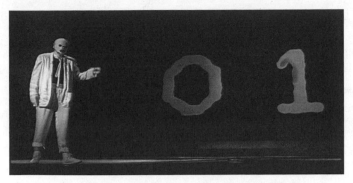

Laurie Anderson's "Zero and One" from *Home of the Brave*.

adds a Dada-like political montage to her signature stylized surrealism. This mix proved provocative enough to occasion viewings that were restricted to late evening on cable venues, especially since the video was read as comparing George Bush Jr. to Hitler and Stalin, in the tradition of John Heartfeld.

In contrast to the often saturated signifiers and baroque onslaught of imagery associated with neosurrealism, many more music videos find their inspiration in two more contemporary forms of art making—minimalism and performance art. Stand-up comedians, storytellers, circus and side-show performers, and dancers provide the historical precedents for performance art. Music video performance, in its carnivalesque, choreographic, and narrative modes thus becomes the perfect site for the migration of museum and stage performance art.

From the start Laurie Anderson's work signaled its potential for music video, notably relative to video's graphic reproduction. Beginning in 1972 with her performances in New York's Soho district, Anderson was one of a group of performance artists and video producers who haunted such venues as the Kitchen, the Paula Cooper Gallery, and 112 Greene Street. Her *United States* began taking form in the performance of some of its parts, such as in the 1981 show at the Orpheum. In 1983 the debut performance at New York's Brooklyn Academy of Music of all four parts of *United States* ("Transportation," "Politics," "Money," and "Love") made this "talking opera" of eight-hour's duration the talk of the downtown scene. Driving and flying, maps, landscapes and astronauts, dreams and biblical references all float as reference points between words and images in this multimedia stage production. *Big Science's* 1981–1982 "From the

Air" would haunt anyone who had witnessed it on every airline flight taken in the 1980s and since. In 1985 "Zero and One" from *The Home of the Brave* explored computer language as yet another language that the poet-musician-visual artist would bring into play. As multimedia performance shaped the 1980s, it would compel recording and mass distribution. The live stage event expanded beyond the television screen through myriad projections of timed simultaneity and juxtaposition, but in order to reach larger audiences, the form ironically had to turn back to cinema and television—the framed formats that in most ways it was seeking to escape.

The combination in 1994 of Anderson's *The Nerve Bible* as a touring show and *The Puppet Motel* CD-ROM represented the different platforms for her work during this period. Both the live act/rear projection format of her staging and lighting magic and the computer graphics/computer allegories demonstrate how an imaginary poetic world can be generated by the simplest of means. For all of her comic flamboyance, the repetition of phrases and the minimalist means by which illusions are overlaid also offer a minimalist aesthetic to be emulated.

Anderson's work in the late 1980s and early 1990s was preceded by, then coincided with, the growth of the playwright, designer, and director Robert Wilson, another artist for whom the Brooklyn Academy of Music proved an important site for innovative staging. In 1969 *The Life and Times of Sigmund Freud* premiered at the Brooklyn Academy. *Deafman Glance* in 1971 links Wilson to the surrealists; as Louis Aragon wrote of Wilson: "He is what we, from whom Surrealism was born, dreamed would come after us and go beyond us."[23] In 1976 Wilson and the composer Philip Glass launched their landmark work "Einstein on the Beach," which was revived for two world tours in 1984 and 1992. More than Anderson, Wilson reframes the stage in reference to the cinematic screen—though it is one in which perspective and figuration allow for perceptual paradoxes and visual puzzles. These visual ideas are translated to video in *Stations*, Wilson's hour-long 1985 experimental performance-art-meets-narrative video. Here the appearance and disappearance of elements in the image, along with their layering, substitute video keying for the transformative stage-lighting effects of Wilson's live works.

Both Anderson and Wilson, along with many video artists not necessarily connected to theater, performance, or music, affect a music video world seeking visual correlates for bands that were emerging from the

MAUREEN TURIM

One of Robert Wilson's "visual puzzles" from *Stations*.

same Downtown club scene. The bands of an earlier 1960s New York underground scene, stretching back to the rise and demise of the Velvet Underground (Sterling Morrison, Mo [Maureen] Tucker, Lou Reed, John Cale), limited their visual signatures mostly to staging and to posters and album covers. The Velvet Underground famously took as their minimalist pop visual emblem Andy Warhol's banana record jacket. Warhol's Exploding Plastic Inevitable, an environmental performance space and dance floor, was saved for posterity in Ronald Nameth's film bearing its name. The Ramones, Patti Smith, and Television followed in this tradition of stylish presentation, yet without fully developing as audiovisual artists. The Talking Heads would take this periods' studied stylistic signature more completely into a visual realm corresponding to the minimalist, performance art, and conceptual installation realm that surrounded them.

Stop Making Sense, Jonathan Demme's 1984 feature release concert film, chronicles the Talking Heads' stage act. *Storytelling Giant*, a compilation of ten music videos made by the Talking Heads during the 1980s, complements the performance documentary by allowing a comparison between the use of visual symbols in performance and in music videos. "Once in a Lifetime" highlights David Byrne's evangelical send-up, as his new wave angular dancing (complete with ticks and jerks of nervous system overload) retains an admiration for a preacher's exuberance while substituting irony for religiosity. The video water forms an abstract ground; multiple Byrne bodies float up at diagonals, recalling Magritte's

Robert Wilson's influence on the video for the Talking Heads's "Burning Down the House."

rain of bureaucrats; and banks of monitors echo images. Byrne's dancing body at points echoes four other versions of himself operating in a separate image plane. The piece, directed by Toni Basil (as was "Crosseyed and Painless") borrows many of the experimental techniques of video art in use at the time. "Wild Wild Life," directed by Byrne (as were the Robert Wilson–influenced "Burning Down the House" and "Road to Nowhere"), uses the minimalist construct of band members sporting stage harnesses that lift them up against a silver-curtained background. This pared-down image is joined by later images of the band members in the harness performing large dance jumps off the rungs of a ladder, which in turn leads to other variations recalling bungee jumping and frame drift. The animator Jim Blashfield created some wonderful circulating images of household objects for "And She Was." For "The Lady Don't Mind," Jim Jarmusch provides a black-and-white minimalist image of a woman in a kimono in a bare room, in montage with night shots of the New York cityscape and the band performing informally but with rear projection.

The Talking Heads clearly believe that imagery in the music video should have a life of its own, following traditions of the visual avant-gardes for which the band's word imagery plays in counterpoint. As Byrne remarks, "We made a couple of Tom Tom Club videos that were purely animation which I was really proud of, but they didn't get shown much because they didn't show the band."[24] Sally Stockbridge notes the similarity between the abstract visuals of the Tom Tom Club videos and the

Michel Gondry's video for "Bachelorette" is both dreamlike and loosely narrative.

films of Otto Fischinger.[25] In *Wired* magazine, David Byrne speaks also of a project making fun of the iconography of PowerPoint: "This whirlwind of arrows, pointing everywhere and nowhere—each one color-coded to represent God knows what aspects of growth, market share, or regional trends—ends up capturing the excitement and pleasant confusion of the marketplace, the everyday street, personal relationships, and the simultaneity of multitasking."[26] The relationship of Byrne's experiments to some of the arrow images of Paul Klee strikes a note for which perhaps we should have been prepared: the dancer on the ladder of "Wild Wild Life" may also be an homage to Klee's figure famously climbing a ladder to abstraction.

With "Human Behaviour" in 1993 Michel Gondry launched what would become Björk's long pursuit of the avant-garde visual arts in her video corollaries for what she conceives of as the avant-garde pop song. Björk plays Goldilocks in a color-saturated narrative that uses animated stuffed bears in much the same way that various installation artists have mobilized toys as elements of symbolic confrontations, for example, Jeff Koons, Kelly Heaton, Fred Wilson, Chris Burden, and David Beck. We might wonder if Gondry had the Porter film of 1903 as a conscious reference, but either way the intertextuality across ninety years of cinema is a fetching avant-garde rhyme.

Gondry's "Isobel" (1995) and "Bachelorette" (1997) are music video's version of the film narrative and sequel, telling the story of a wild child in lush superimposed imagery discovering urban culture through instal-

Sophie Muller and Björk's "Venus as a Boy": a hot pink and orange version of Martha Rosler's "Semiotics of the Kitchen."

lations of toy fighter planes, after which the same girl becomes a woman reacting to her life in the city. In "Hyperballad" Björk continues as a character running through a landscape that simulates that of a computer game, only to throw herself off a cliff. In "Army of Me" (1995) Gondry collages images of Björk driving a vehicle that alternately looks like an overgrown SUV and a science fiction tank; the surrealism is provided by dental imagery that builds toward the blowing up a of a museum. "Jóga" (1997) features a computer-modified ride over the landscape of Iceland. Gondry's videos for Björk increasingly steeping in video art image processing are both dreamlike and loosely narrative.

Björk's videos also have been outlets for other creative videomakers attracted to her mix of pop and artfulness. In "Venus as a Boy," directed by Sophie Muller (1993), Björk's dreamy culinary adventure was purportedly inspired by Georges Bataille's *Story of the Eye* but it is hardly an equivalent eroticization of the egg; in many ways it is more like a version of Martha Rosler's "Semiotics of the Kitchen" colored in hot pink and orange, though Björk's video attempts to rival the look of fashion photography. Similarly, "It's Oh So Quiet" (1995) directed by Spike Jonze riffs on the film musical. Its off-beat send-up of the glamour choreography stage takes a decidedly commonplace setting. Much installation art, including installation video pieces, shares this preoccupation with popular culture, so the two forms seem to easily slide into one another, especially now that some museums have started to curate installations of music videos.

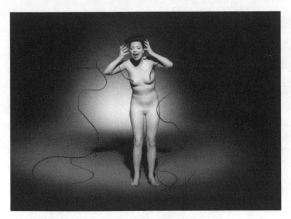

Eiko Ishioka's video for Björk's "Cocoon."

This has been the case especially with Chris Cunningham and Floria Sigismondi, who make installation work in addition to their music videos.

Björk's videos seem most successful, however, when they brush against the conceptual installation. "Violently Happy" (1994), directed by Jean-Baptiste Mondino, features stereotypes of the insane asylum as snake pit, with a padded cell colored in bright baby blue. Its three-wall design seems to present these characters, including Björk, as performers within an installation environment. One of the most avant-garde of Björk's videos, Eiko Ishioka's "Cocoon" (2002), plays with minimalist white for both costume and bleached eyebrows, treating Björk as a geisha whose makeup extends over her entirely nude body. Red translucent threads circulate between her breast and nose, only to finally envelop her in a cocoon.

In "The Erotic Life of Machines" Steven Shaviro addresses the treatment of the posthuman in Chris Cunningham's Björk music video "All Is Full of Love."[27] The video offers another example of white-hued minimalism, while conceptually offering us the love life of identical robots in uncanny symmetry. A strong visual statement, the work operates as if it were an installation piece, with the same sly sense of humor that is evoked by the presence of such setups in museum spaces.

In the preceding pages I have explored how some of the best work in music video is in dialogue with the history of twentieth-century art and current trends in video art and installation. It would be dangerous to end this essay with some high/low polarity—a danger that I have acknowl-

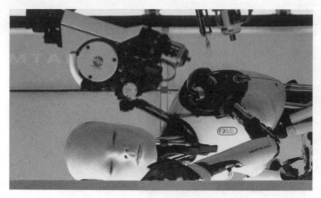

The white-hued minimalism of Chris Cunningham's video for "All Is Full of Love."

edged as latent in much postmodernist art criticism. Yet this polarity is even more pronounced in those who react against postmodernism, and thus other strategies are needed to overcome such latent oppositions. Let me suggest, instead, the dialogue that is occurring between music video and the art world—both of which clearly share their audiences. Through this dialogue we can perhaps move past the notion on the part of the most naive voices within those audiences that each innovation in music video was "invented" by the most recent clip to use it. Perhaps music video's audience will take a new interest in the vital history of the forms they discover through their most recent and most accessible manifestations.

NOTES

1 Fredric Jameson, *Postmodernism, or, The Cultural Logic of Late Capitalism* (Durham, N.C.: Duke University Press, 1991), 18.
2 In 2001 "superflat" was shown at the MOCA gallery, the Pacific Design Center in Los Angeles, and the Walker Art Center in Minneapolis. The bilingual catalogue of the exhibit was published as Takashi Murakami, *SUPER FLAT* (San Francisco: Last Gasp Press. 2003). See also Dana Amanda and Friis-Hansen Cruz, *Takashi Murakami: The Meaning of the Nonsense of the Meaning* (New York: Harry Abrams. 2000); and the interview with Murakami by Mako Wakasa at http://www.jca-online.com/murakami.html.
3 Silke Tudor, "Gogol Bordello's Debauched Gypsy Ferocities, and the Trans-cinema Festival's Mind-Altering New Media," *SF Weekly*, October 9, 2002.
4 David Sinclair, "Blue Pseud Shoes: Radiohead Reckon Their Latest Is Easy

Listening: David Sinclair Has News for Them," *Times* (London), May 30, 2003, 16.

5 "Let the Music Play," *Televisual*, December 2, 2003, 31.

6 David Kleiler and Robert Moses, *You Stand There: Making Music Video* (New York: Three Rivers Press, 1997), 38.

7 Ibid., 38.

8 Ibid., iv.

9 Ibid., 26.

10 Greil Marcus, *Lipstick Traces: A Secret History of the Twentieth Century* (Cambridge, Mass.: Harvard University Press 1990). See also http://www.intuitivemusic.com/tguideavantgarde.html.

11 Tristan Tzara, "Dada Manifesto," in *Dada Painters and Poets*, ed. Robert Motherwell (Cambridge, Mass.: The Belknap Press of Harvard University Press, 1951), 78–79.

12 Cabaret Voltaire interview, quoted in Mick Fish and Dave Halberry, *Cabaret Voltaire: The Art of the Sixth Sense* (London: Serious Art Forms Publishing, 1985). See also Mick Fish and Dave Halberry, *Industrial Evolution: Through the 80s with Cabaret Voltaire* (London: SAF Publishing, 2002).

13 Ibid.

14 Alan Williams, "Pierrot in Context(s)," in David Wills, ed., *Jean-Luc Godard's Pierrot Le Fou* (Cambridge: Cambridge University Press, 2000).

15 Hannah Höch, quoted at http://www.peak.org/~dadaist/English/Graphics/photomontage.html. See also Maud Lavin, *Cut with the Kitchen Knife: The Weimar Photomontages of Hannah Höch* (New Haven, Conn.: Yale University Press, 1994).

16 Joseph Tate, "Radiohead's Antivideos: Works of Art in the Age of Electronic Reproduction," *Postmodern Culture: An Electronic Journal of Interdisciplinary Criticism* 12.3 (May 2002): 37.

17 Nigel Godrich, quoted at http://www.apple.com/hotnews/articles/2001/07/radiohead/paragraphs.

18 Joan D. Lynch, "Music Videos: From Performance to Dada-Surrealism," *Journal of Popular Culture* 18.1 (summer 1984): 53–57.

19 Information on "COME PART MENTAL," an exhibition by Floria Sigismondi at the Museum of Contemporary Canadian Art, September 14 to October 28, 2001, can be found online at http://www.mocca.toronto.on.ca/recent/floria.html, and at http://www.floriasigismondi.com.

20 Lisa Zeidner, "No Mo Po Mo, Or: I Had a Dream," *Tin House* (July 2001).

21 Spike Jonze, quoted from the booklet accompanying his DVD titled *The Work of Director Spike Jonze* (New York: Metropolis DVD, 2003).

22 http://www.director-file.com/cunningham/520.html.

23 Louis Aragon, quoted at http://www.robertwilson.com/bio/bioMaster.htm.

24 David Byrne, quoted at http://www.talking-heads.net/archive.html#interviews.

25 Sally Stockbridge, "Intertextuality: Video Music Clips and Historical Film," in *History on/and/in Film*, ed. T. O'Regan and B. Shoesmith (Perth: History and Film Association of Australia, 1987), 153–58.

26 David Byrne, "Learning to Love Powerpoint," *Wired* 11.9 (September 2003). See also David Byrne, *E.E.E.I.: Envisioning Emotional Epistemological Information* (New York: Steidl, 2003).

27 Steven Shaviro, "The Erotic Life of Machines," *Parallax* 8.4 (October/December 2002): 21–31.

STRANGE PEOPLE, WEIRD OBJECTS:
THE NATURE OF NARRATIVITY, CHARACTER,
AND EDITING IN MUSIC VIDEOS

Carol Vernallis

lthough the field of music video studies has always been richly contested, two central arguments stand out. The earliest writers on the genre, such as Ann Kaplan, David Tetzlaff, and Marsha Kinder, emphasized the discontinuity and strangeness of music video, along with its departure from traditional ways of organizing visual materials. Ann Kaplan's *Rocking around the Clock*, for example, stressed the genre's fragmentary narratives and unusual forms of characterization. The second generation of scholarship, including Andrew Goodwin, John Fiske, and Lisa Lewis, dismissed the earlier readings by stating that they were inattentive to the institutional modes of production and historical practices of musical performance. By focusing on the contexts in which videos were produced and consumed, each writer sought to make sense of what Kaplan sometimes characterized as schizophrenic texts: Goodwin naturalized music video's apparent incoherence by connecting its production practices with those of popular music; Fiske read music videos as standard narratives; and Lewis described the ways that young women—usually regarded as passive viewers—reused the videos they found on MTV. Having looked closely at the ways that videos create visual structures in relation to music and lyrics, and having interviewed directors and others in the field, I believe that the earliest writing had one idea essentially right: music video *is* irreducibly strange. However, the early writing neglected the music's role in shaping a music video's form and shied away from close textual readings. It was therefore unable to account for the ways that the genre's individual parameters function independently and in concert.[1] In this essay I reveal the strangeness of music video through an analysis of three individual parameters:

narrative, editing, and the uses of human figures. I have selected these elements because in music video they are the most striking and problematic.

Before addressing these parameters, I first will provide a way for thinking about music video—one that considers the materials of which videos are composed, the technologies through which they are made, and the ways they work in culture. I would like to return to the question of music's role in music video, and then argue that what separates music videos from other genres such as film, television, and photography *is* the music. Indeed, the music of music video should be taken most seriously, because music videos derive from the songs they set. The music comes first—the song is produced before the video is conceived—and the director normally designs images with the song as a guide. Moreover, the video is intended to sell the song; the video is therefore responsible to the song in the eyes of the artist and record company. Music videos have many ways of following a song. They often reflect its structure and pick up on specific musical features in the domains of melody, rhythm, and timbre. The image can even seem to imitate sound's ebb and flow and its indeterminate boundaries. Through technological advances, such as video editing, digitization, and new pre- and postproduction techniques, the image has become, as Michel Chion suggests, as voluble as speech.[2] Videomakers have developed a set of practices for putting image to music in which the image gives up its autonomy and abandons some of its representational modes. In exchange, the image gains in flexibility and play, as well as in polyvalence of meaning. Many of the meanings of music video lie in this give and take between sound and image and in the relations among their various modes of continuity.

As music videos attempt to fulfill many requirements, such as showcasing the star, highlighting lyrics, and underscoring musical structures, a remarkable thing occurs: any visual, musical, or lyrical element can come to the fore. The viewer may not be able to predict the kind of function that a particular element will perform or the degree of preeminence it will obtain in a video; nor can the viewer assume that its function or status will remain consistent over the course of a video. A video may provide a detailed depiction of some character at the beginning only to abandon him or her later in favor of a rhapsody on green, which may in turn give way to a precise visual articulation of a percussion part—or we may find that the final section reveals a big chair as the video's true subject. It might be helpful to imagine the various elements of music video's mise-en-scène as separate tracks on a recording engineer's mixing board: any element or combination of elements can be brought forward or become submerged in the mix. These elements form a dynamic system in which a change in one part of the mix may be compensated for by a change in another. Inasmuch as any element can come to the fore, the world that a video depicts can become very strange. Some of music video's excitement stems from the sense that anything can happen—even an insightful or progressive image of social relations.

Though many approaches can illuminate the medium, including studies of the industry and audience reception, in this essay I focus on the videos themselves by considering several of the genre's individual parameters. Various methods are helpful in this approach, including close readings of individual clips, investigations of music video directors' oeuvres, and considerations of genre.

PROCESSES, SERIES, CATALOGUES, AND TABLEAUX: HOW AND WHY MUSIC VIDEOS ESCHEW CLASSICAL NARRATIVES

Narrative has often been taken as the prime issue in music video. Some writers on the genre have claimed that videos function like parts of movies or television shows; others have stated that music video is fundamentally antinarrative, that it is a kind of postmodern pastiche that gains energy from defying narrative conventions.[3] In truth, music videos range from those that are extremely abstract, emphasizing color and movement, to those that convey a story; most, however, tend to be nonnarrative. The small percentage of videos that do tell stories do so by specific means that must be placed in context with techniques drawn from other, particularly musical and visual, realms. We should also consider music video's narrative dimension in relation to its other modes, like underscoring the music, highlighting the lyrics, and showcasing the star. Here I will sketch a continuum from narrative to nonnarrative videos by tracing some of the familiar forms and by providing descriptions of particular examples. Next, I consider why music videos most often do not embody narratives. Finally, I offer models for understanding nonnarrative modes like the "process" video, the catalogue, and those that employ a kind of permeability or contagion.

Before I provide examples of videos that fall in the narrative continuum, I would like to offer a definition for narrative, which I take from Aristotle: Narrative occurs when characters with defined personality traits, goals, and a sense of agency encounter obstacles and are changed by them.[4] Still fewer music videos meet the criteria that David Bordwell, in his *Classical Hollywood Cinema*, requires for a story: namely, that all of the events we see and hear, plus those we infer or assume to have occurred, can be arranged by us according to their presumed causal relations, chronological order, duration, frequency, and spatial locations. Even if we have a sense of a music video's story, we may not feel that we can reconstruct the tale in the manner that Bordwell's criteria demand.[5]

Music Video and Narrativity

I begin here on the narrative side of the continuum; in so doing I address Aerosmith's "Crazy" because it flaunts its narrativity more than almost any other music video. Even if it only creates the appearance of a narrative rather than actually delivering one, it suggests how close to narrative videos can come, and it shows some typical devices that they employ to do so. Endowed with some of the proper elements—a beginning and a middle (though not an end)—"Crazy" has characters who possess volition and encounter obstacles. The video tracks the exploits of two teenage girls as they play hooky, shoplift, enter an amateur strip contest, spend the night in a seedy motel, and then drive off to pick up a hitchhiker and skinny dip in a lake.[6]

"Crazy" departs from convention by conveying its tale in the present tense; videos that tell stories most often situate them in the past, in which they string together noncontiguous moments by interpolating images of the artist poised in the act of remembering. Yet already we have a subtle complication—the video seems to occur in the present tense but it also references eras stretching from the 1940s to the 1980s, thus making the temporality of the video unclear. As in many music videos, the narrative elements are established in the opening images, well before the song begins: a "bad" Catholic girl kicks out a door, revealing her underwear as she escapes from school through a bathroom window. Thus, most of what happens during the video proper—the shoplifting and the strip contest—does not represent narrative drive so much as a spinning out of material. Once the characters have committed their greatest transgression—the striptease—there is nowhere else to go. Although a trace of

CAROL VERNALLIS

the premise lingers, the rest of the video veers toward a more episodic structure.

"Crazy" creates the semblance of a narrative through a clever technique: namely, exploiting the fact that the characters lack dialogue. The video alternates between the girls' lip-synch performances and situations in which they cannot or do not speak. Examples of the former include the young women singing along as the Aerosmith song blasts over the car radio, as well as mouthing the lyrics while stripping in an amateur strip contest. When the two girls prepare for the show, they gaze at one another in mutual affection; here, in the throes of a homoerotic moment, they say nothing because words would be superfluous.

Most often in music video the performance footage of the band has the effect of blunting narrative drive; in "Crazy," however, the images of Aerosmith—which are shot so dark that the group is set off from everything else—carry almost no weight, and they almost escape our vision. These barely visible images blend seamlessly with the story footage through match cuts. The lead singer Steven Tyler spits and then so does one of the girls; he throws forward a microphone with attached ribbons, and the other girl tosses her handkerchief into the air. Tyler's own daughter, Liv, plays the role of one of the rambunctious young women, through which in some subtle way a twinning effect is manifested. In "Crazy," the performance and story footage are linked to one another through a family resemblance, thereby creating an unusually rich and layered text. For the father, there are thoughts about a child's actions, as well as a desire to be young again himself; while the daughter dreams of the father who worries about her, or of his bandmate for whom she has an attraction.[7]

"Crazy" delivers much of its material in a compressed, blunt fashion. Drawing from television commercials and movie trailers, the movements of figures within the frame are tightly choreographed, and what might take three shots in a movie is in the video condensed into a single shot. The mise-en-scène of "Crazy" also borrows from the intertitles of silent film. Signs such as those on the nightclub's marquee and on the gas station's sundry store help to show the location; in the conclusion, a tractor plows the word "crazy" onto a field. To advance the story there is a reliance on shots of objects—cars, gas pumps, a photo booth, lipstick, a microphone—and a kind of overgesticulation, or ham acting, that would be out of place in most film genres. Other temporal cues reflect times of day.

The song creates an ambience that allows the image to diverge from the music and lyrics. While the image seems congruent with the song, at certain moments of extreme narrative interest the song as such becomes almost impossible to follow; any effort to concentrate on it in these moments founders, as it might if we were to force our attention onto the soundtrack of a movie during a crucial moment of revelation. Steven Tyler, who wrote "Crazy," has stated explicitly that he now composes music with a potential video in mind, which suggests that he has distanced himself from the pressures and constraints of traditional songwriting, particularly recognizability and novelty. Although Aerosmith's songs are well written within the current context, their comfortable, functional nature does not compel repeated, close listening. As might be expected, music videos are not in business for the purpose of turning our attention away from the song (nor can they afford to), and this is why the video for "Crazy" remains an exception to current practices.[8]

Prodigy's "Smack My Bitch Up" contains several additional narrative devices. The video creates the sense of a narrative in part by presenting the point of view of someone who remains behind the camera. As the camera continually tracks forward, a hand stretches before its lens. Without seeing the body that would ground our sense of this figure, we don't consider the figure's past and future or its aims and desires. The Prodigy song works like techno by bringing elements in and out of a relatively stable mix without establishing sharp sectional divisions. (As such, the videomaker does not need to wrestle with strongly contrasting song sections that might suggest changes of consciousness, activity, or mode of being.) The video's director combines diegetic sound effects with the pre-recorded audio track; these sound effects play against and echo material in the song proper, thereby creating a dense soundscape that rests neither in the song's world nor in the real one. Depicting a single night out, the video unfolds from early evening to sometime at night. The advancing hour is shown through darkening skies and rooms, as well as by people who look more and more disheveled, images of clocks, an increasingly shaky camera, and shots showing the copious ingestion of drugs and alcohol. The drug and alcohol consumption suggests unpredictable shifts in consciousness for which no account need be provided. Several of the strategies that appear in Prodigy's video—the use of diegetic sound, the exploitation of thinly sketched, ambiguous protagonists, a reliance on an unusually relaxed song structure—differ from those employed in

CAROL VERNALLIS

"Crazy." Although such effects might not work as powerfully as those for the Aerosmith video, they do help to establish an engagement in the story.

The many types of narrative range from the most apparent to the most submerged. Most familiar may be those I call "trauma videos," which try to compress a very heated narrative into a small form and close enigmatically, forcing the viewer to watch again and again. In trauma videos, the elements needed for a story—active agents, a sense of time and place, a knowledge of how actions unfold—are confusing or absent. In the next section, I discuss two such videos, Michael Jackson's "Thriller" and Madonna's "Take a Bow," and the ways they exploit music and images' tendency to signify differently, especially in relation to time and space. I consider these narratives to be less strong than the previous ones, in part, because while they elicit a strong engagement with a story, they also brusquely foil that engagement. Other types of narrative forms are those that feature narrative glimpses that are dispersed across the whole of the tape. Good examples include Madonna's "Cherish" and Lenny Kravitz's "Are You Gonna Go My Way." In these cases, performance footage consumes a larger share of the video, and the far-flung narrative sequences need to be connected in order to reconstruct the story. The video's stakes in this story seem to be lower; the connections do not demand a puzzling out.

Sometimes, directors choose narrative imagery reflective of the particular form and scale of a pop song. In Janet Jackson's "Anytime, Anyplace," the singer always initiates a meeting with her lover at the beginning of a verse, sits isolated on the bed in her bedroom during the bridge, and then unites with her lover during the chorus. The minimal nature of the narrative—girl apart, girl together—fits well with the song's three-part structure.

Explaining the Absence of Narratives

Music videos avoid the Aristotelian narrative form and fully drawn stories for several reasons, including the genre's multimedia nature, the lack of appropriateness and applicability of narrative film devices, and the necessity of foregrounding the song's form (in order to sell the song). In the text that follows I discuss these elements in turn.

Videos that foreground a character's change in fortune or that depict strong conflicts often contain ellipses in the narrative that may create a kind of trauma: the viewer takes part in the video's unfolding and notes the shifts of activity, affect, and time, but cannot fill in the context. Music video's multimedia nature may be the major cause of this trauma for a number of reasons. Music, image, and lyrics each possess their own language with regard to time, space, narrativity, activity, and affect. Even when these three media combine seamlessly into a new whole, in the background some aspect of each medium will remain, where it lingers in an almost palpable way. Perhaps directors flaunt the disjunctions among music, image, and lyrics in order to keep the viewer close to the unfolding music; or perhaps the image cannot match the strange spatiality and temporality established by pop songs. (Pop songs are largely determined through postproduction techniques; their sonic spaces do not match those in the real world.) Nevertheless, as we try to understand the relations among media that don't quite fit together, we lose our sense of the piece's larger form. A good example of how music, image, and lyrics each possess their own temporality can be found in Madonna's "Take a Bow" video, in which Madonna falls in love with a bullfighter.

The music for the verses of "Take a Bow" opens with a broad feel and closes with a touch of hesitation. The accompanying images show Madonna, the matador, and the people of the town meticulously preparing for a bullfight over the course of what appears to be a single day. (The music and imagery match closely but not exactly. The music has a sense of grace, yet the image carries the scent of dull, repetitive labor.) A secondary staging presents Madonna standing or sitting alone in a room, hunched below a single light source, or passing her hands in front of a television set; here time seems painful, a suggestion that Madonna has engaged in this activity for a very long time. The music for the chorus, relaxed and lyrical in a ruminative way, could extend over a day or over months. Even more oblique is the imagery featuring hands flowing over the matador's cape and Madonna's face and arms falling through the frame. This imagery is almost completely devoid of temporal markers: these shots might suggest a particular instant, a recurring moment, or a passing thought. Later, when Madonna and the bullfighter have what looks like demoralizing sex, there is no way to draw on what we have learned to tell if the encounter is a one-time fling, a repeated event, or a figment of the female protagonist's imagination.

Each of music video's media—music, image, and lyrics—are, in a way, both blank and shot through with ellipses. Are the lyrics for the viewer, a lover, or are they the singer's personal reflection? To whom do the empty sets belong? What are the music's uses and what spaces should it fill? What happened between the cut from the image of the face to the shot of the fingertips? What happened between the line "She knew me well" to "I've always been there for you," or in the shift from the verse to the chorus?

Music videos obscure narrative as they build up a history. The video often begins with the establishment of a ground and with a sense of stability and coherence. Although I cannot immediately understand the movement from one shot to another, the music begins to give me some feel for it, and the lyrics help me to piece it together. Once the music video starts developing a sense of history, however, and once the musical, visual, or lyrical elements begin to draw upon what the video has presented thus far, I note that I cannot find these sources from earlier in the video. These moments are quite disparate—and between them stretches an archipelago of different events. The moments from the video's past, and the moment in the video's present that has sent me back to them, are linked to other such complexes, each contributing to the present moment's sense of culmination. When trying to learn the patterns inherent in the music, lyrics, and images as well as the relations among these patterns, and when attempting to make conjectures about what happens in the gaps, the viewer creates a template. However, this template (created out of both depicted and inferred material) cannot be experienced in real time because music videos are designed to be almost constantly engaging: the image draws us on as it rushes forward.

We should remember that music videos are short forms, structured around the music and the showcasing of the star, with very little text. Music videos often lack essential ingredients—such as place names, meeting times, a sense of past and present, and fully realized protagonists and villains—and they cannot be described as possessing a classical Hollywood film narrative structure. As a rule, music videos do not help us to predict what will happen in the next shot, or in the following section, or at the close of the tape. To engage the audience in a Hollywood feature film, many directors adopt a technique known as the narrative plank. An appointment is set, after which the character engages in some routine activity in preparation for the important meeting: she or he packs a suitcase and then walks or drives to the next scene. This gives the viewer ample time to predict how the upcoming encounter will unfold. But since the objective of music video is to be continually engrossing, there is little time for such a device. The music demands attention at every instant; a pressing future takes away from an interesting present. Music video typically elicits some protensive activity, most often on a local level within spatial terms or within broadly sketched outlines of interpersonal relations (which also feel spatial). The viewer might chart how long it will take for the melodic line to reach its apex, or for the musical section to close, or for the figure to move across the room, or for one stock character to "get with" another.

Often the imagery that occurs at one of the video's high points will have been disclosed somewhere in the opening third of the video. As we move past the opening imagery, however, we can seldom identify an object, person, or setting as the "marked" material that will round out or clinch the piece. In the moment-to-moment temporality of music video, we don't find ourselves watching the singer, for example, scan a hotel room and then exclaim, "It's under the mattress! Look under the mattress!" The satisfying rhythm of concealment and revelation so crucial to film narrative is less common in music video. Videos almost never provide the information necessary to predict one outcome over another. All outcomes seem possible, including an abandonment of the narrative in favor of a dance sequence.[9]

Music videos are also thin on character. Alfred Hitchcock said that the better the villain the better the suspense. Yet the superficial and brief pop songs seem to be focused on the singer. What space is there for another character, particularly an evil one? In music videos, truly evil antagonists are almost always absent, and background figures can be only mildly threatening; their power and their reasons for implementing that power remain unclear—think of the stonefaced judges in NIN's "Closer" and the factory owner in Madonna's "Express Yourself." Given the absence of villains and, correspondingly, so few elements with which to define them, music video's figures become shadowy.

A music video's star is a phantasmagoric multiple: the songwriter, the musician, and the rock star playing a screen role never cohere, and thus remain echoes of one another and embody different subjectivities. When the video is finally an edited whole the image follows the music, and there is the eerie sense that the music, rather than the subject's intent, animates the figure. In order to match the speed and energy of the music, the image often reflects a more heightened and sustained experiential state than ordinary consciousness, while the actual people in the video become more like automatons.

Music videos are rarely teleological, and the same is true of pop music. A pop song's verse might depict a problem, while the bridge presents a utopian solution, and the chorus offers a crystallization. The director David Fincher noted that when he first started to make videos, he tried to tell straight stories but soon abandoned the throughline approach. Instead he began to create six or seven separate segments, each evoking a unique mood and treated as an autonomous unit.

In a pop song, each musical element can both exist within its own sphere and become transformed over the course of the piece. For example, after a flute line is introduced it will then be varied, extended, or simply repeated so that by the end of the song it stands in a new relation to other musical elements, like the bass line and the voice. Or, if the flute line disappears, it becomes submerged in the unfolding of the piece. There is no complete annihilation of materials in music.

Michael Jackson's "Thriller" is an example in which each shot possesses its own truth value. Jackson performs in a number of roles: a 1970s-style leader of a dance troupe; a self-absorbed moviegoer of the 1980s; a sidewalk escort; a stay-at-home boyfriend who has yellow eyes; a werewolf; and a zombie. Each of these roles is connected to different musical materials: Rod Temperton's funky bass line, Elmer Bernstein's movie music, and an echo of Earth, Wind and Fire's horn and vocal arrangements. Each of these moments is closely linked to the music, as when Jackson shifts from an escort to a zombie (and the muted guitar seems to warm up his character). Viewers may have difficulty hierarchizing fantastical images plus "classic" music versus realistic depictions plus popular music. Not until the video has been watched many times do the different images of Jackson as alternately predatory, flirtatious, and shy each gain coherence and weight.

Types of Nonnarrative

Many videos are devoted to completing a single process: getting everyone to the party on time, ensuring that the plane gets off the ground or that the baby is born, and so on. (Here, we might define "process" as the act of carrying on or going on — i.e., a series of actions, changes, or functions bringing about a result.) A single process placed against shifting song material creates a complex texture. The presentation of this process is fragmented, attenuated abruptly by images of the band performing or lip-synching against an amorphous background. The sustained treatment of the activity comes suddenly, at a time when we do not expect it, and its duration may be unusually prolonged or drastically abbreviated. The video's main project is dispersed across a number of the song's sections. When the footage of this material appears over the course of the video, carrying the process forward, these appearances gain an uncanny sense of return. In such videos the emblematic characters, appearing intermittently with ferocious attention to a simple task, create qualities of volition and determination befitting musical materials that function similarly.

A related type of music video involves categories, series, or lists. The performers might walk through a series of tableaux or separate rooms, or down the street as they encounter different people. The musician might be seen recounting a number of previous relationships. Like the laundry list, the catalogue is not a narrative; events or settings simply fall one after another. The catalogue works well in a music video because the addition of a new yet familiar item can be compared with musical material that returns regularly but also incorporates variation. The travelogue has elements of both the "process" video and the category or list, where the performer is driving, sailing, walking, and seeing or fantasizing things along the way. Another example of this kind is the video that establishes a quasi-mechanical chain of causality in which the camera tracks the flow à la Rube Goldberg's machines.

Music video directors add richness and complexity to the simple structures of processes and lists in several ways. One way is to include a number of such threads in a music video and make sure that at some point at least one becomes linked with another. Many music videos work on the principle of contagion that I referred to at the start of this essay: an element in one of the strands seeps into another, be it a color, a particular prop, or a way of feeling or moving. For example, in Ben Folds Five's "Brick," the splashes of red that appear in the performance space (which function purely as an arbitrary, decorative touch) gradually invade the story space (we see a red Christmas bulb). Rage Against the Machine's "Bulls on Parade" presents a much more complex example. The video weaves eight threads into the texture in an unpredictable way: generic, black-garbed freedom fighters wielding flags make their way up a mountain (à la "king of the hill"); the band performs, becoming more agitated as time progresses; the crowds surge; close-ups of earnest, highly photogenic young people of various ethnicities appear; iconic political propaganda flashes on the screen; text hand-scratched on film jitters on the screen; a printing press churns; an anonymous person writes graffiti on institutional walls proclaiming "Long live the Los Angeles revolution." Many of these threads contain material or processes that seep into the others. The torn red flags that become more worn as the video progresses connect to the last close-up of the lead performer, who stands firm though looking completely exhausted. The red from the flag starts coloring the black-and-white footage of the crowd and the performers. The guitar necks begin to angle upward in the frame, as does the scribbled text, matching the movement of the freedom fighters as they make their way up the hill. (Over the course of the song, the tessitura shifts from low to high.) The director adds complexity by fleshing out and/or reducing various threads. Although visual strands may quickly come together and then depart and head their own way, an elaboration and playing out of material will seem to have taken place. While they clearly inhabit a different space, the youthful mixed-ethnic types begin to bestow greater definition on the generic black-garbed freedom fighters. (A crude line drawing of the graffiti artist strips them bare.)

Many music videos simply extend performance settings: the performer might appear in a dolled-up high school theater, and then some activity will play out backstage or in the wings. Although the depiction may be static, the relation between the performer and the setting can seem unusually charged, as if the activity within the frame is somewhat taboo and the police or a parent might rush in on the scene at any moment. Similar to the performance video is the "slice of life." The slice of life, however, functions in music video more as an extended tableau than as documentary: a single image will be highlighted in time rather than revealed at once, with only one or two elements shifting slightly. Since the slice-of-life footage often contains repetitive, ongoing activity, its placement within the tape seems less crucial and it cuts fluidly against performance footage.

Music videos often suggest a story, but in a somewhat static way: we obtain no more visual information than we might derive from a single narrative painting. "You Oughta Know" shows Alanis Morissette performing in the foundations of a burned-down house, walking around in the desert with a suitcase, sitting on a bench, and lying in a poppy field. The video tells no story, but the faintest allusions to domesticity—to brides, lovers, and housekeepers—are enough to suggest the possibility that a story is being generated.

In music video, what is concealed and what is revealed serve to encourage multiple viewings by engaging the viewer in a process of reconstructing, interpolating, or extrapolating a story behind the scenes that are actually visible. When the narrative mode is present even fleetingly, it creates an aura of mystery, a sense that things need to be puzzled out; it also raises questions of continuity by encouraging an engagement with its human figures. The hint of a narrative draws us into the video, but it is the nonnarrative structures like processes, series, catalogues, and tableaux that dominate it. Music videos encourage us early on to seek out a narrative, and by their close they suggest that something crucial has transpired. But where, when, and how did this transformative event occur? Perhaps the evidence is buried in too many different places, and the clues are too elliptical. How much do we really know about what happens? A viewer may believe that some moment of density and richness is locked somewhere within the videotape. But where is it? And what was it?

As illustrated above, music video's large-scale formal structures differ strikingly from those used to organize classical Hollywood cinema. Additional study will reveal that *all* of music video's parameters—including visual ones such as lighting, editing, space, and props; and musical ones such as text setting, harmony, rhythm, timbre, and so on—take on a special cast. Consider the function of lyrics: some break free from the texture to captivate the viewer's attention, while others sink into the mix to become almost inaudible. Those that break through can seem to possess a shimmer or gloss, and yet the others become almost inaccessible. One of the most striking parameters in music video is editing. (And, in fact, music video editing has been accused of transforming and even debasing classical Hollywood cinema.) In what follows I discuss editing and then move on to the use of objects and human figures; after which I close with a discussion of music video's uncanny features.

THE KINDEST CUT: FUNCTIONS AND MEANINGS
IN MUSIC VIDEO EDITING

Little specific analysis has been done on music video editing. When critics of film and television write that something is "cut like music video" or refer to "MTV-style editing," they might mention quick cutting or editing on the beat, and indeed it is clear that the edits in music video come much more frequently than those in film; that many stand out as disjunctive; and that the editing seems to have a rhythmic basis that is closely connected to the song. These last two features suggest that music video does something different, and a good deal more, than does the editing in film. Music video editing, much more than classical Hollywood film editing, bears a responsibility for many elements.[10] Not only does the editing in a music video direct the flow of the narrative, it can underscore nonnarrative visual structures and form such structures on its own. Like film editing, it can color our understanding of characters, but it has also assimilated and extended the iconography of the pop star. Much of the particularity of music video editing lies in its responsiveness to the music. It can elucidate aspects of the song, such as rhythmic and timbral features, particular phrases in the lyrics, and especially the song's sectional divisions. Because it can establish its own rhythmic profile, the editing can provide a counterpoint to the song's rhythmic structures. More subtly and also most importantly, the editing in a music video works hard to insure that no single element—the narrative, the setting, the performance, the star, the lyrics, the song—gains the upper hand. Music video directors rely on the editing to maintain a sense of openness, a sense that any element can come to the fore at any time. The editing does so in part simply through being noticed. By demanding attention, it prevents powerful images from acquiring too much weight and stopping the flow of information. The editing thus preserves the video's momentum and keeps us in the present. A striking edit can allow us to move past a number of strange or disturbing images without either worrying over them or forgetting them completely.[11]

Music video's rich surface in part derives from the way that editing is sometimes very noticeable and yet sometimes invisible as it draws from the techniques most common in film. Its complexity stems not only from the sheer number of functions it serves, but also from the way that it moves unpredictably among these functions. In fact, the meaning of a technique used in film editing often undergoes a subtle change of valence when used in music video. Since the world of music video editing is so broad and complex, I've divided this part of my essay into five sections, and I provide one or two examples in each. I begin with a discussion of a few shots and edits and show how their functions differ between film and music video. The second section considers the role of editing in creating meaning, narrative, and other forms of continuity. Section three shows how the music video image adapts to the processual nature of sound, and how this adaptation works to hold the viewer's interest. The fourth section explores the ways that music videos treat close-ups of the star. The final section looks at several of the means by which editing can reflect musical features. I argue here that music video editing's varied roles work to enable relations between sound and image.

The Basics: Shots and Edits

When constructing a taxonomy of shots and edits in music video, we can begin with traditional narrative film practices. Within the rather large possible taxonomy of music video edits, it is important to mention one of the most obvious ways of organizing shots—namely, the continuity editing system, which forms the basis of film editing yet is much less common in music video. Common continuity edits in film include the 180-degree rule, which preserves screen direction, as well as the 30-degree rule, which prevents a jump cut between two shots, and also shot/reverse shots, over-the-shoulder shots, and matches on actions.[12] Such edits attempt to naturalize the movement from shot to shot and render the break as seamless as possible. Continuity editing seeks to preserve the flow of time and the coherence of spaces. We are meant to understand that time moves forward between shots. Similarly, one shot should not present a spatial arrangement that another shot contradicts. The ultimate goal of continuity editing is to create a single, clear path through a film's world. Because music videos seem to benefit from providing a multiplicity of incomplete, sometimes obscure paths, continuity editing will serve different functions and govern only isolated sections of a video.[13] Perhaps music videos avoid continuity editing because such techniques would give the visual track too strong of a forward trajectory. The image might seem thereby to overtake the song. The music video's aim is to spark its listeners' interest in the song, to teach them enough about it that first they will remember it, and second, purchase it. Music video editing keeps us within the ever-changing surface of the song. Though a disjunctive edit may momentarily take us out of the tape, as we resituate ourselves within the music and visual texture, we can attend to both musical and visual cues. One of the most narrative music videos, Aerosmith's "Janie's Got a Gun," comes the closest to following the rules of traditional Hollywood continuity, yet it also extends and breaks these rules. In the sequence used in "Janie's Got a Gun," the sightlines do not match. Consequently, it may take a while for the viewer to notice that based upon the position of the characters the woman is watching the man, yet he does not see her. In addition, the 30-degree rule is violated between the medium and close-up shots of the man. Music videos avoid matches on action, often extending or abbreviating a shot to give the sense of a cut in the "wrong place." This effect blunts narrative progress and creates a rhythmic emphasis on the moment when the edit occurs.[14]

One type of music video camera movement that contrasts with the continuity editing system is the tracking shot. In classical Hollywood cinema, the tracking shot is most commonly linked to some vantage point. This might be that of the character, the viewer, the camera, or even an omniscient point of view, but in almost all cases it is tied to some perspective. The shot also provides an opportunity to explore the possibilities of the environment. The tracking shot in music video functions differently. Often used for special emphasis, it frequently dominates a segment toward the middle of the song and is punctuated by a few dissolves. Tracking shots play a crucial role in music video, because they provide relief from a typically shallow sense of space. (In videos, the camera almost never pierces the background or strays far from the star.) The movement of the camera provides a change in point of view: instead of experiencing the music from a stationary position as it rushes past, the viewer can get the sense of running alongside the sound stream. The tracking shot embodies perfectly the music video's attempt to match the energy of the song and to approach its rhythmic drive, even if the music remains just out of reach. The tracking shot can also constitute a distinct rhythmic stratum that will go in and out of synchronization with the song's other rhythmic strata.

Just as editing changes in the shift from film to music video, so does the function of shots. Music videos and Hollywood films share a basic premise: that visual information can best be communicated by cutting among three kinds of shots—long, medium, and close-up. These shots can best be described according to the relation each establishes between the figure and the space around it. In long shots, the space obtains a greater prominence than the figure; in medium shots, the relation is roughly equivalent; and in close-ups, the figure dominates the space. Hollywood film has virtually standardized the cropping of the figures in these shots. Most textbooks recommend that the proportion of the figure to the space in the frame falls within set guidelines to achieve a sense of balance: if too much or too little space surrounds the figure, a shot is said to look awkward. Further, the camera should not frame the body in such a way that the frame's edge passes through a join of the body, such as the neck, elbows, knees, or ankles.[15] Music videos, however, do not follow these rules. Not only is the relation between figure and space frequently off-kilter but the camera bisects the figure in places that would be unacceptable for classical Hollywood film. In film, the framing helps to draw attention to the content of a shot rather than its composition and thus render the editing process invisible. The framing in music video makes us as aware of the edge of the frame (and of what we cannot see) as of the figure itself. This kind of framing can give a shot a precarious quality that the succeeding shot cannot always put right. In this way the image moves forward, matching the momentum of the music.

Within music video's large vocabulary of types of edits, camera movements, and framing devices, the most attractive features may be those that strikingly call attention to themselves, such as extreme jump cuts as well as alternate motion within the frame, graphic matches, and aesthetic edits that interpose a bit of film leader. Also engaging are those effects that resemble edits but aren't quite, such as defocusing or strobing. These raise questions about the ways that editing contributes to the music video's form and meaning. It may be helpful to picture the succession of images in a video, and the edits that join them, not as a chain but instead as a necklace of variously colored and sized beads. This image not only emphasizes the heterogeneity of shots in music video but also suggests the materiality of the edit itself. Indeed, sometimes the edit seems to function as a part of the image and sometimes as a gap between two shots. The varied combinations of these basic kinds of edits, camera placements, and camera movements give the visual track an ability to follow the music and an expressive power in its own right.

Different types of shots and edits can be mixed to create variety. Although it seems that any shot can follow any edit, some shots and edits

CAROL VERNALLIS

are particularly complementary. An edit or camera move can anticipate a gesture in the shot that follows. A tracking shot can complement a subsequent shot of a strutting figure (as in U2's "Discotheque"). A crane shot that starts low and rises through the space seems to match a figure reaching outward. A brusque edit works well preceding a shot that contains a series of sharp rhythmic gestures performed by the dancer or musician. Videos can create this kind of play simply between shots and edits, almost irrespective of what a shot contains. A dissolve can pair nicely with a tracking shot, and the effect of a jump cut can be extended by an unbalanced shot. This isomorphism or exchange of gestures and shapes teaches the viewer to move fluently from parameter to parameter while watching a video. Such movement can occur across many parameters, leading the viewer directly into the structure of the song.

Meaning, Narrativity, and Continuity

The meanings of music videos can be regarded as presenting a puzzle. Most often, music video image is relatively discontinuous. Time unfolds unpredictably and without clear reference points. Space is revealed slowly and incompletely. A video will hint at a character's personality, mood, goals, or desires but will never fully disclose them. We seldom see an action completed—a figure's movement is often cut off by the edit. Stories are suggested but not given in full, and the lyrics do not tell us what we need to know—they may be banal or purely conventional. A famous performer can also pull at the video's meaning—we cannot tell beforehand how or to what extent our knowledge of a star is intended to come into play in a given video.

In *Understanding Comics* Scott McCloud writes about the pleasure of reading into incomplete images.[16] He celebrates the interpretive work needed to transform black-and-white lines or spots of color into meaningful characters. Music video images can provide the same pleasure. We know very little about the figures we see, but we still attempt to make sense of them, based on how they look and what they are doing, as well as the setting, the lyrics, and the music. We must decide whether a figure functions as a character or merely as part of a tableau vivant. In extending the notion of the reader's share in the interpretation of the image, McCloud discusses the gap between panels of the comic. In this gap, the reader calculates the amount of time elapsed, the distance traversed, and any change in the figures. The edits in music videos work similarly. Partly by attending to the song, the viewer decides what has happened in the cut from one shot to another. The disjunctive force of the edit compels this decision: How do these two shots relate? On what basis does the edit link them together? And what is the net effect of these disjunctions on the video as a whole?

A typical video contains a broad range of connection, with the clear and egregiously unclear connections appearing unpredictably. Most edits rest in the middle of the continuum with some aspects of the edit seeming clear, and yet with others less so. We may in a single space see successive shots of people whom we can identify by type, but the people do not acknowledge one other and we cannot determine their relation. Or we might see people in different places and be unable to tell whether they are meant to relate at all. We must often extrapolate from what the shots provide if we are to give meaning to a juxtaposition. The early Russian filmmakers understood that this kind of extrapolation was crucial to cinema, and they argued forcefully that the editing could actually create a meaning in situations where the shots could not themselves provide one. Lev Kuleshov performed an experiment in which he paired shots of an actor and a coffin, an actor and a bowl, and an actor and children. The results showed that the meaning created by placing one shot next to another could be that of a proper emotion directed toward an object: these pairs seemed to signify, respectively, mourning the loss of a beloved, yearning for food, and enjoying children at play. In music video, adjacent shots often relate only loosely; when separated by dramatic edits, each image will seem enclosed within its own semantic realm. Even paired shots of figures often withhold something. Such pairs of shots can resemble the images in the Kuleshov experiment. In these cases, the images stand alone, in isolation, and the affect of the song provides their context. The music cannot define the meaning of objects, but it can surely suggest the animating desire that characters bear toward objects or others. We read emotions into the image before us and, with the help of the song, make connections between this image and others in the video.

Music videos draw heavily on other editing techniques used by these early Russian filmmakers. Shots based on similarity of shape occur only infrequently in a film but with great regularity in music video. These shots contribute to the musical flow and underscore the similar but also varied materials of pop songs. Also common in music videos are instances of Eisensteinian montage, in which two shots edited together create a new

CAROL VERNALLIS

concept. In Kid Rock's "American Badass" a series of match cuts carries over a long crescendo that heads toward the chorus. These match cuts move between men pounding on hanging deer meat still encased in fur, and men draped with centerfold-like women. The crescendo advances inexorably, as if the pounding backbeat were underscoring some moment of truth. The argument is clear: women are meat. The film theorist André Bazin has pointed out that once sound film was invented, the Eisensteinian montage disappeared almost completely from narrative filmmaking.[17] In music video, the forming of a new concept through Eisensteinian montage creates a momentary frisson for the viewer that can play against the music, much the way that the arguably politically objectionable images in "American Badass" create a jolt that becomes recontextualized once placed with the music.

A cursory glance at music video suggests that it does share much with the work of the early Russian film formalists, yet why this might be so may not be immediately apparent. We should remember that the early Russian film directors such as Kuleshov, Pudovkin and Eisenstein worked with minimal resources — film was so valuable that it was recycled for its silver — and they used almost no intertitles because their audiences were largely illiterate. Even though music video directors can command great resources in the era of late capitalist production, they too struggle with limitations. In comparison to the early Russian filmmakers these limitations may seem trivial: music video is a short form; the music and lyrics may be banal; the singer must lip-synch while the rest of the figures remain silent; much time must be spent showcasing the star. Like the early Russians, however, video directors have to make the most of the raw materials of film by making the frames and cuts as expressive as possible.

EDITING AND THE EXPERIENCE OF IMAGE AND SOUND

Theorists like Edward Branigan, Michel Chion, and Walter Ong have reminded us that sound and image possess different properties.[18] Sounds ebb, flow, and surround us. The cinematographic features and mise-en-scène of music video — extreme high, low, and canted angles, long tracking shots, unusual camera pans and tilts, and the lively features within the frame — can mimic sonic processes. The types of shots used in videos do not just reflect sonic processes but also suggest a listening subject as much as a viewing one. We actually see figures turning toward people and objects in the space as if to listen. The camera's perspective often suffices to imply a listening subject. In order best to see something, we might want to be placed squarely before it. If we want to listen attentively to a sound, however, a frontal position is unnecessary. Many positions may be satisfactory—above, below, off to the side. In fact, turning an ear toward the object will take our eyes away from it. One of the most common camera positions in music video—below the subject and to one side—may privilege listening over viewing and grant greater authority to the soundtrack than to the image.[19] The camera in music video also seems to mimic the ways that we direct our attention in a sonic space. The kinds of shots and editing that we see in music video—jumping from one location to another even before an image catches our eye—resembles what we do when we listen.

The camera normally takes time to explore the extent of a video's setting, so that a setting is only partly revealed in any single shot. How does this practice influence our hearing of a song? A pop song creates a sense of a space through arrangement, production, mixing, and mastering.[20] When the song is finally mixed down, to what spaces does it belong? The acoustical properties of this constructed musical space seldom match those in the real world, and they are only tangentially linked to music video's fabricated settings. This lack of fit creates both some confusion and some interest. How could the song's sound world inhabit the space of the video? The camera, as it explores the space, suggests possible ways that parts of the arrangement might be distributed within this environment. Many music videos exploit our curiosity about how a song might sound in the actual space of the music video: walls, floors, and ceilings are placed at odd angles and covered with materials that imply specific acoustical properties; objects that resemble speakers and baffles may be distributed throughout the space. Despite the fact that the camera never quite reaches the sides or the back of the setting, these videos encourage us to imagine the soundwaves rolling into the walls and bouncing off of them, much like dye moving through water.

As the camera explores the space, the viewer begins to gauge how well the sound fits the space. Often spaces in music video are presented serially, and the video can seem to raise questions: What parts of the mix seem best suited to or most intriguing in one place rather than another? Brandy's "What about Us" begins outdoors rather than in an interior setting, but it still presents an opportunity to explore space. The vocalist stands on a huge pyramid of miniature men, and a vast landscape of rolling hills and skies stretches behind her. In the sky hang some miniature trees, and the viewer might wonder how far the song carries, and how far the trees continue to appear into the distance. As the rhythm arrangement kicks in, the camera heads out past the fields, over water and into a winding and metallic tunnel. Suddenly, the voice pad and synthesizer pad no longer capture the listener/viewer's attention; rather, the song's elements that are mechanical and motorhythmic appear to come to the fore.

I've suggested that, in music video, both bodies and space can seem to reflect the experiential qualities of sound. The description that I have laid out thus far suggests that music video creates an experience more like listening than viewing. As such, it encourages some of the receptiveness and sense of connection that sound creates. Music videos draw us into a playful space where attractive objects are distributed across the visual field. In the absence of a strong narrative, videos have other means to maintain a viewer's engagement. The figures, the camera, and the edits each find ways to participate, but they do not always work together harmoniously to achieve this goal; instead, the three often fight among themselves for attention, with the song's formal and rhythmic structures as the stable ground. It does not matter, in a sense, whether an elbow comes forward, an edit occurs, a camera tracks, or a figure walks—all are felt as articulations against the music.

The bodies of the figures are often the first element to engage us. Music video reveals the body as an enormous but incomplete surface. We may feel tempted to extrapolate beyond the edge of the frame in order to fill in the missing arms and legs. At the same time, the intense focus on a fragment of the body invests it with a special expressive weight. We can imagine feelings and desires—a thinking subject—by watching the rate of release in the shoulders or the spring of the hips. As the video unfolds, we piece together what we have seen to make the body whole. We might remember a longer shot of the body, perhaps torso to feet, a close-up of the head and neck, and a high angle shot that captures the figure from above. The image also creates associations with the song by matching sections or other musical features with particular visual materials. We see the body bob up and down during the third verse of the song, say, and we might recall the way it moved during the previous verse. By recalling what we have seen and heard, we create a phantasmagorical body. If a video gives us enough material to create a picture of one body, we can attribute moods to other characters in the space who have been rendered more partially, and who often have been chosen because their carriage and gestures are so different from those of the lead performers. As the video progresses, features of the song become associated with elements of the image: a rhythmic motive with the swivel of the performer's hips; a lilting instrumental melody with a character in the background.[21]

EDITING AND THE MUSIC OF MUSIC VIDEO

Through its varied roles, the editing in music videos loosens the representational functions that filmed images traditionally perform, opening them up to a sense of polyvalent play. The editing thereby places the video's images and the song's formal features in close relation.[22] I doubt that the numerous ways that music and image can be put into one-to-one relations would surprise musicians or pop music scholars. Obviously, editing can reflect the basic beat pattern of the song, but it can also be responsive to all of the song's other parameters. For example, long dissolves can complement arrangements that include smooth timbres and long-held tones. A video can use different visual material to offset an important hook or a different cutting rhythm at the beginnings and ends of phrases. And, of course, these effects can switch from one-to-one relationships to something that is more contrapuntal.[23] Before offering an example of this element, I want to describe something more sophisticated. By emphasizing certain sounds and images, a videomaker can provide a path through the song. For example, in music video our attention to the song shapes the way we perceive the image; to an equal extent, however, what we attend to in the image helps to determine how we hear the music. When a star jams his or her face in front of the camera, or when a hand or foot threatens to break through the viewing plane, we suddenly hear the music in a different way. We become aware that we should pay attention right now. If the same moment in the song were accompanied by a less assertive image—say, a long shot—we would more likely attend to the overall arrangement of the song than focus on any particular element. This experiment can work in reverse, with the music influencing our attention to the image. Imagine a scenario with two types of music. The first contains a city scene with people walking down

CAROL VERNALLIS

a busy street in slow motion in a medium long shot so that we see them from their knees to just above their heads. Let us say that the song contains a pounding jungle beat and short synthesizer flurries. We might notice the intensity of the pedestrians' faces or the muscled bodies of one or two people. On the other hand, if we hear a flowing synthesizer pad with a minimal rhythm arrangement, perhaps some innocuous "CD jazz," we might attend instead to the spring and sweep of the bodies in motion, and to the flow of the crowd as a whole.

The musical or visual element with the sharpest profile tends to claim the viewer's attention. As a video unfolds, our attention shifts continually among music, image, and lyrics, as each provides novelty at some point and then recedes into the background. This competition among media helps us understand the look of music video. The image can guide our attention from one musical feature to another by shifting among long, medium, and close-up shots. Close-ups often appear as a song reaches the hook line, for example. When the voice stops singing and the instrumental backing comes to the fore, the image frequently emphasizes the background of the set. The careful deployment of mixed shot types can thus establish a path through the formal and timbral space of the song. As we move toward a moment of culmination in the song, the editing can tease us with the possibility of spoiling the peak moment's arrival, or feign disinterest by drawing attention to other features of the song. By anticipating what the song will do next, the image can create a sense of expectation. A change of shot types can allow us to circulate within a musical parameter-like rhythm or the arrangement. We might first notice the music's smallest rhythmic value and then jump down one level to the basic quarter note pulse. If we see a long shot of performers in the background against an ornate curtain or a waterfall, we might attend to the microrhythms of the music. Imagine that the video cuts next to a medium shot in which the singer's face and chest are foregrounded and her head moves side to side, while she crosses and uncrosses her arms as if clocking to the music. The two shots together might encourage such a leap.[24]

I have tried here to offer a window onto the world of music video editing. Editing constitutes one parameter of many that influence the look of music video. It exists on an equal plane with other elements—like color, narrative, and the treatment of the star—that sometimes vie for attention and sometimes recede into the background. At the same time, editing plays a uniquely superordinate role. When we follow the changing surface of a video, we can try to remember that a momentary effect that claims our attention is part of a structure that traverses the whole of the video, and that this effect is created within the context of that structure: it may mark the high point of some value or constitute a departure from a traditional role. If a video seems discontinuous, it is not because the image track consists of autonomous shots that do not relate to one another, it is because the video interlaces a number of such structures in an unpredictable way. The sheer density of this interlace provides one of music video's greatest pleasures.

I hope that I have been able to show how narrative and editing in music video work in unusual ways. I began this essay by pointing to the uncanniness of music video, and these uncanny qualities can be found in music video's edits or use of narrative. Edits often interrupt a character's gesture and seem to prevent the viewer from reaching the walls; the editing can maintain a sense of off-screen space as impossible to map. But the easiest way to gain a quick sense of what is strange in music video lies in tracking the functions of characters and props. In the service of music, both objects and people in music video *become strange*. Objects separate from their subjects, thereby rendering the status of both uncertain and unstable.

ONE SINGS AND THE OTHER DOESN'T: MUSIC VIDEO AND STARS, BACKGROUND CHARACTERS, AND PROPS

Music Video's Props

As our attention fluidly crosses over the video's surfaces, from a lyric to a vocal timbre or a drum solo, from the person as actor to the person as performer, from an inkling of a narrative to a focus on spectacle, from hearing the music alone to hearing music in relation to image, and so on, we might suddenly notice a prop. As with narrative and editing, a prop's status can be fluid and unstable. Most interesting is the inscrutable nature of costuming accessories and handheld objects: What does it mean in a video when the performer darkens his hair and wears black lipstick and nails? How do we interpret a dangling monocle, cross, bone, or pacifier? What about the moment when the star shakes a big walking stick (as is done in so many videos from the early 1990s). What about the strange suit with beaded embroidery, or the thick eyeglasses or gold-rimmed, tinted shades? Props, like clothing and accessories, can seem to contain a secret that the video never discloses. The film theorist James Naremore argues that props in classical Hollywood film support stage business — and he therefore calls props expressive objects.[25] The way that an actor fusses with a briefcase, dangles a cigarette, or fluffs a pillow helps her to submerge herself inside her character, suggesting both a character type and a nuanced portrait within the confines of a character type. In music video, however, we seldom know how to read the costume accessory. Perhaps the cigarette that the protagonist holds is there for thematic purposes, as an emblem, as an item that looks cool, or as an indication that the performer is a smoker.

That the role of the blemish, disability, mark, or imperfection already suggests the function of strangeness in music video becomes obvious when we consider the treatment. In narrative film, a funny detail — a crooked hat, a facial scar, a limp — helps define the character and, no matter how gruesome or startling, it does not usually break the surface of the film. In music video, however, such details can remain unintegrated; they can buzz around the performer aggressively, asserting their own bizarre presence. As the image conforms to the soundtrack, the musical forces — the thrust of harmony, melody, arrangement, and rhythm — fracture the image into individual components.[26]

The fact that objects recur in videos of a particular genre or period suggests the gradual development of generic repertoires functioning within a sign system unique to the medium. Objects seen in videos of the mid-1990s include thrones, couches and chairs, canes, heads of animals (pigs and wolves), clowns, and toilets. In the 1980s there was a prevalence of diaphanous cloth, wind, figures dancing in formation, big hair, sketchily drawn windows and doors, canted stages, and horses. As time passes, the visual codes loosen from their musical and social context and the meaning becomes more obscure. What is interesting here is not the answers to the question of what these objects "mean"; rather, it is the role that this question plays, how persistently it is asked, and whether — in different genres and periods and in individual videos — it is answerable.[27]

Objects in music video can also carry an excess of meaning and exist outside the flow of the tape. As such, they take on a heightened role. Like the ballet slippers in *The Red Shoes*, they appear to possess a mysterious power, as if their silence contained some truth about the video beyond what the characters embody. Certain props come to the foreground as mysterious but unknowable, graspable but unobtainable. Often these are set off in isolation—sometimes they literally float in the frame: witness the needle, blouse, bowl of water, and glove in Madonna's "Take a Bow"; the glittering and metallic butterfly in Smashing Pumpkins's "Bullet with Butterfly Wings"; the twirling trumpet in TLC's "Creep"; the crystal ball in Boyz II Men's "Water Runs Dry"; the pig's head and apple, and the chair onto which is nailed an impaled heart, in Nine Inch Nails's "Closer"; the pears, bowl, and coins in Live's "Lightning Crashes"; the speaker, picture frame, and bowl of milk in Madonna's "Express Yourself"; and the record player in Janet Jackson's "Anytime, Anyplace."

Music video sets are usually stripped down to the essentials; only occasionally are they dolled up, and the few items that are brought to the fore tend to stand in isolation. This strategy is taken to an extreme in some videos from the late 1980s and early 1990s, where the frame is stripped to a nicely painted wall and empty windowsill, or to a corner of a room. Natalie Merchant's "Wonder" simply shows a woman's hands dangling over a washbasin and a praying mantis resting on a woman's forearm. The effect of such a shot's featuring of a single gesture—and being separated from the video's stream of events—is that the object and performer are both made strange. Each defines and limits the other's meaning, the object more lifelike and the performer less so. Music assists us in understanding this uneasy relation by revising our assumptions about the object, its uses and purposes, and its internal disposition and rhythms in relation to spaces and persons. Without much narrative drive, character development, or dialogue, the meaning is derived in part from the music and the way that the object is placed in relation to the performer.

Music Video's Characters

Anyone who has even casually watched music video would notice that in most cases the star performer is foregrounded in bold relief. The camera highlights every curl of the fingers and bend of the elbow, every wrinkle of the brow and blink of the eye. A close-up captures for our own private scrutiny every emotion that crosses the star's face. In contrast, the supporting characters in music video typically have an indeterminate nature, and they often seem strange and uncanny. As a whole they are music video's underclass; as if they come from a caste different from that of the lead performer.[28] Some of the reasons for the laconic nature of supporting characters are obvious; other reasons are surprisingly subtle. In the former case, the supporting roles have no lyrics and therefore no dialogue. The resources with which these characters can assert themselves are much more meager than those of the star—mirroring the fact that we, as a society, are predisposed toward speakers (and all able-bodied individuals) and away from the mute, passive, or silent. Understandably, record companies want to tie the band to the song, and since the lead singer most often sings the hook line, we can see why the star is placed under our immediate gaze. Yet it is also true at times that a character's move to the background will have to do with the formal properties of music and lyrics. To explain why, let me lay out some types of background figures—for example, those who, at least for a moment, resemble the bit players in a movie, and those who are silent or in a position where they cannot speak, including mannequins and statuary.

When a video's scenario has a strong narrative charge, the supporting characters can look real, fleshly, and unaffected by the music. If those in R. Kelly's "Down Low" resemble real people, it may be because the video is a rare example of a full-blown narrative. (It relies on breaks in the soundtrack to make way for movie music, a long, dialogue-rich introduction with the plot clearly laid out, and occasional moments where the characters silently mouth dialogue). The two subsidiary roles, Mr. Big's white girlfriend and the number-one hit man, both of whom are extremely small, are derivative of roles that we know from movies; they are placed strategically within key moments in the musical and visual flow, and their parts are full of emotional charge—one with imagery of miscegenation, the other of violence. In this case, the viewer may be supplying much that has been gathered from films in order to construct a character. Another character we see in "Down Low"—Lila, the girlfriend of R. Kelly—is a type that exists somewhere on the continuum between full personhood and a mannequin. Perhaps overcome by infatuation from having just received a stroke on the cheek or a bouquet of flowers, she is unable to speak. Here, her silence is naturalized; she is mute, but she can be nuzzled or receive gifts. At other moments, her silence seems like a wound conveying helplessness—she is put in a position where she cannot speak, and the lead performer must articulate the feelings for both of them.

Sometimes one solitary figure will be especially emblematic—for example, an old man wearing overalls and sitting in a rocking chair in the middle of a bar. Placing such a figure in the background compels the viewer to search him out, as in Dr. Dre's "Keep Their Heads Ringing," in which a copilot, shrouded in darkness, with curlers in his hair and bird-like gestures, speaks in a high squeaky voice. A comparably unapproachable type, this time set in the foreground, is the custodian in Nirvana's "Smells like Teen Spirit," a figure who, in his own setting, churns a mop obsessively in a pail.

For all the emphasis on beauty in music videos, there are a surprising number of characters who are plump or grossly overweight; who might be called ugly or too old; and who stand in as stereotypes for class, ethnicity, sexuality, gender, avocation, or occupation; or who seem freakish, comical, or absurd. Such figures are essential to the genre in part because their tempo differs from that of the principal performers; they possess a different force against the music. Nothing can enable the viewer to experience the range of materials in a pop song as successfully as a variety of people mingling together. For example, in the beach-party scenes in Coolio's "Fantastic Voyage," the camera, tilted up from below the sand's surface, reveals a series of figures emerging from the trunk of a car. Alternately, we see the bikini-clad crotches of beautiful young women, and then the front torsos of a much more varied group of men—dumpy, slovenly, exotically dressed (as mariachi musicians), or shrimpy. Such a contrast encourages the viewer to feel a graceful flowing movement as well as something awkward and leaden against the music. At the beginnings of phrases, an obese African American man appears against the noisy, even flatulent, bass line; a woman or a figure holding a small child appears at the ends of phrases—highlighting the upper register. Our attention is drawn to particular elements on the musical surface, as well as to stereotypical notions about the ways these bodies move and feel. We might hope that this broad range of humanity would increase the viewer's sensitivity to others, but their presence does not seem to serve this function. Unlike the star over whom the camera lingers, and who appears from a variety of angles, the background figures are experienced most often in passing; the viewer literally glances over them. In so doing, the background figures help to define what the star is not, thereby setting the outer limits to a system of representation. Looking through the video for characters that color our relation to the star is an important part of understanding how music video works as a whole.

This brings us to one of the most common and most striking types of supporting figure in music video—namely, that of static emblems like mannequins, statues, or robotic workers. By placing such figures in libraries, prisons, mental asylums, schools, offices, and factories, video directors make calculated use of these figures' inability to speak. Directors also exploit this muteness by introducing what can be called "paraspeak": that is, gestures that resemble speaking— such as opening and closing mouths, chattering teeth, or broad gesticulations. Fine gestures are generally reserved for the star; indeed, the movement of the star's hands before her or his face provides the most useful example of refined expressivity because it closely reflects speech and can also possess the rhythmic qualities of dance.

How does the relegation of supporting characters to the background help show off a pop song? Most obvious is the tendency, through choices made at all stages of production—composing, arranging, and producing—to bring the voice forward over other sonic elements. If the star performer begins to stand for the primary voice, other figures may become associated with the accompaniment and slip beyond our attention. Rudolph Arnheim, in *The Power of the Center*, describes how the frame exerts a centrifugal force upon any object depicted within it.[29] The moving image extends the force-field metaphor much further. In film, not only are there moments of stress and relaxation created by the ways that visual material falls within the frame, there also are spatial and temporal nodes of stress.[30] In addition, the music exerts its own qualities of pressure: harmonic pulls, metrical accents, changes in dynamics, rises and falls in melodies. All of these elements create pockets of tension and release in the image. If a subsidiary figure lacks authority (is not dancing or performing) and is devoid of charisma, he will, like a doll, seem to be danced by the music, or, worse, left aside by the momentum of the music and the lyrics, as if he did not have sufficient energy to rail against an unceasing flow. (By contrast, the lead performer seizes the music; he is slightly in front of—pushed onward by—the music, as if he were catching hold of and riding a tiger.)

In possessing a stillness that complements some of the more extroverted qualities of the star, mannequin figures can also mediate between silence and becoming. Videos establish a continuum from stillness and silence to constant flux: the inanimate decor and the quiet out of which the song begins; still figures and the slowest tempos; moderate physical movements such as shallow knee bends, heads turning to one side, or steps forward; frenetic visual elements such as the showy, fluttery gestures of the star, the rapid movement of small turning objects, and shifting patterns of light. If a music video reflects a world where no object or person acts quite as we expect, the still figures help to bridge the gap between inanimate and animate—the gap between setting and star. Another reason that directors make such use of the mute figure is that these figures help to create a more richly nuanced psychological portrait of the star. They play the Hyde to the performer's Jekyll. When the lead character is lip-synching and carrying out all kinds of demonstrative moves, it is helpful for others to hold down the scene and act as a receptive audience (even when they are not listening, their bodies are turned receptively toward the star). The use of background figures as a type of Greek chorus is exemplified in Neneh Cherry's "I've Got U Under My Skin" and En Vogue's "Whatta Man."

The music theorist Richard Middleton has argued that one of the defining features of popular music is its high degree of repetition—rhythms, timbres, iconic materials, and sectional divisions repeat endlessly and build to a state of jouissance.[31] At some level, the whole and parts of a music video's character also become material to be used for musical purposes. With such a small palette to work with—a short, circular, and episodic form and little narrative or dialogue—the distinction of the video becomes secondary to the characters' controllable parameters—namely, props, hairstyle, costume, color, and makeup. Hundreds of photographs and hours of tape will be scanned to find extras with the right look. After choosing physiques and facial features that play off, echo, or complement those of the star, the video's director will have created one more type of visual/thematic variation to support the varied representations of the lead performer: the varied iterations formed through posters, TV appearances, Claymations, statuary, photographs, and extreme close-ups; the musician performing and the musician in dramatic situations, the musician wearing one type of clothes or hairstyle versus another. If the star constantly shifts between something that we might recognize as a narrative character or a real person to something that hardens into a close-up shot, so too does the background character become alive and then dead, hard and then soft—functioning thus as a second layer of articulation. The relation between star and subsidiary character creates a bleed-through; as in many elements in music video, the local connections across parameters first link and then supersede larger formal devices, thereby weaving a vast subtle network, a fine skein. In Robbie Williams's "Rock DJ" video, representations and transformations between lead character and supporting figures run thick through the texture. Williams, sporting black-slashed tattoos, dances with a woman dressed in a zebra-striped costume. He showcases his tiger-headed underwear, and then the video cuts to an African American woman dressed in gold lamé. Williams's groin becomes fuzzed out, and then we see a woman with soft, blurry underwear. The star pulls back his pink flesh to reveal red, bloody musculature underneath, and the video then cuts from a woman dressed in pink-tinged glasses and a baby-pink halter and shorts to a woman with gaudily painted matte-red muscles with striated yellow veins.

The supporting characters—women roller skaters—in "Rock DJ" exemplify a key principle of music video: that almost every musical and visual parameter, such as props, camera movement, lighting, melodic hooks, and lyrics, can serve a dual purpose. How much do the parameters serve to accentuate a musical function? And to what extent do they work as cultural objects—things that try to tell us how we should get on in the world? In the end, we never find out. And, in fact, the most magical moments in music video occur when a parameter simultaneously fulfills both functions in a virtuosic manner—the activity of the figure furthers the story (often through a transgressive gesture intended to undermine a socially contested norm) and also illuminates the musical structure. The visual element becomes magical because it can negotiate between two worlds—a real world and a musical world. At the end of the section in "Rock DJ," when the women nod their heads as they stand in the doorway, we are unsure if they do this because the video wants to make a social point—that women, as much as men, objectify and judge the other for their sexual attributes as commodities—or because it wants to draw our attention to interesting musical material—the break when the rhythm arrangement comes to the fore.[32]

And here, finally, we may be able to touch upon the uncanny in music video. Earlier in this essay I suggested that the people who appear in music videos can resemble automatons. What makes them seem mechanical? The forces of music, editing, and framing make music become more spatialized, while the temporal qualities of space also come to the fore. These forces of space and time can be imagined as casting a grid across the video's frame. As performers find a place on this grid, so do they move in and out of synch with the music, and to and from a balanced position in the frame. In this way they flicker between the human and the mechanical.[33] In addition, music video's characters inhabit a strange world that bears some resemblance to reality but also to a realm with another phenomenology—a musical world where sound structures events. In this world, the unfolding landscape appears to reflect the music's teleology: objects such as pixie dust, cloth, and tumbleweeds fall away after musical entrances, suggesting a cause-and-effect relation. A wandering or slithering camera turns in response to the music. The music seems to be a good thing for the viewer to identify and follow. Sound structures music video's world, determining the paths of its characters. Stanley Cavell claims that sounds "are warnings, or calls; it is why our access to another world is normally through voices from it; and why a man can be spoken to by God and survive, but not if he sees God, in which case he is no longer in this world."[34] As Cavell suggests, a world structured by sound might become an eerie, uncertain place, where we cannot know for certain what animates the figures. Music video characters also become automatons through the ways that they exist in a heightened state. In singing and dancing they are placed on display. Song and dance can be thought of as extreme forms of everyday talking and walking: in music video speech is song and all movement becomes dance. The incisive probing of the camera, as well as the work of editing and framing, capture the most performerlike gestures and construct phantasmagorical bodies.

Sound's power over the image, the spatializing and temporalizing of the image and the theatricalization of the characters, makes music video a distant cousin to cinema. Videos do not always present a worldview. They can even refuse to suggest a life beyond the frame. While we might worry about what happens to characters once a film ends, we almost never do so in music video. Here we tap into the strangeness of music video. Even as we gaze at figures who are more allegorical than human, the music reveals something personal—the characters' insides, what their bodies are sensing. Film suggests, at a further remove, how to understand a character's situation. During music video's heightened moments, I have the illusion that I directly perceive the rhythms of the body before me, the contours of that body's affective life. But music videos present more purely formal features as well. Directors like Mark Romanek, David Fincher, and Francis Lawrence reward our efforts to follow the camera and the music as they trace paths across bodies and empty space.

CAROL VERNALLIS

1 I attempt to cover this ground in my *Experiencing Music Video: Aesthetics in Cultural Context* (New York: Columbia University Press, 2004).

2 Michel Chion, *Audio Vision: Sound on Screen*, ed. and trans. Claudia Gorbman (New York: Columbia University Press, 1994), 162, 163.

3 John Fiske interprets music videos as stories; Marsha Kinder does not. See John Fiske, *Reading the Popular* (Cambridge: Cambridge University Press, 1989); and Marsha Kinder, "Music Video and the Spectator: Television, Ideology and Dream," *Film Quarterly* 38.1 (1984): 2–15.

4 The Aristotelian definition is narrower than many. Some people shear off an Aristotelian definition, requiring only some elements—for example, a cause-and-effect relation or a number of events in an ordered sequence such as a setting of the scene, introduction, character, rising action, crisis, intensifying action, major crisis, and denouement. Narrative can also be defined etymologically as anything that is recounted or told.

5 David Bordwell and Kristin Thompson, *Film Art: An Introduction* (New York: McGraw-Hill, 1997), 482.

6 The relaxed, episodic structure of "Crazy"—one in which events are pleasurable but little is at stake—raises challenging questions. Could it be that female rather than male lead characters are cast because women have been represented traditionally as possessing fragmentary, nondevelopmental lives? Are we meant to think that the girls were fine before they left school, and that they can always return? Hollywood film narrative gains steam from sending the protagonist on a twofold quest—solving a problem and finding a mate. The activities in Aerosmith's "Crazy" are compressed into a single trajectory—the girls act naughty to have fun and sex.

7 Shared genes play a significant role in "Crazy." In Marty Callner's and Bon Jovi's "Always," two sisters struggle to capture some male attention while the band sings on. Despite having the same director, musical style, and premise as "Crazy," "Always" loses its narrative drive, thereby exhibiting the intermittent plot structure that most other videos possess.

8 "Crazy" is just one in a series of unusual videos that Aerosmith has been able to make because they are an unusually long-lived and beloved group. The band does not have to lay claim to the new or the special, nor does it need to depart from earlier material. Although Aerosmith's songs are well written within the current context, their comfortable, functional nature does not compel repeated, close listening. The song title "Crazy" suggests a desire for an instant classic. (Willie Nelson's more famous "Crazy" was recorded not only by Patsy Cline, but also by a host of other country and pop artists.) The Aerosmith version functions more as a subtle echo of this earlier composition than as a song with its own agenda. Steven Tyler, the lead singer who wrote "Crazy," says explicitly that he now composes music with a potential video in mind, which suggests that he has distanced himself from the pres-

sures and constraints of traditional songwriting—particularly recognizability and novelty.

9   The viewer's impulse to guess at what will happen becomes strongest when the video closes its borders by establishing a clearly demarcated space, a restricted setting, and a limited assortment of props. In Solo's "Heaven, Right Here on Earth," in which the band performs inside a bus, items such as a swing, a twirling bass, a conch shell, a globe, and a butterfly appear in the aisles and on the seats, with some objects toward the front and some toward the back. We feel anticipation about what will appear next, whether it will fit in with the other items, and whether the video can play itself out well until the end. Other examples of this phenomenon are U2's "Numb" and Madonna's "Human Nature," which place the performer before a stark background in which only a few other characters appear.

10 Film editing must bear responsibility for many elements: it must maintain spatial and temporal continuity, disguise cuts, employ cross-cutting to build suspense or create thematic associations, and so on. Music video editing does all this, but just as often it does the opposite. Editing can carry a video's narrative and become like the "invisible editing" of classical Hollywood film; just as often it becomes purely formal, however, and highlights its own aesthetic properties such as its rhythmic drive. The power of music video editing comes from the fact that there is no predicting what a video's edit will do. An individual edit in music video can also carry great weight, perhaps more than in cinema. In music video, shifting a shot *by a single frame* can dramatically alter the feel of the tape: it can determine the way that subsequent shots relate to earlier ones, and it can also shape what the viewer notices in the music.

11 Theorists such as Roman Jakobson have noted that in classical Hollywood film all elements—lighting, editing, music—are subsumed by the narrative, which functions as the dominant through line. Roman Jakobson, "On Realism in Art," in *Readings in Russian Poetics*, ed. Lataslav Matjeka and Krystyna Pomorska (Cambridge, Mass.: MIT Press, 1971), 38–46. In music video, on the other hand, the narrative is only one element among many: any parameter can come to the fore, grab our attention, and then quickly recede from view. We do notice the editing in Hollywood films, but only rarely, as during a frenetic action sequence or at the heightened moment when the camera suddenly peers down a gun barrel.

Here I refer to classical Hollywood editing in its most generic sense, akin to how Janet Staiger, Kristin Thompson, and David Bordwell define it in their *Classical Hollywood Cinema* (New York: Columbia University Press, 1985), 284–85. There are, of course, a number of directors who highlight editing as a stylistic feature, such as Sergio Leone and Sam Peckinpah, and those who break the rules, like Carl Theodor Dreyer and Yasujiro Ozu. Music-video editing has influenced contemporary filmmaking such that the border between media has become less distinct. The contemporary directors best known for a style reminiscent of music video—Paul Thomas Anderson, Spike Lee, Quentin Tarantino, and Wong Kar-Wai—make frequent use of popular music, and long stretches of their work can resemble music video. These directors achieve some of music video's effects, such as a sense of postmodern play and a type of frisson, but not others, such as the foregrounding of the song's structure.

I do not intend to minimize the ways that editing contributes to a narrative film's organization and its effect on spectators. One very good piece on the subject is Ayako Saito's "Hitchcock's Trilogy: A Logic of Mise en Scène," in *Endless Night: Cinema and Psychoanalysis—Parallel Histories*, ed. Janet Bergstrom (Berkeley: University of California Press, 1999), 200–49. Saito argues that three films that Hitchcock made in close proximity to one another, *Vertigo, North by Northwest*, and *Psycho*, each focus on a different theme—namely, melancholia, mania, and schizophrenia. Such states of consciousness are evoked almost purely through editing, camera movement, and framing. What makes music video different from film is that the casual viewer notices the edits.

Editing tends to be an undertheorized area of film studies. The most significant texts on film editing are Karel Reisz, *The Technique of Film Editing* (Boston: Focal Press, 1988); and Ken Dancyger, *The Technique of Film and Video Editing* (Boston: Focal Press, 1996).

12 Classical Hollywood cinema follows several rules in its attempt to create a seamless world where the viewer moves forward through time and in space. The 180-degree rule involves an invisible line that crosses between two or more characters. The camera must remain on one side of the line or the image will appear to jump. (If the 180-degree line is breached, the camera should be shown moving across it.) Another guide is the 30-degree rule, which states that if the camera records an image of a person and then moves in or out for a subsequent shot, the camera needs to be displaced 30 degrees. Without this displacement, the viewer experiences a lurch into the image. "Match on action" is another editing technique. When moving between wide and close-up, an editor will cut on a character's movement as well as include a two-frame overlap. This renders the most seamless effect possible. Shots of people also tend to include shot/reverse shots, in which characters glance at one another from within the isolated space of their frame. (Their glances appear to intersect across the edits.) These are complemented by over-the-shoulder shots, where shooting is done, in accordance with the 180-degree rule, from opposing shoulders. Most commonly in classical Hollywood cinema, a scene begins with a wide shot and then the camera moves gradually closer in. This gives the viewer a sense of visual prowess. As the scene progresses and the camera draws nearer to its subject, more story information is revealed. The viewer gains a wider base of knowledge (as secrets and

disclosures are revealed through dialogue), an understanding of the ways that characters belong to the setting, and a greater intimacy with the characters. Music videos, however, are free to break all of these rules.

David Bordwell notes that "graphics, rhythm, space, and time . . . are at the service of the filmmaker through the technique of editing. . . . Yet most films we see make use of a very narrow set of editing possibilities — so narrow, indeed, that we can speak of a dominant editing style throughout Western film history. . . . The purpose of the system [continuity editing] was *to tell a story* coherently and clearly, to map out the chain of characters' actions in an undistracting way. Thus editing, supported by specific strategies of cinematography and mise-en-scène, was used to ensure *narrative continuity*. . . . The basic purpose of the continuity system is to create a smooth flow from shot to shot. All of the possibilities of editing . . . are bent to this end. First, graphic qualities are usually kept continuous from shot to shot. The figures are balanced and symmetrically employed in the frame; the overall lighting tonality remains constant; the action occupies the central zone of the screen. Second, the rhythm of the cutting is usually made dependent on the camera distance of the shot. Long shots are left on the screen longer than medium shots, and medium shots are left on longer than close-ups. The assumption is that the spectator needs more time to take in the shots containing more details" (Bordwell and Thompson, *Film Art*, 280–81).

13 Music videos seldom present a clear path through their structure. Sustained sequences of pure cross-cutting are rare (the classic example is a shot of a man on a horseback racing to the train, then the speeding train, then back to the man on horseback), as is a figure chasing another in a single shot. More levels of activity may be necessary to underscore the heterogeneous quality of the song. At first glance, The Clash's "Rock the Casbah" seems like a simple chase — Egyptians chase Israelis. However, a closer examination of the video reveals that the armadillo that runs at the bottom of the frame complicates the relations among the figures and the music.

14 Videos establish a sense of continuity on the surface partly by using dissolves. Smoother than cuts, dissolves provide a fuzzy articulation, rather than a sharp one, against the song. They do not therefore require a strong rhythmic commitment to a single musical feature. The director David Fincher's background is in graphic art. In an interview in spring 1998, he told me that when he shot music videos he purposely avoided learning the information commonly taught in film schools. He believed he would make more interesting work by not sharing a common background with other filmmakers.

15 "As filmmaking developed, a universal system for classifying shots evolved. These provide convenient quick reference points for all members of the production team — especially for the director and the camera operator. A series of 'standard' terms have evolved for the most effective shots of a single *person*. . . . If in doubt, remember how these shots are framed; e.g. 'cutting *just*

below the waist,' *'just below* the knees.' Avoid framing that cuts through the body at natural joints" (Gerald Millerson, *Television Production* [Boston: Focal Press, 1999], 99).

16 Scott McCloud, *Understanding Comics* (Northampton, Mass.: Kitchen Sink Press, 1994), 66–72.

17 André Bazin observes that the use of the graphic match atrophied once sound became used in film. He notes that the shots of women talking and then chickens clucking in Fritz Lang's *Fury* are a holdover from silent filmmaking. See Andre Bazin, *What Is Cinema?* (Berkeley: University of California Press, 1971), 34.

18 Edward Branigan, "Sound and Epistemology in Film," *Journal of Aesthetics and Art Criticism* 47 (1989): 312–34; Chion, *Audio Vision*; Walter Ong, *Orality and Literacy: The Technology of the Word* (London: Methuen, 1985).

19 The low-angle "stage front" shot that magnifies the performer (which was parodied in *This Is Spinal Tap*) could be seen as simply a convention of rock performance cinematography. Nevertheless its popularity relates also to the way an imposing resonating body suggests an enormous sound and vice versa.

20 Most commonly, when a pop song is recorded each instrument is miked in its own separate space, to then be allocated a particular placement within the stereo field. Numerous modifications in postproduction can be made to the sound including reverb, equalization, flanging, and overdubbing. Additional sound sources, either synthetic or analog, can be added to "sweeten the mix."

21 Classical Hollywood cinema has long presented imagery of body parts in order to encourage the viewer to fashion phantasmagorical bodies out of them. However, Hollywood uses bodies in a slightly different way than does music video. When we see the femme fatale in long shot, we anxiously await her close-up, so that we can gauge whether she is as beautiful as we had anticipated. One of my favorite examples of cinema's fragmentation of the body and how the viewer participates in its reconstruction is Alfred Hitchcock's *The Lady Vanishes*. In one of the film's first scenes, the camera reveals a woman's legs as she tiptoes on a table. We as viewers may have the pleasure of thinking about the woman—even as we are reminded, as the camera follows an elderly male servant's entrance into the room, that we might feel some shame in doing so. In a subsequent tighter shot the woman's head pops into the top of the frame—a move in which the director and camera inform us that this is a girl who, while she would not be flustered by our watching, might not approve of a too salacious eye. In music video, the viewer's censor remains more submerged, in part because as the viewer pieces together parts of the body, he or she must imagine how these move against the music, and in doing so, he or she will be asked to dance alongside the figures on the screen. Deprived of the power of a punishing narrative, or even of speech outside that of a few song lyrics, figures cannot threaten the

viewer in the way that they can in classical narrative cinema. Relative to film, a gaze that is freer, greater in scope, or more stoic is possible in music video.

22 Music video directors often covet particular editors. Marcus Nispel admires his editor's special sensitivity to the ways an edit falls on or off the beat, perhaps gained from years as a professional drummer. Music video editing demands skills not taught in film school.

23 Although some types of shots and edits appear more frequently in some genres than in others (e.g., a slow-mo, low-angle, long tracking shot followed by a dissolve appears most frequently in rap), the language of shots and edits does not differ greatly from one musical style to another. Even in country videos (such as Shania Twain's "Looks Like We Made It"), the rhetoric remains within the same language. In addition, editing has not changed noticeably in music video's short broadcast history. While a number of early 1980s videos, such as INXS's "What You Want," may not be as densely articulated as some videos today, many of the same editing techniques and strategies are present. Further study of editing based on genre, period, or director would be a fruitful undertaking.

24 Both music video and film use editing to maintain a sense of rhythm and flow. Yet it is only music video that uses editing so concertedly to highlight musical structure. Anyone who has edited a narrative scene knows how influential edits are in determining a scene's pacing. In a series of variations upon a two-person scene, if one actor remains constant while a number of alternate performers are substituted in, the edits most likely will fall at different moments, based on the new rhythms created through the varied vocal inflections and physical gestures performed by both actors. A good example of how editing creates a sense of pacing can be seen through a consideration of one of the greatest directors of the two-person scene, Howard Hawks, who kept his shots long, his camera work fairly simple, and his attention on the actors' performances. In the first encounter between Philip Marlowe and Vivian Sternwood (Humphrey Bogart and Lauren Bacall) in *The Big Sleep*, the editing and physical gesture set up a rhythm. The middle part of the scene features two major points of articulation. Bacall starts the banter, with her voice set at a regular and predictable pace, and then the first sharp edit comes up as Humphrey Bogart snorts on her words. For a moment, the banter turns toward the playful and relaxed, and the subsequent edits are loose. Then Bacall says, "Get it yourself" (meaning "get your own damn drink") while jabbing her elbow, and the cut and articulation are as hard as the earlier one with Bogart's snort: the woman stands tall to the man. Here we have two tight edits bookending some looser ones. The first and last fall strongly on the beat, while the inner ones have more play. A different pattern might not suggest such enticing and confusing relations—these two characters are perhaps comrades in arms, lovers, or well-matched sparring partners.

25 James Naremore, *Acting in the Cinema* (Berkeley: University of California Press, 1990), 84–87.

26 A list of videos with odd, isolated details includes Nina Howard's "Freak Like Me" (long fingernails), Madonna's "Human Nature" (black hair in cornrows); Ol' Dirty Bastard's "Fantasy" (silver-capped teeth); Queen Latifah's "Just Another Day" (woven Peruvian hat); Method Man's "Bring the Pain" (glass eye); Aaliyah's "One in a Million" (eye patch); Green Day's "Misery" (pierced tongue and extracted tooth); Nirvana's "Heart-Shaped Box" (obese woman with painted body suit, and old man on cross with Santa Claus hat); Mötley Crüe's "Primal Scream" (necktie without a shirt); and Bush's "Everything Zen" (pig's head).

27 Not only props but other visual touches become associated with particular eras. In the early 1980s a musical phrase often ended with a freeze frame. Did the still image reflect the zombie-like look of the performers? Were the freeze frames a response to anything in the music, like the big drum sounds? Lighting can reflect periods (and genres) as well. Think of the use of color and light in Hype Williams's rap and R&B videos of the early 1990s.

28 Note, however, that the relationship between the rapper and his posse is often less wide than that between the performer and complementary roles found in other genres, but rap is closer to speech. Perhaps the gap between speaking and silence is less than that of song and silence.

29 Rudolph Arnheim, *The Power of the Center* (Berkeley: University of California Press 1988), 53–55.

30 Herbert Zettl describes these as vectors. Zettl, *Sight, Sound, Motion: Applied Media Aesthetics* (San Francisco: Wadsworth, 1998), 106.

31 Richard Middleton, *Over and Over: Notes Towards a Politics of Repetition*, http://www2.hu-berlin.de/fpm/texte/middle.htm.

32 Other Janus-faced instances include the moment when the rhythm arrangement drops out and the star covers his crotch. Both the singer and the music have lost the phallus.

33 The attraction may resemble that of wind-up dolls, marionettes, and the actors in Elizabethan masks. What is alive, and what is not?

34 Stanley Cavell, *The World Viewed* (Cambridge, Mass.: Harvard University Press, 1979), 18. William Rothman and Marian Keane provide an excellent reading of this text in their *Reading Cavell's* The World Viewed: *A Philosophical Perspective on Film* (Detroit: Wayne State University Press, 2000).

Philip Hayward

The nation of Papua New Guinea (PNG) comprises the eastern half of the island of New Guinea along with a number of adjacent islands (including New Britain, New Ireland, and Bougainville). The majority of the population (currently approaching five million) is Melanesian, but its cultural and linguistic diversity is highly marked— the island is home to between seven hundred and eight hundred separate languages (or 25 percent of the world's total). The main language of national communication is an English-derived pidgin referred to locally as *tok pisin*. Standard English is also still widely used as an official medium of speech and written documentation. Papua New Guinea was administered by Australia up until 1975, when it was hurriedly prepared for independent statehood. One of the most remarkable aspects of the new nation has been the manner in which (despite local rivalries and occasional unrest) it has embraced cultural diversity. In this regard, diversity has not been seen to undermine the basis of nation-statehood but rather has given PNG a distinct character as a culturally pluralist environment. Modern popular music, utilizing Western instruments and electronic amplification, developed from the 1960s on, blending imitated Western styles of pop and rock with local musical traditions and repertoires. Local language and recognizable local musical "trademarks" remain important aspects of popular music and have not been effaced in any attempt to create a standardized sound and lyrical format for PNG pop.

After several years of intense public debate, television broadcasting was introduced into Papua New Guinea in 1987. One of the main concerns held by its opponents was television's likely impact in light of PNG's great diversity in language and in regional and local culture more generally. An allied concern was whether Western (and, specifically in this case,

Australian-owned) television companies could be trusted to produce material that reflected PNG culture. Television broadcasting commenced in January 1987 with the launch of the short-lived NTN (Niugini Television Network).[1] The network ceased operating in mid-1987 and the national broadcasting franchise was taken over by EM-TV. During the late 1980s and early 1990s the fears of many appeared to have been justified: EM-TV developed as a highly commercial service with close similarities to its Australian parent company, Channel Nine. Although it began producing a series of impressive station "idents" (short nonnarrative sequences ending with the EM-TV station logo) showing scenes of PNG culture and landscapes in the mid 1990s, it has otherwise produced or shown little in the way of local material and it has not supported the production of local TV drama. The television diet it offers comprises mainly Australian, British, and American commercial programs.

The impact of such programming upon the local population is more difficult to gauge. Although Western culture, social values, and economics are rapidly changing the perceptions and lifestyles of all but the most remote tribal communities in PNG, these changes do not necessarily imply imminent cultural collapse. Similarly, there is as yet little evidence to demonstrate that there is a simple and unequivocal Westernization of PNG culture underway. Indeed, it is possible to argue that PNG culture continues to show signs of diversity, development, and accomplishment both in the face of and, more significantly, *through* the agencies of its "modernization." As Malcolm Philpott has outlined, this cultural diversity has nowhere been so obvious as in the case of popular music, which has thrived over the last twenty years.[2] Local music has also been culturally significant in another sense, too, as it has come to constitute a powerful presence amid the (foreign-dominated) schedules of EM-TV through TV music video shows.

Since its development as a marketing tool in Britain and the United States in the late 1970s and early 1980s, music video has developed into an international form. Western videos (primarily Anglo-American) are now widely broadcast in European, North American, and Australasian markets and in parts of Latin America, Asia, and Africa. Many of the countries in these regions have also begun to produce their own music videos, usually intended to promote locally produced music tracks in local or regional (as opposed to global) markets. Since the introduction of television broadcasting, PNG has followed this model by becoming both a consumer of Western music videos and, more recently, a producer of videos of its own. There has been a widely voiced sense in the West that the early phase of music video production, from the late 1970s to the early-to-mid 1990s constituted something of a golden age of experimentation, creative autonomy, and budgetary flexibility. This is the period in which artists such as Madonna, Michael Jackson, and Peter Gabriel were most spectacularly and memorably visualized by music video directors. The period 1990 to 2005 has been regarded by some as marked by increasing standardization and functionality (and various chapters in this volume address this perception in various ways). A similar sense pervades the critical perception of PNG music videos — a perception that is substantiated by a consideration of the processes of client control and budgetary management that have developed over the last decade. The vital phase of PNG music video is usually regarded as the early 1990s and is closely connected with the output of one particular directorial auteur, Titus Tilly.

Focusing on this in the first sections of this essay I address Tilly's role in the development of music video in Papua New Guinea, and I examine how his initiation and development of music video production in the nation reflected a perception of the medium as a strategic site for the development of contemporary forms of PNG culture. The concerns I express in this essay parallel those of Nancy Sullivan's discussion of the emergence of film and television production in PNG, first by looking at the way production has been used as a tool for local cultural development and "for casting the local in terms of the national and even the international . . . 'indigenizing' television as they 'naturalize' its mode of production"; and, second, by examining the extent to which local production has "been subject to innovation along local patterns of social organization and local empowerment."[3] Subsequent sections analyze the nature of more recent music video production and the images and impressions of contemporary PNG culture that they convey.[4]

CONTEXT

As Philpott describes in his essay "Developments in Papua New Guinea's Popular Music Industry," the PNG music industry began to take off in 1977, when NBC (the National Broadcasting Corporation) commenced releasing cassettes of locally produced pop music. In 1980 the first two commercial labels were established, Chin H Meen (CHM), now the largest PNG label, and Soundstream (which folded two years later). In 1983 the Pacific Gold label also entered the market, where it was CHM's main commercial competitor in the 1980s and 1990s. Regular broadcasts of music video began in 1989–1990 in the form of the Australian-franchised MTV program, which mixed Australian and Anglo-American material with MTV-USA "stings" and packaging. The first locally produced music show, *Mekim Musik*, which was closely modeled on the MTV format, was introduced in October 1989. Packaged by EM-TV at Boroko (a suburb of the capital city of Port Moresby), and sponsored by Coca-Cola, the show was hosted by a local VJ in standard MTV style. For its first two years of operation the show broadcast a selection of Australian and Anglo-American videos and later added locally produced clips when they began to come on stream. Music video production in PNG was initiated in 1989 by the local independent videomaker Titus Tilly, who was encouraged by the readiness of EM-TV's director, John Taylor, to broadcast early clips.[5] The increasing availability of PNG clips in 1991–1992 (financed by the two major PNG recording companies) led EM-TV to introduce a second music video program in February 1993, which showed entirely local material. The prime mover behind this program was Raymond Chin, the managing director of CHM.[6] Prior to the introduction of this second program (named *Fizz* in allusion to its sponsor, Pepsi), CHM had paid EM-TV for airtime to run music videos (largely as extended ads for CHM music cassettes). *Fizz* thus gave CHM (and its competitors) access to broadcast airtime as well as a regular and identifiable TV slot for PNG music.

One element that differentiates PNG music video from Euro-American productions is the conscious national-cultural project that informed its early days. In a manner similar to that of the PNG music industry — which was initially set up as an initiative to preserve and promote PNG music — music video production was conceived as a way of boosting local music and breaking the dominance of foreign products on the screens of EM-TV. In the hands of Tilly, at least, it was also conceived as a means of preserving and re-presenting traditional music forms and local customs in the era and arena of broadcast television. Tilly's key role in this narrative reflects his generation and the significance of that generation in the establishment of cultural identity and the culture industries following independence. Tilly was born in 1958, in Pum on the island of Yela (formerly known as Rossel Island) in the far east of the Louisiade archipelago in Milne Bay Province. He was educated in mission schools before going on to join, following independence, the first generation of students to undertake higher education courses at the National Art School (NAS) in Port Moresby. Tilly's diploma in visual arts included work in drawing, painting, and photography. The diploma courses at NAS taught at this time in subjects such as music and visual arts had a strong orientation to traditional PNG culture and emphasized the virtues of preserving that culture, rather than simply attempting to reproduce displaced Western models and aesthetics. Art students were, for instance, required to go on fieldtrips to examine and work with ideas from traditional local cultures, and music students were encouraged to learn traditional instruments and to become familiar with the diversity of PNG's music forms.

Tilly's fellow students at the NAS at this time included Tony Subam, who while still a student founded the "pan-traditional rock band" Sanguma.[7] As Michael Webb has detailed, Sanguma was not simply a group that drew on the various and diverse PNG traditions as part of their musical and visual appeal; rather, they were an ensemble that consciously attempted to develop and promote a new PNG identity that drew on and perpetuated traditional culture while embracing Western influences. Although Sanguma was never as popular in PNG as acts such as George Telek or Painim Wok, they toured internationally in the 1970s and acquired a reputation as the "official music representative of Papua New Guinea."[8] As Don Niles has emphasized, Sanguma was important in bringing "attention to traditional music in the light of the fact that many young people are turning their back on traditional music and are more interested in either imitating western music or composing their own western-type music. Sanguma demonstrated . . . that there are a lot of interesting things to be found in traditional music that may be used as a basis for popular music within the country."[9] While numerous personnel and industrial factors prevented Sanguma from achieving success in the world music market in the 1980s and 1990s, the band's creative agenda was echoed in other areas of PNG cultural production.

THE EMERGENCE OF PNG MUSIC VIDEO

During the 1980s, when the PNG music industry began to take off, Tilly worked on government-sponsored radio projects and as a press photographer before moving into video production with the short-lived NTN in

PHILIP HAYWARD

1987. After working for EM-TV, Tilly left the organization in late 1989 to join the independent company Pacific View Productions, which was set up by the former NTN production manager, Craig Marshall. During Tilly's time at EM-TV he became convinced that PNG should produce music videos to counter the monopoly held by Anglo-American-Australian products via their presence on the MTV show. In order to convince PNG record companies and audiences of the potential of local ("indigenous") music video production, Tilly produced a demonstration piece that became PNG's first music video.

The music for the video was produced by Pius Wasi and Jeff Chalson, who were former NAS students and members of the band Tambaran Culture. The only directions given to these musicians was that the music should be "traditional . . . in a new style." The track that they developed, titled *Kame*, opens with a gentle flute and keyboard passage that fades to a keyboard and bass interlude before moving into the song's main form — a choppy, syncopated, mid-tempo instrumental groove over which the two vocalists sing unison melody lines. To this soundtrack Tilly shot both traditional and modern images to illustrate the "two worlds" of PNG music and culture. After an opening sequence showing a landscape of lakes and hills — complementing the delicate flute introduction — the video mixes sequences of Wasi and Chalson on location in the forest (wearing traditional garb) with sequences of the musicians working in the studios and lip-synching the vocals wearing "sharp," city-style clothes. The video also makes extensive use of Fairlight effects (image multiplying and color blurring and distorting) to create gentle patterns in the traditional scenes and dynamic background graphics for the lip-synched studio sequences. In unconsciously adopting an approach pursued by what is commonly regarded as the first Western music video (David Mallet's 1976 clip for Queen's *Bohemian Rhapsody*) and a series of subsequent videos, Tilly used the Fairlight effects to "excite the audience . . . excite them with some magical images that they wouldn't be used to."[10]

Tilly completed the clip in July 1990 and showed it to EM-TV's Taylor, who, he remembers, was "very excited and very pleased" by it. Rather than show the video as an isolated item, Taylor agreed to Tilly's suggestion that the video should be dropped (unannounced) into *Mekim Musik* (which, until then, was comprised of entirely foreign-produced material). According to Tilly, "viewers were so excited that they called the station immediately asking about the clip and asking to see it again . . . it stayed very popular and was shown many times over the next year" (despite the fact that the music was not released on audiocassette to "support" the video). The publicity and public buzz over the video, which far exceeded Tilly's expectations, was sufficient to convince CHM and Pacific Gold to begin to produce videos for their own artists' releases and, as might be expected, Tilly was an immediate beneficiary of their commissions. Following this first production Tilly worked exclusively for CHM where he shot, directed, and edited in excess of 150 videos before withdrawing from music video production in 1996.[11] The average budget for video production in the early 1990s was around 500 kina (equivalent to about US$575)—a miniscule sum by international standards, but one that must be considered in light of the markedly smaller size of the PNG music market.

Following Tilly's initiative, the filmmaker Albert Toro—who codirected and starred in the first feature film to be directed by a Papua New Guinean, *Tukana: Husat i Asua?* (1982)[12]—began to produce music videos through his company Tukana Media.[13] Reflecting his interest in drama, Toro's video clips usually featured (skeletal) enactments of the song's emotional themes or miniscenarios, which were performed by the singer or by other band members or "extras" in a mode similar to, if not derived from, mainstream Anglo-American music videos. This tendency was also evident in the small body of videos produced by the National Art School's video unit (as a commercial sideline), as well as in several videos produced by Vanessa Daure for Pacific Gold prior to her death in 1992.

Although a number of Tilly's videos also use this approach, he felt compelled to explore other approaches to music video production. As he states: "We in PNG do not yet have the skills in our actors and singers to do these types of dramas, this 'song acting,' in a convincing way—we might in the future but I don't think it works very well for the kind of productions we can do now . . . on our budgets and our limited shooting times." Several of Tilly's videos eschew pseudo-realist set pieces and instead demonstrate an attempt to develop synchronic, "poetic" uses of images to illustrate and complement the lyrical themes of songs. This is perhaps most marked in the traditionally orientated Ronnie Galama trilogy, with its emphasis on traditional dance (discussed below), but it was also explored in videos for more contemporary-style songs such as Lamaika's *Baba* (1993).

Tilly dismisses arguments that music video is a form overdetermined by its Western origins, styles, and applications. He explains that his work in the medium is strategic and functional; as he argues: "You've got to capture and have some kind of archival history of your culture — and TV and music video are one medium for doing this, for capturing movement, sound, image and colours . . . Music videos are one means of recording history." While such claims for the importance of music video may appear unusual and overstated to those familiar with Western media, they need to be considered in the context of PNG and its media environment. Given the almost complete dearth of indigenous drama (filmic or televisual), music video (together with television advertising and station idents) became the prime televisual site for the representation of PNG culture in the 1990s. The textual practices of music video, however prescribed by their promotional function, can be understood as "enabled" audio-visual spaces and thus as strategic sites for expression.

TILLY'S PRODUCTIONS

Tilly's 1991 clip for Hollie Maea's song *Kerema* is an attempt to further develop *Kame*, the popularity of which, as noted above, Tilly attributes to the mix of traditional-style music and the technological "magic" of the video. *Kerema* was already one of the most popular on the band's 1990 cassette album, and it had been played widely on the radio for more than four months before CHM decided to repromote the song and cassette. Unlike *Kame*, *Kerema* is an assertive, up-tempo, "funky-pop" PNG song, with prominent lead guitar lines and lyrics sung in pidgin. The song's principal theme is the government's neglect of the Kerema region (in the Gulf of Papua). Aspects of the song's lyrics are directly visualized in the video, most notably when the names of other ("favored") cities such as Rabaul, Madang, and Goroka appear as graphic backdrops at appropriate points in the verses. Given the considerable amount of postproduction time that Tilly's ideas for the clip required, he secured a budget of 750 kina for the video. Unlike many of his later location videos, Tilly decided to shoot Hollie Maea performing the song in a high-tech chromakeyed visual environment (the "development" level of which was thereby far more marked than that of the Kerema region itself). After shooting images of the lead singer Robert and his backup singers and dancers in the studio against a blue screen, Tilly produced the rest of the images using the Fairlight. The final video featured vibrant swirling effects backgrounds behind the male members of the band lip-synching the lyrics, intercut with four female dancers shot in both group formation and solo.

Like *Kame*, the video was a major success with audiences, who responded to the technological "wow" factor. Indeed, it repromoted the Hollie Maea cassette so successfully that the cassette sold out in Port Moresby after the video's first broadcasts. Although the success of the video prompted a number of bands to request similar videos from Tilly, he resisted making such a move. As he noted: "Particular songs need different treatments, ones appropriate to their music, their song themes and their atmosphere. The chromakey and Fairlight suit some songs not others . . . I had to educate the artists and try and get them to think creatively about it." While this statement is obviously based on the director's own taste rather than any objective criteria, it reflects Tilly's attempts to interpret music tracks creatively rather than simply packaging them in the most obvious or highly demanded styles.

In a fashion similar to that of some Western videomakers, Tilly differentiates his video productions as standard commissions or as those he regards as special creative projects — "artistic videos which I make as an artist."[14] Although Tilly has emphasized that he takes seriously all of his video productions and that he perceives his work as an "important view on PNG's cultures for its audiences," he regards projects such as the trilogy of clips he produced for Ronnie Galama in 1991–1993 as his "most important work." Galama, who also is a former NAS student, recorded three cassette albums for CHM in the early 1990s: *Ronnie Galama, Volume One: Saidi* (1991); *Volume Two: Saidi — Very Best* (1992); and *Volume Three: The Legend of Naviu Marona* (1993). These recordings feature traditional songs from Maopa in Central Province, arranged in various styles, alongside more syncretic PNG pop.[15] In a manner similar to that of the Australian band Yothu Yindi's use of traditional Gumatj material, Galama's use of traditional Maopa songs and dances was sanctioned and encouraged by clan elders. As Galama has explained, the elders saw his music as one way of ensuring that the traditions can "stay alive" and appeal to young people who otherwise "only listen to contemporary PNG pop or overseas music."

As the house director for CHM, Tilly was asked to make as a standard production commission a video of one of the tracks on Ronnie Galama's first cassette album. Upon listening to the album, Tilly was struck by a "traditional"-style track called *Rinunu*, a vocal chant sung over a slow, emphatic bass guitar riff (with continuing, faster-paced percussion "fill-ing in" the rhythm spaces), and he chose to work with *Rinunu* instead of the album's more pop-orientated pieces. Although due to the traditional orientation of much of his music Galama was not considered by CHM as a potential major selling artist, Tilly was encouraged to submit an imagina-tive treatment for the song and, on acceptance of the treatment, he was awarded an unusually high production budget for the video. The CHM di-rector Raymond Chin describes the budget of 1,500 kina (now equivalent to about US$1,725) as a "gamble" on his part; one that was based on both Tilly's ambitious proposal for the video and CHM's interest in developing Galama as an artist who might have international appeal (with the video therefore also intended to function as a potential promotional piece for international record companies).

Rinunu picked up on one of the strands of the *Kame* video by featur-ing the singer and dancers in traditional clothes performing traditional dances. *Rinunu* was, however, stylistically more complex than *Kame*. Completed in October 1991, it blends the singer's lip-synching with dance sequences (featuring Galama and a group of female dancers) and brief narrative vignettes. The song's narrative tells the story of a proud young man who is driven out of his village and speared by his uncle before flee-ing to a beach, where he meets three beautiful, mysterious women. He marries them and eventually returns to his village as a "big man." Tilly interprets the story present in the lyrics through a series of brief visual motifs—sequences that do not lend themselves to easy linear interpre-tation. This was a conscious move on the director's part since, as he ex-plains, "I try not to just tell a story from A to Z by following the vocals on the soundtrack. I like to mix the story up, select and juggle it around. The story lines are there but they are in themes, images . . . It's my artis-tic interpretation and the audience is able to interpret the images in the way they want . . . maybe differently. In this way I try through my videos to add levels to the song."

The *Rinunu* video opens with the image of a face and chest rising up out the sand, and then cuts to a spearing and shots of a young man run-ning away and falling exhausted on a beach. Three women come up to the man and turn him over, after which the vocals begin, lip-synched by Galama and the female dancers. Galama is featured as a vocal performer and actor in the narrative, and shots of the spearing and the man's rise from the sand recur throughout the video as its narrative develops ellip-

Planting crops in Tilly's video for Ronnie Galama's "Rinunu."

tically (and does not reach the [lyrical] conclusion of the hero's return to his community). Alongside these sequences are images of the women's slow group dance, sequences where they are shown as if planting crops, and images of their faces and bodies. Three of the women appear both as dancers/members of the vocal chorus and as the women in the narrative who restore the hero to health. The video works thematically and atmospherically rather than as conventional narrative.

The role and prominence of the dance and dancers in the *Rinunu* video is particularly significant in light of Galama's and Tilly's conscious cultural project. In traditional PNG cultures, songs, music, costume, dance, and ritual are not separate, semiautonomous practices but rather part of an "organic" social practice. As Anne Gee has emphasized, "traditional music in Papua New Guinea, with very few exceptions . . . always involves singing, dancing and musical accompaniment."[16] The dances associated with songs have ritual and/or symbolic meanings, and if they are separated from the songs and dispensed with in "modernized" musical versions they diminish the re-representation of the traditional form. The inclusion and prominence of the dance in *Rinunu* (and other) videos thereby retains at least a trace of the basic symbolism and significance of the live dance accompanying traditional performances of the songs. In this manner, the sequences of the dance in the *Rinunu* clip serve to reinforce one of the "messages" of the song (which Galama summarizes as "not hating each other while we are alive because we can't say sorry when we are dead") with the linked arms and unison movement of the dancers

PHILIP HAYWARD

Galama in Tilly's video for "Goruna."

symbolizing clan bonding and friendship. Despite the obvious contrasts between music video (and the broadcast context of EM-TV) and forms of traditional Maopa culture, members of Galama's community were keen to participate in the production of the videos of *Rinunu*, *Goruna*, and *Uana*. As Galama recalls: "My people were happy to appear in the videos before they passed away — they wanted to keep their image alive so that they would be there after, in the future, for their children and those that come after." This enthusiasm also extended to their subsequent broadcast: "My people liked the videos a lot when they saw them on TV. They made their memories come, made them sad as the songs and dancers made them remember their ancestors who passed away."

The stylistic approach developed by Tilly for *Rinunu* continued in his video for *Goruna* (first screened in February 1993), a song on Galama's *Volume Two* cassette. Although credited to Galama alone, *Goruna* principally comprises a female vocal chorus singing over a mid-tempo *kundu* drum pattern. Made on a similar budget to that of its predecessor, *Goruna* is performed onscreen by Galama and the dancers who appeared in *Rinunu* (together with two male percussionists). Like the *Rinunu* clip, the video's scenario is based on the song's lyrics, which tell the story of a chief's sister who breaks her brother's magic wooden charm. Although he tries to punish her by spearing her, he misses and turns her into an eagle instead. This story is visualized through a fleeting and fragmentary introductory sequence and, subsequently, through an exchange of looks between Galama (as the chief) and a dancer (as his sister), as well as images

Tilly's video for Galama's "Uana."

of a spear and of an eagle's face and claws. Much of the video's effect comes from the slow, repetitive (collective) motions of three groups of dancers on the beach—movements that create an intense, trance-like visualization of the vocal performance. This atmosphere is further heightened by shots of a mysterious, processed image of a ghostly male face.

The video for *Uana*, a track off the *Volume Three* cassette, differs from the *Rinunu* and *Goruna* videos in its choreography (with dancers ranked in several parallel lines); its more literal visual depiction of a specific event; and its high (3,000 kina) budget.[17] Made in October 1993, the video mixes two strands: the performance of a traditional Maopa song, sung by Galama and the women of Vali Pakuna Clan, and images of fire and destruction. The latter sequences illustrate the song (whose lyrics mourn and commemorate the accidental burning down of a village in the 1920s) by realizing the lyrics through reenacted scenes staged for the clip. These reenactments involved the construction of a replica set close to the site of the original village, which was then set on fire, with Tilly shooting footage of village members running through the smoke and burning wood. In this manner, the aural-linguistic and melodic record of a traumatic community event became reenacted, reinscribed, and perpetuated by another nonliterary medium, video.

In complete contrast to videos such as *Kame* and *Kerema* (as well as much Anglo-American production) *Rinunu*, *Goruna*, and *Uana* have a slow, stately, sparingly edited, visual "ambience" that makes them resemble particular styles of video art rather than standard industry rock

PHILIP HAYWARD

Villagers in the "Uana" video.

clips.[18] Video art, understood as a Western practice with its own histories, genres, and contexts, is of course alien to PNG, which has only recently emerged into the video-filmic era. In this manner, the Galama trilogy can perhaps be better understood as examples of a nascent indigenous "music-video-art" that circulated, paradoxically, within a highly commercial TV system primarily reliant on Western programming.

LOCAL GENRES

For all of the accomplishment in Tilly's work, some aspects have been problematic within their originating cultural context. One of the problems faced by producers emerging in a new medium such as PNG music video (let alone its more self-consciously artistic versions), concerns issues of audiences and critical responses. Tilly can be seen to have been both a key agent in the establishment of music video in PNG and a producer who has attempted to make more complex, traditionally orientated versions of that form. There is a sense in which the direction of his trajectory has been premised on a cultural project that is both outside the standard operation of music video (both in PNG and internationally) and the nature of EM-TV's standard (commercial, import-dominated) programming. Although Tilly describes the Galama trilogy as significant and culturally innovative works, he also has pointed out that some of his most popular videos with audiences were the early "technology-heavy" ones such as *Kame* and *Kerema*—videos made in a style that Tilly was reluctant to repeat. In this manner, the Galama videos are exceptional in address and orientation (as well as accomplishment), being made, in many ways, without an audience in mind. As noted above, when viewed as a kind of indigenous music-video-art they can be seen to be out of context when broadcast on the *Fizz* show with its repeated and heavily emphasized ads and plugs for Pepsi and with its upbeat style of VJ presentation. As Galama himself has commented: "Old people and people who like the traditional ways like the videos [i.e., the Galama trilogy] best—the young people don't like them so much, they are not all 'fast,' they are not the kind of stuff they like today."

As discussed above, videos such as the Galama trilogy require more reflective readings than is conventionally provided by either the broadcast context or the target audience for TV music shows. This is *not* an attempt to simply characterize PNG viewers, PNG youth, or the international audience for music videos as innately deficient or superficial in their viewing, but rather to point to the manner in which broadcast material is a form watched contextually by all but its most academic audiences. The industrial logic that invariably relegates unusually subtle, complex or experimental TV programming to ghetto slots is not simply one of conservative overcaution on the part of broadcasters but rather one that acknowledges audience expectations and schedule-related context and flow.

It is therefore hardly surprising that Tilly's most complex work has not been imitated or equaled by successive videomakers working in a local industry where budgets and aesthetics soon became standardized. Indeed, Tilly's pieces have an exceptional place in PNG music video as "classics" of the genre. This status continues to be affirmed. Visitors to CHM's Web site in recent years have been able to navigate their way to a page that includes extracts from six music videos. Despite a sizable output of video clips since the early 1990s, two of the featured videos are *Goruna* and *Rinunu* and the remaining four conform to what might be referred to as the "clan/location" genre established by Tilly.

The central element in the clan/location genre is the lip-synched performance of a song by its singer in his or her village or rural location accompanied onscreen by fellow clan members, usually dressed in traditional ceremonial costume and body paint, performing traditional-style dances that have been edited to fit the rhythm of the singer's pop/rock track. This genre has become a standard form of video on PNG television over the last decade, and there have been several hundred works produced in this style. The cumulative effect of these resembles annual events such as the Mount Hagen gathering where large numbers of clan performers meet to dance traditional dances in local costumes. One major difference between the individual performances at shows and those in the music video texts is that while the dancers in the latter form are traditionally attired they are accompanied by nontraditional music. Another difference is that at the gatherings the dances are not performed in a neutral showground area, but rather on location and thereby "rooted" in a manner similar to that of the Galama videos. There are, therefore, divergent tendencies present in the clan/location genre. On the one hand, precontact and/or earlier generations of postcontact traditions are discarded in the music tracks of the genre; on the other hand, locations and costume are inscribed—and thereby memorialized—in the visual track. While to non-PNG viewers there is a degree of sameness about the videos' style and contents, the examples of this genre are readily identifiable in terms of broad location and culture for domestic audiences and the videos might be read as an exemplary inscription of the local within a national media space.

While the mid-1990s saw a variety of styles of music video produced by independent videomakers such as Tilly, Toro, and Vincent Ain for CHM, Pacific Gold, and other minor music labels, experimentation soon gave way to standardization as CHM gradually came to dominate the domestic market while Pacific Gold downsized its operation and investment in music video production and broadcasting. As a result, PNG music video production became a highly centralized activity in the late 1990s and in early 2000. Over the last five years the overwhelming majority of videos have been produced for artists signed to the CHM label. In response, CHM has subsumed the small group of individual videomakers into its company operation. Raymond Chin now serves as executive producer on all video clips, and location camera operators are employed to shoot footage that is subsequently edited at CHM Video Production under tight budgetary constraints. The low-budget craft and ingenuity that typified Tilly's early work has thus been replaced by rapid production schedules that allow camera operators and editors little scope for creative treatment of their material.

Along with the clan/local genre, there are several other broad types of PNG music video.[19] One category is the in-concert clip, which is comprised either entirely by a performance shot live at a concert or includes a mixture of concert footage and specially shot sequences. The latter type of video tends to resemble Western music videos of the same type—although usually with a limited range of available camera angles and lighting variations. Another broad area of music video production shows sequences shot in urban locations. These overwhelmingly feature performers and extras in Western garb and usually employ lip-synching in urban locations and/or enacting micronarratives. One genre that has rarely been produced in the late 1990s and early 2000s (presumably due to its demands on postproduction resources) is the high-tech image processed clip.

The production-line approach to music video making taken by CHM has come to resemble that of its music studios, which are well known for their rapid production schedules and 24/7 operating hours. This ability to produce a high volume of product has in turn secured CHM even greater prominence in the PNG media as the result of changes to EM-TV's scheduling in 2002. Following the resignation of the longtime Australian manager John Taylor, EM-TV's schedules were revamped to include a far larger number of hours of music video broadcasting and, in particular, midnight-dawn slots on Saturday and Sunday mornings. As a result, PNG music videos (and thereby CHM product) enjoy a significantly increased exposure.

PACIFIC INTERNATIONALIZATION AND LOCAL CULTURE

As outlined above, during the 1990s PNG music video succeeded on two fronts. First, the form established itself as a node of indigenous culture in a television environment otherwise dominated by imported Western programming. Second, it largely avoided the simple imitation of established Western music video styles. In this sense it can be seen to have validated the optimistic prediction made by an editorial in October 1986 in *Pacific Islands Monthly* that "fears of a population gorged on Coca Cola culture to the exclusion of its own heritage are probably unfounded . . . most island cultures are vital and dynamic and probably well able to recover from the initial shock of broadcast television. They are not, as some people fear, unable to look after their traditions."[20]

But while Westernization may have been mediated and "glocalized" in music video production, some Papua New Guineans recently have perceived another cultural threat—one that stems from the popularity of Polynesian/Pacific pop music and music videos and the influence that these forms have exerted on local artists and video styles. In the mid-1990s CHM began actively cultivating links with Pacific artists and record labels. One of the first licensing deals was with the California-based West Maui Recordings for their Fijian Caribbean-influenced pop performer Danny Rae Costello. During the mid-late 1990s CHM formed further links with producers and artists from Fiji, Samoa, and Vanuatu, and the company also released material by the Australian-based Melanesian/ Polynesian music project Siva Pacifica. The success of this material with local audiences served to refresh interest in those PNG artists, largely from the south and southeast coasts, whose music, traditional dress, and dance routines are closest in style to Polynesian forms. Similarly, other artists have been inspired to follow this musical and visual "style guide" in developing new product. The showcase for this form in the early 2000s has been the CHM-sponsored EM-TV *South Pacific Music* show.

The program has featured acts such as the long-running PSII, which has progressively emphasized the Polynesian aspects of its members' visual and dance style. Also showcased are recently emerged artists who have created their musical and visual personas within this Polynesian/ Pacific aesthetic. The images presented in their music videos are markedly different from those of established mainstream 1990s videos. Some commentators have perceived such videos to be effacing the Melanesian identity of the nation while representing PNG within Polynesian/Pacific frames of reference. The following letter published in the national daily *Post-Courier* newspaper in 2002 summarizes this perspective:

> Watching the South Pacific Music Show on EM-TV recently was a real turn-off. The first five numbers were all Pacific Islands Polynesian songs performed by PSII and then Moses Tau and Lakwa Haru. To top it off, PSII were dressed in flora shirts, lava lavas and danced if they were from Polynesia rather than Paramana or Barakau.
>
> Just what is wrong with PNG music? Can't we write and arrange our own PNG brand of music? Shame on those artists who sing other people's songs to gain fame. Shame on those groups that perform songs and dances from other Pacific islands. And shame on those producers who steal other people's art and con the television audience into believing that this is "Paradise Live" PNG.

The PNG-born singer O-Shen in the "Meri Leva" video.

No wonder PNG is becoming full of second hand music, cars, clothes, food and even recycled second hand Pacific islanders.[21]

One of the most prominent artists who has been promoted with a Polynesian-type image is a young, PNG-born Caucasian named O-Shen (pronounced "ocean"). Singing in pidgin with occasional English phrases, O-Shen's musical style is a soft reggae-rap-pop hybrid. As Nancy Sullivan notes, he sings "of loving the country and the people, his friends, family—all the true PNG values."[22] Videos such as *Meri Leva* exploit O-Shen's photogenic qualities and twin his romantic image and performance with sequences of a young, slim, female solo dancer, dressed Polynesian style, performing a slow, hip-swiveling hula. The video is notably more "polished" than standard CHM videos in terms of the accuracy of its lip-synching and its image quality, and it shows O-Shen paddling a canoe through the vivid blue waters of a frond-lined creek. The images and musical style offer no clues as to the location of the clip and the national-cultural origins of its performers. Indeed, in this regard it is possible to take the cultural critiques advanced above further to characterize the video in terms of its delocalized tropical exoticism—a product and style directly antithetical to that which cultural activist pioneers such as Tilly pursued in the early 1990s.

This nonspecific visual exoticism reflects the manner in which O-Shen has increasingly been developed as a Pan-Pacific star by his (now West Australian–based) management, which has targeted Hawaii, New Zea-

PHILIP HAYWARD

A dancer dressed Polynesian style performs a hula in "Meri Leva."

land, Noumea, and Fiji as his first domestic market—hence the inclusive title of his latest album release *Kanaka Pasifika* (2004). O'Shen's music videos play a prominent role in promoting his act across a dispersed marketplace linked by expensive air routes, and his Web site, O-Shen.com, features various video and sound clips that profile his product and his success in gaining regional music awards.

It is difficult at this point to gauge how long the Polynesian/Pacific vogue might continue, as well as what long-term effects it might have on PNG music, culture, and cultural identity. It is, however, significant in pointing to the manner, in an increasingly internationalized environment, in which products, influences, and/or "threats" do not simply flow from the West to "the rest" but rather occur between various national and regional groupings.

The short history of PNG music video constitutes a significant strand of the nation's postcolonial cultural history. Although Tilly's work can arguably be seen to comprise the artistic high point of the form (to date), the aggregate of the considerable number of music videos produced over the last decade provides an archive of impressions that show the manner in which the highly commercialized PNG music industry, increasingly dominated by CHM, has pursued a cultural agenda that draws on the legacy of the early postcolonial period (and, specifically, the broad project of the NAS) in pursuing its commercial trajectory. However standardized the styles of music video production might have become, the range of musical talent and different cultural groups featured in its images and music tracks has provided a series of visual-musical "snapshots" of contemporary PNG culture. The fact that this achievement in cultural representation has received little scrutiny either in Papua New Guinea or internationally illustrates the manner in which music video is still regarded as an ephemeral and/or fringe form in a global context that continues to lionize feature film productions as credible peaks of audiovisual culture.

NOTES

Thanks to Denis Crowdy, Michael Hannan, Don Niles, Gima Rupa, Nancy Sullivan, and John Taylor for their assistance with the research for this essay.

1 Due to the financial difficulties experienced by NTN's Australian owner, Kevin Parry, the network shut down in March 1988. Shortly before going off the air, the network's production manager, Craig Marshall, had gained approval for a weekly PNG music magazine show—a format that EM-TV did not develop until *Fizz* in 1993.

2 See Malcolm Philpott, "Developments in Papua New Guinea's Popular Music Industry," *Perfect Beat: The Pacific Journal of Research Into Contemporary Music and Popular Culture* 2.3 (1994): 98–114.

3 Nancy Sullivan, "Film and Television Production in Papua New Guinea: How the Medium Became the Message," *Public Culture* 11 (1993): 533.

4 Note that throughout the text all quotations by Titus Tilly are from interviews conducted with the author in Sydney and Adelaide in February 1994; all quotations by Ronnie Galama are taken from an interview with the author conducted in Port Moresby in September 1994.

5 The enthusiasm of EM-TV for PNG video material derived both from *Fizz*'s ability to deliver cheap local programming (on a network dominated by Australian and U.S. product) and from the interest in local music and culture held by the Australian-born director John Taylor.

6 The association of CHM with EM-TV dates from 1989 when CHM began providing EM-TV with background music for EM-TV's test pattern broadcasts.

7 Michael Webb, *Lokal Musik: Lingua Franca Song and Identity in Papua New Guinea* (Boroko, PNG: National Research Institute, 1993), 61.

8 This was a description given to them by PNG's ambassador to the United States, Renagi Lohia (cited in Webb, *Lokal Musik*, 62).

9 Mark Worth, unpublished interview with Don Niles, 1991. It should be noted, as Niles also emphasized in the same interview, that "Sanguma's experiments did not [at the time] ignite the country into wanting to do similar things."

10 For a detailed discussion of the first music videos, see Philip Hayward, "In-

dustrial Light and Magic: Style, Technology and Special Effects in Music Video and Music Television," in *Culture, Technology and Creativity* (London: John Libbey Press/Arts Council of Great Britain, 1990), 124–49.

11 In addition to music videos Tilly worked on documentary projects for PVP, including items for ABC-TV Australia's *Foreign Correspondent* program.

12 The first feature film usually credited as a local production was Oliver Howes's *Wokabut Bilong Tonten* (1973).

13 See Sullivan, "Film and Television Production in Papua New Guinea," 537–39, for further discussion of Toro's film work.

14 An example of such an effort by a Western company is the Sydney-based video production group Axolotl, which claims to have subsidized productions to which its members felt a strong artistic attraction (interview with the author, Sydney, March 1989).

15 Galama has characterized Maopa music as "songs of our place, we don't have harsh sounds, singing . . . rhythms. Our songs are soft like the soft southerly wind that blows on our place . . . With the songs they have a tune, a flow — people are not so excited by song melodies but the lyrics . . . what they mean, the poems we sing . . . what the songs give you a feeling of" (interview with the author, Boroko, PNG, September 1994).

16 Anne Gee, "Contact, Change, and the Church," dissertation, University of New England, 38.

17 Chin identifies the extra costs on *Uana* as a result of factors such as the need to hire a vehicle and driver to travel to the location; (unspecified) payments to the village community to ensure their collaboration and participation in making the video; and the cost of constructing the structures built for (and burned down in) the video.

18 It was in this context as a video artist that Tilly was for the first time introduced to an overseas audience, when at the 1994 Adelaide festival he spoke in a forum titled "Video as Open Form," which was organized as part of the Festival's Artists' Week.

19 Inevitably there are also various individual videos that do not conform to this typology.

20 *Pacific Islands Monthly* (Suva, Fiji), October 1986, 4.

21 "Shame on Our Pacific Pretenders," Papua New Guinea *Post-Courier*, September 2002, http://www.postcourier.com.pg.

22 Personal communication, September 2002.

Antti-Ville Kärjä

The Finnish forests, lakes and seasons have left their
imprint on painting and music.—ERKKI SALMENHAARA, "Birth
of a National and Musical Culture in Finland"

The beginning of 2002 was a gloomy one for Finnish music video. After airing daily for six years, the television program *Jyrki* was terminated. Since its launch in September 1995, it had been the major outlet for Finnish music videos, for which the question of visibility, and thus also the meaningfulness of their production, has been a major issue. On *Jyrki*, a ninety-minute local music show modeled on the Canadian music channel MuchMusic, domestic music videos could receive up to three screenings a week; otherwise, Finnish music videos were at the mercy of weekly entertainment and variety programs. A few lucky productions might make their way through to the rotation of MTV Nordic, but for the bulk of Finnish music videos the premiere was also the closing night.

The mid-1990s represented a turning point for Finnish music video. This was a result of several factors. First, videos and their makers began in 1992 to be officially awarded with Muuvi prizes by Suomen Ääni- ja kuvatallennetuottajat ry ÄKT (the Finnish National Group of the International Federation of the Phonographic Industry). Second, the success of one particular video, 22-Pistepirkko's *Birdy* (1993, directed by Mika Taanila), in MTV Europe's *Counter-Eurovision Video Contest* created faith in the quality of Finnish music videos. Third, in 1994, a top 40 countdown program, *Lista*, was launched on Finland's national television. During its first year, the videomakers Tommi Tikka and Aulis Moisio were hired to manufacture one hundred domestic music videos for the program. In 1994, Finnish music videos gained yet another outlet in the form of the Oulu Music Video Festival, an annual event awarding videos with Pumpeli prizes. Finally, 1995 saw the emergence of *Jyrki*.

Through the combination of these factors, by 1995 Finnish music video had risen from public opprobrium to a reasonable level of esteem. This recognition resulted gradually in the funding of videos by the Finnish subsidiaries of multinational record companies. Prior to this moment, an average budget for a Finnish music video would have been around 5,000€ (approximately $6,400), but then budgets began to rise significantly. In 1998 BMG reputedly spent 100,000€ on the video "Wicked Game" (directed by Markus Walter) for the "love metal" group HIM (a.k.a. HER in the United States). By 2001 the estimated costs for the band's video "Pretending" (directed by Kevin Godley) had doubled. All this happened, however, in close connection with the so-called breakthrough of Finnish popular music into the international market. As HIM was conquering the German charts, the electro-house act Bomfunk MCs and the techno wizard Darude were challenging their British counterparts. The latter was even rumored to be planning a collaboration with Madonna. In any case, it seemed that a lifelong dream for Finnish popular music performers and promoters had finally come true.

For video production, this new success resulted in a clear distinction between the videos targeted at international distribution and those made for domestic exposure. At the lowest level there are the "five pence videos," as video producer Hannu Koro labels them, which are made most often as drills and exercises (and practically for free) for emergent or low-profile artists. Koro feels that for many it is this category that has been, and perhaps still is, most representative of Finnish music videos.[1] The question of the Finnishness of videos is indeed an intriguing one, and not only because of the medium's history as an overtly Anglo-American form. With the abolition of *Jyrki*, the production of Finnish-language videos is even more vulnerable than it was previously. The major outlets at the moment seem to be Moon TV, an anarchist cable channel distributed in the largest metropolitan areas only,[2] and MTV Nordic, the regional subdivision of MTV Europe that is by no means a national channel. The only other significant outlet for these videos is the Internet.[3] All of these outlets suggest an urban audience, which in itself is greatly at odds with traditional conceptualizations of Finnishness. Thus it would seem that the depictions of Finnishness in these contexts are much more complex than we might initially have imagined.

How is it possible for a video to be considered Finnish when it is directed and produced by German or English personnel and sung in English? Surely it would be more reasonable to disregard any national labels and treat these videos as emblematic products of supranational popular culture industries? If this is so, why are these videos eligible to compete with other Finnish music videos for Muuvi and Pumpeli prizes? The Web site for ÄKT directly states that a video is permitted in the Muuvi competition if its composer, performer, or production company is of Finnish origin.[4] The Oulu Music Video Festival is somewhat more strict in its regulations: the contest "is open to all music videos that have been made by Finnish directors for Finnish bands or artists."[5] These prerequisites form the core of an institutional definition of Finnish music video: a rather normative way to define certain cultural forms maintained by diverse organizations, public discourse, and, especially, the media.

Another pertinent reason for the discussion of Finnishness in music videos is the fact that in the world of popular music, nationalities and cultural identities play a crucial role. As John Street writes: "In the rhetoric of rock writing, origins matter; and in the business of making music, places matter. . . . The unstated assumption of this rhetoric is that we cannot understand the music unless we know where—physically—it is coming from."[6] After gaining this understanding our actions are directed by it, and the results may not be all that favorable for the representatives of places outside the Anglo-American nexus of popular culture. Koro provides an example of this when he explains how the production of HIM's video "Pretending" was given to an English company and director, even though for the same money a Finnish company could have supplied a substantially greater amount of postproduction work. He maintains that the reason behind this kind of decision is not the real but rather the imagined differences between British and Finnish video production. In short, there is no faith in Finnish production—or at least not yet.[7]

This brings us closer to the qualitative aspects of Finnishness. Of course, after the poststructuralist revolution in cultural theory it has become customary to think that the search for any essence of a given culture is a meaningless task. From a theoretical point of view, this results mostly from the emphasis on articulation theory and radical contextualism, which involves "the construction of one set of relations out of another" and where "every context is a piece of other contexts and vice versa."[8] From a more empirical perspective, it seems that the various effects of postwar globalization—for example, mediatization, transnational commerce, migration, tourism—have created cultural atmospheres where it is increasingly difficult to maintain traditional conceptions of stable and unified collective identities. For example, according to Stuart Hall instead of declining national identities it is more likely that the processes of globalization will lead to an emergence of new "identities of hybridity." In light of this, he notes the ethnic minority "enclaves" created by Third World refugees in Western nation-states as well as the consequent "pluralization" of national identities.[9]

This line of reasoning is also echoed in most of the work done by Finnish cultural theorists. For instance, the folklorist Anna-Leena Siikala asserts that the present-day field of experiences has been expanded in an unparalleled way by the culture industry, and that instead of Finnishness we should talk about Finnishnesses.[10] The sociologists Pertti Alasuutari and Petri Ruuska complete this view by stating that one "patria" is supplanted by multiple "patrias," or communities with differentiated cultures.[11]

However, as the cultural historians Hannu Salmi and Kari Kallioniemi argue, there seems to be a wide gap between the national identity located by research and the one expressed in public opinions.[12] Apparently, while in cultural theory and academic discourse there is a will to subscribe to the multicultural view, in more popular discursive domains the traditional perceptions of authentic Finnishness still prevail.[13] Arguably the most influential of the latter is the so-called Topelian idea of Finnishness, which dates back to the latter half of the nineteenth century.

Topelian Finnishness derives from the account by the writer, journalist, and professor Zachris Topelius (1818–1898) in his *Maamme kirja* (The book of our country), which originally was published in Swedish (*Boken om Wårt Land*) in 1875. Following Topelius, the national character of Finnish people can be summarized as being comprised of the following qualities: "Fear of God; perseverance, toughness and strength; patience, self-denial and vitality; calmness; heroism and fitness for battle; tenacity and stubbornness; obedience to authority; phlegm and hesitation; love of freedom; and thirst for and love of knowledge."[14]

One could argue that the Topelian view of the people has been canonized as the "real" Finnishness, and that it is still highly valued and thus has a significant impact on present-day conceptions of Finnish-ness.[15] Siikala, for example, reminds us of the fact that modern folklore, including women's magazines and the hymn book as well as oral tradition, still supports the Topelian ideas.[16] The composer and musicologist Mikko Heiniö's findings about music reviews in the daily press advocates this view. According to him, the notion of "Finnishness" for many commentators refers to music that is "by nature Finnish, e.g. gloomy, melancholy, leisurely." Heiniö contends, quite rightly I think, that these kinds of "speculative aspects" are very difficult to ascertain as matters of fact, but as they seem to be at the core of qualitative elements of Finnishness, what becomes essential is that there is a general belief in the existence of such natural characteristics of Finnish music.[17] This kind of belief also has been sustained by the most acclaimed composers and scholars, as the epigraph to this essay suggests. So, while the music theorist Ilkka Oramo deems the Finnishness of music "an illusion or a fallacy based on the listener's knowledge of the composer's nationality,"[18] conceptions of national identity and culture clearly are a matter of much dispute and deep investments. In addition, as the musicologist Lars Lilliestam points out, for many they appear as quite unproblematic and "true," and they are important aspects in the construction of personal identity.[19]

Coming back to the possible formation of hybrid national identities caused by globalizing forces, it is germane to note that Topelius himself acknowledges the mixed nature of the people, as "during the centuries there has been blending between the Finnish, Swedish and Lappish as well as other nationalities." Yet the amalgamation of these "pure races" is subjected to political geography; it is those who love the country of Finland as their fatherland and who abide by its laws and work for its prosperity who constitute the Finnish people.[20]

Despite this very early perspective on multicultural Finland, as it were, similar accounts are relatively sparse in later commentary on Finnishness. Indeed, only during the last five years or so, fueled by the everyday situations facing refugees, has the discussion about multicultural Finland really proliferated. Still, it may be that "after a tight upbringing into an integrated society it is hard to build a multicultural country out of Finland."[21] Also, Ruuska is rather skeptical toward the formation of plural or hybrid ethnic identities in Finland. He refers to the "ethno-nationalist" nature of Finnishness, by which he means that the bond between people and state is exceptionally strong in Finland, and therefore

ANTTI-VILLE KÄRJÄ

it is possible that any articulation of ethnic identity will be connected to a territory and power. This in turn means that any deviation from ethnicity that is conceived as the essence of Finnishness is treated as a threat. In other words, in Finland ethnicity and nationalism seem to be the same thing.[22]

What might very well be at stake here, too, is the strengthening of national and local identities through resistance to globalization and its pluralizing impulses. This contradictory nature of globalization can be conceived through a tension between "tradition" and "translation"—that is, an opposition between attempts to restore the purity of identities and an acceptance of identities being subject to, as Hall states, "the play of history, politics, representation and difference." Indeed, the proliferation of possible new hybrid identities is met by a forceful revival of "ethnicity," which in turn often represents itself either in the form of crude and essentialist particularistic nationalism or religious fundamentalism.[23]

The sociologist Les Back likewise argues that while new "inclusive" forms of ethnicity that "defy boundaries of race and ethnicity" are emerging through constant negotiations in the "liminal spaces" of young urban people, they can be possessed by "egalitarian processes . . . alongside the most brutal forms of racism." These "ever more complex forms of racial power and domination" may make questions about national identity seem meaningless. Yet nationness carries substantial institutional and political weight because "the frame of the state" is easily covered with the "organizational skin" of the logic of cultural purity. However, Back suspects that the nation might be important "only in the moment where its cultural imperatives are being carnevalized, subverted and challenged."[24]

It seems to me that there are two basic positions from which to investigate the alleged Finnishness of Finnish music videos and popular culture in general. The first of these would be to hold onto traditional Topelian conceptions of Finnish characteristics and mentality and to ponder how Finnish music videos might be supporting these notions. The second option would be to argue in favor of theories of new ethnicity and to advocate them as the backbone of the cultural identity of Finnish music videos. A major question, however, is how to execute such an investigation; that is, through which elements and dimensions of music videos is the national-cultural quality exposed? Such a question calls for theoretical and methodological solutions.

As an audiovisual form, music videos combine both aural and visual symbolic material and representations. I therefore find it highly reasonable to consider both realms when discussing the qualitative aspects of music videos, regardless of the more specific scope of analysis. These kinds of accounts are still relatively sparse in music video research, and prior to the 1990s and the increased interest in the form by (ethno)musicologists they were virtually nonexistent. Instead, a considerable amount of attention has been directed only toward the visual aspect of music videos. Quite often this attention has been accompanied by a certain kind of concern about videos' representations and impacts; the focus has been, for example, on the sexist and oppressive portrayals of women, stereotypical "racial" depictions, and violent imagery. Also, when the analysis has been less moralistic, it has often been conducted as if there are virtually no aural elements in the videos.

Further aggravating the issue is the fact that popular music, the bedrock upon which music videos most commonly rest, usually involves singing. Consequently, it has been and still is common to take song lyrics as the point of departure when attempting to interpret music and its meaning. Where this has taken the form of rather quantitative content analysis, it may be criticized for overlooking contextual matters, especially the interaction between music and lyrics.

Taken together, these two dilemmas point to the theoretical conclusion that what is desirable is a form of analysis that will take all three dimensions of music video into consideration: visual imagery, music, and lyrics. I believe that there are at least four routes to this form. The first path is that of structural analysis. The arguments along these lines suggest that most videos are edited straightforwardly according to the music's rhythm,[25] and that in practice all music videos consist of movement and editing synchronized to a basic pulse and of shorter rhythmic episodes following the accentuation of music.[26] Although useful, these kinds of analyses tend to be highly detailed and therefore fairly uneconomical, especially if the aim is to examine a large group of videos. Furthermore, while these endeavors may provide quite a few fertile starting points for an investigation of music-image relations, they nevertheless are of little use when considering cultural identity.[27]

The second path is that of synaesthetic analysis. Following Andrew

Goodwin, it may be stated that the concept of synaesthesia is instrumental for understanding music videos, since videos are based on the soundtrack's visual associations.[28] Yet to discuss associations here may cause some problems. Nicholas Cook, for example, accuses Goodwin of falling for the lures of "quasi-synaesthesia" and "contextual associations that really have nothing to do with synaesthesia at all."[29] For Cook "synaesthesia proper" is exclusively a psychological phenomenon where "an input in one sensory mode [excites] an involuntary response in another," and it should be kept separate from historically determined "quasi-" or "cultural synaesthesia."[30] Cook, however, seems to be relying on a rather normative conception of synaesthesia, which for its part supports the idea of absolute, nonrepresentational music. The implication of his discussion is that the "true" forms of music-image synaesthesia come only in the form of perceptions of color or light when hearing a certain musical sound. Goodwin's use of the term is also warranted by the strict dictionary definition, according to which synaesthesia involves the "production, from a sense-impression of one kind, of an associated *mental image* of a sense-impression of another kind."[31] Therefore, his list of various "sources for the iconographies stored in popular cultural memory" appears highly relevant: "(a) personal imagery . . . (b) images associated purely with music itself . . . (c) images of the musicians/performers; (d) visual signifiers deriving from national-popular iconography . . . and (e) deeply anchored popular cultural signs associated with rock music."[32]

While structural analysis is primarily based on the "hard data" that can be retrieved from a video through the careful transcription of both music and image, synaesthetic analysis is dependent on the more subjective qualitative evaluation of music-image relations, especially in relation to the sounds *as sound* (not as notated intervals and durations). This usually is linked to structural observations, on the level of form in particular, as the examples given by Goodwin suggest: musical tempo vs. visualized speed, rhythm vs. editing, arrangement vs. mise-en-scène, and harmonic development vs. thematic changes in the imagery.[33] An obvious example of synaesthetic relations between music and image in music videos is provided by the pop band Aikakone's (now known as Aika, after switching to English) video *Keltainen* ("Yellow," 1996), which begins with sitar sounds accompanied by yellow-toned psychedelic bubble figures, those "gaudy, colorful, surreal images" that for Goodwin represent the most outstanding synaesthetic phenomenon within rock culture.[34]

The third path is that of intertextual analysis. In fact, the synaesthetic analysis outlined above can be approached from the perspective of intertextuality. In the case of *Keltainen*, for example, both the sitar sounds and liquidlike imagery, as distinctive systems of textual signification, form an intertextual relation within the broader context of psychedelia. A significant difference between the concepts of intertextuality and synaesthesia is, however, that the former can include relations between diverse phenomena within the same sensory register. In actual analysis this mostly seems to be the point of departure. When examining the intertextual dimension of particular moving images, for example, the sub/intertexts are usually sought from another particular set of moving images. This is true also for Goodwin, as his examples of intertextuality in music videos consist almost without exception of visual references to films and television, in one form or another.

Goodwin's account does not help much in studying the intertextual dimension of music in videos, but the principles he outlines both in relation to synaesthesia and intertextuality are applicable to the intertextual analysis of popular music. Additional support is offered by Lilliestam, as he has adopted intertextual analysis in his attempt to find out what it might be that constitutes Swedishness in Swedish popular music. He searches primarily for discernible songs, stylistic features, styles, and expressions, but he also allows musical references to be something other than a quotation, an allusion, or a recognizable structure; they can also be merely a feeling that "this reminds me of something." Thus, an intertextual analysis carries a substantial weight of subjective interpretation, and therefore it may be somewhat vague.[35]

I nevertheless suspect that the "popular cultural memory" that Goodwin mentions in relation to synaesthesia is of great relevance here,[36] as it to a certain extent ensures that there is a ground for shared interpretations. In other words, following Michael Riffaterre, we could posit "aleatory" intertexts—that is, subjective interpretations of intertextual relations—against "obligatory" ones, or relations presumably recognized by a large number of people.[37] By way of illustration, let us take a look at the video "East Is Red" (1994) by the hard-rock band Havana Black. As the title of the video itself suggests, orientalist references abound. Lyrically, they come in the form of placenames such as Bombay and Kashmir, as well as in an explicit partial quotation from *The Homeric Hymn to Demeter*, which is spoken in the very beginning of the song: "Blessed of earth-bound men is he who has seen these things, but he who is without a share of them, has no claim ever on such blessings, even when departed down to the moldy darkness." Visually, the East is represented through ruined amphitheaters, mosaic pictures, and a tabla drum. Musically, the Eastern elements include, in addition to the obvious sound of tabla, a synth string pattern derived from the Beatles's *Within You Without You*. It seems clear that all of these references are easily recognizable to a great many people.

The fourth route is provided by genre analysis. Instead of more or less clearly demarcated intertexts, now we deal with a group of texts that have something in common. A genre is "invented" by producers, critics, and audiences.[38] Generic features operate on different levels, although the inclusion in or exclusion from a popular musical genre may be based mostly on sonic solutions. The process of genre determination should not, however, be thought of as an arbitrary one because it is heavily conditioned by various conventions. Simon Frith groups these conventions under four rubrics: sound, performance, "packaging," and ideology.[39] In other words, when a musical piece enters the world it is met by expectations about what it should sound like, in what kind of situations and media it should be performed, how it should be sold and marketed, and what it stands for or what values are inherent to it.

It is especially through this set of conventions that a connection is made between music as material sound and conceptions of collective identity. David Brackett notes how genres are tied to "connotations about music and identity which may encode specific affective qualities . . . and they may encode a whole variety of social characteristics including race, class, gender, place, age and sexuality."[40] Obviously, from race and place it is a short passage to national or cultural identity. And very often commentators are keen on linking certain genres to particular locations and cultural values. In so doing, the complexity of genres is routinely sold short, as they are assigned by critics and performers alike to only one place and one ethnic group, whether for economic, political, ideological, or other reasons.[41] Thus, for example, salsa is essentially seen as Latin, reggae as Jamaican, gamelan as Indonesian—and *iskelmä* as Finnish.[42]

Thus genre analysis is party to a major problem of many analyses of music's cultural identity. Often the question has been approached by disregarding the possible representational nature of music and by referring exclusively to the expressive qualities of words, be they song lyrics or commentary about music. Heiniö, for example, asserts that "Finnishness is something which is produced and reproduced in *speech and writing*." For him, the structural analysis of both art and folk music is most likely to reveal the common Western tradition rather than anything else.[43] Additionally, Whittall writes that the more we try to define a music's national quality in technical terms, "the more determinedly the national characteristics recede and the more likely we are to point to comparable melodic, harmonic and rhythmic features."[44]

Another way to approach this dilemma has been to conduct the qualitative analysis of Finnish music from the point of view of intonation theory, as defined by Mikko Heiniö. Heiniö sees it as exceptionally suitable for the analysis of certain kinds of popular music, and he clarifies his point as follows: "According to Boris Asafyev, music is the accumulated experience of different generations, a 'fund of intonations,' part of the collective awareness of a given time and place. It therefore seems sensible to imagine that the Finnish element in a composer, society, history, in other words, the cultural environment as a whole, is what makes music Finnish. But I believe the Finnish element is to be found not in the recent art music but in the popular music (not in the rock but in the tango and slow dance music). This music is very close to the everyday lives of people, it depends very much on our language and it can hardly be imported to other countries."[45]

In the field of Finnish popular music research, Asafyev's ideas have been most forcefully promoted by the composer and historian Pekka Jalkanen, whose poetic account on the basic elements of Finnish popular music is worth quoting here in length:

> Between the opposing poles of European and Afro-American music, the Finnish minor-key popular song has proved its persistence . . . Its prevailing moods are anguish and nostalgia, the subconscious roots of 'arctic hysteria.' Repeated from one stylistic period to the next, they represent inseparable twin myths, the fear of hell and the dream of heaven.
>
> The musical representation of anguish is the descending fifth, sol-do, the oppressive *katabasis* figure defined in the Baroque doctrine of affections. . . . By the 19th century, the *katabasis* fifth had been adopted in secular songs as the symbol of negative emotions and events—deceit, jealousy, separation and pain. . . . Its ultimate crystallization came in the Finnish evergreen tango *Satumaa* (Fairyland) by Unto Mononen (1930–68); the shadow of the *Kyrie el-*

ANTTI-VILLE KÄRJÄ

eison looms behind this piece, which gives perfect expression to Finnish self-destructiveness. The same note of anxiety is struck by the 'confessional songs' of the 1970s, describing affliction, drunkenness, divorce or thoughts of suicide . . .

The counterpart to the *katabasis* is the ascending minor-key sixth, sol-mi. . . . It was assimilated into the Finnish hit song as the symbol of Chekhovian nostalgia, autumn leaves, quiet village roads and moonlit nights. . . . Thus audiences are soothed by the immutability of the world as depicted in the conservative hit song, a form of layman's therapy emphasizing permanence, and thus making life easier to live.[46]

Yet while the intonation theory is attractive in its emphasis on culture as a whole, it seems that the kind of connections that Jalkanen draws are based on heavy generalizations and, in fact, are stereotypical in themselves. Furthermore, although he utilizes music analysis in his examination, he is working all but solely with melody. In addition, it is worth asking whether the predominance of the ascending minor sixth is an emblem of Finnishness, or merely of the minor key.[47]

In relation to popular music, I am therefore likewise dubious about the applicability of thorough musicological analysis in these matters. However, while it may be that Finnishness in its various forms is explicated in verbal utterances only, it is questionable to abandon the consideration of other forms of symbolic expression in relation to it. Verbalizations are tied to the same discursive formation—a genre, we might put it—as both visual and aural representations, be the latter musical or not. Representations are a key element in sustaining or subverting traditional conceptions of national and cultural identity, and they are the very basis against which possible presuppositions are tested. They form the material foundation for interpretations, which, in exchange, conditions the material existence of representations.

I would therefore welcome any analysis of Finnishness in (popular) music that not only examines what was said but also what was done. Mäkelä provides an elementary example of this in his analysis of Ismo Alanko's song *Kun Suomi putos puusta* ("When Finland Fell from the Tree," 1990). Mäkelä considers how the sonic features of the song participate in the processes of meaning formation, and he also describes how the song is filled with antithetical utterances on the lyrical level, thereby evoking images of Finnish society struggling in a structural change between old and new. He analyzes how these verbal contrasts are accompanied by musical solutions: no distortion, dissonances, or heavy rhythms but rather descending melancholic melodic lines resembling folk song style, the use of *kantele* (Finnish zither) and harmonium, and the inclusion of a chainsaw as a background noise. In his view, the power of this particular song probably resides in its offer of a felicitous portrayal of Finnish society at a turning point. Through its lyrics, it yearns for the past in musical terms.[48]

ANALYZING FINNISH MUSIC VIDEO

In the actual analysis of Finnish music videos it is difficult to ascertain whether or not some "purely" musical features in most of them signify Finnishness, or any other cultural/national identity for that matter. No doubt the guitar/synth solo in the goth metal band Nightwish's "Over the Hills and Far Away" is intended to connote (mythical) Celticness, but even this connection cannot be established through structural music analysis; rather, it is the outcome of intertextual relations that have been instituted over the course of time. Closer to the idea of the Finnishness of certain musical structures is the pop-duo Nylon Beat's "Syytön," as the first eight bars of its verse in their D to G melodic progression seem to meet Jalkanen's criteria of the descending-fifth katabasis motif, supposedly representing the anguish of Finnish mentality.

In terms of synaesthetic analysis, it is likewise hard to say which features of the videos would constitute Finnishness in any clear sense, since there obviously are not any objective yardsticks for determining this fact. Ostensibly, we could perhaps argue that the slow musical pace and tranquility of delivery in Tapani Kansa's iskelmä "Salaisuudessain" (2002) aligns with its editing and the overall "misty" mood. But to prove beyond a reasonable doubt that this is somehow emblematic of Finnishness is a questionable matter. To interpret this particular performance as Finnish becomes more problematic when we realize that the song, in fact, is a cover of Leonard Cohen's "In My Secret Life" (2001). And just as with structural analysis, the implications of a synaesthetic relationship between music and visuals in terms of cultural identity lie not so much on those relationships per se, but instead on their historical intertextual affinities.

An important aside here concerns stardom. While Cohen might more

ANTTI-VILLE KÄRJÄ

appropriately be included in the singer/songwriter category, Kansa's career of thirty-plus years is that of an iskelmä artist, and occasional changes in repertoire cannot change this established reputation. Furthermore, the cultural connotations of these genres differ from each other, as iskelmä is consistently located at the core of the Finnish mentality, whereas singer/songwriters most prominently call to mind Anglo-American folk sentiments. This is not to say that the latter category would be absent from Finnish popular music, but the fact remains that those artists who have worked most consistently in the singer/songwriter mode, especially during the late 1960s and early 1970s, did follow the Anglo-American model quite consciously. More recently, the mantle of singer/songwriter has been taken up by Emmi, a young female rock artist. Her performances are characterized by soft and relaxed vocal delivery, indie-style moderate guitar distortion, symmetrical musical structures, and facile melodic contours; for some she even has become "a bit worryingly close to MTV middle-of-the-road pop."[49] Interestingly, the video for her song "Crashing Down" (2001) demonstrates how these kinds of sounds and the genre she represents are still very much connected to an American ethos. Visually, the video mostly depicts a taxi ride, accompanied by occasional images of a rainy metropolis seen through the window of a skyscraper. And the taxicab itself is, of course, a regular Detroit dinosaur complete with a speedometer that reads MPH. Only a glimpse of the license plates reveals that the car in fact is registered to the Finnish Central Motor-Vehicle Registry.

In any case, when looking at videos intertextually, the possibility to discuss their relationship to issues of identity becomes much broader. Here we are entangled in the web of reference points both within the various textual elements of a particular video and in larger contextual factors. An example of the former would once again be provided by "Over the Hills and Far Away." Like many other metal performances, it is filled with multiple connotations of power: Celtic hooks, operatic vocal style, Viking imagery, and a ruined fortress in visuals.[50] The network of intertextual connections created by these features may once more be difficult to assign to any distinctive form of national identity; rather, it points to a certain generic identity.

Genres are irrevocably tied up with the process of naming. The purpose of naming is basically twofold: on one hand, genre labels are epithetic, and, on the other, they are utilized in order to distinguish a certain type of music from other types of music.[51] In some cases, genre labels signify local forms of music, either through language or direct placenames. As such, the clearest examples would be provided by iskelmä and *Suomi-rock*. Otherwise, it is astonishing to note the extent to which the field of Finnish popular music is penetrated by English-language labels (e.g., rock, punk, electro house, love metal) or Anglicisms (e.g., techno becomes tekno). Nevertheless, it is significant that judging the alleged Finnishness of popular music most often takes place in close relation to these labels and the webs of auditory, visual, and ideological factors that they imply.

A simple commutation test proves my point. Anne Mattila, a young female *iskelmä* vocalist, is, in her video "Valokuva" ("Photograph," 2002), surrounded by images of the countryside in the summer. Musically the song is an echo of 1950s "jazz-iskelmä"[52] with "old-time fox-trot"[53] rhythms and petite chromatism. The traditional countryside image seems to be central for Mattila, since in reviews and popular articles it is frequently emphasized that she herself is a genuine country girl.[54] In comparison to Mattila's apparent "niceness" we can take a closer look at Lordi's "Would You Love a Monsterman?" (2002), which musically is a tribute to 1980s heavy metal and visually an homage to horror movie makeup artists.[55] The heavy distortion, roaring vocal delivery, penetrating synth accompaniment, and catchy choruses that comprise this particular performance would be virtually impossible to juxtapose with the visuals of "Valokuva." The generic conventions are so strong that there are no power chords in flickering birch leaves.

However, we must not overlook the fact that genre labels are also closely connected to the commercial purposes of the music industry. According to Frith, generic terms are used to solve the record company problem of "how to turn music into commodity."[56] This also explains something about the prevalence of the English language in the Finnish music market; when the bulk of the music in that market comes from Anglophone countries, it is handy to classify the domestic acts according to the same naming system. But also it works the other way around: it is easier to export domestic artists to international markets when the generic labels are common to both sides. Selling iskelmä abroad would not be easy, I suspect; at best it would receive attention as something exotic and bizarre. Mäkelä, in fact, puzzles over the conditions and prerequisites that face Finnish performers wishing to break through to the global

ANTTI-VILLE KÄRJÄ

arena; should they sell "exotic Finland" or dispel all national traits? In his view, the first alternative results at most in cult status, whereas the acts with the most success abroad are, in both music and image, something other than what has been regarded as characteristically Finnish. Bomfunk MCs, Darude, and HIM, he claims, are products of that part of Finnish culture that does not draw upon the national past and imagery of Finnishness, but instead borrows from the dialogue with ostensibly global popular music.[57]

Yet recent evidence of more traditional conceptualizations of Finnishness has been provided by the television program *Levyraati*. After seeing the members of the nu-metal band Ruoska ("The Lash") naked in a sauna and the snow, slapping themselves with a *vihta* (sauna whisk), and pouring ash over their bodies, one jury member stated that "Finnishness is always good."[58] This view is sustained by the band themselves; their Web site notes that "Ruoska is indeed a genuine Punishment Rock group. A band that cannot be born anywhere else than in Finland, in the shade of great spruces, in the middle of dark winter, machined by anxiety, vexedness, and booze."[59] Interestingly, the video "Myrskylyhty" by the singer Mikko Mäkeläinen also aroused discussion about its apparent traditional Finnish values.[60] Musically, the song is something like country-iskelmä, comprised of clear electric guitar melodies with extensive tape echo and a low, sonorous vocal quality. The visuals, in turn, center exclusively on performance and backstage imagery. While the songs are markedly different from each other, they both seem to coalesce around aspects of authenticity, and hence together with the commentary they enforce the idea of Finnishness as something with ancient and honest traditions.

DO NOT LET THE CULTURE POP!

Again, then, we are faced with the alternative of either Topelian Finnishness or new ethnicities. In the study of the era of globalization much attention has been devoted to the latter, especially in terms of hybridization. Undeniably, the pace in which this hybridizing process is taking place has increased tremendously during the past few decades, but it is worth remembering that this state of affairs applies predominantly to "Western" societies. While there is no denying that it would affect "other" societies, too, there are certain differences. As Stuart Hall writes: "Societies of the periphery have *always* been open to Western cultural influences and are now more so. The idea that these are 'closed' places—ethnically pure, culturally traditional, undisturbed until yesterday by the ruptures of modernity—is a Western fantasy about 'otherness': a 'colonial fantasy' maintained *about* the periphery *by* the West, which tends to like its natives 'pure' and its exotic places 'untouched.' Nevertheless, the evidence suggests that globalization is impacting everywhere, including the West, and the 'periphery' is experiencing its pluralizing impact too, though at a slower, more uneven pace."[61] It is reasonable to assume that Finnish popular music has been open to various influences for quite some time. In fact, this is basically the stance of the popular music historians Jalkanen and Kurkela, who insist that Finnish popular music is a product of three "parent traditions": classic-romantic art music, nineteenth-century folk music, and Afro-American music.[62] Additionally, the musicologists Juha Henriksson and Risto Kukkonen, in the study of the musical style of perhaps the quintessential Finnish tango composer, Toivo Kärki, are adamant in their attempt to show how Kärki drew influences from such various sources as Karelian (or "Kalevalan") music, church music, 1930s jazz, Tchaikovsky, and Slavic folk music.[63]

Without a doubt, new musical pieces owe something to their forerunners, and in that sense the impulse to examine them in terms of possible influences is understandable. This kind of examination nevertheless has a tendency to stultify music, and especially when executed in relation to the intentions of certain musicians it tends toward a simple affirmation of creative genius in certain individuals, with little regard for the underlying institutional structures and power relations. Salmi and Kallioniemi point to the search for influences as one common way to conceptualize Finnishness in popular culture; another way would be the accused "aping" of international phenomena. In their view, the "Finnishnesses" born this way have passed unrecognized. Instead of making moralistic accusations about the copying of mass-produced international commodities, they would rather see the creativity in "Finlandizing" international phenomena be recognized and investigated. Furthermore, they feel that there is a need to address the tensions among nature, rusticity, and urban youth, as these represent the "mythical Bermuda triangle" of Finnish popular culture and music especially.[64]

When it comes to music videos, however, we cannot overlook the impact of MTV. Arguably, it is this particular television channel that has established the overall aesthetic norms for the music video form. There is a tremendous range of music videos produced in various locations, reaching from Bulgarian *tshalga* videos to clips from Papua New Guinea.[65] Despite this variety, videomakers who hope to get paid are to some degree obliged to model their expression on MTV-style aesthetics.

It nevertheless needs to be acknowledged that this particular aesthetic norm is subject to a considerable amount of commercial pressure. In transnational contexts, finding a common appeal for advertisers and audiences alike can prove difficult. Regarding MTV Europe, the most desirable yet elusive outlet for Finnish music video, Robert Hanke writes about the development of a "pan-European" concept for programming as a part of MTV's global strategy of "localization." In his view, rock music has been used in this way to overcome linguistic and cultural differences; music television has constituted its audience as a social group united by a "rock lifestyle." The strategy of localization also involves "regionalizing" practices, since production centers, VJs, and playlists are also "localized." With advanced communications technology, an affiliate can provide more local contributions while maintaining "a core of international and pan-regional programming."[66]

Hanke also points to the ease of seeing the local versions of MTV in light of the cultural imperialism thesis. According to this viewpoint, the "new language of MTV, even if it speaks or sings in the native tongue, is regarded as the same old imperializing one, producing a convergence of international musical taste that marginalizes [local] music, or standardizes [it] as a segment within a homogeneous international style of popular music." But such concerns can be accused of relying on problematic notions about authenticity in indigenous musical expression, and Hanke, for one, would rather approach the puzzle of localized MTV from the point of view of transculturization. Hence, localized music videos can be seen as hybrid results of a dynamic dialogue between local musics and American rock.[67] In sum, as Hanke notes: "While much of [local] music may never enter [MTV's] playlist, the network does open up a new and important space for those who are successful in getting 'heavy rotation.' As musicians continue to work on the [local] mix and extend their praxis to the making of music videos, they gain access to an important means of representing the 'rock and roll apparatus' . . . and are able to achieve a kind of affectivity they could not otherwise have. The practice of making music videos is an aesthetic, expressive practice of translating the infinite possibilities of mutating, hybrid sound into images that travel across time and space."[68]

The transculturization model that Hanke offers as opposed to the cultural imperialism thesis seems to rejoice in the positive aspects of cultural globalization, particularly as embodied by MTV. Echoes of this kind of enthusiasm for the empowering effects of global symbolic exchange can also be heard from Kallioniemi's assertion that the act Pansonic represents "a perfect contemporary cultural metaphor for Finnishness." Indeed, "it combines the two extreme points of Finnish culture that have been adjusted against each other with uttermost tension during the 1990s: the mythical, simple, sylvan elementality and the ultramodernization led by Finnish technological development."[69] Yet I find these kinds of declarations problematic. It may very well be that MTV and music videos in general, be they Finnish or not, provide people with positive points of identification, but it seems to me that this empowerment is nevertheless conditioned, as Hall notes, by age-old "patterns of unequal cultural exchange," as the global networks are dominated by the products of "Western" cultural industries, and the "proliferation of identity choices" is broader in the "Western" centers than in the postcolonial peripheries.[70] Furthermore, it appears that instead of supporting the idea of "new ethnicity," most music videos instead reiterate stereotypical ethnic images, or "no ethnicity" at all.

For example, Hayward writes about the way in which the Aboriginal rock of Yothu Yindi has been "domesticated" in mainstream media by the use of their major hit song and video "Treaty Now." In the more "mediafriendly" version the band is, according to Hayward, distanced from the political concerns of present-day Australia through exoticization in various ways, including vernacular lyrics, remote milieus, and an emphasis on indigenous musical instrumentation. As a result, the cultural authenticity of the Other is praised, and the mainstream culture can "congratulate itself on its new-found tolerance and receptiveness to [the Other]." The Other is made safe by bringing it to visibility only within the delimited context of safely distanced, exotic representations.[71] The Other is a creature of the night on MTV as well.

My previous findings are in accord with this argument. In an examination of the twenty finalists in the 1996 and 1997 Muuvi competitions, I was surprised by the relatively large number of black people visible in the videos. Their presence was noteworthy, especially when considered in relation to the paucity of black performers in the field of Finnish popular music at that time. They may have very well been representing the "compulsory negro" in (Finnish) music videos of those days, as one student put it.[72] Nonetheless it is also notable that the genres of popular music that are mostly associated with blackness — soul, funk, R&B, rap — were, with one or two examples, absent from my sample. In other words, while the black musical idioms may have been lurking beneath the surface of Finnish popular music, blackness in a more explicit sense was used, it seems, merely as an exotic ingredient. It was there to prove that Finnish music video, too, was tolerant and receptive and, perhaps more important, that it had a vivid connection to the "authentic core" of popular music.

But the blackness of these videos was a particular kind of blackness; that is, it was American blackness, not African; or at the very least, it was West African blackness, not East African; it was Christian blackness, not Islamic. To be blunt, it was the blackness of imported basketball players, not Somali refugees. The latter would have come too close — the Other needs to be kept secured. This is one element of the popular cultural logic of late capitalism. Indeed, it is hardly a new phenomenon in Finnish popular music. As Jalkanen notes: "Since the 1970s, the Finnish popular song has sought to strike a balance between translated cover versions, a suave middle-of-the-road style and Finnishness. Traditional hit songs, particularly tangos, are the evergreen favourites of the record-buying public. Folk and rock music have won the nation's favour only when the traditional melody in minor key could be detected behind their modish exterior. The reason must be in part sociological: the man in the street or country-dweller has a non-analytical attitude to music and demands safe repetitiveness from songs. Period styles . . . show that a securely conservative approach is the recipe for success."[73]

Popular culture in general is and has been comprehended as a regime of secured Otherness. There are at least two sides from which to approach this issue — either by psychological factors or by means of economic considerations. In other words, one is first of all dealing with very general human principles of how to encounter the Other, as charting unknown regions is always a risky business. The domain of popular culture is, of course, restrained by the fact that what is already familiar will probably sell better.

Consequently, the question concerning power over cultural representations such as music videos is conditioned by this particular form of
Otherness. Put differently, the politics of ethnic representation in music video are by their very nature secured, in terms of both interpretation and production. There may be an even more explicit sense of politics
involved here; Mäkelä, for his part, sees that the lack of international
success of Finnish popular music has represented, in a sense, the last
obstacle in the narrative of Finland's quest for being part of Europe and
Western culture in general.[74] As Finnish acts have gradually found success, various actions have been taken and organizations established to
enhance this prosperity. The most recent example of the latter is Music Export Finland, which was instituted in late 2002 for the purpose of
enhancing the possibilities for the export of Finnish (popular) music.
It remains to be seen how these organizations locate themselves in the
field of tensions between domestic and international representations,
but nevertheless it seems that nation-states play, despite their apparent
ideological flaws, a crucial role in this effort to export culture. As Oramo
claims, "as long as states take care of their own cultural policy and do not
leave it to be decided by some EC directives, there will be national differences in music just as in any other field of culture."[75]

Locality may indeed be a significant factor behind the decisions about
making a music video. Interestingly, this is not solely a question of representation. As the music video director Tommi Pietiläinen sees it, the
demand for novelty, when combined with relatively limited monetary
resources, has favored the development of certain narrative structures
in Finnish music videos. When there is no chance to make strong statements or shock the viewer with special effects, Finnish music video directors have turned to extraordinary storylines.[76] Pietiläinen himself has
executed one video in the semidocumentary dogma style, and Tuukka
Temonen is quite famous for his endeavors in music video narration. For
example, the video "Hallaa" (1998), which was done for his own band Ap-
ulanta, caused some controversy because of its violent content. Although
its splattery aesthetic is realized with rather clumsy detached limbs and
spines, it was banned from *Jyrki* (to give it a boost in the markets, some
might say). This, in turn, means a shift from the question of what kind of
Finnishness the videos support to the question of what kind of Finnishness the videos construct.

It seems to me that the emphasis on the positive force of local reinterpretations and subversions of seemingly global representations is a bit naive. Like Keith Negus, I would be hesitant to discount the persistence of cultural imperialism, as it apparently is "a useful concept for understanding the world-wide movement of music, providing that it is employed without assuming that it refers to 'effects' (impacts *on* culture) but to the *processes* and struggles through which dominant power is exerted."[77] Currently, it also seems that such imperial power remains in play in the way this same dominant power is exerted in military actions. This is, without question, finally more disturbing than any kind of secured Otherness in popular cultural forms.

NOTES

1 Hannu Koro, phone interview with the author, Helsinki/Espoo, September 20, 2001.

2 Furthering the dearth of outlets for videos by domestic acts, Moon TV declared bankruptcy on July 1, 2003.

3 See, for example, http://plazatv.fi.soneraplaza.net:800//; and http://elisa.net/elisatv/.

4 See http://www.ifpi.fi/palkinnot/muuvit/.

5 See http://www.omvf.net/en_kotim_kilp.html.

6 John Street, *Politics and Popular Culture* (Cambridge: Polity Press, 1997), 99.

7 Koro, interview with author.

8 Lawrence Grossberg, *We Gotta Get Out of This Place: Popular Conservatism and Postmodern Culture* (New York: Routledge, 1992), 54, 58.

9 Stuart Hall, "The Question of Cultural Identity," in *Modernity and Its Futures*, ed. Stuart Hall, David Held, and Tony McGrew (Cambridge: Polity Press, 1992), 300, 307.

10 Anna-Leena Siikala, "Suomalaisuuden tulkintoja," in *Olkaamme siis suomalaisia*, ed. Pekka Laaksonen and Sirkka-Liisa Mettomäki (Helsinki: Suomalaisen kirjallisuuden seura, 1996), 148–49.

11 Pertti Alasuutari and Petri Ruuska, *Post-Patria? Globalisaation kulttuuri Suomessa* (Tampere: Vastapaino, 1999), 7–8.

12 Hannu Salmi and Kari Kallioniemi, "Pohjan tähteiden tuolla puolen: Suomalaisuuden strategioita populaarikulttuurissa," in *Pohjan tähteet: Populaarikulttuurin kuva suomalaisuudesta*, ed. Hannu Salmi and Kari Kallioniemi (Helsinki: BTJ Kirjastopalvelu Oy, 2000), 7–8.

13 Jari Ehrnrooth, "Mentality," in *Finland: A Cultural Encyclopedia*, ed. Olli Alho, Hildi Hawkins, and Päivi Vallisaari (Helsinki: Finnish Literature Society, 1997), 208–10.

14 Z. Topelius, *Maamme kirja: Lukukirja Suomen alimmille opilaitoksill* (Köping: Bokförlaget Oden, 1980), 151–52; translated in Ehrnrooth, "Mentality," 208.

15 Päivi Rantanen, "Hevosenkaltainen kansa—suomalaisuus topeliaanisessa diskurssissa," in *Me ja muut: Kulttuuri, identiteetti, toiseus*, ed. Marjo Kylmänen (Tampere: Vastapaino, 1994), 17–24.

16 Siikala, "Suomalaisuuden tulkintoja," 147.

17 Mikko Heiniö, *Karvalakki kansakunnan kaapin päällä: Kansalliset attribuutit Joonas Kokkosen ja Aulis Sallisen ooperoiden julkisuuskuvassa, 1975–1985* (Helsinki: Suomalaisen Kirjallisuuden Seura, 1999), 41–42, 45; see also Mikko Heiniö, "The Main Trends in Finnish Music in the 1970s and 1980s and the Problem of 'Finnishness,'" in *Music and Nationalism in Twentieth-Century Great Britain and Finland*, ed. Tomi Mäkelä (Hamburg: von Bockel Verlag, 1997), 183–89.

18 Ilkka Oramo, "Beyond Nationalism," in *Music and Nationalism in Twentieth-Century Great Britain and Finland*, ed. Tomi Mäkelä (Hamburg: von Bockel Verlag, 1997), 35–43.

19 Lars Lilliestam, *Svensk rock: Musik, lyrik, historik* (Göteborg: Bo Ejeby Förlag, 1998), 45.

20 Topelius, *Maamme kirja*, 150 (my translation).

21 Siikala, "Suomalaisuuden tulkintoja," 146 (my translation).

22 Alasuutari and Ruuska, *Post-Patria?* 210–12.

23 Hall, "The Question of Cultural Identity," 309, 311–13.

24 Les Back, *New Ethnicities and Urban Culture: Racisms and Multiculture in Young Lives* (London: UCL Press, 1996), 244–51.

25 Simon Frith, *Music for Pleasure: Essays on the Sociology of Pop* (Cambridge: Polity Press, 1988), 219.

26 Alf Björnberg, "Sign of the Times? Om musikvideo och populärmusikens semiotik," in *Svensk tidskrift för musikforskning*, Årgang/volume 72 (Göteborg: Svenska samfundet för musikforskning, 1990), 63–84.

27 For exemplary structural analyses of music videos, see Alf Björnberg, "Structural Relationships of Music and Images in Music Video," in *Popular Music* 13.1 (1994): 51–74; and Carol Vernallis, "The Aesthetics of Music Video: An Analysis of Madonna's 'Cherish,'" *Popular Music* 17.2 (1998): 153–85.

28 Andrew Goodwin, *Dancing in the Distraction Factory: Music Television and Popular Culture* (New York: Routledge, 1993), 50.

29 Nicholas Cook, *Analysing Musical Multimedia* (Oxford: Clarendon Press, 1998), 76 n.53.

30 Ibid., 25–29, 49.

31 *OED Online*, http://dictionary.oed.com (my emphasis).

32 Goodwin, *Dancing in the Distraction Factory*, 56.

33 Ibid., 60–68.

34 Ibid., 52.

35 Lilliestam, *Svensk rock*, 241–42.

36 Goodwin, *Dancing in the Distraction Factory*, 56.

37 See Judith Still and Michael Worton, introduction to *Intertextuality: Theories*

and Practices, ed. Judith Still and Michael Worton (Manchester: Manchester University Press, 1990), 26.

38 Lawrence Grossberg, Ellen Wartella, and D. Charles Whitney, *Mediamaking: Mass Media in a Popular Culture* (Thousand Oaks, Calif.: Sage, 1998), 159.

39 Simon Frith, *Performing Rites: On the Value of Popular Music* (Oxford: Oxford University Press, 1996), 94.

40 David Brackett, "(In Search of) Musical Meaning: Genres, Categories and Crossover," in *Popular Music Studies*, ed. David Hesmondhalgh and Keith Negus (London: Arnold, 2002), 66.

41 See Patria Román-Velazquez, "Locating Salsa," in *Popular Music Studies*, ed. David Hesmondhalgh and Keith Negus (London: Arnold, 2002), 210–22.

42 In general terms, *iskelmä* refers to middle-of-the-road entertainment music, which is sung in Finnish. Plenty of songs associated with the Tin Pan Alley tradition have been recorded in Finnish as *iskelmä*. According to the popular music historian Pekka Jalkanen, "There are basically two versions of the genre: a sentimental love song and a humorous narrative. In both cases, the worldview is regressive, escapist, and nostalgic. Musically *iskelmä* tends to be formulaic with a strict verse/refrain structure, a tonal melody, occasional sequences of fifths, and minimal modulations." See Peter Jalkanen, "Popular Music," in *Finnish Music*, ed. Kalevi Aho, Pekka Jalkanen, Erkki Salmenhaara and Keijo Virtamo; trans. Timothy Binham and Philip Binham (Helsinki: Otava, 1996), 225–28.

43 Heiniö, *Karvalakki kansakunnan kaapin päällä*, 12, 44 (my translation, emphasis in original).

44 Arnold Whittall, "Personal Style, Impersonal Structure? Music Analysis and Nationality," in *Music and Nationalism in Twentieth-Century Great Britain and Finland*, ed. Tomi Mäkelä (Hamburg: von Bockel Verlag, 1997), 23–24.

45 Heiniö, "The Main Trends in Finnish Music in the 1970s and 1980s and the Problem of 'Finnishness,'" 188.

46 Jalkanen, "Popular Music," 225–28.

47 Juha Henriksson and Risto Kukkonen, *Toivo Kärjen musiikillinen tyyli* (Helsinki: Suomen Jazz and Pop Arkisto, 2001), 127.

48 Janne Mäkelä, "Ismo: Suomalaisen rock-auteurismin jäljillä," in *Pohjan tähteet: Populaarikulttuurin kuva suomalaisuudesta*, ed. Hannu Salmi and Kari Kallioniemi (Helsinki: BTJ Kirjastopalvelu Oy, 2000), 226–31.

49 See the review of Emmi's *Solitary Motions* in AfterDawn.com, http://www.afterdawn.com/mp3/albums/151.cfm. See also *Musical Discoveries* (2001) http://www.musicaldiscoveries.com/digest/digest.php?v=2andis=6#EMMI.

50 See Robert Walser, *Running with the Devil* (Hanover, N.H.: University Press of New England, 1993).

51 Jason Toynbee, "Mainstreaming, from Hegemonic Centre to Global Networks," in *Popular Music Studies*, ed. David Hesmondhalgh and Keith Negus (London: Arnold, 2002), 149–63.

52 According to Jalkanen, "Popular Music," 233, this style was derived from klezmer tunes and was an invention of one particular record company in the early 1950s.

53 Pekka Nissilä, "A review of Anne Mattila by Anne Mattila," *musa.fi* 5 (2002): 50.

54 See, for example, http://www.extraviihdepalvelut.fi/amattila.html; and http://www.ruokamessut.fi/2002/artik_anne_mattila.asp.

55 See, for example, http://www.lordi.org/.

56 Frith, *Performing Rites*, 76.

57 Janne Mäkelä, "Yhteinen sävel vai riitasointu? Globaalin ja lokaalin suhteista populaarimusiikissa," in *Muuttuvat asemat: Kompassi integraation arkeen*, ed. Maija Mäkikalli and Katriina Siivonen (Turku: Kirja-Aurora, 2000), 37–38.

58 Quote from the journalist Wallu Valpio, in *Levyraati*, December 22, 2002, on MTV3 about the video *Kiroan* ("I Curse").

59 Ruoska, 2002, http://www.ruoska.net/historia.php (my translation).

60 *Levyraati*, January 16, 2003, on MTV3.

61 Hall, "The Question of Cultural Identity," 305 (emphasis in original).

62 Pekka Jalkanen and Vesa Kurkela, "Populaarimusiikki ja historia," *Musiikki* 1 (1995): 20. See also Jalkanen, "Popular Music," 206.

63 Henriksson and Kukkonen, *Toivo Kärjen musiikillinen tyyli*, 18–23.

64 Salmi and Kallioniemi, "Pohjan tähteiden tuolla puolen," 8–11.

65 See Vesa Kurkela, "Bulgarian tshalgavideot, poliittisuus ja orientalismi," in *Etnomusikologian vuosikirja*, ed. Jarkko Niemi (Helsinki: Suomen etnomusikologinen seura, 2001), 91–113. See also Philip Hayward's essay in this volume, as well as his "A New Tradition: Titus Tilly and the Development of Music Video in Papua New Guinea," in *Sound Alliances: Indigenous People, Cultural Politics and Popular Music in the Pacific*, ed. Philip Hayward (London: Cassell, 1998), 142–57.

66 Robert Hanke, "'Yo Quiero Mi MTV!' Making Music Television for Latin America," in *Mapping the Beat: Popular Music and Contemporary Theory*, ed. Thomas Swiss, John Sloop, and Andrew Herman (Malden, Mass.: Blackwell Publishers, 1998), 223–27.

67 Ibid., 232–37.

68 Ibid., 237.

69 Kari Kallioniemi, "Onko sijaa ylväälle dandylle Suomenmaassa? Englantilaisuuden vaikutuksia suomalaisessa popmusiikissa ja siitä käydyssä keskustelussa," in *Pohjan tähteet: Populaarikulttuurin kuva suomalaisuudesta*, ed. Hannu Salmi and Kari Kallioniemi (Helsinki: BTJ Kirjastopalvelu Oy, 2000), 90.

70 Hall, "The Question of Cultural Identity," 305.

71 Philip Hayward, "Safe, Exotic and Somewhere Else: Yothu Yindi, 'Treaty' and the Mediation of Aboriginality," in *Sound Alliances: Indigenous People,*

Cultural Politics and Popular Music in the Pacific, ed. Philip Hayward (London: Cassell, 1998), 190–98.

72 There has been much discussion of the use of the word "negro" (*neekeri*) in Finnish in recent years. Some insist that it is a neutral term, but it is increasingly seen as a politically incorrect way of addressing certain groups of people, notably Somali refugees. I find these discussions somehow emblematic of the tensions within the contemporary becoming-multicultural Finnish society.

73 Jalkanen, "Popular Music," 225.

74 Mäkelä, "Yhteinen sävel vai riitasointu?" 37.

75 Oramo, "Beyond Nationalism," 41.

76 Tommi Pietiläinen, interview with the author, Oulu, August 26, 2000.

77 Keith Negus, *Popular Music in Theory: An Introduction* (Hanover, N.H.: University Press of New England, 1996), 164.

"COMING TO YOU WHEREVER YOU ARE":
EXPLORING THE IMAGINED COMMUNITIES OF
MUCHMUSIC (Canada) AND MTV (United States)

Kip Pegley

T he American-based MTV Networks (MTVN), a highly successful group of designers, regulators, and disseminators of music television, are the undisputed gatekeepers of international video, with stations scattered from Japan to Brazil and from Finland to Australia. One market, however—Canada—remains irritatingly elusive; MTVN spokespersons have repeatedly expressed their frustration at their inability to permeate the Canadian border. From MTV's perspective, the challenges posed by Canada exist on several levels: first, since 1984 Canada has had its own nationally broadcast music video station, the Toronto-based MuchMusic. Second, television licensing in Canada falls under the powers of the Canadian Radio-Television and Telecommunications Commission (the CRTC), whose policies forbid new stations to compete with existing ones if they intend to offer simply a similar product. To bypass these regulations, MTV joined forces with the Calgary-based Craig Broadcasting and attempted its first "affiliation" with a digital Canadian channel in fall 2001, giving it initial (although limited) access to Canadian cable subscribers. Despite such efforts, however, MTV is likely to be perpetually frustrated north of the border. As long as MuchMusic continues to satisfy the requirements of the CRTC and receive high viewer ratings, a full-fledged "MTV Canada" will never reach Canadian viewers.

The absence of an MTV station from Canadian cable packages, while troubling for MTV, is less problematic for the many Canadians who intuit that MuchMusic—self-identified as "the nation's music station:—is in fact substantially different from MTV and is a worthy source of music videos and popular culture. I for one have been among MuchMusic's supporters: my long-held perception, after years of viewing from my home in Canada and during my visits to the United States, was that Much-Music consistently aired more videos than MTV and featured performers representing a wider range of races and ethnicities. In contrast, MTV had always seemed less pluralistic and more restricted by its heavier (that is, more repetitious) video rotation schedule, which resulted in a smaller number of videos and a narrower range of genres. The stations' contents—from their video repertoires to their televisual flows—seemed to construct different types of relationships with viewers, which in turn contributed to what I perceived, following Benedict Anderson,[1] to be two distinct constructions of imagined (national) communities: whereas the Canadians seemed to be addressed as a pluralistic collective, American viewers were distinguished by their unique individualism.

But were the stations as different as I believed or wanted to believe? Is it possible that MuchMusic altered the content and style of music television—originally designed by MTV—to communicate what I perceived to be distinctly Canadian cultural narratives? To address these questions, I conducted a study in late 1995 based on a one-week simultaneous sample of the two stations (336 hours of footage), in which I analyzed their video repertoires and televisual flows—that is, the entire sequence of televisual events including programs, station identifications, commercials, trailers, and so on.[2] That week the two stations showed approximately 2,500 videos: MTV aired 248 different videos, most of which were repeated, resulting in 1,033 video events, and MuchMusic aired 400 different videos, which, when repeated, resulted in a repertoire of 1,457 video events.[3] I also examined in detail a twelve-hour extra-musical sample targeting everything that was aired between the videos, from visual and sound trailers to commercials to station logos, all of which were coded in time intervals of seconds. A week-long sample, of course, is far too small to be considered representative of either station, and that it was recorded in 1995 deems it a historical study of the two stations.

Any number of televisual parameters could be used to explore the differences between MuchMusic and MTV.[4] Here, I focus on a facet of music video dissemination that has received little critical attention—namely, the stations' extra-musical content. With few exceptions,[5] there is no careful consideration of the programming, VJs, visual and sound trailers, commercials, station identification tags, and so on and how these components participate in establishing a station's relationship with the viewer.

My exploration here targets MTV's and MuchMusic's stylistic distinctiveness and content discrepancies, the sum of which I will argue contribute to the construction of different nationally inflected imagined communities. Several parameters in particular contribute to these constructions. I begin with an analysis of the stations' programming grids and means of disrupting "household flow." Rick Altman previously defined this term as an individual's actual living practices;[6] as he argues, television's sound component is intentionally designed to interrupt household flow and redirect our attention to the television set. Here I explore how MuchMusic and MTV bring our attention back to the program being aired and how these practices contribute to the manufacturing of different viewing communities. I then move on to explicate the role of the VJs, guest artists, video repertoires, and commercials and how they contribute to imagined alliances, and I conclude by summarizing the stations' overall differences vis-à-vis the intersection of media biases and nationhood.

Despite the movement toward media globalization over the last decade, it might seem slightly surprising that television stations remain so decidedly nation bound. As Ien Ang points out, "The categories of national identity and national culture are invested with formal, discursive legitimacy and are . . . dominantly used as a central foundation for official cultural and media policies."[7] This may be even more true today than it was when the current sample was taken in 1995: in the days and weeks following September 11, 2001, music television stations became important portals through which audiences and media tried to make sense of the attacks, by defining "us" and "them" and by solidifying unified national positions from which "we" spoke. The ability to observe nation-based ideological constructs pre-9/11 goes far to help us critique current ideological practices, some of which have intensified recently because of the need for national support during an unpopular war in Iraq. We have long been constructed throughout our media as unified imagined communities of Canadians and Americans, and nowhere is this more crucial in our age of increasing international uncertainty than on seemingly natural and untainted youth-oriented stations like MTV and MuchMusic. In this study I seek to expose some of the deeply embedded ideological mechanisms on these stations and to illuminate how they were relevant to audiences from 1995 as well as why they continue to be so today.

First, and at the most basic level, the stations' televisual styles can be differentiated by comparatively examining their programming grids. This was evidenced more than twenty-five years ago when Raymond Williams attempted to identify the differences in flow on public versus commercial television stations.[8] When program content—one parameter of televisual flow—was examined according to the daily "listings," Williams noted that the evening sequences of the public broadcasting stations moved between disparate themes, from war dramas, to news, to regional programming on agriculture, and so on. These segments demonstrated the sharpest mood contrasts. The commercial stations, meanwhile, featured programs that were more thematically related, thus fostering a homogenized mood and, ideally, capturing the viewers' sustained attention.[9] According to Williams's research, the programs aired on public broadcasting were more likely to be selectively viewed as opposed to those shown on commercial television where the viewer was encouraged not to turn off the television set.

In implementing Williams's model of analyzing programming vis-à-vis thematic genres, I examined my sample to compare MuchMusic's and MTV's thematic programming. There are any number of ways to compare and contrast the thematic content of different shows on music television stations, the most obvious of which is to organize it by musical genre. Accordingly, I divided the musical genres into six categories, including (from the largest to the smallest category), rock, alternative, pop, rap, urban, and "other" videos, and then charted their programming over an average twenty-four-hour period.[10] On both stations the musical genres were sometimes featured exclusively (alternative videos were shown as a separate block on MTV's *Alternative Nation* and MuchMusic's *The Wedge*), but more often the genres were combined within individual programs.

From midnight to about 7:00 AM MTV was domintated by alternative, rock, and, to a lesser degree, rap and pop/rock, creating a seven-hour block. At 7:30 AM, urban and rap were the most frequently heard genres on the show *Most Wanted Jams*; the music shifted back to rock, pop, and urban from 8:00 to 10:00. At 10:00 another break occurred: MTV *Jams*, which aired from 10:00 to 12:00 noon, featured urban and rap videos. From 12:00 to 3:00 PM, the general video flow featured alternative music mixed with rock and some rap. Between 4:00 and 5:30 on the weekends, urban and rap dominated (during the week this time slot was mostly syndicated shows) and after 5:30, the programming became mixed and the video rotation became lighter as other syndicated shows were introduced into the flow (*Singled Out*, *Road Rules*, and so on).

There were both similarities and dissimilarities found in MuchMusic's programming. From midnight until 1:30 AM there was a mixture of alternative, rock, urban, and some "other" videos. At 1:30, however, I encountered a series of genre "surges": one-half hour shows featuring rap (the program *Rap City*), alternative (*The Wedge*), and metal (*Power 30*), followed by a surge indicating "other" videos. Later, between 4:00 and 5:30, rock was the most prominent genre in the flow.

At 6:00 there was a surge of pop/rock, but this surge needs to be differentiated from the others: it represented the show *French Kiss*, which featured French-language videos only. These were not mainstream North American pop videos because not only were they in French but they featured mostly Quebecois artists who were generally not Top 40 performers on English stations. The argument I am making here is that the English-speaking viewers of pop/rock shows may or may not have been drawn to this one-half hour show; I believe it indicated a definite break from the rock videos that preceded it. From 6:30 to 10:00 AM rock and alternative dominated, and from 10:30 to 11:30 "other" and rock videos were aired most often. The surge at 11:30 AM representing *French Kiss* stands alone again. Between 12:00 and 4:30 PM, rock and alternative once again dominated for what may be viewed as one of MuchMusic's longest thematic periods of four and one-half hours. From 4:30 to 6:30 the genres changed quickly and decisively. At 7:00 the music news show *Fax* was aired, followed by one final mix from 7:30 to 10:30 with rock and alternative leading once again.

According to this analysis, MTV's programming underwent seven significant thematic changes per day whereas MuchMusic, because of its numerous surges, underwent seventeen. Temporally, the airtime segments on MTV were thematically longer with less "interruption" from other genres, thus discouraging the interested viewer from turning the channel. In this way MTV both reflected and extended the dominant American commercial model identified by Williams that encourages the homogenization of both televisual content and the viewing audience. MuchMusic, meanwhile, more closely resembled the early public broadcasting model developed in Britain and Canada in which the programs were intended to be more selectively viewed. In other words, MuchMusic targets disparate audiences made aware of one another as its programs collide in the daily listings, particularly at the half-hour level. As a result, MuchMusic's viewers are constantly informed of the plurality of their imagined community in contrast to MTV viewers, who are more often reminded of viewer similarities and shared musical tastes.

HOUSEHOLD FLOW

After programming flow, the second critical televisual discrepancy between MTV and MuchMusic involves the manipulation of household flow. As Altman has pointed out, the sound component of television is responsible for interrupting our everyday lives (our "household flow") and redirecting our attention to the television. The soundtrack is largely responsible not only for luring us back to the television set, but for enticing us not to turn off the set altogether. Interrupting household flow is critical to the highly competitive station for one simple reason: ratings systems. The Nielsen ratings assume that when the television set is on the viewer is actively watching. This, of course, is not necessarily the case: intermittent viewing is equally probable while viewers cook in the kitchen or do their homework. But because many rating systems today track the operation of television sets rather than actual viewer practices, and because stations seek high ratings for advertising dollars, it is in the best interests of the networks for viewers to keep the television set on, even if the viewer is not watching. So how did the two stations attempt to interrupt our household flow and repeatedly draw us back into the televisual image? Here I will consider six means: sound and visual trailers, silence, station identification tags, the use of direct address, the extended video format, and the presence or absence of VJs.

Trailers are announcements of programs, videos, or events to be aired at a future date. The use of trailers, Raymond Williams notes, was a result of intensified competition, when broadcast planners wanted to "capture" the audience and keep them watching their particular channel for upcoming events or events later that day, week, or month. Their usage has differed among stations and countries: "In conditions of more intense competition, as between the American channels," Williams argues, "there is even more frequent trailing, and the process is specifically referred to as 'moving along,' to sustain what is thought of as a kind of brand-loyalty to the channel being watched."[11]

How then did the two stations insert trailers, and how did this result in different levels of household flow interruption? During the extramusical sample, I coded the trailers that announced events to be aired in the immediate future, later that same day, in the upcoming week, and later that month. The trailers were either visually based (written text, usually accompanied by music) or reinforced with a voiceover by the VJ or a non-VJ. Table 1 outlines the number and types of trailers used by the two stations.

1   Visual and Sound Trailers in MTV and in MuchMusic

	MTV	MuchMusic
Number of trailers	89	87
VJ voiceover	57	51
Non-VJ voiceover	32	30
Without voiceover	0	6

That week MTV aired 89 trailers, of which 57 were done with a VJ and 32 without; MuchMusic, meanwhile, aired 87 trailers, 51 with a VJ and 36 with a non-VJ voiceover. A total of 36 trailers without a VJ were aired on MuchMusic, 6 of which did not carry any voiceover component. All of MTV's trailers had a textual component, which indicates a high degree of household flow disruption because the trailers used a voice to prompt the audience back to the screen. As Altman points out, for the interruption of household flow to be effective "there must be a sense that *anything really important* will be cued by the sound track."[12] If sound cues are absent, the viewer is less compelled to pay attention.[13] The 6 trailers without an aural text on MuchMusic were significant because they risked losing the viewer to (other) household activities. The same principle applies to the videos themselves, and a difference also was recorded here: the week of the sample every one of MTV's videos included lyrics while MuchMusic aired 6 instrumental videos. I would argue that for many viewers, lyric "sound cues" prompt them to look at the singer to share the musical experience, particularly if they are singing along. These 6 videos, evidence of MuchMusic's expanded repertoire (including nonmainstream work), risked the viewer-television connection by possibly losing the audience to other household activities.

While musical sounds and voices draw the listener into the televisual flow, the absolute lack of sound (a "dead track") can also prompt viewers' attention. As Joseph Boggs points out, within the filmic context the "dead track" provokes us to pay even more attention to the visual stimulus; with sounds in film so "naturalized," their absence creates tension; we await the next sound so that we can relax.[14] I would argue that music video dead tracks similarly fulfill the function of creating tension and encouraging attention.

A noteworthy difference in the use of absolute silence existed between the two stations. On MuchMusic, absolute silence was used in 56 videos, usually at the beginning, simultaneous with the visual narrative but before the music entered. Combined, these 56 videos comprised 3.8 percent of the repertoire. On MTV, however, 95 videos incorporated this technique—that is, 9.2 percent of the video repertoire. This means that compared to MuchMusic, an average of 5.5 *more* videos interrupted household flow daily on MTV by means of absolute silence, thus contributing to MTV's overall pattern of attracting listeners' attention back to the station.

Another means of interrupting household flow was accomplished vis-à-vis station identification tags. Tags feature station logos as the focal point of the visual image; their objective is to present these logos in as many different and interesting forms as possible. MuchMusic's station tags featured a stationary "M" symbol that was invariably featured throughout the entire clip. The logo either changed colors or "shimmered" over the duration of the tag to hold the viewer's interest. This was usually accompanied by some sort of sound like a conga drumbeat or a bass beat. The image and sound were usually static and nondeveloping.

Like MuchMusic's practice, some of MTV's tags featured its logo (a large "M" with an embedded "tv") in the opening frame, where the logo although colorful, remains stationary. Most often, however, MTV incorporated its logo into a mininarrative that emerged only at the end of the clip. One ten-second animated tag featured a man seated in a dentist's chair while the dentist pulls his tooth; when turned upside down the tooth is revealed to be the MTV logo. In another tag, animated characters with protruding neck veins are shown straining; there is a sound of something being released, and the logo falls into water. These mininarratives are intended to engage the viewer: we watch and wonder when and how the logo will emerge. The narratives are usually accompanied by sounds, if not by words: sounds of splattering or popping draw us into the plot. Relative to MuchMusic, the narrative techniques used by MTV were more purposeful and designed to keep us watching for the logo to emerge while simultaneously drawing us into the slightly raw—and usually humorous—aesthetic. In short, they were specifically designed to pique our interest and encourage us to continue watching until the narrative's conclusion.

The viewers' relationship to household flow was also shaped by particular modes of televisual address. All of the VJs on both stations engaged in direct address with the viewer, that is, they looked directly into the camera. Visiting celebrities on MTV also engaged in direct address with the viewer. On MuchMusic, however, the celebrities looked at the VJ or at the audience, but never at the camera. This discrepancy is significant: when celebrities on MTV looked into the camera, it was as if the viewer were being "summoned." As Kurt Danziger notes, direct address is "another way of calling [the viewer]."[15] The viewer, in turn, was encouraged to reciprocate with equal intimacy and attention; this again pulled us back to the television. On MuchMusic, however, we were not addressed directly by the stars; this enabled us to listen without being visually "called in," possibly allowing us to continue with our household activities with more ease. This practice also points to different modes of celebrity construction on the two stations; I shall return to this point later.

Losing the viewer to household flow was also risked more frequently on MuchMusic because it occasionally aired longer videos. While MTV consistently aired the standardized video length, MuchMusic included a number of longer songs including Barnes and Barnes' "Fishheads" (4:40) and Passengers' "Miss Sarajevo" (5:59). By extending the standardized video length, MuchMusic risked the attention of those viewers more accustomed to shorter video texts with more formulaic structures.

Finally, the two stations' household flow strategies differed vis-à-vis the presence or absence of VJs. What role might VJs play beyond the sound of their voices announcing upcoming events? Andrew Goodwin has pointed out that when the television personality is not present—for instance, on stations like Juke Box—a clear station identity cannot be made.[16] Following Danziger's assertion that direct address invites the viewer to reciprocate by looking back, I would also argue that when the VJ is absent from a show, leaving the viewer with only the sound of voiceovers, the audience is likely to watch the television set differently. The week of my sample, MTV aired only one show without a VJ: *Best of the 90s*. This program instead featured a split screen allowing viewers to write online communications that appeared underneath the video images (titled "Yack Live"). This arguably makes the viewer attend to the visual image even more attentively than usual as they simultaneously watch the video and the commentary about the video and artist. Although all of the other shows on MTV featured VJs, during my sample MuchMusic aired two shows without a VJ: the *MuchMusic Top 20 Countdown* (with a voiceover by VJ Bill Welychka but no visual image of him) and *Rap City* (for four of the five airings the show was "under construction" and in search of a new VJ). As such, the viewers were less likely to be drawn back visually to the television set when the videos were being introduced.

While each of these discrepancies between the two stations individually may seem unavailing, their sum contributes significantly to our understanding of how they established their televisual flow. That MTV engaged in a higher level of flow is not surprising: as Altman notes, "flow is related . . . to the commodification of the spectator in a capitalist, free enterprise system"; in highly competitive markets, networks, because of their open competition for viewers, engage high levels of flow, while public stations work at much lower levels.[17] High degrees of flow also parallel more developed ratings systems; nowhere is this more clearly seen than in the United States. Within Canada, commercial stations similarly engage in extremely competitive modes, yet MuchMusic's degree of flow, while higher than most other Canadian stations—including both music and nonmusic programming—resisted imitating the competitive American commercial model. It could be argued that MuchMusic, while undisputedly commercial, was inflected with the public broadcasting ideology (a pervasive model in Canada perpetuated largely vis-à-vis the Canadian Broadcasting Corporation), which attempted to serve a wide demographic of Canadian viewers of varying styles and tastes.

Ranging from factors such as the varied programming on the half-hour level to fewer demands on the audience to return their attention to the set, I have argued here that MuchMusic did not match MTV's American-style coefficient of network flow. I now turn to the function of VJs and guest artists, the video repertoire, and station commercials to assess their contributions to the formation of distinct national communities.

IN FRONT OF THE CAMERA: VJS AND CELEBRITIES

The function of the VJ has received little attention within academic scholarship. To readdress this paucity, Goodwin has pointed out a number of ways in which the VJs serve to "anchor" the MTV text. Of particular interest here is his argument that the VJs serve as individuals with whom the viewer can identify, thereby providing the familiar, friendly component against the backdrop of the superstars (the unreachable).[18] As part of his analysis, Goodwin cites John Langer's essay "Television's Personality System" (1981). Langer, borrowing from film analysis, argues that the models used to understand the construction of film stars, while useful for television, must be modified because there are distinct differences between the film and television celebrity. The film star traditionally has been separated out from our everyday lives, and accordingly we exit our daily routine to view a film that appears to us "larger than life" on screen. In addition, we often do not know when the star will release another film until we see it advertised. The stars appear, as Langer writes, within the realm of "the spectacular, the inaccessible, the imaginary."[19] Television's personality system, however, is structured in opposition to that of film. "Good television," according to Langer, "personalizes whenever it can, rarely using a concept or idea without attaching it to or transforming it through the 'category of the individual.'"[20] In other words, it is the television personality that mediates television codes and transforms its symbolic discourses. It is through these personalities that events on television are "encoded" and "made intelligible," thereby allowing the medium to operate ideologically.[21] Correlating ideas or opinions with television personalities requires that the TV personality be more reliable, consistent, and familiar than the film star. The television personality should be predictable and somewhat regular; ideally, they should be scheduled at the same time each day or week.

So how did the two stations schedule their VJs? During the selected week, MTV featured 22 different VJs, 8 regularly scheduled VJs and 14 guests (a list of VJs and their respective programs appears in table 2). The guests included musicians like Coolio and nonmusician celebrities like Shaquille O'Neal, Cindy Crawford, and Adam Oates of the Boston

2   VJs on MTV, November 4–11, 1995

Regular VJs	Programs
Simon Rex	*Music Videos*, *Most Wanted*
John Sencio	*Music Videos*, *Rude Awakening*, *Top 20 Video Countdown*
Bill Bellamy	*MTV Jams*, *Most Wanted Jams*, *MTV Jams*, *Countdown Weekend*
Kennedy	*Music Videos*, *Alternative Nation*
Erik Palladino	*Dreamtime*
Matt Pinfield	*120 Minutes*
Daisy Fuentes	*Top 20 Video Countdown*
Idalis	*Prime Time*

Bruins. Each of the regular VJs or guest VJs appeared either on their own or in combination with another person, or both. On MTV, regular VJs often were associated with a particular genre and/or time of day. The VJ Simon Rex, for instance, appeared on the general video flow program called *Music Videos* and on the show *Most Wanted*. Because VJs took turns hosting *Music Videos*, the viewer was never sure if Rex would appear on the program, but he always appeared on his own prime-time show *Most Wanted*. John Sencio, in addition to his appearances on *Music Videos*, appeared daily on the morning show *Rude Awakening*, and Erik Palladino was the nightshift VJ appearing exclusively on the program *Dreamtime*. Time-specific shows (i.e., programs while the world sleeps or wakes up) were possible on MTV because it prerecorded its segments in a decontextualized, timeless loft setting and showed them at the same time of day across the United States. Thus a viewer in Miami saw John Sencio on *Rude Awakening* at 6:00 AM eastern time, and a viewer in Los Angeles saw him at 6:00 AM Pacific time. The VJ appearances were temporally consistent and reliable, thus creating the impression that they were more familiar and, as a result, perhaps even more trustworthy. This was accomplished, as in the case of newscasters, without disclosing personal information about themselves to the audience. But, as Langer has pointed out, it is not necessary for the personalities to convey personal information about themselves in order to be received as familiar and accessible: every time a personality appears, even if he or she is not conveying personal information, he or she is still contributing toward a "knowable" self.[22] Whereas stars play "parts," someone new and possibly unfamiliar each time we see them, personalities play themselves, "distinguished for their representativeness, their typicality, their 'will to ordinariness,' to be accepted, normalized, experienced as familiar."[23]

This familiarity allows the personality to work ideologically; in this particular MTV case, it enabled the VJs to call attention to specific videos, generate interest, and even influence video popularity without seeming overly imposing. During my sample week, the hard-edged VJ Kennedy pointed out, on her alternative late-night show *Alternative Nation*, the poor reception of the newly released Smashing Pumpkins unit *Mellon Collie and the Infinite Sadness*. During the week Kennedy made further references to the album and the lead video "Bullet with Butterfly Wings," inviting us to "call in and let us know what you think" and asking us "is it really that bad?" The enthusiasm generated by Kennedy's remarks — coupled with the substantial airplay — culminated in its appearance on the *Top 20 Video Countdown* by the end of that week.

On MTV, then, programs often were linked not only with musical genres but also with VJ personalities; this deflected attention away from the mechanisms of power involved in selecting and orchestrating the video repertoire, implying instead that the video choices were "natural" ones. "The effect of structuring television around personalities," Langer writes, "suggests that the world, first and foremost, is constructed through the actions of individuals behaving as free agents rather than by the complex relations among classes, institutions, and interest groups."[24] The time-specific programming of MTV facilitated VJ-program-viewer associations; as our connection with the television personalities strengthened and their appointment appeared increasingly more "natural," their power to influence the viewer from a seemingly "personal" space expanded and MTV's corporate-driven obligations became less conspicuous.

On MuchMusic, during my sample week 10 VJs were featured: 8 were regular VJs and 2 were guests (the program *Rap City* was done without a VJ; see table 3 for a list of VJs and shows). It would be reasonable to assume that because MuchMusic featured fewer VJs, a more stable and perhaps more predictable schedule would result. MuchMusic, however, unlike MTV, did not adjust programming to accommodate time zones: the station taped live for eight hours, then shuffled and repeated programs to make a twenty-four-hour cycle. All of this material was aired simultaneously across the country, making nationwide time-specific shows impossible: for example, when it is 6:00 AM in Newfoundland, the furthermost eastern point of Canada, it is only 1:30 AM in the West.

3   VJs on MuchMusic, November 4–11, 1995

Regular VJs	Programs
Diego Fuentes	*Video Flow, R.S.V.P.*
Sook-Yin Lee	*Video Flow, The Wedge*
Mike Campbell	*MuchEast*
Terry David Mulligan	*MuchWest*
Natalie Richard	*Video Flow, French Kiss*
Master "T"	*Da Mix*
Bill Welychka	*Video Flow, Cliptrip, Intimate and Interactive Preview, Daily R.S.V.P., MuchMusic Countdown* (voiceover only)
Teresa Roncon	*Video Flow, Power 30, Daily R.S.V.P.*

At least three significant differences between the two stations can be noted here. First, although MuchMusic aired the same shows at the same time each day, the VJ appearances were not always predictable: if I tuned in on Monday morning, Diego Fuentes was the video flow VJ, but on Tuesday morning it was Sook-Yin Lee. (On MTV it was always John Sencio, who started my day with a cup of coffee in hand.) Second, the fact that MuchMusic aired simultaneously across the country in different time zones resulted in different repertoires for its viewers: the videos that a teenager saw after school in Ontario were not what a British Columbian saw when she or he arrived home several hours later. Texans who watched MTV during their dinner hour, however, were watching the same repertoire as Californians sitting down several hours later. Finally, the farther the Canadian viewer lived from the Toronto studio the more they were temporally marginalized: a viewer in Vancouver might be sitting in darkness while a MuchMusic VJ broadcasted live in daylight. MuchMusic's airing schedule, like its program listings, served to remind the viewer that they were one among many. MTV, meanwhile, insisted that the individual viewer's time zone overrode all others and that he or she was always the intended viewer.

And the "many" that comprise Canada's ethnic and racial mix were represented in more depth on MuchMusic by a diverse pool of regular VJs, including Natalie Richard (a Francophone), Sook-Yin Lee (of Chinese Canadian descent), Master "T" (of African Canadian descent), and Diego Fuentes. MuchMusic, in fact, drew attention to this diversity in its commercial promo for Diego Fuentes the week of the sample: Fuentes was introduced as the winner of a cross-Canada VJ search; in the commercial he stated, "I was born in Chile where it's hot, and moved to Canada, where it's not." To accentuate this geographical shift, he was shown sweating on sand for the first phrase and shivering in a sweater while holding hockey skates during the second. Here, Fuentes clearly was identified (and celebrated) as part of Canada's Latin American immigrant population. The fact that MuchMusic was filmed at street-front level in Toronto is also significant: Toronto repeatedly has been identified by the United Nations as the most multicultural city in the world. The richly varied fans who crowded the studio or watched from outside were reflected daily by the lineup of diverse VJs. Conversely, on MTV, with the exception of the Cuban American Daisy Fuentes who hosted one show the week of my sample, the station featured regularly scheduled VJs of either African or European descent.

A further distinguishing feature between the VJs, in addition to scheduling differences and ethnicity, was their accessibility vis-à-vis their physical locations and their mode of address. MTV was recorded in a decontextualized studio setting; where exactly it was filmed is only speculative for the viewing audience member.[25] Moreover, the VJs (and guest celebrities) used teleprompter cues, such that they did not appear to be reading the information but rather simply reporting it. On MuchMusic, the VJs were shown reading charts and sheets with printed information. In addition, the cameras were often moving in the "interactive" environment: MuchMusic employees were viewed working in and around the set with the street-front setting in the background, and the VJ was shown moving about and picking up information to be read to the home audience. The mechanical technology here was thus intentionally exposed.

These differences illustrate well Erving Goffman's notion of "front" and "back" regions, or conceptual boundaries that can help differentiate on the two stations the power relations between VJ and viewer.[26] In this particular context, the front region included the VJs' performances on camera, whereas the back region was the "behind the scenes" activity. MTV made a clear separation between the preparation of information and its dissemination; MuchMusic, however, collapsed front and back regions. What might be the significance of this difference? Joshua Meyrowitz has pointed out that hierarchical structures depend to different degrees on concealing or revealing back regions: highly hierarchical roles usually conceal backstage preparation, rehearsals, and practice. The higher the status the more the denial of even the existence of a backstage.[27] Here lies one of the significant hierarchical differences between the two stations: on MuchMusic the VJs appeared to be more like "us," they read (or sometimes misread) prepared texts, thereby giving the impression that they learned the information simultaneously with the viewer. On MTV, however, the VJs were "already knowing." This discrepancy between the VJs results in two distinct degrees of status: As Meyrowitz argues, "The information possessed by very high status people must appear to be not only 'unknown,' but 'unknowable,' wherein hierarchical roles involve both mystery and 'mystification.'" As he argues further, "The greater the ability to hide the time and effort needed to maintain a high status role . . . the greater one's seeming power and omnipotence."[28] On MuchMusic, the VJs were chosen in part because of their ability to represent a plurality of racial and ethnic backgrounds; their style of dissemination reinforced their ordinariness, thereby further enabling the viewers to read themselves into the role of the VJ.

MuchMusic's VJs once again resembled their viewers more so than those on MTV: their role was demystified and common, preparing their way to function as the mediator between the viewer and the visiting celebrity. This leads to another distinguishing feature between the two stations in their constructions of imagined communities: the role of the guest celebrities. Two primary stylistic differences separated the stations with regard to guest participation: live musical performances and the use of direct address. On MuchMusic, guests usually performed live (and live-to-air) in the studio.[29] The week of my sample, MuchMusic featured live musical performances by Meatloaf, Melissa Etheridge, and others on programs like *Intimate and Interactive*, where audience members can ask questions and talk both with the performer as well as within the general video flow. The fans, by extension, were also shown within the studio setting, sometimes only inches away from the performer (see figure 1). Meanwhile, the members of the audience overflow who braved the weather outside on Queen Street looked through the huge "windows" for a glimpse of the celebrity, or, in many cases, the celebrity exited through these windows to interact with the fans outside. In each case the celebrities were interviewed by the VJ with questions posed by the audience. The presence of the audience here is significant. As David Marshall has pointed out within the forum of television talk shows, the audience "constructs an atmosphere of an event that is particularized in time and

Usher greeting the fans outside the MuchMusic studios in Toronto.
(Photo courtesy of MuchMusic)

place."[30] I would extend this argument to MuchMusic and suggest that the audience contributed to these moments of temporal specificity. MTV, however, did not feature live musical performances in the loft and no audience appeared. Guest stars like Coolio, Elastica, or Killah Priest even replaced regular VJs, whereas on MuchMusic, the VJ was always retained to mediate between the viewer and the celebrity.

One further difference between the interactive styles of the guest stars on the two stations concerns the use of direct address. Direct address was discussed above with regard to the interruption of household flow, but it also affects hierarchical structures between the viewer, the VJ, and the celebrity. The differentiation here between the two stations is straightforward: visiting celebrities on MTV looked directly at the camera; guests on MuchMusic, other than a quick glance, never did. Why should this matter? Kurt Danziger, as I noted previously, argues that it is through direct address that the celebrity seems to be taking the viewer into account, of speaking directly to him or her. He continues by stating, "[In] appearing to reduce distance through intimacy the personality system operates to mask the gap between the powerful and the powerless, ensuring that the real unities of power, class, prestige and interest can continue relatively intact and unexamined."[31] The fact that MTV celebrities talked to the viewers directly blurred existing hierarchies, making our ascension from viewer to VJ to celebrity slightly more plausible, despite the overwhelming odds to the contrary. The gap between the powerful and powerless is minimized as the star speaks directly to the viewer as an individual.

I would argue that the parallel to MTV's direct address was for Much-Music the appearance of the crowd. The significant difference is that the celebrity on MTV spoke to the individual viewer. This suggests that with some effort the distance between the celebrity and the viewer could be overcome, thus evoking a form of American individualism. On Much-Music, meanwhile, the star who addressed the VJ and/or performed for the crowd (and, by extension, for the television viewer), was speaking to the viewers as a whole—that is, a Canadian collective. The distance between viewer and celebrity was not elided and the hierarchy from viewer to audience member to VJ to star, from the most powerless to the most powerful, may be argued as more realistic than that depicted on MTV.

THE VIDEO REPERTOIRE

The fact that on MuchMusic the audience members were encouraged to imagine themselves as part of a broader collective is a crucial distinguishing feature between the two stations. I would like to support this argument by commenting briefly on two features of the actual video repertoires—namely, variance of language and historical depth.

Stations reinforced the viewing population's uniformity or diversity through language. Of the 1,033 videos shown on MTV that week, only 4 video events were not in English: one French video, "69 Année Erotique" by the East Coast–based Luscious Jackson was aired four times that week. The languages from MuchMusic's video repertoire were more varied: 1,357 in English, 63 in French (mostly on the show *French Kiss*), 14 in Spanish, and 7 in languages other than these three, including, among others, Ukrainian and Punjabi. Needless to say, MuchMusic's repertoire contained significantly more linguistic diversity than did that of MTV.

Second, the imagined communities were constructed differently vis-à-vis the historical depth of the video repertoires. MuchMusic's repertoire included a considerably greater number of older videos, whereas MTV's was extremely current. As part of my analysis, I coded individual videos according to their "special video identifications": new videos on MTV were called "Buzz Clips"; on MuchMusic they were labeled "Fresh New Vibes" or "New Power 30" videos. I then collapsed these labels and ar-

	MTV	MuchMusic
New videos	87	36
Exclusive videos	24	0
Featured video	30	28
Requested videos	0	26
Indie videos	0	4
Dated videos	0	39

rived at six categories, shown in table 4. Compared to MuchMusic, MTV was more aggressive in airing new videos. In addition, MTV informed the viewer when it had bought a video's exclusive rights (over other American stations), whereas MuchMusic didn't engage in this practice due to less direct competition. Each station had one featured video per week, which in total was about the same (30 on MTV, 28 on Much), and MuchMusic aired requested videos whereas MTV did not.[32] The most striking difference between the two is the discrepancy between the videos from the 1980s and the very early 1990s: there were 39 on MuchMusic and 0 on MTV. It should be noted that MTV did show a few older videos, although they were not identified as such; these videos included a portion of Michael Jackson's 1983 "Billie Jean" and UB40's 1983 release "Red Red Wine" (which charted in the United States later in 1988). With only a few exceptions, however, the vast majority of MTV's video repertoire was taken from the 1990s, predominantly from 1993–1995. On MuchMusic, meanwhile, a total of 39 older videos were aired, including Bon Jovi's "Runaway" (1984) and Cameo's "She's Strange" (1984).

How was MuchMusic able to show a relatively wide range of videos? The answer is that they showed more videos overall during the sample (1,457 to MTV's 1,033) and they used a slower rotation. This means that the top artists were shown more frequently on MTV than they were on MuchMusic. In fact, the top twelve artists on MTV were featured in 35.4 percent of all the videos shown, and the top twelve on MuchMusic accounted for 20.1 percent of its repertoire. Thus the effort to slow the rotation and show more videos by a wider range of artists overall allowed for the possibility of an expanded repertoire.

It should be noted, however, that MuchMusic might be expected to feature an expanded repertoire because of the Canadian content regulations determined by the CRTC. Further, it has less network competition and thus is able to target a wider demographic market. MuchMusic's primary competitors in 1995 were country music stations and video programs shown on Black Entertainment Television (BET). In MTV's case, in addition to the country stations and BET it also competed with VH1 (a co-owned station with an older target demographic of ages twenty-five to forty and a more pop-based playlist), the Box, MuchMusic USA, and Z Music Television (a Nashville-based Christian video network) among others. With this group of competing stations, MTV might have been expected to narrow its playlist to appeal to the younger ages twelve to twenty-four demographic. Yet, consider how much of the video market was actually controlled by MTV: in 1993 it had 57.4 million subscribers in the United States; that same year, VH1 had 47.2 million viewers.[33] Targeting the ages twenty-five to forty group, however, proved difficult for VH1; in fact, ratings have been so low that Viacom (the owner of MTV and VH1) has grappled with selling the two stations together only as a package, knowing that operators can't afford to lose MTV.[34] In short, MTV simply had a stranglehold on the U.S. market for all demographics in 1995. I point this out simply because we might not surmise this from MTV's limited playlist, which, like the programming flow discussed earlier, reinforced the perception of a relatively narrow range of viewers.

STATION COMMERCIALS

To conclude, I would like to briefly address how the differences in station commercials also contributed to distinctive imagined communities on either side of the border. During my twelve-hour sample, MTV featured a total of five station commercials. These can be further divided into two subgroups: the first of which includes commercials that attempted to depict MTV in a lighthearted, playful, and even irresponsible light. In one commercial, an artist paints a gentle outdoor landscape, commenting on his process as he adds scenery and wildlife. By the commercial's end the artwork is revealed to be in the shape of the MTV logo, and the artist comments: "MTV: it's all just fluffy white clouds." Thus MTV is purposefully (and ironically) presented as an unthreatening presence.

Juxtaposed with this style is another more purposeful one intended to align the station specifically with the young viewing audience. Several different commercials aired during my sample week show this style. In one, MTV's president, Gwendolyn VanDeerlin, is shown in a black dress with her hair partially down, lying comfortably (and seductively) on a sofa. The music accompanying this image is in a minor mode with fast, suspenseful arpeggiation in the upper keyboard register. From her sofa, VanDeerlin states: "Hi, I'm Gwendolyn VanDeerlin, president of MTV. As you know, MTV has always been against censorship, but the growing number of multiple-career MTV families has made parental supervision more difficult [the camera pans the room, a piece of paper and a pair of glasses are shown on furniture, reminding the viewer of her professional status]. That's why we recommend the MTV chip [the chip is shown, held in hand]. This simple device inserted in your TV set will allow you to limit the amount of time your parents watch MTV [the image of adult is shown in front of television with remote in hand]. Don't let the government control what your parents can watch. That's your job" [a male voiceover and text is shown on screen: 'MTV: It's a right and a responsibility']." In addition to its satirically humorous content, this commercial also functions in establishing at least four distinct groups: the parents, the viewers, MTV (in alliance with the viewers), and the government, which oversees all. In this instance, the viewers are homogenized and treated as a single unity that must band together to "save" the parents and protect themselves from the government's dangerous directives.

MuchMusic's commercials, meanwhile, tended to be more playful and did not identify collectivities. In "The Mime" commercial, for instance, a mime unsuccessfully performs a series of movements, including the moonwalk and the robot; he is then hit with a brick at the end as "MuchMusic" and "Express Yourself" are written across the screen. MuchMusic's commercials, while arguably subversive, were extremely playful and self-identified as "low budget," and they refused to take any sort of overt stance on any topic. Unlike the MTV commercials that carefully delineated the viewing audience by making distinctions between them, their parents, and the government, MuchMusic tended to include humor but did not strive for shared cohesiveness of viewing subgroups.

TIME, SPACE, AND MEDIA BIASES

In this rather detailed analysis I have attempted to delineate how the musical and extra-musical parameters on MuchMusic reinforced the perception of a wide-ranging audience. These parameters include the station's programming on the half-hour level, the presence of both the studio audience and the VJs who represent Canada's multiethnic plurality, and the twelve-year historical depth of the video repertoire. I would argue that through these initiatives MuchMusic evoked and reinforced discursively produced Canadian narratives of plurality and collectivity. In contrast, on MTV the programming did not delineate musical preferences so sharply, and the individual rather than the collective was always prioritized. In addition, on MTV the VJs and the guests spoke to the individual viewer while they announced artists and videos (with either a cup of coffee in the morning or surrounded by candles at night), the current video repertoire was always foregrounded, and the commercials identified the viewer as youth who (even if only satirically) should be wary of authority figures.

The sum of these differences can be more broadly identified by each station's media biases, which in turn indicate additional national inflections. For insight into these partialities, I borrow from the work of the communications theorist and historian Harold Innis.[35] In *The Bias of Communication* Innis details how Western communications media privilege space over time. Kim Sawchuck, in his essay "An Index of Power: Innis, Aesthetics, and Technology," states that Innis's "concepts of space and time articulated a theory of power for both realms: hierarchical (temporal . . . based in the oral tradition) and decentralized (spatial . . . based on the eye)."[36] In other words, time-biased media emphasize interpersonal, short-distance communication whereas space-biased media, which include print media, telegraphs, and, today, communication technologies such as computers and satellites, facilitate the control and quick dissemination of information over far-reaching geographical spaces. Easily replaceable and hypercurrent, these technologies accentuate what Innis calls "the modern obsession with present-mindedness,"[37] while their users propagate the myth that newer is not only better but necessary.

When MTV's 1995 programming is considered within a space and time model, the station's bias is clear: its determination to interrupt household flow illustrated its concern with the visual realm; the ear, secondary to the eye, was used between the videos as a mechanism to direct the viewer back to the visual stimuli. Space was further biased by MTV in its rapid dissemination of videos, its currency, its adaptability through its own timelessness (separate from that of the viewer), its placelessness, and its erasure of collective cultural history. As a result, MTV was extremely mobile. As the station's slogan proudly asserted: "MTV: Coming to you wherever you are."

As Jody Berland puts it, the sacrifices for space bias are significant: "The American empire's predilection for conquering space through media . . . is expressed in its extension of the modernizing, visualizing, and rationalizing space-bias of paper and print . . . obliterating media appropriate to memory, tradition, spirituality, dialogue: all aspects of oral culture that have been appropriated and transformed through the production of technological space."[38] A time-biased medium, as Berland points out, facilitates a sense of history and memory, thus enabling the individual to situate herself or himself within that history. While MuchMusic obviously could not operate as a time-biased medium, orality was clearly injected into their style and content, particularly when they attempted to make explicit the hierarchical positions between the celebrity, the VJ, and the viewer by retaining the VJ to speak to the celebrity on behalf of, and alongside, the viewing audience (MTV elided these unequal positions through techniques like direct address and the absence of an audience). On live performance shows like *Intimate and Interactive*, orality was brought into clear focus as audience members were invited to ask questions of the celebrity by phone, e-mail, or fax or in the form of face-to-face dialogue within the studio. As Innis notes, "The oral tradition involves personal contact and a consideration of the feelings of others,"[39] and this is precisely what MuchMusic attempted to capture in their programming vis-à-vis emotionally intense and engaging personal discussion. When viewed alongside their historically broader video playlist and their explicit temporal and geographical specificity within downtown Toronto, MuchMusic clearly privileged the hierarchical time-biased model articulated by Innis a half century ago.

Unlike viewers who tuned into MTV, MuchMusic's Canadian audience members frequently were reminded that the videos they enjoy represented only a fragment of a wide range of musical styles, and that their generation was but one of many that cross musical tastes, linguistic boundaries, and multiple time zones. By reinforcing discursively produced narratives of cultural diversity and social collectivity, MuchMusic inflected MTV's highly successful format to create new, vibrant, and uniquely Canadian imagined communities, where individuals were invited to participate in a collective celebration of popular music and musical life in Canada.[40]

I thank Rob Bowman, Jody Berland, Beverley Diamond, and Susan Fast for their helpful criticisms of this work, and I also would like to acknowledge the support of the Social Sciences and Research Council of Canada.

1 Benedict Anderson, Imagined Communities: Reflections on the Origin and Spread of Nationalism (London: Verso, 1983).

2 The seminal essays in televisual flow and program analysis can be found in Raymond Williams, Technology and Cultural Form (New York: Schocken Books, 1974). The video sample could either be discrete, meaning specific programs are taped over a period of days, weeks, or months and are examined as a set or, conversely, as continuous samples of an entire day, series of days, or a week. In this study I was not interested in examining particular programs but rather the range of each stations' programming; as such, a simultaneous continuous period of time was deemed most appropriate. The week of November 4–11, 1995, was chosen because it fell between two important events: Halloween and Thanksgiving in the United States. The sample, then, reflected the programming of the stations without being overly skewed by images related to American or Canadian seasonal events.

3 During the taping of the sample, approximately two hours of MTV videotape was mistakenly erased; the programs affected were Rude Awakening and MTV Jams on Tuesday morning, November 7. This accounts for approximately twenty additional videos.

4 For an analysis of gender construction on the two stations, see my "'Simple Economics'? Images of Gender and Nationality on MuchMusic (Canada) and MTV (US)," Women and Music: A Journal of Gender and Culture 4 (2000): 1–17.

5 For exceptions, see Andrew Goodwin, Dancing in the Distraction Factory: Music Television and Popular Culture (Minneapolis: University of Minnesota Press, 1992); and Williams, Technology and Cultural Form (New York: Schocken Books, 1974).

6 Rick Altman, "Television/Sound," in Studies in Entertainment: Critical Approaches to Mass Culture, ed. T. Modleski (Bloomington: Indiana University Press, 1986), 39–54.

7 Ien Ang, Living Room Wars: Rethinking Media Audiences for a Postmodern World (London: Routledge, 1996), 145.

8 See Williams, Technology and Cultural Form.

9 Ibid., 99.

10 The videos originally were divided into twelve categories (the five primary categories of rock, alternative, pop, rap, urban, and a smaller number of videos—such as industrial, folk/traditional, dance, etc.—that did not fit into these categories). Graphing this level of detail, however, did not provide statistically significant results for the smaller genres. Accordingly, the smaller categories were collapsed into one grouping titled "other" videos.

11 Williams, Technology and Cultural Form, 93.

12 Altman, "Television/Sound," 42 (emphasis in original).

13 I would argue that sound (music) without a verbal text allows the viewer to return to household flow, whereas music with a verbal text draws the viewer back into the television flow. Ironically, nondiegetic silence (a portion of a video with no sound whatsoever) also draws the viewer back to the television set: silence is very disruptive and prompts many viewers to explore what is "wrong."

14 Joseph Boggs, The Art of Watching Films, 3rd ed. (London: Addison-Wesley, 1991), 234.

15 Kurt Danziger, Interpersonal Communication (New York: Pergamon Press, 1976), 66.

16 Goodwin, Dancing in the Distraction, 141–42.

17 Altman, "Television/Sound," 40–41.

18 Goodwin, Dancing in the Distraction Factory, 140.

19 John Langer, "Television's Personality System," Media, Culture and Society 4 (1981): 355.

20 Ibid., 352.

21 Ibid., 351.

22 Ibid., 357.

23 Ibid., 355.

24 Ibid., 363.

25 The move by MTV to its Times Square studios in the late 1990s, however, created a new sense of geographical situatedness for the network, particularly during its daily request program, Total Request Live. This flagship program features frequent shots of the New York cityscape and the ever-present crowd of screaming teens gathered on the street below. The studio itself is encased in large windows and the VJs are surrounded by a live studio audience.

26 Erving Goffman, The Presentation of Self in Everyday Life (Garden City, N.Y.: Doubleday, 1959), 22–30.

27 Joshua Meyrowitz, No Sense of Place: The Impact of Electronic Media on Social Behaviour (New York: Oxford University Press, 1985), 64–66.

28 Ibid., 65.

29 The performances are in fact live, usually in front of an audience.

30 P. David Marshall, Celebrity and Power: Fame in Contemporary Culture (Minneapolis: University of Minnesota Press, 1997), 125.

31 Cited in Langer, "Television's Personality System," 354.

32 The videos included here are those that had a "request" logo shown at some point before or during the video.

33 Jack Banks, Monopoly Television: MTV's Quest to Control the Music (Boulder, Colo.: Westview Press, 1996), 127.

34 David Tobenkin, "The All-Music Channels," Broadcasting and Cable 126/127 (1996): 38.

35 Harold Innis, The Bias of Communication (Toronto: University of Toronto Press, 1951). I would like to thank Jody Berland for suggesting Innis's work.

36 Kim Sawchuck, "An Index of Power: Innis, Aesthetics, and Technology," in Harold Innis in the New Century: Reflections and Refractions, ed. C. Acland and W. Buxton (Montreal: McGill-Queens University Press, 1999), 371.

37 Innis, The Bias of Communication, 76.

38 Jody Berland, "Space at the Margins: Colonial Spaciality and Critical Theory After Innis," Topia 1 (1997): 65–66.

39 Innis, The Bias of Communication, 372.

40 While both stations have changed stylistically since 1995, this is particularly true of MTV: after the launching of MTV2, a station dedicated primarily to airing music videos, MTV continued to diversify its programming beyond the video repertoire. As a result, MTV now airs considerably more (often syndicated) programs at the half-hour level, while MTV2 features longer video segments. Moreover, the addition of more recent programs to MTV's lineup suggests that they have been moving toward MuchMusic's time-biased model. Total Request Live is a case in point. This is not to suggest that Total Request Live has adopted MuchMusic's format verbatim: the aired videos are abridged while e-mailed viewer messages are scrolled across the bottom of the screen—all of which is intercut with enthusiastic "live" messages from audience members who momentarily displace the videos both visually and sonically. It could be argued, then, that while some of MTV's programming has moved toward MuchMusic's model (available to American viewers via MuchMusic USA), the station has developed—vis-à-vis the audience— unique and effective strategies to draw the viewers' attention back to the television screen itself, thus sustaining a high level of televisual flow.

ELVIS FROM THE WAIST UP AND OTHER MYTHS: 1950S MUSIC TELEVISION AND THE GENDERING OF ROCK DISCOURSE

Norma Coates

lvis Presley's third appearance on *The Ed Sullivan Show* on January 6, 1957, is commonly accepted as the birth—and the death—of rock and roll on network television. Rock and roll mythology de-emphasizes Presley's many other appearances on television variety programs in 1956. Presley's national television exposure began with multiweek appearances on the Dorsey Brothers' *Stage Show* in January and continued with appearances on *The Milton Berle Show* and *The Steve Allen Show*. Sullivan finally consented to book Presley after losing to Allen the weekly ratings battle in his time slot in the week of Presley's appearance. The fact that Presley's whole body graced his first two Sullivan appearances—or cultural critic Gilbert B. Rodman's well-supported contention that Presley's most risqué 1956 appearance occurred on Milton Berle's show—is minimized, despite the easy availability of visible evidence.[1] Instead, Presley's third Sullivan appearance is invoked to immediately position rock and roll music and culture in opposition to conservative and feminized mass culture, represented in this case by television. Even respected chroniclers of rock and roll history fall into this trap. For example, Charlie Gillett, in *The Sound of the City: The Rise of Rock and Roll*, originally published in 1970 and still one of the best accounts of rock and roll history, avers that "Sullivan allowed Presley on his show provided he wore a dinner suit and the camera was kept above waist level."[2] Again, visual evidence that refutes this is easily available on video anthologies and on cable channels.

Because rock criticism and even rock scholarship exist in something of a vacuum, little has been written about the impact of television, or any other media besides FM radio, on the transformation of gender- and race-inclusive "rock and roll" to white masculine "rock." The cultural critic

David Shumway is one of the only scholars to recognize the importance of the visual aspect of Elvis Presley's appearances on television in defining rock and roll.[3] With this essay, I continue to fill the critical void about the important relationship between television and rock and roll long before the advent of MTV. In particular, I focus upon the impact of television rock and roll in the 1950s on later discourses that inscribed normative masculinity into rock and roll culture.

The selective historiography about Elvis on television in 1956 symbolizes the active exclusion of the feminine from rock and roll discourse, especially as discursive formations emerged around rock and roll in the mid-1960s. This is not a literal exclusion, of course, as women have played significant roles (in one way or another) throughout rock and roll history. The mechanics of this exclusion can be observed in the inaugural issue of *Crawdaddy* magazine in February, 1966. *Crawdaddy* was the first magazine devoted to the critical analysis of rock and roll. Its editor, a Swarthmore undergraduate named Paul Williams, was very clear that his magazine was for those who took rock and roll "very seriously indeed," not the fans who "would debate over who was greater, Elvis or Fabian."[4] Williams's references to two of the major targets of teenage female adulation in the late 1950s, as well as his choice to ignore the enormous appeal to male as well as female audiences of Elvis in 1956, clearly identifies those who would take rock and roll seriously as male, with the implication being that teenage girls did not embrace rock and roll for its aesthetic merits.[5] Williams's 1966 broadsides in the hand-typed pages of his dorm-room magazine marked the beginning of the discourses of rock and roll exceptionalism and authenticity that continue to be reiterated and thus retain their abjecting power.

Given the obvious entry, or at least belated recognition, of women as active participants in most aspects of rock and roll music and its industry, why do the masculinized mythologies of rock and roll remain so active and potent? In this essay I posit one possible answer to this not-so-simple question by focusing on the relationship between the television and music industries in the pre–rock and roll and post–rock and roll 1950s. My primary argument is that the gender roles within rock and roll and, indeed, its masculinization were heavily influenced by prevailing social norms as reiterated and reinforced through television programs and representational, industrial, and economic practices in the 1950s. This influence was especially potent at the point where television intersected with rock and roll, beginning, for this argument as for so many others, in 1956 and continuing through the end of the 1950s. I examine several programs, notably *The Ed Sullivan Show*, *The Big Beat*, and *American Bandstand*, in terms of their reception in the trade press at the time, their fit with the industrial imperatives and conventions of American television in the 1950s, and their later insertion into developing discourses that naturalized a particular inflection of heterosexual masculinity in rock and roll culture. I assert that in critical hindsight these programs, especially *American Bandstand*, caused considerable damage both to the reputation of rock and roll on television and to the primary audience for these programs, teenage-girl music fans. Later rock critics blamed the female fans as much as the performers and the music industry itself for encouraging the musical blandness of the late 1950s.[6]

Rock and roll mythology (along with its implicit demonization of television) remains influential, as indicated by the treatment of the conjunction of the two forms of media in the book *Station to Station: The History of Rock and Roll on Television* (2000), written by the rock critic Marc Weingarten. In light of this point, I offer from Weingarten's book an extended quote about rock and roll on television in the 1950s:

> TV's ultimate mission—to sell things—essentially hasn't changed over the last half century, which makes it the most culturally intransigent electronic medium ever created. We need only track the programming history of the big three networks—CBS, NBC, and ABC—against the cultural and social currents that have roiled America over the past four decades to discover how out of touch TV has been in reflecting the other cultural impulses taking place "outside the box." Rock and roll, on the other hand, was created to provide the insurgent teen culture with a voice and an attitude at variance with mainstream values. It was supposed to stir things up and rage against the decade's complacent, smug ethos, not propagate the status quo. Rock and roll was loud, brash, and impudent; TV was soothing and polite. Rock and roll was sex; TV was violins. Rock and roll was Elvis Presley; TV was Robert Young. TV was black and white; rock and roll was Technicolor—it was black *and* white only in the sense that it accommodated the miscegenation of pop and R&B. If kids wanted to see youth run wild, they had to go to the movies.[7]

Weingarten's analysis speaks to an image of 1950s television that ignores its historical and other contexts, as well as its ongoing relationship with popular music, including the rock and roll genre. To address this issue, I discuss in this essay the industrial, social, and economic contexts in which the television industry launched these and other music programs of the 1950s in order to complicate the notion that television watered down and thereby "feminized" rock and roll in order to exploit and contain it. An understanding of the context in which these programs and presentations of rock and roll were created and launched is less a narrative of co-optation and containment than it is a story of a new medium trying to negotiate between numerous economic, social, cultural, moral, and industrial imperatives.

The television networks, sponsors, and variety-show hosts of the 1950s needed the audience drawn by Elvis Presley and, subsequently, by rock and roll artists, but they did not need the controversy generated by Presley's unbridled performances. I turn now to a discussion of *The Ed Sullivan Show* in the 1950s and how it and other programs, particularly *American Bandstand*, came to represent the feminizing impact of television on rock and roll. I examine *The Ed Sullivan Show* because of its enduring link and importance to the spread and popularity of rock and roll music in the 1950s and 1960s. For example, Elvis Presley appeared on many other programs in 1956 before he was finally invited onto *The Ed Sullivan Show*. His performances on the Dorsey Brothers' *Stage Show*, starting in January 1956, are arguably the most radical and sexualized of Presley's 1956 performances. These performances capture Presley while he was still identified as a rockabilly artist on the Sun Records label, just before he signed with RCA. After his move to RCA, Presley's music acquired a more polished, popular sound. His *Stage Show* appearances also capture his rawness and vitality, which would soon become more of an act as he gained awareness of his power. But Presley's signing by Sullivan meant that he—and rock and roll—had become commercial forces to be reckoned with. Moreover, it is *The Ed Sullivan Show*, not the others, that has become a part of popular memory and consciousness, in large part because of its association with rock and roll.

By 1956 *The Ed Sullivan Show* was an institution. It had no "brow" as it breeched promiscuously the boundaries of high-, low-, and middle-brow culture. For most Americans, the Sullivan show represented the best of culture from both the U.S. and abroad. It drew a huge audience every Sunday night. For performers, an appearance on the program guaranteed mass popularity; for the sponsor, it guaranteed great profit. It was incumbent upon Sullivan, then, to deliver an inoffensive program that would meet the needs of his entire constituency. Presley, and rock and roll, disturbed the equilibrium that Sullivan had coaxed out of television's inherent conflict between the public good and private profit.

The Ed Sullivan Show, originally titled The Toast of the Town, premiered in 1948, the same year as the Texaco Star Theater. Sullivan's program outlasted all of the other "great" variety shows of the era, and it remained on the air virtually unchanged in format until 1971, when it was canceled by CBS along with other programs lacking so-called urban appeal. Sullivan was hardly an avuncular figure. He was an ungainly, tongue-tied, nationally syndicated New York gossip columnist. Oddly, this persona contributed to his appeal. That a gossip columnist could become television's most successful variety program host is not surprising. Sullivan may have succeeded where arguably more talented individuals did not because of his particular inflection of the variety program. In many ways, Sullivan's program was closer to the spirit of traditional vaudeville than were the more well-known, arguably better, variety shows of television's early years. Your Show of Shows and Texaco Star Theater focused on sketch comedy, which was only a part of a typical vaudeville show. Each weekly edition of The Ed Sullivan Show contained the same main components as a basic vaudeville show, as well as "something for the youngsters." As the vaudeville historian Albert F. McLean Jr. asserts, "At one time or another vaudeville brought just about every form of entertainment known to man under its umbrella, but its main components were those drawn from early variety shows—skits, songs, dances, and comic monologues— together with some of the minstrel show's humor and the staples of circus programs—acrobats and animals."[8] Here McLean could have been describing a typical Sullivan hour, minus the overt minstrel routine.

The Ed Sullivan Show and Ed Sullivan the persona epitomized the dual nature of 1950s culture. The program's elevation, in nostalgic hindsight, to the position of sacred text, as well as exemplar of a kinder, gentler time in American culture, is evidence of Sullivan's skill in submerging the contradictions covered over by the veneer of benign pluralism.[9] The Ed Sullivan Show helped to ease the introduction of television into the American home with its (and Sullivan's) particular vision of "something for everyone." Every Sunday night, viewers would be treated to acts as disparate as opera and rock and roll, serious dramatic readings and children's puppets. Sullivan also brought his audience overseas to Europe in an effort to showcase acts that he considered the best that the "high-culture" continent had to offer to American families. Sullivan's archived papers indicate that he was passionate about his vision and thus took the lead role in finding and booking acts for his show.

As much as Sullivan avowed to focus on pleasing the American people, he was most motivated by the weekly Trendex ratings detailing the number of viewers tuned into messages for his sponsors. Numbers and dollars thus dictated Sullivan's vision of "family entertainment" or "cultural enlightenment." For example, Sullivan canceled a contract for a multiweek series of vignettes by the Metropolitan Opera after the ratings proved to be abominable. Sullivan could rail against certain acts or individual performers as being in bad taste or inappropriate for his core family audience, but he would do a quick reversal whenever he lost the ratings race in his time slot. The paramount example of Sullivan's fluctuating definition of good taste was his very public refusal to book Elvis Presley on the show in 1956. Sullivan had been quoted as saying that Presley "would never go on our show. Ours is a family show. If I were selling cigarets, maybe I'd book him, but how many Elvis Presley fans are going to buy new cars?" (a direct reference to his sponsor, the Lincoln-Mercury division of Ford Motor Company).[10] Elvis, apparently, went from being in bad taste to being in good taste, as well as a great car salesman, as soon as his appearance on *The Steve Allen Show* helped that program beat Sullivan in the ratings one Sunday night. Sullivan soon booked Presley for three appearances, paying him an unprecedented fee of $50,000.[11] By the mid-1960s, Sullivan was taking credit for discovering Presley.[12] His later published comments about this and other "discoveries" reveal an artificiality and duplicity that later rock critics would attribute to television as they constructed it, its programs, and even its performers as an inauthentic compared to "real" rock and roll.

Nevertheless, Ed Sullivan and his eponymous program have stuck in American cultural memory for a role that Sullivan played inadvertently, that of rock and roll impresario. An appearance on the Sullivan show in the 1960s catapulted bands into public consciousness, and in the case of the first U.S. appearance of the Beatles on February 9, 1964, it fueled a cultural revolution. But rock and roll's association, indeed need for, Sullivan and his program was fraught with tension, a tension central to the relationship between the television and music industries over the presentation of rock and roll. By the 1960s, Sullivan's program was a necessary evil for rock artists seeking to find an audience or to promote their latest release. Sullivan's concerns for propriety would translate into a further revilement of television by counterculture critics, especially rock journalists. Their contempt would feed into their ongoing scorn for television as a feminine and feminizing medium.

Rock and roll was a necessary evil for Sullivan, too. Throughout his television career he frequently found himself caught between a vision of his moral mission to maintain an archaic conception of cultural propriety and his overwhelming need to win each week's ratings race in his Sunday-night time slot. *The Ed Sullivan Show* embodies tensions between the public and private inherent in commercial television from the 1950s to the present time. Rock and roll, particularly in the 1950s, posed thorny problems for program hosts like Sullivan, along with his sponsors, and the network and stations that distributed his program, in that it was discursively constructed as an outlaw form of entertainment. It was therefore consistent with the public-interest responsibilities granted to television stations to withhold rock and roll from America's television screens. At the same time, television's sponsors sought to make the most money they could from the medium, and it was the responsibility of figures like Sullivan to make it for them. Rock and roll attracted the lucrative teenage audience to the screen in an unprecedented manner, and thus profit-making trumped public interest—to an extent. By the mid-1950s, Ed Sullivan had established himself as America's paternalistic arbiter of family entertainment. His "blessing" of Presley as "a real fine boy" after an appearance on his program helped to establish a place for rock and roll on television. It also helped later rock critics to blast television as a corrupter of authentic rock and roll.

As noted above, Sullivan's ability to manage the inherent contradiction between television's public and private imperative was ultimately tested, and compromised, by the advent of rock and roll music in the form of Elvis Presley. Presley was more than a performer—he was representative of an increasingly powerful social group, the teenager, and their economic power. Sullivan, along with other television variety-show hosts, were thus forced to choose between social propriety and winning ratings. Ever the scoop-loving newspaperman, he chose ratings. In the meantime, his program, and the errant nostalgia that figured it as a symbol of tradition and ultimately an enemy of progress, inadvertently set the stage for the gendering of rock and roll as a white heterosexual male form. This process would be greatly assisted by other rock and roll music programs of the late 1950s.

Before addressing these other programs, I first want to note that it is important to understand the various contexts in which rock and roll on television was situated. Televised rock and roll highlighted points of friction between two media that were at the same time complementary and often incompatible. Popular music was an integral part of television from the dawn of network programming, but it was difficult for television programmers to provide an effective visual treatment of music on television outside of variety-show appearances or the insertion of songs into dramatic programs. Rock and roll exacerbated this problem, because its performance was almost too visual: rock and roll artists wiggled the wrong way, or were the "wrong" color and threatened to wiggle the wrong way, for family television. Performances of rock and roll thus challenged the television industry and its sponsors' avowed desired to deliver "appropriate" entertainment into the sanctity of the (white) American home, and in so doing opened the medium to popular, critical, and political attack.

But rock and roll drew teenagers, an important "market in training," to the television set in an unprecedented manner. Rock and roll was therefore an economic godsend for the television industry and its sponsors; indeed, its money-making ability could not be denied or ignored. Ed Sullivan and others who lived and died by the Trendex ratings found themselves in the midst of a Hobson's choice: feature rock and roll performers and risk a degree of public disapproval, or ignore rock and roll and lose money. Needless to say, they chose the former. The trade press of the mid-1950s documents that it was widely supposed that rock and roll was a fad that would quickly die out. Therefore, why not make the money and run? The "solution" to the challenge posed by rock and roll on television was to water it down—that is, to make it more acceptable for mass consumption while the fad was at its peak, then wait for the fad to die out on its own. There was no reason to suppose that rock and roll would not do so, as music fads such as the popularity of crooners in the 1930s and the bobbysoxer mania for Frank Sinatra in the 1940s were contained and faded away. The fact that this move was "contextually consistent" given the era's social and cultural mores, as well as its audience expectations and interests, was ignored by later rock critics who mapped the countercultural values of the 1960s that they espoused onto the very different public values of the 1950s. Thus the rock and roll television of the late 1950s, beginning with the treatment of Elvis on both the Ed Sullivan and Steve Allen variety shows, and the representative youth music program of the era, *American Bandstand*, was to shoulder the blame for the near-death of rock and roll.

As noted above, the critical hindsight about 1950s music programs espoused by 1960s and 1970s rock criticism was complicit in naturalizing rock and roll music as a white, male, and heterosexual cultural form. As I will demonstrate, much of this programming was targeted to prepubescent females (the much-maligned "teenyboppers"), their older teenage sisters, and young housewives. Because masculinity was not immanent in rock and roll in this (and any other) period, it was constructed into the form as discourses about "authenticity" were created, circulated, and reiterated in the 1960s. As part of these discourses, television came to symbolize the artificial and, in a critical schema ruled by binary thinking, the feminine. Televised rock and roll became representative of the inauthentic, and its feminine, or more accurately feminized, audience was placed in a marginal position in rock and roll culture and discourse.

Rock and roll discourse, emanating as it does from a link to and concern with the industrial, social, and cultural dynamics of popular music in the 1960s, does not take into account the parallel dynamics of the television industry in the 1950s. Television in the mid-1950s was well on its way to becoming a truly mass medium, but utopian hopes and visions for its future still remained. This period has since been constructed as television's "golden age" of anthology drama, strong writing, and the hallowed virtue of "liveness" that provided it with a degree of cultural legitimacy that it has not been able to obtain since.[13] A decision to "water down" rock and roll, if it were a conscious decision at all, was not made in a vacuum. Rather, social, cultural, economic, and audience expectations all came to bear upon programming decisions and conventions.

Rock and roll was a programming challenge on many levels. It was connected to two important changes that would have an enormous impact on all aspects of American life: the economic birth of the teenager, and the civil rights movement. Rock and roll was a musical form that appealed to the new white, suburban, affluent teenager, and it was directly descended from the rhythm and blues music that had been popular in African American communities for a decade. If that weren't problematic enough, the music also had strong roots in the "hillbilly" music of the

American South and the folk music popularized by the left-leaning intelligentsia (who were not the most popular people in the mid-1950s). Through its lineage alone, rock and roll threatened the cozy picture of American political and social life as comfortably pluralistic yet oddly homogeneous, thus espousing a key contradiction at the core of American civic life. As the music historian Trent Hill observes, rock and roll provided a means by which "subterranean social forces" could assert themselves. While rock and roll, he argues, "may have been fine for the kids, for their parents and the other authorities rock & roll was a threatening reminder of the existence of others and otherness that set a dangerous precedent that had to be examined, understood, criticized and controlled."[14]

Perhaps the biggest threat of rock and roll was its overt recognition of the plausibility of racial miscegenation. Musical miscegenation could to some extent be contained, as it had in jazz, but rock and roll had a much wider appeal. It was a short step from the fear of musical miscegenation, the primary effects of which were between the ears, to the fear of racial miscegenation, concerned with feelings lower down the body. Rock and roll thus challenged and put into crisis the prevailing racial and sexual mores of the day.

Indeed, rock and roll gave rise to a "dangerous" mixing of the races, physically through the mixed-race revues popularized by leading disk jockeys, and aurally through the widespread broadcast of rhythm and blues music on the radio. Such mixing threatened to upset the prevailing racial norms of the 1950s, in the North as well as in the South.[15] Rock and roll was also, and often incorrectly, articulated to juvenile delinquency, in part because of the visual iconography of black leather jackets, black or blue jeans, and outlaw hairstyles circulated by the spate of movies produced in the mid-1950s to capitalize on rock and roll's appeal to youth.[16]

The problem for television programmers and variety-show hosts like Ed Sullivan was that rock and roll's white teen audience was too large and too wealthy for them to ignore. This was compounded, if not confounded, by the fact that the teen audience was hard to reach as well as hard for television sponsors to rationalize. Articles from various industry and business magazines of the era indicate that although there was much eagerness to capture the teen audience, there was great uncertainty as to why. That this was a market with great potential spending power was clear: a 1956 article in *Sponsor* quoted a study by the Gilbert

Youth Research Organization, the leading market research firm specializing in teen tastes and trends in the 1950s, which estimated that year's teenage buying market to be between nine and ten billion dollars.[17]

This article, published at the height of Elvis Presley's popularity in 1956, grappled with whether or not Presley and other rock and roll artists could sell basic consumer goods. Rock and roll could do so, the article concluded, but only for a while. As a trend, it would soon die out. In the meantime, rock and roll could "plant for the harvest," that is, condition youth to brand names as they prepared to become adult consumers. Radio was deemed to be the best medium for reaching teens with product messages, particularly about items such as shaving products, cosmetics, personal hygiene products, milk, ice cream, and soda, which were perceived to be staples of teenage life that would carry over into adulthood.[18]

The article also claimed that teenage girls spent more time than their male counterparts listening to rock and roll on the radio. Girls were also responsible for a slim majority of record purchases. Radio and television sponsors, the article implied, would be well served by targeting the teenage girl audience. Given the young average age of marriage in the 1950s, these girls would soon be nineteen-year-old homemakers and mothers. Or, if they chose to go to college instead, they would spend an average of $456.22 as a college freshman to outfit themselves and their dorm rooms.[19] But teenage girls, according to a 1955 Ohio State University study quoted in the article, lost their taste for "hot" music once they assumed adult responsibilities and purchasing power. By their late teens, "their taste veers to the sweet and 'schmaltzy' (*viz.* Lawrence Welk, Liberace)."[20]

The teen audience, especially teenage girls, was well worth capturing, but rock and roll was a potentially dangerous lure, the use of which could backfire on sponsors and stations. Radio play was bad enough, but teens would shortly outgrow rock and roll and move on to more appropriate music, or so it was thought. Rock and roll radio could, therefore, be tolerated in the short term in order to make money for sponsors and radio stations. Presenting rock and roll on television in a noncontroversial manner was much more problematic, for economic as well as social reasons. That television was seen as well as heard opened the medium, the networks, and its sponsors to greater scrutiny and criticism. Rock and roll was more potent, and thus more dangerous, on television. The potential sales impact of Elvis Presley's 1956 television appearances was clear early on. Rock and roll, particularly in the person of Presley, drew the teen audience to the television screen. It also drew great criticism, which was aimed more at the television industry than at Presley himself.

Jack Gould, the influential television critic for the *New York Times* in the 1950s, fired a damaging broadside at the television industry in an article written for the widely read Sunday edition, published September 9, 1956, after Presley's first appearance on the *Ed Sullivan Show*. Presley had been appearing on national television since January of that year. Gould wrote a short article about Presley on June 6, 1956, describing the performer "as a rock-and-roll variation on one of the most standard acts in show business: the virtuoso of the hootchy-kootchy."[21] In this second article Gould, whose *New York Times* pulpit made him perhaps the most influential critic of the era, placed the blame for rock and roll and its attendant evils on the television industry's pursuit of profit at any moral cost. The headline said it all: "Elvis Presley—Lack of Responsibility Is Shown by TV in Exploiting Teen-Agers." The full brunt of Gould's wrath fell on Presley's performance on the previous week's *Ed Sullivan Show*. Gould grudgingly acknowledged that television was not alone and that the magazine and recording industries shared the blame for casting rock and roll upon the national scene, as well as white teenage affluence, mobility, and hormones. But in his analysis, television, as a medium created and programmed by adults who should know better, had the most opportunity—and necessity—to act responsibly to stem the spread of rock and roll and its attendant social maladies. Television was free, providing easy access to its wares. Therefore, young children as well as teens could be "overstimulated" by Presley's bump and grind. Gould was especially critical of a "perennial weakness in the executive echelons of the networks . . . their opportunistic rationalization of television's function." He characterized the industry's code as giving the public what they want, and he condemned them for abrogating their social responsibility to that end, fulminating that "when this code is applied to teen-agers just becoming conscious of life's processes, not only is it manifestly without validity but it, alas, is perilous. Catering to the interests of the younger generation is one of television's main jobs; because those interests do not always coincide with parental tastes should not deter the broadcasters. But selfish exploitation and commercialized overstimulation of youth's physical impulses is certainly a gross national disservice."[22]

Whether Gould's condemnation inspired Sullivan and his producers to present Presley from the waist up in a subsequent appearance is unclear.[23] Gould's implicit condemnation of network executives and his reminder of their social responsibilities likely influenced the subsequent presentation of rock and roll on network television. They could not stop showing rock and roll, as it drew a desired audience for potential sponsors, but neither could they continue to take the blame for disseminating and furthering the cause of a perceived social ill. In turn, making rock and roll acceptable for network television meant moving it further away from its roots in rhythm and blues — thus literally whitening both the composition of its groups and its sound, regardless of the race of its performers.

Moreover, by 1957 it was clear that rock and roll would be more than a fleeting fad, thus making it in the television establishment's best interest to exploit it for profit while they could. Accordingly, the ABC television network — still in the shadows of the giant networks of CBS and NBC and trying to establish a niche for itself — decided to experiment with rock and roll programming in a stand-alone format. Their first attempt involved signing Alan Freed (the Cleveland disk jockey who popularized the term "rock and roll" to make rhythm and blues more palatable to the white audience) for a thirteen-week stint as the host of *Alan Freed's Big Beat*. The program premiered on Friday, July 12, at 10:30 PM eastern time. Freed was signed by ABC after a rock and roll program hosted by the disk jockey scored a solid 13.3 rating earlier that year. The network took special care, according to its programming chief Ted Fetter, to ensure that "the show was acceptable as family fare — screening lyrics and inviting a selected studio audience, culled from Freed's own fan club." Fetter also mentioned that the network had not received any viewer complaints about the racially mixed talent lineup.[24]

Nevertheless, the program's late prime-time slot owes as much to the fear of televising rock and roll as to ABC's hunting for an available slot. *Billboard*'s review of the initial program of the thirteen-week series states that there were no commercials, thus indicating that ABC had not yet found a sponsor brave enough to bankroll a rock and roll program. The reviewer, Charlie Sinclair, opened his critique by gently but decidedly castigating both rock and roll and ABC for the program's mediocrity: "The Big Beat" is hygienic rock and roll. Under the watchful eye of ABC's network censors, the show's cameras view the acts from the waist up.

Forced thus to stand or fall primarily on its minor musical merits, this Alan Freed package frequently stands around with egg on its electronic face." Sinclair continued in this vein, criticizing the program's flaccid presentation of rock and roll while also criticizing the music itself and its audience. Sinclair also questioned ABC's wisdom in presenting a program with little adult appeal that was instead "slanted toward teenagers—who seldom watch TV anyway." Sinclair's pen threw acid on the host itself, too, describing Freed as combining "the unctuous charm of Ralph Edwards with the manic gymnastics of Jerry Lewis."[25] A bad audience combined with bad music made for, in Sinclair's view, bad television.

Freed's program did not stay on the air long. This was not due to its quality or the lack of an audience, but because it transgressed television's—and 1950's society's—racial boundaries. Freed had long flirted with trouble by staging gala rhythm and blues and later rock and roll revues that drew racially mixed audiences. Often, the races were physically separated within the host auditoriums to prevent contact, especially mixed dancing. Although it was especially important to maintain this division on television, doing so did not seem difficult because the programs were open to white audiences only. African American performers were not excluded, and indeed they comprised many of the popular bands. According to Freed's biographer John Jackson, the program was after the third week immediately canceled by ABC because of the public uproar caused when its cameras caught the African American performer and show guest Frankie Lymon dancing with a white teenage girl.[26] As I discuss below, ABC's timidity and subsequent treatment of Freed would add fuel to the critical condemnation of the payola scandal that ruined Freed's career in the early 1960s, and from which another television disk jockey, Dick Clark, escaped with his reputation even enhanced.

Despite this setback, ABC went ahead with its plans to introduce an afternoon rock and roll dance program. Dance programs targeted to teenagers were a staple of early local and network programming. The renowned bandleader Paul Whiteman was ABC's music director in its early days, and he hosted its TV-Teen Club dance program for years. Local stations in big cities throughout the country, including Chicago, Detroit, and Minneapolis, presented afternoon dance parties for teenagers.[27] As reported in Billboard late in 1956, "Altho record shows have yet to gain general acceptance at the network level, the TV disk jockey format has become increasingly important in the local station market in the last year."[28] The foray by ABC into the world of dance programs launched a television institution—and gave rock and roll on television a bad reputation among the rock cognoscenti until the dawning of the cable era.

Of the many stations that produced local disk jockey programs, none was more successful than WFIL in Philadelphia, home of *American Bandstand*—an afternoon "dance party" featuring local teens dancing to the lip-synched beat of their favorite rock and roll bands. *American Bandstand* premiered as *Bandstand* on October 6, 1952, and it "was a sensation from the start."[29] From the start, *Bandstand* was little more than visual radio, fitting into the early television category of "disk jockey program." It drew high ratings, as local teens did not seem to tire of watching other local teens dancing. Moreover, dances seen on the program would soon spawn local dance fads. Although primarily a venue for the saccharine white pop music of the day, *Bandstand*, encouraged by some of its teenage regulars, occasionally experimented with African American rhythm and blues music and artists—a trendsetting and taboo move for television in the pre–rock and roll era.

Much of *Bandstand*'s early energy and success came from its host, the experienced Philadelphia disk jockey Bob Horn. A sex scandal involving a teenage girl ended Horn's career in 1956, just as rock and roll was beginning to make its impact. A young and ambitious WFIL disk jockey, Dick Clark, was tapped to take Horn's place. Clark's tenure with *American Bandstand* began on July 9, 1956, and did not end until March 1989. The show itself ended six months later. Clark's public persona was squeaky clean, as was his vision of the show. When the sex scandal involving Horn broke open in 1956, Clark used his "choir-boy" image to disassociate his program from it. This effort also entailed keeping the show clean and free of any untoward physicality. John Jackson quotes a 1990 interview in which Clark claimed that had Bandstand been "a snake pit of writhing bodies," it would have been "off the air in a week."[30]

American Bandstand premiered on ABC as an afternoon program just as *The Big Beat* was imploding. According to a recollection printed in Leonard Goldenson's autobiography (Goldenson was ABC's chairman in this period and was instrumental in its establishment as the third major network), his president, Ollie Treyz, was responsible for bringing *American Bandstand* to network television. Treyz, an advertising industry veteran, enjoyed poring through ratings books. On one of his forays into audience numbers, he was struck by the consistently high ratings garnered by a local afternoon entry on Philadelphia's WFIL television station. He contacted an associate in Philadelphia and requested a kinescope of *American Bandstand*. As Treyz recounts: "I saw the Kine, and I thought, I can see why. I had a 16 mm Kine projector at home, so I showed it to my kids, and they liked it. I told them, Bring in all your school friends, the girls, get them to come over. I was interested in the girls' reaction, because I saw girls dancing with girls. And they loved it. They asked to see it again. They loved that kind of music and the dancing, the Twist and all that. 'Would you come home and watch that right after school?' Oh, yes, they would."[31] If this recollection is correct, it is notable because Treyz's children, both boys, were nine and five at the time.[32] Their "school friends" would have been prepubescent junior high and elementary school students, or "teenyboppers," not teenage rock and roll fans. *American Bandstand* and, by association, music on television would suffer at the hands of later rock critics and aficionados for being aimed at teenyboppers, preteens who had not yet developed "good" musical taste.

In its network incarnation, *American Bandstand* helped ABC—and local stations—solve a number of problems. *American Bandstand* and local dance programs reached the elusive teenage audience in unprecedented numbers.[33] On October 7, 1957, *Billboard* reported that *American Bandstand* was the number one program in its time period (3:00–4:30 PM eastern time) according to the September, 1957, Trendex report. According to Trendex, the program's 5.7 rating and 35.6 audience share were 62 percent higher than CBS's numbers and 35 percent higher than NBC's during those time slots.[34] Regionally broadcast and syndicated dance programs were also doing well.[35]

Indeed, *American Bandstand* drew the teen audience. The program highlighted performances (usually lip-synched) of hit songs by the original artists, white or African American.[36] A set of regular dancers soon developed, and the romances and friendships between them became as much of the program's appeal to teen viewers as the music. *American Bandstand* also drew an unexpected bonanza to the screen—homemakers who were not interested in game shows or soap operas, the other afternoon fare.[37] The younger average age of marriage in the 1950s meant that many homemakers were barely out of their teens, if they were out of them at all. *American Bandstand*'s success in pulling this audience also disproved the idea that women turned to Lawrence Welk for musical pleasure upon marriage.

American Bandstand's best asset, in terms of its appeal to television executives, was Dick Clark. A 1958 *Variety* article attributed Clark's success to his "underemotional, relaxed 'all-American boy' personality."[38] These same qualities would later be used in rock culture to diminish Clark and his program's achievements. Even more heinous in the eyes of rock critics, Clark was a one-man record promotion giant. A representative of the Dealers of Greater St. Louis, a trade organization of music store owners, called Clark "the greatest stimulant to the record business we as dealers have ever known."[39] *American Bandstand*'s Trendex rating of 5.6 topped both NBC and CBS in the 4:00–4:30 PM time slot just two months after its national introduction on ABC.[40]

Sponsors were eager to jump on the Dick Clark bandwagon, too. Although the half-hour version of *American Bandstand*, presented on Monday nights at 7:30 PM from October 7, 1957, to December 30, 1957, failed miserably, ABC created a new vehicle for Clark.[41] *The Dick Clark Show* was essentially a half-hour version of *American Bandstand* combined with a liberal sprinkling of *Your Hit Parade*. One of the program's attractions was the weekly "*American Bandstand* Top Ten," a preview of the songs that would be featured on the afternoon program during the following week. Unlike *Your Hit Parade*, only the hit performances of featured songs were offered, and they were performed, or more often lip-synched, by the original artists.[42] *Variety*, normally no friend to rock and roll television, published a glowing review of the program's premiere. The review was particularly sanguine about Clark, whom it called "a young wholesome type who makes with hip chatter," and his ability to "gain a hefty adult quotient" for the program.[43] Accordingly, the audience for the Saturday night *Dick Clark Show* was estimated to be over half adult. The other half, teenagers, comprised 40 percent of the market for chewing gum, thereby leading Beech-Nut Gum to sign on as its sponsor two weeks into the program's run. An early 1959 article in *Printer's Ink* forecast that the company would soon announce a sizable gain over the previous year's sales. The article quoted a company spokesman as declaring, "I can tell you quite frankly, we hope we'll be associated with Dick Clark for a long time. He's an outstanding salesman, the kind that a company like Beech-Nut welcomes."[44]

This very attractiveness to sponsors, and what was later perceived as the program's, and Clark's, championing of the prefabricated "teen idols" of the late 1950s, particularly Fabian and Bobby Rydell from Philadelphia, caused the program's contributions to the spread and legitimization of rock and roll to be obscured and ignored. That is not to say that *American Bandstand* did not "sanitize" rock and roll to some extent. Indeed, the program was complicit in the relegation of most African American artists, except those who could emulate a white pop sound, to the newly reghettoized rhythm and blues category. *American Bandstand* cemented rock and roll as a white musical form. The racial implications of this move on what would become rock and rock culture were skirted over later by white rock critics who turned rock into a signifier of white masculinity and authenticity and denied the implications of its African American roots as much as did Clark's programs.

Dick Clark and *American Bandstand* cannot shoulder all of the blame for the whitening and mainstreaming of rock and roll. Certainly, the program circulated wholesome images of rock and roll and popularized artists who were more congruent with the conservative sexual and social mores of the late 1950s than were rhythm and blues artists and first-wave rock and rollers like Elvis Presley. The cultural historian Brian Ward's observation that the program "stood both as a testament to rock and roll's rapprochement with white middle-class values, and as an example of the dominant culture's capacity to absorb, transform and ultimately commodify 'threatening' sub-cultural styles in accordance with its own core values" exemplifies the usual critical assessment of the program.[45]

Ward's point is accurate but incomplete. The mainstreaming of a cultural form is neither complete nor irreversible. Mainstreaming will always create insiders and outsiders, and not necessarily those that are obvious. For example, the mainstreaming of rock and roll turned it into a predominantly white form of popular culture. This point is generally acknowledged. At the same time, this operation turned rock and roll into a predominantly male and heterosexual preserve of "authenticity" and resistant culture, positioned against the feminized "other" of "inauthentic" and commercialized popular culture—and music—promoted on television. That is, the same white middle-class values cited by Ward as an inauthentic and feminizing influence on rock and roll drew on the middle-class gender politics of the 1950s to do so. Rock's "counterculture" may have run counter to mainstream middle-class values in some ways, but it depended upon and reinforced them in others.

It was, and remains, easier to place the blame on television, teenyboppers, and teen idols for rock and roll's "mainstreaming" in the late 1950s than to scrutinize the internalized value systems of those who defined the discursive boundaries of "rock culture" in the 1960s. This is not to claim that there were no efforts to contain rock and roll. For example, it may be compellingly argued that it was the payola scandal of 1959 and 1960s, coming on the heels of the television quiz show scandals, that forced some of the pioneering rock and roll deejays, most notably Alan Freed, off the air. Payola, a practice in which disk jockeys received money from record companies to play new songs, was a long-standing practice that preceded rock and roll by almost a century. The music historian John Jackson, for example, traces payola back to 1863. According to Jackson, representatives of ASCAP, the composer and publisher's organization associated with the pre–rock and roll music industry, took advantage of the political and popular outrage engendered by the quiz show scandals in an attempt to shut down rock and roll and its primary publisher, rival BMI.[46] The only notable rock and roll disk jockey to survive the payola scandals with his reputation—and job—intact was Dick Clark. It is well documented that Clark's business interests were very much entwined with the recordings of many performers featured on *American Bandstand*.[47] That Clark came out of the payola hearings unscathed while others suffered grave consequences is marshaled as evidence of his fiscal importance to big broadcasting, notably ABC. Jackson reports Alan Freed's opinion that "because Dick Clark grossed about $12 million a year for the ABC network, compared to Freed's $250,000 yearly figure for the local WABC radio, there was no doubt in his mind that ABC had a double standard for him and for Clark."[48]

I have no doubt that Clark's utility to ABC, and the television magnetism and savvy that each day attracted teenage and adult female audiences to *American Bandstand*, influenced more than a little the outcome of the payola hearings. I argue, however, that rock and other cultural critics overemphasize *how* hegemonic tactics contained rock and roll in the late 1950s. A more interesting area to explore is *why* it was so easy to do so.

Blaming the mainstreaming of rock and roll on television genres, conventions, and programs and foisting prefabricated teen idols onto unsophisticated female audiences solves but a part of the puzzle. I suggest that the culture was not ready for the generational rebellion and massive social changes that pushed rock and roll firmly onto the scene in the 1960s. Programs such as *American Bandstand*, *The Ed Sullivan Show*, and

Ozzie and Harriet may be perceived as mainstreaming rock and roll, but they can also be seen as paving the way for the cultural importance of 1960s rock and roll. Mainstreaming, particularly of cultural forms, is a much more contradictory process than generally is considered. I suggest that the answer has as much to do with cultural receptiveness as with a program, organized or otherwise, of cultural repression. Hegemonic forces can always be marshaled to wipe out or decrease the power of an oppositional cultural form, but, as in the 1960s, they do not always succeed in full. Why did this work, to some extent, in the late 1950s?

Articles in the music trade, business, and "lifestyle" magazines and newspapers of the late 1950s confirm that rock and roll was very popular among teenagers, generally defined as belonging to the 12–18 age cohort. But while we can comfortably assert that rock and roll was the primary form of popular music embraced by teenagers in the 1960s, their counterparts in the 1950s were not as parochial in their listening habits. Mitch Miller, the artists and repertoire head of Columbia records, noted in 1956 that teens still had a fondness for conventional pop music, for which he cites the enduring popularity with that audience of more mainstream artists such as Johnny Ray and the vocal group the Four Lads. Miller, portrayed in the trade press as an outspoken critic of rock and roll, sought to disavow or at least temper that image by stating, "What is necessary is a balanced viewpoint and a long range view." Miller also noted that rock and roll's popularity "reminded us [the mainstream music industry] of the necessity of stressing the element of rhythm in our pop recordings."[49] Miller is often pointed to as the exemplar of industry opposition to rock and roll in the 1950s. These observations indicate much more of a rapprochement with rock and roll, not on substantive or creative grounds but on economic ones. Contrary to rock and roll mythology, the music industry did not try to kill rock and roll on moral or economic grounds. They were justifiably uncertain about its "staying power" and its ability to retain the interest of the teen audience as it aged. Given that rock and roll remains discursively constructed as youth music, and that the social pressure, from both sides, is to grow away from it as one ages, Miller's concern is not an idle one. The incorporation of a "heavy beat" into standard pop songs may be viewed as mainstreaming rock and roll, but it may also be viewed as a capitulation to popular tastes.

By the end of the decade rock and roll's circulation via television and radio helped to loosen the grip held on it by censors. June Bundy, in a January 1959 *Billboard* article, asserted that a survey of network continuity-acceptance heads and recording librarians showed that the "public is becoming more broadminded and censors are becoming more lenient about the lyric content of songs aired over both radio and TV (both local and network) every year."[50] Such leniency may be interpreted as a result of the success of a concentrated effort to mainstream rock and roll, but it is equally valid to surmise that rock and roll was becoming accepted as a valid form of popular culture.

An obvious point that is apparently lost on those who criticize the teenybopper audience for Fabian and his ilk in the late 1950s is that these same prepubescent girls would form the core of the audience for the British invasion and other rock and roll bands of the 1960s. More was done, then, to "prep" the audience for rock culture than is generally acknowledged. Indeed, in the 1960s rock culture was created and promoted by college students. In the 1950s, this same age cohort, according to studies and surveys, had little use for rock and roll.[51] Girls have always bought more records than boys; without this audience, rock and roll may never have achieved the power it held for some time.[52] Men were responsible for the discursive gendering of rock and roll in the 1960s, but in the 1950s girls and women drove it economically with their purchases as well as their influence as consumers.

The critical narrative that blames rock and roll programming targeted to teenyboppers, teenage girls, and young adult women for the decline of rock and roll in the late 1950s ignores the salient facts that do not support such a claim. For example, Ed Sullivan is not the only person who "neutered" Elvis Presley. Sullivan, by ordering that cameras be trained on the upper half of Presley's body, provided the crucial visible evidence that is privileged as "truth" of the operation. Little if any blame is placed on Elvis's manager, Colonel Tom Parker, who engineered Elvis's every professional, and occasionally personal, move. In volume two of his painstakingly researched definitive biography of Presley, the cultural historian Peter Guralnick claims that during Presley's stint in the army (1958–1960), Parker undertook a "campaign of scarcity" by withholding new releases to provide the impression that Presley was busy serving his country. The savvy Parker also believed that he was protecting Presley's reputation in the wake of a general slump in the recording industry.[53] Guralnick also chronicles Parker's plan to move Presley to the middle of the

NORMA COATES

road through a series of B-movie vehicles and Parker's choice of mediocre pop songs as Presley's post-army recordings. Parker's impact on Presley's post-army decline has been eschewed by critics who favor a narrative that constructs a dictatorial teenybopper and teenage audience that demanded pop rather than rock and roll.

Many factors contributed to the mainstreaming of rock and roll in the late 1950s, but these have been selectively recalled in order to support the naturalization of the masculinity in rock and roll in the service of myths about the popular form's authenticity and exceptionalism. Rock and roll is no longer the leading music genre favored by or representing youth; in fact, many claim that it no longer exists. If it does exist, it does so in its most extreme forms, championing hyperbolic masculinity and sexuality while reaching out to a small audience of teenage boys. Youth music is fragmented, and if any form now unifies youth as rock and roll did in the 1950s and 1960s, it is rap music, which also is constructed as a masculine preserve. Although rock has fragmented into hundreds of subgenres that often barely resemble the original, it is still regarded as a male form. The male gender of "rock" is no longer as blatant as it was from the 1950s through the 1970s, but the dynamics of its naturalization are still at work in, for example, the use of the term "women in rock" when discussing female rock musicians. The logical semantic mate, "men in rock," is not used when discussing male rock musicians. As I write this essay, the best-selling youth music in the United States falls into the rap and the teenybopper categories. Teenybopper artists such as Britney Spears and the "boy bands" N'Sync and the Backstreet Boys, primarily appeal to prepubescent and teenage girls. Accordingly, these groups, on cable as well as on network television, are the butt of critical and cultural jokes and even some moral panic. Their female fans are as often as vilified as their grandmothers were in the late 1950s. Rock and roll may have fragmented, but its myths, and its constructions of insiders and outsiders, remain curiously potent.

NOTES

1 Gilbert B. Rodman, *Elvis after Elvis: The Posthumous Career of a Living Legend* (New York: Routledge, 1996), 153.
2 Charlie Gillett, *The Sound of the City: The Rise of Rock and Roll* (New York: Pantheon, 1970), 207.

3 David Shumway, "Rock and Roll as a Cultural Practice," in *Present Tense: Rock & Roll and Culture*, ed. Anthony DeCurtis (Durham, N.C.: Duke University Press, 1992), 125.

4 Paul Williams, "Along Comes Maybe," *Crawdaddy*, August 1966, 22.

5 By 1966, Elvis had not appeared publicly for nine years, and his music had moved in the direction of Vegas pop. His touted "comeback" (via television, ironically) was still two years away.

6 For example, the critic Greg Shaw, writing in *The Rolling Stone Illustrated History of Rock & Roll*, the first attempt to create a canon of rock and roll performers, blamed this music on "the teenage girls, the ones in the suburbs who wanted big fluffy candy-colored images of male niceness on which to focus their pubescent dreams." "Teenyboppers" thus remain a convenient villain for critics decrying the sorry state of popular music. See Greg Shaw, "The Teen Idols," in *The Rolling Stone Illustrated History of Rock & Roll* (New York: Rolling Stone Press, 1980), 96–100.

7 Marc Weingarten, *Station to Station: The History of Rock and Roll on Television* (New York: Pocket Books, 2000), 3.

8 Albert F. McLean Jr., *American Vaudeville as Ritual* (Lexington: University of Kentucky Press, 1965), 21–22.

9 See, for example, John Leonard, "Ed Sullivan Died for Our Sins," in *Smoke and Mirrors: Violence, Television, and Other American Cultures* (New York: New Press, 1997).

10 *New York Post*, July 13, 1956.

11 Sullivan's dismissal then embrace of Elvis Presley in 1956 is well documented in many journalistic accounts of the time as well as in recent cultural history and criticism. See, for example, David Halberstam, *The Fifties* (New York: Fawcett Columbine, 1993), 476–79; Peter Guralnick, *Last Train to Memphis: The Rise of Elvis Presley* (Boston: Little, Brown, 1994), 301, 351–53, 378–79; and Gilbert B. Rodman, *Elvis after Elvis: The Posthumous Career of a Living Legend* (New York: Routledge, 1996), 146–54.

12 In a letter to Sir Lew Grade, the talent manager of a number of "British invasion" rock and roll groups, Sullivan claimed to "discover" Presley's drawing power "in a 1956 incident [during] my public appearances throughout the United States for Lincoln-Mercury, in the South. I read newspaper headlines in Southern papers about the then unknown Elvis Presley who was drawing record crowds to Fairgrounds. Because I am a newspaperman, whenever a Page 1 phenomenon occurs—whether it involves and [sic] unknown Presley—or the unknown Beatles . . . my newspaper training instinctively translates a Page 1 story into a Page 1 showbiz attraction." Sullivan spun quite the yarn to Grade, given that his initial opposition to Presley was well documented, as was Presley's previous appearances on network television in 1956 prior to his relatively late-in-the-year initial appearance on the Sullivan program.

13 William Boddy's *Fifties Television: The Industry and Its Critics* (Urbana: University of Illinois Press, 1993) provides an insightful account of the critical and industrial tensions as television grew into a mass medium in the 1950s.

14 Trent Hill, "The Enemy Within: Censorship in Rock Music in the 1950s," in *Present Tense: Rock & Roll and Culture*, ed. Anthony DeCurtis (Durham, N.C.: Duke University Press, 1992), 45–46.

15 This is not to claim that rock and roll had any direct effect on the civil rights movement or in changing the minds of young white Americans regarding racial equality. In fact, Brian Ward, in *Just My Soul Responding: Rhythm and Blues, Black Consciousness, and Race Relations* details a number of incidents of battles between African American and white fans after rock and roll concerts in the mid-1950s, not in the South but in Newport, Rhode Island, and Boston, Massachusetts.

16 See, for example, Thomas Doherty, *Teenagers and Teenpics: The Juvenalization of American Movies in the 1950s* (Boston: Unwin Hyman, 1988); and John A. Jackson, *Big Beat Heat: Alan Freed and the Early Years of Rock & Roll* (New York: Schirmer Books, 1991).

17 "Can Elvis Sell Soap?" *Sponsor* 10.21 (October 15, 1956): 33.

18 Ibid., 106–8.

19 Ibid., 96.

20 Ibid., 108.

21 Gould's identification of Presley with a traditionally female role indicates anxiety at Presley's displacement of traditional 1950s gender roles, subverting the norms of heterosexual masculinity, while at the same time representing sexual potency on the television screen. See Jack Gould, "TV: New Phenomenon—Elvis Presley Rises to Fame as Vocalist Who Is Virtuoso of Hootchy-Kootchy," *New York Times*, June 6, 1956, 67. The cultural critic David R. Shumway characterizes the reaction to Presley's "hootchy-kootchy" as "feminization," arguing that Presley "became feminized because he displayed his body as a sexual object," thus violating gender boundaries. For Shumway, Elvis's self-feminization is transgressive. Rock critics of the 1960s and beyond, I suggest, did not acknowledge the transgressiveness of Presley's gender performance because it did not fit their model of rock and roll as heterosexually masculine, modernist, and out of the mainstream. Instead, their reading of Presley in the 1950s privileged Presley's sexual and racial transgressions as the major points of conflict with mainstream culture. It was also easier for rock critics to displace part of the blame for television's neutering of Presley and rock and roll onto over half of the audience, teenage girls, who were pathologized even by supporters of rock and roll. Those who privileged Presley's sexual threat found it easy to blame those who most needed to be "protected" from it for television's subsequent turn to bland rock and roll programming and performers, most notably characterized by *American Bandstand*. See David R. Shumway, "Watching Elvis: The Male

Rock Star as Object of the Gaze," in *The Other Fifties: Interrogating Midcentury American Icons*, ed. Joel Foreman (Urbana: University of Illinois Press, 1997), p. 127.

22 Jack Gould, "Elvis Presley: Lack of Responsibility Is Shown by TV in Exploiting Teen-Agers," *New York Times*, September 16, 1956, part 2, p. 13.

23 Ed Sullivan's coproducer Marlo Lewis claims that the controversial choice to film Presley from the waist up was due to a circulating rumor, allegedly confirmed by an eyewitness. The rumor had it that "Elvis has been hanging a small soft-drink bottle from his groin underneath his pants, and when he wiggles his leg it looks as though his pecker reaches down to his knee!" Presley was therefore shot from the waist up to ensure that his prosthetic self-endowment would not grace America's living rooms. I question the veracity of this account, in that Lewis and Lewis place Presley's first televised appearance on the Sullivan show as occurring in 1955. Presley did not appear on national television until January 1956. Lewis and Lewis also place that appearance as Presley's second on the show; many other sources assert that it was his third appearance. See Marlo Lewis and Mina Beth Lewis, *Prime Time* (Los Angeles: J. P. Tarcher, 1979), 146.

24 "Web Reports Solid Rating for First ABC-TV R&R Show," *Billboard*, May 13, 1957, 34.

25 Charlie Sinclair, "'The Big Beat' Rocks, Rolls—and Stumbles," *Billboard*, July 22, 1957, 20.

26 Jackson, *Big Beat Heat*, 55–56.

27 John A. Jackson, *American Bandstand: Dick Clark and the Making of a Rock and Roll Empire* (New York: Oxford University Press, 1997), 18–21.

28 June Bundy, "TV-D.J.s' Status Up at Local Level," *Billboard*, Novermber 10, 1956, 62.

29 Jackson, *American Bandstand*, 19. I am indebted to the Jackson book for much of my descriptive account of *American Bandstand*.

30 Ibid., 37.

31 Oliver Treyz, quoted in Leonard H. Goldenson (with Marvin J. Wolf), *Beating the Odds: The Untold Story behind the Rise of ABC: The Stars, Struggles, and Egos that Transformed Network Television by the Man Who Made It Happen* (New York: Charles Scribner's Sons, 1991), 162.

32 "ABC-TV's Oliver Treyz: Daring Young Man with a Mission," *Printer's Ink*, June 20, 1958, 56.

33 Technically a local program, *American Bandstand* in this period was a two-hour broadcast on WFIL in Philadelphia. It was transmitted daily by ABC for an hour and a half, leaving the remaining time to local sponsors.

34 "TV Jock Finally Comes into Own," *Billboard*, October 7, 1957, 28.

35 Ibid., p. 32.

36 This was not unproblematic, as we will see, and it may have led, in part, to the reghettoization of rock and roll performed by African American artists to the post–rock and roll rhythm and blues category.

37 Jackson, *American Bandstand*, 75.

38 Bob Rolontz, "From Radio Jock to Nat'l Name—How Clark Does It," *Variety*, Mach, 24, 1958, 4.

39 "TV Jock Finally Comes Into Own," 28.

40 Rolontz, "From Radio Jock to Nat'l Name—How Clark Does It," 4.

41 John Jackson theorizes that *American Bandstand* failed as a weeknight prime-time offering for two reasons. First, the teens and housewives drawn to the afternoon version of the program were otherwise occupied at that time. Second, male breadwinners had control of the television dial by 7:30 in the evening, and they were not interested in watching the program.

42 Jackson, *American Bandstand*, 105.

43 Review, "The Dick Clark Show," *Variety*, February 19, 1958, 31.

44 "Beech-Nut Hitches Its Sales to TV Star," *Printer's Ink*, January 30, 1959, 72.

45 Brian Ward, *Just My Soul Responding: Rhythm and Blues, Black Consciousness, and Race Relations* (Berkeley: University of California Press, 1998), 168.

46 Jackson, *Big Beat Heat*, 244.

47 See, for example, Jackson, *American Bandstand*, chapters 5 and 9.

48 Jackson, *Big Beat Heat*, 280.

49 "'Teen Buyers Grow Up,' Warns Miller," *Billboard*, September 8, 1956, 17, 22.

50 June Bundy, "Censorship Eases on Aired Lyrics as Acceptance Grows," *Billboard*, January 19, 1959, 2.

51 "Can Elvis Sell Soap?" 108.

52 According to a 1956 survey of 4,000 teens (12–18) conducted by Scholastic Magazines, 73 percent of boys and 79 percent of girls owned radios, and 60 percent of girls owned phonographs. In addition, 61.7 percent of girls in junior high and 48 percent of girls in senior high purchased records on a monthly basis, compared to 46.6 percent and 41.9 percent, respectively, of their male counterparts. See June Bundy, "Gals Best Disk and Phono Buyers in Teen-Age Bracket," *Billboard*, August 25, 1956, 15, 20.

53 Peter Guralnick, *Careless Love: The Unmaking of Elvis Presley* (Boston: Little, Brown, 1999), 29.

Lisa Parks and Melissa McCartney

Lisa writes: In Hawaii a few years ago, I witnessed a scene described by travel agents as the most authentic Hawaiian luau on the island of Kauai. After standing in line outside the Coconut Palace for over an hour, I was seated with a table of newlyweds. We did typical tourist things like eat roasted pig and poi, sip watery mai tais, put on leis, and watch singers and dancers as they performed on stage. But when I heard an ensemble of Hawaiian men begin singing "Tiny Bubbles" and "Blue Hawaii" with ukulele accompaniment, I felt a little poi gurgle up in my throat. Perhaps naively, I honestly didn't expect to hear Lawrence Welk and Elvis songs at the most authentic luau on the island. This *hapa-haole* music (i.e., music from half-Caucasian outsiders) has become a genre of contemporary Hawaiian music whose hybrid characteristics reproduce Hawaiian struggles for cultural survival as much as they articulate the Western appropriation of Hawaiian sounds.[1] As I later learned, perhaps among the most "authentic" moments in Hawaii's recent music history are Don Ho's almost parodic performances of "Tiny Bubbles" at Duke Kahanamoku's supper club in Waikiki.[2] And Elvis's "Blue Hawaii" has become a standard cover in most collections of contemporary Hawaiian music; collections that one Hawaiian music historian sardonically calls tidal waves because of their association with Western popular music styles.[3] Indeed, few mainland figures have made such a splash on Hawaii's musical shores as Elvis, the king of rock 'n' roll.

The film critic Gerry McLafferty suggests that "Shooting *Blue Hawaii* marked the beginning of a long love-affair between Elvis and the 50th state."[4] In 1961, the *Honolulu Star-Bulletin* described the film as a boost to Hawaiian music because it was viewed by more than twenty million people around the world.[5] Not only did Elvis star in three films set in

Hawaii (*Blue Hawaii*, *Girls! Girls! Girls!*, and *Paradise, Hawaiian Style*), he performed two benefit concerts, one for the USS *Arizona* Memorial Fund and another for the Kui Lee Cancer Fund, and he visited the islands frequently on holidays. The unlikely melding of the iconic American pop star and the newest U.S. state culminated in the second of these benefits — the 1973 *Aloha from Hawaii* concert, which was broadcast live via satellite to over forty countries worldwide.

In this essay we analyze Elvis's *Aloha from Hawaii* concert in the context of discourses surrounding Hawaiian tourism and Hawaiian music during the 1970s, and we further consider the live-via-satellite concert format popularized by this unusual show. The live satellite concert, we suggest, should be considered as part of a broader genealogy of global music television because it helped to establish the technical infrastructure, consumer markets, and discursive parameters for programming formats that are often misunderstood as emanating solely from MTV. Hawaii's tourist industry boomed in the seventies as land developers remolded the rugged cliffs and lava beds of places like Oahu's Kawela Bay and Turtle Bay into four-star resorts and orchid-lined golf courses. As a tourist destination, Hawaii has become, in the words of David Baker, "one of the most extensively depicted, lavishly described and heavily promoted places on the globe."[6] As the tourist trade strengthened its hold on the new state, representations of Hawaii were increasingly shaped by a touristic gaze invested in a facile image of Hawaii as the "paradise of the Pacific." As Rob Wilson explains, "'Paradise' remains a white mythological trope" used to "structure and integrate Hawaii into the mainland and transnational tourist flow."[7] To a large degree, *Aloha's* representation of Hawaii reinforced this mythology of integration. Wilson, however, encourages us to challenge the Hawaii-as-paradise myth as a "de-historicizing fantasy of a dominant culture expanding its telos of development-driven material prosperity — at whatever cost to indigenous or local culture."[8]

While the tourist's gaze fixated on a travel-poster simulacrum of Hawaii, the islands' local communities were engaged in a veritable cultural renaissance, reviving musical traditions such as *hula ku'i* chants and songs of the early 1900s as well as the traditional dance chants (*mele hula*) of the mid to late nineteenth century.[9] As Shirley Sebree writes, "In the 1970s, when minority groups [in Hawaii] began searching for their roots, a new contemporary Hawaiian sound evolved and recording activity experienced a new surge."[10] Musical groups like the Sons of Hawaii and Sunday Manoa emerged, along with soloists such as Peter Moon and Palani Vaughn, and the tourist-friendly, hapa-haole music of Don Ho and Kui Lee gave way to more traditional Hawaiian *mele*—that is, the chanted poetry of pre-European Hawaii that has historically expressed the values, wisdom, and history of the islands' indigenous peoples and celebrated the physical surroundings and spiritual forces affecting their lives.[11] In 1971 George Kanahele formed the Hawaiian Music Foundation, an organization that, Sebree explains, "grew out of deep concern for the rapid decline of professional Hawaiian musicians and composers; the dwindling number of steel guitar and slack-key players; the lack of time devoted to Hawaiian music through the electronic media; [and] the lack of interest in Hawaiian music by the musicians and scholars of other Western cultures."[12] The foundation successfully cultivated a renewed attention to Hawaiian music in the local broadcast media. In 1974 the Hawaiian public television station KHET released a six-part documentary series called *Mele Hawaii* that explored the historical progression of Hawaiian music. And the radio stations KCCN and KKUA were recognized by the foundation for their work in "perpetuating and promoting Hawaiian music."[13]

Two countervailing tendencies marked Hawaiian music in the 1970s: while a growing tourist trade demanded hapa-haole songs of blissful island paradise, a traditionalist movement was producing highly politicized musical forms tied directly to Hawaii's history of cultural struggle. Within this context the live global satellite broadcast of *Aloha from Hawaii* technologized and extended practices of Hawaiian tourism while suppressing local Hawaiian musical influences. Indeed, Elvis's *Aloha* concert—much like his earlier films—positioned Hawaii as a peaceful paradise and a place of romance and beauty. In an act of reverse tourism, *Aloha* brought Hawaii to one billion viewers and inscribed the newly annexed state into the satellite-regulated space of global modernity. In the process, the show suppressed the neotraditional musical influences so prevalent in local Hawaiian culture at the time. In this way, *Aloha* functions to establish the continuities between an "eternally primitive" Hawaii and the "fully modern" American nation, and it does so in a way that elides the social struggles that would necessarily attend such a transformation. The figure that negotiates this cultural alchemy—that mediates this tension between an ahistorical idyllic past and a technologized global future—is Elvis.

The live-via-satellite concert is a unique cultural format that emerged in the early 1970s after a decade of experimentation with live satellite broadcasting—including such events as the Kentucky Derby (1962), a Sotheby's art auction (1965), the Tokyo Olympics (1964), and *The Town Meeting of the World* (1965). In the late 1960s and early 1970s, several Western nations also initiated a handful of satellite "development" projects aimed at "modernizing" third world countries. In 1967 the European Broadcasting Union and the BBC organized a live satellite program called *Our World*, which relayed scenes of third world overpopulation, hunger, and urban crowding to viewers in eighteen nations. In 1973, the same year as the *Aloha* concert, NASA helped initiate the Indian Satellite Television Experiment (SITE) in an effort to catapult that country's rural populations into a quantum leap toward modernization. Finally, producers at National Educational Television in the United States organized satellite television exchanges geared toward the development of American Samoa. In sum, satellite technology was used during the 1960s and 1970s to experiment with new international television formats and in an effort to assimilate the world's developing societies into an imagined "global modernity."

Musical performers had appeared live on television since the 1950s. In April 1956 Elvis himself performed "Heartbreak Hotel," "Blue Suede Shoes," and part of "Shake, Rattle and Roll" on *The Milton Berle Show* telecast live from the USS *Hancock* naval ship in San Diego. The installation of communications satellites during the 1960s had the effect of electronically transporting live acts across continents, expanding the potential size of the audience as well as the performer's international exposure. The live-via-satellite concert became a lucrative format during the 1970s and 1980s because it could be used to showcase a popular music performer in a novel way before an enormous international audience. It also generated a "live" recording that could be released after the show—one that had already been internationally promoted in the context of the satellite spectacular.

In addition to these experiments, there were two live-via-satellite musical performances that helped to establish the feasibility of the Elvis extravaganza. The Beatles had appeared in the live satellite broadcast *Our*

World on June 25, 1967, playing "All You Need Is Love"—a song written by John Lennon expressly for this satellite broadcast—from a BBC studio in London before an unprecedented audience of 350 million viewers. Televised live to viewers around the world at the very same time it was being recorded in the studio as a single, "All You Need Is Love" went on to become a number one hit not only in the United Kingdom and United States but also in other countries such as Argentina, Australia, Canada, Denmark, Ireland, and Poland. The event suggested that the venue of live-via-satellite performance could both generate an instant hit and attract a global market for pop music recordings.

Three years later on May 10, 1970, the fifteenth annual Ivor Novello Awards Show, later known as *Musical Festival 70*, was beamed from the Talk of the Town in London to pop music lovers around the world as a pay-per-view concert hall show. Handbills and posters plastered all across New York City touted the news that followers of the Rolling Stones, Peter Sellers, and John Lennon and Yoko Ono could see their pop idols receive statuettes "'Live,' by Satellite . . . Direct, In Color From London."[14] Venues in the United States, France, Spain, Australia, Holland, and Venezuela sold thousands of tickets to fans eager to witness this innovative musical event that traversed continents and concert halls. The show included performances by the Beatles, Blue Mink, and Dusty Springfield, and turned popular musical performance into a form of traveling culture—an electronic signal that would be ricocheted from the BBC in London to satellite transponders, then down to satellite receivers and out to viewing rooms scattered across both Northern and Southern Hemispheres. Crowded into concert halls and movie theaters, spectators joined the audience at the Talk of the Town, becoming a part of history as the night's events unfolded live before them. The distance from London to spots around the globe was bridged by the signal that instantly crossed immense gaps in time and space, replacing stage with screen. The broadcast evening's crowning moment came when David Bowie, the recipient of the Special Award for Originality for Best Song, performed his hit single "Space Oddity," accompanied by the Les Reed Orchestra. Bowie's manager Kenneth Pitt saw this concert as an opportunity to "give [Bowie] his first major exposure in the US and in several other countries of the world, which [he would] exploit."[15] With over sixty reception locations in the United States alone, including Carnegie Hall, a live satellite broadcast meant that Bowie could reach thousands of viewers with one show and one song. His live-via-satellite performance turned the awards event into his own headlining show, and he was able to maximize his exposure with minimal resources.

Live satellite television provided an ideal way for pop music stars to enter the global spotlight by exploiting assets already in place. A single person on a stage—in any part of the world—could be transported internationally by means of satellite transmission; the technology was easily adaptable to different settings and events with the simple use of a satellite link, a transmitter, and a television camera. Thus, as Kenneth Pitt insisted, Bowie didn't just perform for a packed house in London but played for a packed world, bringing to his global audience both his music and the experience that went along with attending the Ivor Novello Awards. Live satellite spectatorship brought pleasure to the viewer in the form of scenes from far-off places filled with well-known celebrities, conveniently packaged through the television screen, while generating "valuable exposure" for the performer as well.[16]

ALOHA FROM HAWAII

Both the Beatles's *Our World* spot and Bowie's *Musical Festival 70* appearance were instances in which live musical performance was integrated within variety and award show formats, but the 1973 *Aloha* event was the first time a concert was aired live via satellite in its entirety. On January 9, 1973, Elvis flew by helicopter into Honolulu's Hilton Hawaiian Village and spent the next few days rehearsing and preparing for the first live global concert. According to the *Honolulu Star-Bulletin*, Elvis was greeted by a "surge of fans" including a flock of bikini-clad women, "Tahitian dancers [who] sprang into action," and "Hawaiian beauties who were [eager] to kiss him."[17] Nervous about a breakdown with the satellite system, Elvis demanded extra rehearsals in the days preceding the broadcast. While the band and backup singers worked out the music arrangements, Elvis held secret rehearsals with a select group of musicians in the Hilton Hawaiian Dome. The intensity of these rehearsals was confirmed when RCA decided to tape the sessions for future record releases.[18] The recording of the January 12 dress rehearsal was, for instance, released on video in 1996 as *Elvis: The Alternate Aloha*.[19]

The production costs of *Aloha* totaled $2.5 million and required the financial support of RCA president Rocco Laginestra, who understood the concert as an "unprecedented opportunity to merchandise Presley's records."[20] Indeed, as the first concert (as opposed to award show) ever to go worldwide, *Aloha* became a profitable new album. It qualified as a gold disc even before the show was transmitted, on advance orders alone.[21] And after its release in late January, *Aloha* soared to number one on the Billboard Pop Album Chart and stayed on the chart at various positions for fifty-two weeks.

Although RCA envisioned *Aloha* as a venue for big record sales, the concert had a humanitarian underpinning as well. Kui Lee, one of Hawaii's best-known songwriters, had recently died of cancer at age thirty-four. Elvis, who sang "I'll Remember You" as a tribute to Lee, donated ticket admissions from the morning show and another dress rehearsal to the Kui Lee Cancer Fund, thereby raising $75,000 for cancer research. The day after the concert the *Honolulu Advertiser* published a two-page photograph of Elvis with thanks to him and Colonel Parker for their efforts, and an editorial lauded Elvis's charity by calling him "a great, good friend of Hawaii."[22]

On January 13, 1973, the Honolulu International Center, reportedly "jammed with 6,000 Hawaiians," was transformed into a "supersized TV studio for the hour-long spectacle."[23] The concert was televised live at 12:30 AM Hawaiian standard time to one billion viewers in nearly forty nations—including Japan, Australia, Korea, New Zealand, the Philippines, Thailand. and South Vietnam.[24] Fans in Europe watched a slightly delayed *Aloha*, but the program was not shown in the mainland United States and Hawaii until April 4, 1973, when NBC rebroadcast it as a ninety-minute special. To the U.S. version, NBC added Elvis's covers of five Hawaiian songs. The network announced that the program attracted an unprecedented 57 percent of the viewing audience, beating out the popular sitcom *All in the Family*.[25] Indeed, the *Aloha* concert was seen in more American households than Neil Armstrong's first walk on the moon.

As a space of live international entertainment, *Aloha from Hawaii* foregrounded the theme of transport using an array of space motifs, thus discursively linking Elvis and Hawaii to the wonders of space communication. Both Elvis and Hawaii were sent on tour around the world via satellite, while at the same time the largest TV audience to date toured Hawaii as a live electronic space—a hybridized site that combined kitschy Americana (in the guise of Eagle-winged Elvis in his pseudo planetarium) with caricatures of island beauty. The program opened with an image of

LISA PARKS AND MELISSA MCCARTNEY

the spinning blue earth. As the camera pulls out to reveal an orbiting satellite, we hear the beeping of live signals and watch them relayed to different spots on the planet. After the satellite transmits the message "Elvis:
Aloha from Hawaii" in ten different languages (including French, Spanish, Japanese, and Arabic), the space-age modernism of global satellite
communication is abruptly interrupted with the comparatively primal
sound of a pounding drumbeat followed by a rapid cut to the pulsating
torso of a Hawaiian dancer whose pelvic tremors prefigure Elvis's aging
but still volatile body. The sequence not only evokes McCluhan's "global
village" metaphor so prominent at the time, but also articulates global
futurism and local primitivism together around the satellite-relayed image of Elvis. Indeed, it is Elvis — the American pop icon in orbit — that is
used to mediate the odd convergence of the ancient and the modern. As
the Polynesian drumbeat fades we hear Elvis sing out, again and again,
"Hawaii: USA!" thereby integrating the island (which became a state in
1954) within a discourse of U.S. assimilation and nationalism.

Set designers overhauled the Honolulu International Center to appear
as a giant planetarium containing a night sky filled with a myriad of flickering stars. Mirrored panels framed both sides of the stage, not only sim-
ulating the reflective solar panels of a satellite — suggesting that Elvis's
body itself was in global orbit — but also giving the spectator enhanced
visual access to his live performance as cameras captured his movements
in mirrored reflections. *Aloha* began in complete darkness as "Thus Spake
Zarathrustra" heralded Elvis's entrance onto the stage. "Zarathrustra,"
the opening fanfare from Richard Strauss's 1896 symphony based on
Nietzsche's lengthy poem, had become a hallmark of space-age wonder
and spectacular awe as the theme to Stanley Kubrick's 1968 film *2001: A
Space Odyssey*. The song had also become a standard opening for many
arena rock acts during this period.[26] Thus the concert's own "aloha," or
greeting, drew on the space-age futurism of *2001* and the classicism of
the German Enlightenment, positioning the locale of Hawaii and the
body of Elvis with one foot wandering the frontier of outer space and the
other strapped beneath the weight of Western culture.

Aloha was marked as much by intense American nationalism as it was
by global futurism. Dressed in his custom-made American eagle outfit —
a white star-spangled, flare-legged suit — Elvis sang a mélange of popular American classics including Frank Sinatra's "My Way," Roy Orbison's
"It's Over," Peggy Lee's "Fever," Carl Perkins's "Blue Suede Shoes," and

Chuck Berry's "Johnny B Goode." Perhaps the most nationalistic of his performances was the "American Trilogy," an odd medley of "Dixie," "Battle Hymn of the Republic," and "All My Trials." Elvis's passionate performance of this number near the show's finale reportedly sent "several hundred fans to their feet."[27] The show closed with a tribute to Hawaiian fans, in which Elvis sang his *Blue Hawaii* hit "I Can't Help Falling in Love with You." Just before the song he flapped his American eagle cape around his shoulders, preened on the catwalk before his fans, and then flung the cape into the audience as if he were the national bird incarnate. It was this moment that prompted one biographer to describe Elvis as "the living symbol of freedom and light."[28]

The NBC broadcast of the *Aloha* concert in the U.S. mainland three months after the live show gave network executives ample time to repackage and promote it. Producers added five hapa-haole songs to the lineup (*Blue Hawaii, Ku-U-I-Po, No More, Hawaiian Wedding Song*, and *Early Morning Rain*) and inserted special sequences using graphic devices that split the frame into four sections, each of which contained either close-ups of Elvis's singing face or picturesque Hawaiian landmarks. While elements of Hawaiianness were incorporated into the *Aloha* special, the program squarely positioned Hawaii as a product of the tourist imaginary—as an exotic place of romance and tranquility. The "Blue Hawaii" segment, for instance, features palm tree silhouettes and a warm sunset as the background for a Hawaiian hula dancer, whose gestures illustrate Elvis's Hollywood lyrics.[29] Another frame encases a blonde tourist in a blue muumuu staring at a tropical bird in a grass cage. Her image is replaced by a panoramic view of blue ocean and rocky bluffs. The "Hawaiian Wedding Song" and "Ku-U-I-Po" sequences feature similar postcard montages of fern grottoes, cascading waterfalls, kissing lovers, blooming orchids, and bikini-wearing beauties.[30] The composition of these sequences, especially the use of graphic boxes, contains Hawaii as an exotic playground by mapping the visual conventions of the vacation postcard onto the electronic space of television and the theatrical space of live musical performance. And the sequences narrativize Hawaii as a stream of lyrics that all too easily roll off Elvis's tongue.

Although these five Hawaiian songs are favorites among American tourists, they also hold significance for many Hawaiian people and offer some recognition—however problematic—of a distinct Hawaiian music culture. Ultimately, however, the addition of these songs and visual sequences was not so much a nod to the culture of the newest American state as it was yet another co-optation of Hawaiian music to support touristic fantasy. Indeed, as Elizabeth Tatar suggests, the tourist industry has appropriated Hawaiian music as a promotional commodity since the late nineteenth century. As Tatar explains: "Western concepts of entertainment usually play a greater role in determining the presentation of traditional music and dance than do the more complex Hawaiian concepts associated with these traditions."[31] Tourism constructs its own "authenticity" and is predicated on a willful ignorance of history.[32]

While likely motivated by an economic decision to streamline Elvis's live show, the producers' exclusion of these Hawaiian songs from global view is symptomatic of a refusal to represent Hawaii as a place of active cultural production. Furthermore, the erasure of these Hawaiian songs from the live satellite relay suppressed the potential within Hawaiian music to vocalize resistance to the U.S. (and worldwide tourist) appropriation of Hawaiian territory and culture. This is a particularly significant exclusion in light of the revival during the 1970s of the historical and cultural specificity associated with Hawaiian music and dance. Thus while the neotraditionalist movement of the 1970s sought to reattach Hawaiian cultural expression to specific political and cultural struggles, *Aloha's* postcard snapshots exoticized Hawaiian culture by freezing it as an image of eternal Edenic bliss detached from the unraveling of history and divorced from the raw potential of live satellite expression.

While *Aloha* works to conceal and contain a Hawaiian musical discourse that recounts territorial struggle and cultural conflict, many Hawaiians were deeply attached to Elvis and profoundly moved by the concert. Honolulu's mayor, Frank Fasi, and his wife proudly occupied front row center seats. And not only did Elvis receive a standing ovation at the end of the concert, but in a royal semiotic twist he was crowned a modern-day Hawaiian king. Elvis's cover of "I'll Remember You," brought the haunting presence of Kui Lee, a musician renowned as Hawaii's "rebel without a cause," into global view. Though Lee's songs ("Rain Rain Go Away" and "Going Home") continued the hapa-haole "break with the past" by blurring distinctions between mainland and island sounds, he is said to have "strayed from but never abandoned his Hawaiianness," and he is celebrated by Hawaiian music scholars for exerting a strong influence on the substance, style, and especially the mood of Hawaiian music. According to George Kanahele, Lee's "frustrations and joys, resentments and affections, were all tied to his efforts to protect and sustain his island heritage."[33]

Finally, we might consider the fleeting nonnarrativized instances of Hawaiianness within the concert text in relation to the Hawaiian term *kaona*, which refers to layered meanings and hidden poetic references embedded within Hawaiian mele. When *Aloha* opens with the mele hula of a Hawaiian dancer, we are witnessing a shaking of the hips that is perhaps as much about the celebration of Hawaiian genealogy and landscape as it is a feast for the eyes of Elvis and the world's spectator-tourists. And in the concert's title is the word "aloha," which as the activist Haunani-Kay Trask reminds us has very specific meanings to Hawaiian people, meanings quite contrary to tourists' reinventions of it. This is not to say that Hawaiians naively hailed Elvis as a savior of Hawaiian culture. Rather, the concert might have simply been a discursive entry point—a site through which Hawaiians could consider and critique their relationship to U.S. nationalism as well as locate themselves within an emerging global media culture. And while Elvis's appropriation of Hawaiian songs clearly advanced the interests of a developing tourist economy, that music had a long cultural history that preceded Elvis's triumphant landing on Hawaiian shores. Indeed, the lyrics of "Ku-U-I-Po" and "Hawaiian Wedding Song" can be traced back to the royal composers of the late nineteenth century and early twentieth. In other words, the images and sounds that Elvis so effectively co-opted may have also carried kaona quite beyond the perception of the touristic gaze.

CONCLUSION

Where *Aloha* introduced mainlanders to a seemingly idyllic island life, later showmen used global satellite television networks to be the purveyors of a less paradisal message. What Elvis did for cancer research and Hawaiian tourism by joining his music with island backdrops, Bob Geldof and a slew of musical celebrities tried to do for famine relief in Africa through an event staged on July 13, 1985, called Live Aid. The pop music powerhouses George Michael, Bono, Phil Collins, Sting, and dozens more aided Geldof with his crusade to turn a mere awareness of the rapidly deteriorating situation of drought and starvation in Ethiopia into an event designed to catalyze collective action. Born out of circumstances

LISA PARKS AND MELISSA MCCARTNEY

surrounding the hit single "Do They Know It's Christmas,"[34] Live Aid constructed a daunting portrait of "third world Africa" by juxtaposing glamorous rock stars against "stark images of millions of people starving to death in Ethiopia"[35] The musicians' televised cry for help was intended to rattle viewers from silent complacency and move them to action, which ranged from consumer purchases of the Live Aid album to charitable donations to the Live Aid fund to general awareness of hunger issues in Africa. All of the donations generated by Live Aid went to relief efforts in Africa, but the show did not result in any structural changes to address the problem of world hunger.[36]

Live Aid, a much larger event than *Aloha*, aired live on MTV for sixteen continuous hours as producers intercut feeds from simultaneous shows staged at Wembley Stadium in London and at JFK Stadium in Philadelphia, employing thirteen satellites and twenty-two transponders to broadcast the show,[37] which attracted more than 1.4 billion television viewers in 170 countries worldwide.[38] Feeds of live performances were also beamed in from the Netherlands, Japan, West Germany, Austria, Yugoslavia, the Soviet Union, and Australia. As the producer Hal Uplinger insisted, "The fact that we did a live 16 hour continuing broadcast utilizing most of the satellite transmission facilities that were available in the world at that time was certainly a breakthrough!"[39] Indeed, the fact that Live Aid managed to use global satellite television facilities to transmit sixteen hours of continuous music programming while spotlighting an important humanitarian theme was no small feat. What was odd, however, was the show's meager inclusion of African musicians (with the exception of the African American blues artist BB King), its paternalistic tone, and its continual construction of African people as "starving victims." Indeed, Geldof periodically reminded viewers that "if you do nothing, millions of people will die."[40] Major sponsors such as Chevrolet, Pepsi, and AT&T ran ads imploring viewers to join the fight against world hunger; AT&T donated a live call-in line for charitable donations and aired an ad featuring images of famine victims while an off-screen chorus sang "reach out and touch some one . . . some one whose only hope is you."[41] While the show's producers may have had noble intentions, such statements and mottos were ideologically problematic as they cast the pop stars, consumers, and corporations of the industrial world as the inevitable saviors of "helpless" and "hungry" Africans. As in the case of the *Aloha* show, the live satellite concert claimed on the sur-face to be a gesture of good will and cultural integration, but it worked at the level of representation to reinforce elitist cultural divisions by revel-ing in the rock 'n' roll liberal humanism and technological bravado of the West.

Still, both *Aloha* and Live Aid demonstrated that the live satellite con-cert could be both effective and profitable, and they spawned a multitude of comparable benefit shows of a similar theme and design. Bob Dylan suggested at Live Aid that a similar project would be useful in the United States to assist family farmers; thus Farm Aid hit the stage six weeks later in September. Tickets sold out immediately and the success of Live Aid was re-created. The then-new cable network TNN picked up the broadcast in an effort to increase its market share and has continued to air it every year since, raising a total of $17 million.[42] By 1999 the Internet had been commandeered to the cause of poverty and hunger relief with the advent of Net Aid. Drawing on Geldof's original concept of multiple, simulta-neous shows, three concerts were staged in New York, London, and Ge-neva. This time they were broadcast over the Net in order to reach even greater crowds in still more remote places, along with synchronized live casting on MTV and VH1. Echoing Uplinger's views in 1985, the program manager Diane Merrick noted, "Technically, nothing like this has ever been put together."[43] The Web site received more than sixty million hits during the show, raising significant funds.[44]

The lure of pop superstars has not dulled since Bowie, the Beatles, and Elvis were first transformed into electronic signals traveling through the ether to satellite receivers and onto the screen. By 1973, when El-vis told the world aloha, this ability to bring unknown people and places right into homes throughout the globe meant that promoters could book worldwide gigs at only the cost of satellite airtime. Bowie, Elvis, and even Bono could be in every living room in the United Kingdom, while at the same time bringing a glimpse of London or Honolulu to the far reaches of South Africa and Nepal. The advent of Pay-Per-View cable and satellite television in the 1980s afforded concert promoters, media conglomer-ates, and advertisers the ability to sell virtual tickets. In order to watch, viewers had to shell out for the signal beamed to their local cable or satel-lite provider. As one of the earliest live satellite concerts, the *Aloha* show is symbolic because it offered a formula for interweaving pop music, tele-vision, charity, and tourism. As such it serves as a site through which we can begin to understand how these industries helped to develop the global music television economy even before the launch of MTV. By the late 1980s and 1990s satellites were used regularly to relay live concerts and to transmit streams of music videos to cable and satellite providers around the world. The success of MTV as a global network can be traced back to some of these early experiments, because the live satellite concert reinforced global consumer desire for televised pop music performance and "live" recordings.

By carrying Live Aid in its entirety, MTV was able to promote itself as a brand glued not only to hit pop music, but also to an amalgam of humanitarianism, consumerism, and tourism. By the early 1990s MTV jumped beyond the U.S. market and began to aggressively globalize, first being packaged as part of Sky TV direct satellite broadcasting services in Western Europe and then being folded within an enormous Asian footprint as part of Star TV's offerings. Since then, MTV has gone on to develop a series of "glocal" channels such as MTV India, MTV Japan, MTV China, and so on.[45] Occasionally MTV programming reveals some lingering commitment to humanitarian concerns (with AIDS/HIV awareness, for instance), but, for the most part, the network has become the centrifugal force of a global youth consumer culture. Thus while *Aloha*, Live Aid, and MTV have used satellite television technology to different ends, they can all be understood as part of a genealogy of music television since contemporary formations are derivative of early live global concerts and their mixings of pop sounds and spectacles with international humanitarianism, tourism, consumerism.

NOTES

1. According to Shirley Sebree, country and folk rock are widely represented in hapa-haole music, which includes songs such as Marcus Schutte's "Paniolo Country" and "Waimea Cowboy," and Jerry Santos's "Kulu Home O Kahalulul" and "O Mailia." See Shirley Sebree, *Pele's Tears: Reclaiming the Lost Gems of Hawaiian Music in Western Music Styles* (New York: Vantage Press, 1994), 153.

2 George H. Lewis, "Storm Blowing from Paradise: Oppositional Ideology in Popular Hawaiian Music," *Popular Music* 10.1 (1991): 53–68.

3 Sebree, *Pele's Tears*, 162.

4 Gerry McLafferty, *Elvis Presley in Hollywood: Celluloid Sell-Out* (London: Robert Hale, 1989), 66.

5 *Honolulu Star-Bulletin*, November 11, 1961; quoted in Sebree, *Pele's Tears*, 178.

6 David J. Baker, "*Ea* and Knowing in Hawai'i," *Critical Inquiry* (spring 1997): 645.

7 Rob Wilson, "*Goodbye Paradise*: Global/Localism in the American Pacific," in *Global/Local: Cultural Production and the Transnational Imaginary*, ed. Rob Wilson and Wimal Dissanayake (Durham, N.C.: Duke University Press, 1996), 320.

8 Ibid., 320.

9 Elizabeth Tatar, *Strains of Change: The Impact of Tourism on Hawaiian Music* (Honolulu: Bishop Museum Press, 1987), 19.

10 Sebree, *Pele's Tears*, 153.

11 Richard Trimillos, *Musics of Hawai'i* (Honolulu: State Foundation on Culture and the Arts—Fold Arts Program, 1994), 20.

12 Sebree, *Pele's Tears*, 183.

13 Ibid., 173.

14 *Music Festival '70*, advertisement poster.

15 Kenneth Pitt, *Bowie: The Pitt Report* (London: Omnibus Press, 1985), 215.

16 Ibid., 214.

17 Bob Barr, "Presley's Benefit Concert Viewed in 36 Countries," *Honolulu Star-Bulletin*, January 15, 1973, A17.

18 Howard A. DeWitt, *Elvis: The Sun Years* (Ann Arbor: Popular Culture Ink, 1993), 11.

19 This show was recorded at 8:30 PM on January 12, 1973, in case something went wrong with the satellite. The back-up show was made for Japanese television.

20 DeWitt, *Elvis*, 11.

21 The initial local order in Honolulu was 20,000 copies, and Japan's first order was for 100,000 ("Listening Post," *Honolulu Star-Bulletin and Advertiser*, January 21, 1973, A4; see also Peter Jones, *Elvis* [London: Octopus Books, 1976], 84).

22 "Thanks to Elvis," *Sunday Advertiser*, January 14, 1973, A24.

23 Wayne Harada, "Gold Crown Awarded to 'King' Elvis," *Honolulu Advertiser*, January 15, 1973, C3.

24 Bob Barr, "Presley's Benefit Concert Viewed in 36 Countries," *Honolulu Star Bulletin*, January 15, 1973, A17. The live broadcast attracted 37.8 percent of viewers in Japan, 91.8 percent in the Philippines, 70 percent in Hong Kong, and 70–80 percent of the viewers in Korea (http://www.elvis-presley.com/ologyp2.html).

25 DeWitt, *Elvis*, 12.

26 Robert Matthew Walker, *Elvis Presley: A Study in Music* (Tunbridge Wells, U.K.: Midas Books, 1982), 95. Groups like Rush and Grand Funk Railroad, for instance, opened with "Thus Spake Zarathustra."

27 Wayne Harada, "Gold Crown Awarded to 'King' Elvis," *Honolulu Advertiser*, January 15, 1973, C3.

28 W. A. Harbinson, *The Illustrated Elvis* (New York: Grossett and Dunlap, 1976), 140.

29 Bing Crosby first performed "Blue Hawaii" in the 1937 film *Waikiki Wedding*. It was written by Leo Robin and Ralph Rainger, both of whom were staff composers for Paramount Pictures during the 1930s. The song also became the title track of the 1961 Elvis film *Blue Hawaii*. See George S. Kanahele, ed., *Hawaiian Music and Musicians: An Illustrated History* (Honolulu: University of Hawaii Press, 1979), 46.

30 "Hawaiian Wedding Song" was written by one of Hawaii's most prolific composers, Charles E. King, who was born in Honolulu in 1874 and became a legislator, educator, and conductor in the Royal Hawaiian band. Hawaiian tour guides have performed his song since the 1950s. "Ku-U-I-Po" ("My Sweetheart") was written by one of the least recognized royal composers — Princess Miriam Likelike — during the late nineteenth century. See Kanahele, *Hawaiian Music and Musicians*, 226.

31 Tatar, *Strains of Change*, 27.

32 See Baker, "Ea and Knowing in Hawaii."

33 Kanahele, *Hawaiian Music and Musicians*, 223.

34 Written by Boomtown Rats lead singer Bob Geldof and Ultravox lead singer and guitarist Midge Ure, "Do They Know It's Christmas" was recorded by nearly forty musicians for free under the title Band Aid. The single was released December 7, 1984, and soon became the fastest-selling single ever in recorded history. Geldof then immediately set about creating Live Aid featuring many of the same artists present on Band Aid.

35 *Live Aid: The Show That Rocked the World*, BBC News, April 5, 2000, http://news.bbc.co.uk/1/hi/uk/702700.stm.

36 The goal of the Live Aid producers was to raise $50 million, but at the end of the show only $40 million had been donated. See "Robert Hilburn and Dennis McDougal, "Star-Studded Concert Raises Funds for Africa," *LA Times*, July 14, 1985, 32. By 1993, $127 million had been generated from the event and sales of the recording.

37 Jon Eklund, "Interview with Mr. Hal Uplinger," April 7, 1993, National Museum of American History, Smithsonian Institution, Washington, D.C.).

38 "Live Aid 10th Anniversary," BBC Television, July 1995, http://www.oneworld.org/tvandradio/live_aid.html.

39 Eklund, "Interview with Mr. Hal Uplinger."

40 Esther B. Fein, "Stands and Phone Lines Jammed for Aid Concert, *New York Times*, July 14, 1985, 14.

41 Hilburn and McDougal, "Star-Studded Concert Raises Funds for Africa," 32.

42 For more information about the history of Farm Aid, see the project's Web site at http://www.farmaid.org.

43 "Bytes for the Hungry," ABC News.com, October 1999, http://more.abcnews
    .go.com/sections/tech/dailynews/netaid990921.html.
44 Ibid.
45 For further discussion of music television in Asia, see Lisa Parks, "Satellite
    Rhythms: Channel V, Asian Music Video, and Transnational Gender," in *Rock
    Over the Edge: Transformations of Popular Music*, ed. Roger Beebe, Denise Ful-
    brook, and Ben Saunders (Durham, N.C.: Duke University Press, 2002).

Warren Zanes

I f the popular music industry is frequently associated with bloating and fatigue, as of late it is unpredictability that is its defining feature. Even for those who have witnessed a number of the industry's transformations and can thus claim of it an insider's knowledge, it has become difficult to venture prophesy regarding the restructuring that lies ahead. While downloading and its effects are perceived by some as a healthy disruption that might force an evolution, we can only speculate as to what piracy practices, today so much a part of the music fan's everyday life, will finally mean to both record companies/retail bodies *and* the rights of recording artists. But despite the potential effects of Internet piracy, when we consider today's increasingly corporatized commercial radio, it is the post-Napster Internet that seems the site most likely to provide a diversified and open musical public sphere as things unfold.

While it would be difficult to say with any kind of assurance what lies in store for either the monolith of commercial radio or the Internet as an alternative to it, at present the tension between the two modes of transmission marks this as another moment in which "underground" tactics and DIY projects are pitted against the homogenizing pressures of a corporate structure. Given this situation, it would seem that the old divide between the "commercial" and the "underground" would be experienced as being wider than ever.[1] But such is not the case, at least not to an extent that reflects the extremity of the situation. And it is this matter, not the much-discussed issue of piracy, that interests me here.

The merger of several years ago that brought Geffen, Interscope, and A&M records under one umbrella, with Seagrams behind it all, gave an ever-greater sense of the commercial music industry as Goliath. Clear Channel's grip on the radio and touring industries, which has done much to erase any sense of the *local* in local music, underscores this point. Amid the industry's tumult and the buyouts that find corporations growing evermore grotesque in their proportions, we would expect a healthy romanticism that dwells upon the *slaying* of the giant. But that romanticism, so right for the moment, is curiously absent or, at least, muted. While the explanations for this are many, one explanation has to do with the underground's changing relation to video. At one time, video was the very thing that gave energy to what in my title I refer to as the "theater of purity."

The "theater of purity" has roots in art world discourses. It is the process through which artists define their own, sometimes lofty, mission in relation to what they implicitly propose is a less art-directed operation. And, of course, artists often have much help in establishing this difference. It is easy enough to imagine early advocates of Jackson Pollock at play in the theater of purity, slamming the "superficial" illustrations of Norman Rockwell as they describe the creative depth at which Pollock works. Witness Clement Greenberg in "Avant-garde and Kitsch."[2] Such an approach was—and is—common enough. In music culture it is almost a reflex, used to substantiate, to elevate, to validate. It is a declaration of difference that condemns one in order to celebrate another. And when the one being celebrated is an underdog figure, working away in the shadows of mainstream culture, romanticism has its toehold. The theater of purity is underway. At one juncture in popular music history, video was particularly useful as an object of difference, a thing against which to define purportedly more substantial work. It played a crucial role in the theater of purity.

In this essay I will consider a number of issues relating to the theater of purity; for its play of differences has been an activity endemic to popular music culture in the rock era. Always generating dichotomies, the theater of purity's favorite antagonist is, of course, mainstream commercial culture. Romantic in flavor, it posits an underdog creating in the margins, invisible to the masses and beyond that mainstream commercial culture. With discursive roots in the world of the visual arts, this romanticism involves a curious—curious *because* drawn from the visual arts—"denigration of the image." When its rhetorics gain momentum, even begin to spiral a bit, certain byproducts are generated (often inadvertently) by the theater of purity. The "denigration of the image" is one such byproduct that emerged as twentieth-century art world discourses worked madly to establish the territory of the avant-garde artist.

When the underground musicians of the early 1980s pointed to video as a medium hopelessly bound to a flaccid mainstream culture, they channeled much of the energy associated with an earlier avant-garde impulse. Their position was, in effect, supported by a certain artistic history — they had the support of a powerful lineage. In turn, when in the late 1980s and 1990s video was established as a part of music culture in general, and not just mainstream music culture, the energy of the earlier art world discourses was not as easily accessed and the fire of the underground rhetorics dwindled. Put another way, a moment arrived in which the underground, no longer able to use video as an object of difference, lost force in its project of self-definition. Following this logic, then, the underground needs new models of artistic self-definition. No longer able to draw power from the particular avant-garde, *anti-image* discourse, there is in the underground a sense of floundering that is still with us today despite the wide gulf between a bloated corporate culture and the realm of the artistic underdog.

To reiterate: video, released from its strict association with the commercial mainstream, drifted from a position in which it could be used for underground self-definition. In the process, the romanticism of the underground lost a crucial object of difference, and it also lost a connection with an earlier art world discourse that provided substantial energy to an oppositional music culture. When many among the underground construed video as a tainted medium, a medium almost hopelessly attached to commerce rather than to "art," something was working. For better or for worse, there was a force behind underground self-definition that is largely absent today.

The argument here is not that the underground, in order to recover its oppositional energy, must make a return to that way of thinking, but rather that new models of artistic self-definition might bring new life to a moment in which an underground sensibility is *lacking* definition. A study of an earlier phase of video's history, the early 1980s, provides insight into the project of underground self-definition and reveals something of video's historical trajectory — more importantly, it illuminates the tie between the one and the other, betraying video's role as an object of difference in the underground's theater of purity.

In order to consider the theater of purity and its effects, it is necessary to grasp the historical, discursive roots of the potent art/commerce opposition that has so often structured the value assignment in music culture. It is an opposition that is both archaic and nonsensical when applied to an industry that is intrinsically commercial; but it is an opposition that returns with remarkable consistency. Most strikingly, it is the world of modern painting, itself a reservoir of romantic conceptions of the artist and art making, that contributed something to the project of underground self-definition. In reproducing an avant-garde "denigration of the image," a bridge was created between two cultural and historical worlds, creating a discursive alliance over time.

In order to understand this curious situation and a particular moment in video's history, I will devote a good bit of space to consider the language and the anti-image rhetoric that have traveled from the world of the modern visual arts to music culture.

BUT FIRST: MILLER'S MADE THE AMERICAN WAY

While memoir has alternately been favored and frowned upon in the context of academic fashion, my own relationship to the situation of video leads me to a bit of memoir (sounds harmless, eh?). It was while playing in a band in the 1980s, a band called the Del Fuegos, that I saw video become crucial as a tool of promotion. Associated with the Los Angeles company Slash Records that spawned the Germs, Fear, and X, my band signed to the label and spent considerable time opening for other Slash acts, including the Blasters, X, the Gun Club, and Los Lobos. On some level, X was still the label's emblematic band around the time we joined Slash. Though X had recently signed with Elektra Records, their shadow loomed large at Slash and in American underground music more generally. Through John Doe and Exene Cervenka, the band's songwriters, Slash maintained a kind of lifeline to the punk ethos. And for some time, the Del Fuegos adopted just this ethos.

Doe and Cervenka were outspoken politically and helped to define both an activist sensibility and a musical aesthetic that were far-reaching in their influence. They often described a music business fraught with grim possibility for any artist seeking to preserve his or her integrity. An us/them structure colored their view of life in the music business. Regarding video, they expressed, at least, uncertainty. Cervenka describes

L.A. punk culture's reception of the medium thus: "Nobody liked [video]. Nobody wanted to be a part of it. Everybody was dragged kicking and screaming into it . . . it was just a necessary evil and everybody had to do it."[3] The medium of video is here implicitly differentiated from record making, with the latter being a realm of potential artistic statement as opposed to a "necessary evil," or something one resists. Art, this suggests, does not thrive equally well in both mediums. This a point to which I will return.

The romantic view of the artist as underdog working within a corrupt system, which X both promoted and seemed to embody, was attractive to my band. On some level, we already knew the rudiments of such a view from Bruce Springsteen, Elvis Costello, Bob Dylan, the Sex Pistols, Woody Guthrie, and many others, all of whom (if to varying degrees and in very different ways) represented a real street credibility that could be opposed to commercial artifice. However diverse this grouping, they all exuded the all-important if intangible *authenticity* that seemed a part of any important music. Thus, as a band we were aggressive in constructing our own authenticity so as to fit into this tradition, even if we did so without any measure of self-reflexivity. If our efforts involved what Robert Cantwell refers to as "social theater," we certainly did not conceive of it as such—at least not any more than we conceived of Woody Guthrie's act as "social theater."[4] The artifice of our street credibility did not strike us, despite its obviousness in such practices as our conscious concealment of the fact that three out of four band members attended a prestigious eastern prep school (to be sure, on the occasions when that information did come out, we were quick to explain that we were scholarship students, closer to the "real thing" because lower on the economic ladder). Even Bruce Springsteen's constructed street credibility had only just started to become more obvious to us. We were a long way off from the kind of ironic disposition that foregrounded self-awareness, a disposition that proliferated in nineties music culture.

This much said, if initially associated with the "underground," with the vestiges of a punk tradition, and with the authenticity that underground status conferred, after signing to Slash we rather quickly did an about-face and embraced the idea of commercial success and all it took to achieve it. As a historical document that (embarrassingly) betrays our turn, the inaugural issue of *Spin* featured a story on both the Del Fuegos and the Replacements, a story highlighting our new interest in—I'll resort to euphemism here—*broadening our audience*. While in the article the Replacements openly reject the mainstream, the Del Fuegos profess a desire to clean up their act in order to see what could happen in that mainstream context. At the heart of the story, not a great intellectual affair, was the question of how much beer one should drink before playing a show—we rather disingenuously suggested limits whereas the Replacements suggested no such thing. As early as the time of that article, there were those among the Del Fuegos's advocates who got the sense that we were betraying the very audience that had set us on our way. There was, of course, plenty of truth to this appraisal. More importantly, in regard to video, the matter at hand, the Replacements would go out of their way to reject the medium. The Del Fuegos welcomed it, even yearned for it. At the time, video was perhaps one of the most significant signposts along the road to mainstream acceptance; video emblematized the world beyond the underground. Eventually, our dreams realized, the Del Fuegos made a handful of largely forgettable videos.

In that era, there was certainly no question that a mainstream audience wanted videos of the songs they liked. Thus, if a band hoped for such an audience, to embrace video was imperative. The other side of this logic was that if a band wanted to preserve its underground status, video was a risky proposition, a medium tainted; hence the ambivalence with which a band like X approached the medium. Videos, *particularly* those that played with narrative and pulled their storyline directly from song lyrics (an approach associated with heavy metal), reeked of the mechanics of advertising. At that time, commercial advertising (with the exception of album advertising) was certainly off-limits for bands that wanted anything to do with the lineage of Springsteen, Costello, X, and Dylan to which I refer above. These were the days before a Dylan/Victoria's Secret collaboration could seem subversive, even artistically savvy. Thus we might explain the Del Fuegos's choice to do a Miller Beer commercial as born out of a profound state of cluelessness. For we did indeed want to be a part of that lineage of authenticity. But the decision to do a television commercial would, of course, all but sever the band from that lineage. While cluelessness was certainly a factor in our decision making, the nature of that cluelessness is worth considering.

Two things strike me here. First, having already embraced rock video, the Del Fuegos knew they were consciously making a bid for mainstream success. There was no "kicking and screaming" involved in our relationship with video. Rather than see video as marking a boundary between the underground and the mainstream, we saw it as inherently mainstream. This understanding of the medium was something we, like the Replacements, brought with us from the underground (the bands merely responded differently to the same belief). So, rather than consider the television commercial our downfall, we saw it as an extension of the visual campaign already underway. In fact, both the band and the advertising firm that produced the commercial referred to it as a "sixty-second video." Second, the Del Fuegos were indeed clueless (or, at least, cocky) when it came to playing with the historically determined guidelines or codes that performers follow in order to be a part of the lineage of authenticity. While such guidelines are unwritten and certainly fluid, at that time commercial advertising was strictly taboo for those, like my band, hovering between the underground and the mainstream. We weren't excommunicated from the underground for doing a video, so we thought we might be able to do the commercial, reap the rewards, and survive. Not so.

For bands and performers, constructing and maintaining authenticity requires following certain guidelines and making strategic decisions in relation to those guidelines so as to insure authenticity. We can bend such guidelines, hence their shifting nature, but not avoid them altogether. Our beer commercial, while somewhat unusual in its aesthetic and approach (it involved a hand-held, pseudo-documentary feel and pseudo-documentary content), was impossible to redeem, at least at that moment. Choosing to do it amounted to blasphemy. Naive, the Del Fuegos embraced the commercial world in ways that were then forbidden. Dave Marsh, the longtime Springsteen champion and biographer, publicly castigated the band. Elvis Costello, suggesting that young bands could use advertising money to keep the show on the road, publicly defended the Del Fuegos's choice. Feeling our pain, people gave us tapes of famous bands doing advertising (not insignificantly, most of it European[5]), such as Cream's Falstaff commercial. But none of these things mattered one way or the other. In that phase of authenticity construction, a young band just starting its career was making a stunning mistake in doing a commercial, if, that is, that band was interested in the kind of authenticity we hoped to cultivate and maintain. In the end, we got our wider audience at a price. In hindsight, the commercial was a mistake.

The proximity of video to commercial (and particularly *televisual*) advertising certainly made video a potentially dangerous medium for those, like my band, playing the authenticity game in the early to mid-eighties. If doing commercial advertising could mean a fall from grace, video was always potentially part way there. What interests me here is the manner in which the "sell out" designation, the ultimate charge of guilty that the underground could make, was more apt to happen the closer one got to the *visual* realm of mainstream culture. Video did indeed function as a boundary marker of sorts, the other side of which was the deep (visual) trouble of the kind my band got into. If the guidelines of authenticity were thick with paradox, they were guidelines nonetheless. For instance, while being on a label like Slash/Warner Brothers meant being a part of a corporation, a radical differentiation between *that* corporate alliance and something like the Del Fuegos's corporate *advertising* alliance meant that the latter was strictly taboo while the former was a matter far less problematic. The visual aspects of the whole record-making and record-promoting process were uniquely prone to negative categorization, to being viewed as intrinsically related to the commerce side of the art/commerce split. This factor played a constitutive role in determining the guidelines of authenticity to which my band did not, in the end, adhere.

THE HISTORY OF A DISTINCTION

However much the simplistic underground/corporate (art/commerce) dichotomy remains operative in music culture, there is finally no position of purity in the business of music. The music business is, alas, a business. Despite this, the language of purity often persists in the espoused high ideals with which many pop musicians decorate themselves and their careers. And, as I have argued, music culture's romanticism and the language of purity that it generates have at times given rise to a significant "denigration of the image," the roots of which can be traced back to the art world rhetorics that have been adopted in music culture. Most notably, and perhaps surprisingly, the discourse I refer to as *modernist aestheticism* at one time entered popular music culture and, absorbed into its rhetorics, resulted in the hierarchical differentiation between the visual and aural with which this essay concerns itself.

While writers such as Simon Frith, Greil Marcus, and Lawrence Grossberg have gone to great lengths—and rightly so—in noting the ways in which some of the more radical cultural practices of the twentieth century (from the art-into-life movement of the Russian avant-garde to the pointedly disruptive maneuvers of Dada negation to the irony of postmodernism) have resurfaced in popular music culture, often with art schools as one crucial nexus between the art and music worlds, less attention has been given to the inheritance in music culture of what are, at least from our historical vantage point, the more conservative rhetorics of modernist aestheticism. Modernist aestheticism is associated most notably, though certainly neither originally nor exclusively, with the aforementioned Clement Greenberg.[6] While Frith and Andrew Goodwin, echoing a common enough sentiment, note the "central place of romanticism (its language of art and genius) in rock ideology," such an insight has not led to close analysis of how romanticism's particularities, channeled through a range of twentieth-century art world ideologies, have finally taken root in popular music culture.[7] Part of this failure is due to the fact that some of those twentieth-century art world ideologies are more than others far more appealing to the cultural studies camp with which Frith and Goodwin are associated. But it is in considering the inheritance in music culture of the less-appealing principles of modernist aestheticism that we can better understand the complicated place that was at one point assigned to the visual register.

The romanticism of popular music culture, crucial to what might be called the classical version of authenticity (which I have associated with a range of performers, from Woody Guthrie to Bruce Springsteen and beyond), has been shot through with modernist thought: how and why did this lead to a certain "denigration of the image" within rock and pop's fluxuating definitions of authenticity? If, as I suggest above, cultural studies writers have frequently celebrated punk's "cut-and-paste" approach, rightly noting the irony and irreverence with which punks ransacked commercial culture's visual materials and reordered them for the purposes of subversion or, at least, for the meaningfulness of meaninglessness, there remains another, entirely different mode of punk's confrontation with the visual materials of commercial culture, a mode that is captured in X lead singer Exene Cervenka's description of L.A. punk's reception of video. Implicit in Cervenka's statement is the notion that video is a tainted form, not simply another cultural product with which punks could *have their way*, appropriate, defile, and, in some way, subvert. Indeed, Cervenka slides into a telling geographic metaphor meant to describe the *place* of video: one must be "dragged kicking and screaming into it." The suggestion, common enough, is that there is a place *outside* of video's realm, outside of mainstream popular culture, that is implicitly a scene of authenticity and art rather than commerce and its unfortunate necessities.

In Cervenka's description, something quite different from the cut-and-paste, dive-into-popular-culture-tear-it-up-and-make-new-meanings-of-it mentality is being expressed. Indeed, what is conveyed is an attitude that both arose in punk's first wave and reemerged later when artists spoke a language of purity in order to position themselves against the commercial presence that was nonetheless intrinsic to music culture. Again, such a rhetorical maneuvering *cannot* easily be related to the artistic strategies of Dada, for instance, or to the Russian avant-garde, or to postmodern play with irony and appropriation, at least not as easily as it can be related to modernist aestheticism.

If Peter Burger divides modern art practices into, first, an avant-garde impulse and, second, a modernist aestheticism, with Burger privileging the avant-gardist approach as one "whose aim it is to reintegrate art into the praxis of life," Cervenka's use of the geographic metaphor to suggest video's distance from art relates not to the rhetoric of the avant-garde but to that of the modernist aestheticians.[8] What Burger celebrates as the capacity of the historical avant-garde to "reintegrate art into the praxis of life" is defeated in the moment that Cervenka implicitly opposes video/mainstream popular culture to an elsewhere, to the *art* of punk. Which is to say, rather than bridging art and everyday life, she (and, of course, so many others among punk's heroes) sanctifies a zone outside of the mainstream—the mainstream, where, for most of popular music's audience, everyday life is lived. Thus, while the historical avant-garde is often presented as the model for, among other things, punk practices, the rhetorics of modernist aestheticism are just as often and just as consistently in evidence in popular music, whether in punk or in classical versions of rock authenticity. Any overemphasis on the inheritance of avant-gardist method in music culture finally inhibits an analysis that seeks to understand how modernist aestheticism's rhetorics have been adopted in that same place and, in turn, how such rhetorics have determined the uneasy marriage of sound and vision therein. Thus it is in order to better understand popular music culture's language of purity and the place sometimes assigned to video in that language's system of differences that I consider the modernist rhetorics that provide many of the basic grammars and idioms for that language of purity.

The giant-slaying romanticism inherent in music culture's oft-told story of a little *us* versus a powerful, institutional *them* is, of course, nothing new; histories of modern art are punctuated by narratives that have at their center just this us/them structure. In the history of the history of art, short though it may be, stories of *innovation* are most often told in relation to this us/them structure, innovation celebrated as the individual's noble betrayal of the institution's codified modes of artistic creation. Indeed, it is the ghost of art history's proclaimed divide between the rule-bound, oppressive academy and the radical, truth-seeking modern artists that lurks about in and informs rock and pop ideologies — the ghost emerges in the form of an opposition made between the commercial and the underground, an opposition worshipped and defended despite concrete evidence that this border has always been both highly permeable and much-trafficked by "artists."

In analyzing music culture's debt to the rhetorics of modern art, we can begin to appreciate not only the place that the visual has assumed in certain popular music rhetorics but also the curiously elevated status that the modern visual arts have given to music. In the introduction to the collection *Rock Over the Edge*, that volume's editors make the point that the "die-hard persistence of the authenticity myth . . . indicates just how difficult it is to discuss rock music apart from rock's rhetoric; it is as if rock would cease to exist without the opposition of 'real' and 'fake' musics to underwrite it."[9] Without a doubt, the "authenticity myth" has at times, and in an explicit aping of modern aestheticism's rhetorics, used the figure of the visual (particularly video) to represent the category of the "fake." In doing so, "underground" rock and pop music's curious "denigration of the image" has been advanced.

In *Gardner's Art through the Ages*, a text that has assumed canonical status in relation to art history survey classes, descriptions of the modernist project typify what might be called a mainline conception of modernism in the visual arts. Modern artists are presented as aiming to "advance the cause of artistic innovation and engage in a running battle with a largely unsympathetic public and hostile authorities." "The prophet of the Modernist doctrine," the authors insist, "was Cezanne, and the principal heroes of the movement were Seurat, van Gogh, and Gauguin."[10] The language is unambiguous: new, important "battles" demanded of the modern artists a profound and often solitary heroism, while in the midst of it all the ossified institutions and ignorant popular audiences failed to comprehend (sometimes even attempted to suppress!) that heroism and the innovations it yielded. Of course, the art historian, cognizant of it all (albeit in hindsight) is flattered by his or her knowingness. In *Gardner's* description of the fauves, we read of artistic discoveries that "led the [the fauves] individually into paths of free invention and away from the traditions of the Renaissance."[11] If in the academy artists were enslaved to traditions based in Renaissance systems of representation, *outside*, in the cafés and other spaces of bohemian everyday life, a revolution was taking place. Of course, this "outside" status becomes a crucial earmark of the innovator, with "outsidedness" being at the heart of the geography through which the story of modernist innovation is told. The geographic metaphor returns again, if much later, in the celebration of the "outsider artist."

Gardner's volume is hardly unique in presenting the story of modernism in such terms. As heroic artists exercising what might be described as an epic individualism, when modernism is the subject these creatures pop up everywhere, with the repressive institution positioned as the true artist's antagonist. If *Gardner's Art through the Ages* offers the "mainline" view of modernism, Clement Greenberg is the critic, as frequently revered as he is reviled, most commonly cited as the key explicator of modernism's character, historical trajectory, and agenda. His critical insights gave strength to modernist aestheticism's rise to postwar glory. However, what in Gardner's volume is discussed as painting's movement "away from the traditions of the Renaissance," Greenberg describes more precisely as the narrowing of the modern painter's interests, a narrowing that ultimately finds the painter involved only with the qualities and characteristics particular to his medium. The world beyond the canvas does not pertain to such a painter's mission. With Greenberg's guidance, the autonomy of art and the discrete character of art's various mediums are established as modernist doctrine. And in asserting the notion of an art that involves itself only with itself, Greenberg describes and defends an artistic strategy that is very, very different from what *Burger* describes as the avant-garde art-into-life approach. Greenberg's is an art that beats a hasty retreat from everyday life. Famously, Greenberg defines modernist painting as that which escapes the tendency to simulate three dimensions on a two-dimensional surface and, instead, embraces the medium's unique fact: flatness. In "Modernist Painting," an essay first published in 1961, he puts a fine point on his career polemic: "It quickly emerged that the unique and proper area of competence of each art coincided with all that was unique to the nature of its medium. The task of self-criticism became to eliminate from the effects of each art any and every effect that might conceivably be borrowed from or by the medium of any other art. Thereby each art would be rendered 'pure,' and in its 'purity' find the guarantee of its standards of quality as well as of its independence. 'Purity' meant self-definition, and the enterprise of self-criticism in the arts became one of self-definition with a vengeance."[12]

In Greenberg's writing we often find the aim of modernist aestheticism described in terms that suggest that a certain moral imperative is attached to modern painting's investigation of its own unique properties. That is, the modernist abandonment of classical modes of representation is given a moral charge, where the move toward abstraction is equated with the good. "Purity" and "truth" are terms bandied about in descriptions of this modernist project. Importantly, in making a connection between the abandonment of classical modes of representation and a new morality, Greenberg's argument recalls those passages in Plato's *Republic*, such as the following, in which painting's mimetic function is condemned as a practice of falsification: "I said that painting or drawing, and imitation in general, when doing their own proper work, are far removed from the truth and the companions and friends and associates of a principle within us which is equally removed from reason, and that they have no true or healthy aim."[13] Though Greenberg argues that the "proper work" of painting, the investigation of the medium's unique characteristics, *is* actually the medium's "true and healthy aim," whereas Plato delivers a blanket condemnation of painting as a practice (painting is not to be allowed in his utopia), the shared ground between Greenberg's conception and the Platonic view is made plain in their common belief that the effort to portray three dimensions on a two-dimensional surface is a move away from the truth, a lapse.

While this suggests a certain symmetry of thought between premodern philosophy and modernist aestheticism, there is still another respect in which Platonic thought presages the value systems of modernist aestheticism. Alongside a contempt for the mimetic arts, the Platonic account celebrates music as an art that escapes the pitfalls of mimesis: "Musical training is a more potent instrument than any other, because rhythm and harmony find their way into the inward places of the soul, on which they mightily fasten, imparting grace, and making the soul of him who is rightly educated graceful."[14] This celebration of music as a language that plays directly upon the soul, as an unmediated language, resurfaces with great force in modernist art theory. If modernism is widely represented as an advance away from the illusionism of Renaissance traditions, such an advance is *toward* abstraction and is often described in terms of modern painting's increasingly musical quality, its affinity with music. This is, despite Greenberg's insistence that modern painting's evolution can be described in terms of the medium's increasing self-referentiality, the medium attending to itself on its own terms, music is frequently referenced in descriptions of that very modernist project. Music, understood as a nonreferential, abstract language, was seen to embody all that painting was itself striving for as it overcame its reliance on mimesis. Indeed, in the movement toward abstraction, modern visual artists regularly took music as their ideal and paradigm.

In his *Concerning the Spiritual in Art*, Wassily Kandinsky insists that art must approach the condition of music in order to achieve new heights in spirituality. As the artist strives toward the "abstract, the non-material," it is music, Kandinsky demands on a Platonic note, that is "the best teacher."[15] Thus does illusionism/mimesis come to be equated with a movement *away* from the spiritual (Kandinsky's position is argued, as is Greenberg's several years later, along implicitly moral lines). In providing the visual arts with a model of a nonreferential, affective art form that in its abstract nature need not make a circuit through the material world (at least not commonly at the level of reference), music becomes a rhetorical figure that is used to suggest what the visual arts, too, might become (and here is the great paradox): an art of pure feeling, an art that might, though of necessity ocular, transcend the eye's connection to the material world. Following this line of thought, true art, it seems, is felt more than it is seen. In figuring Renaissance-based academic work as an art that is slave to the eye—the eye, pulled to the external, material, *non-spiritual* referent—Kandinsky describes an art born of the *feelings*, of the *soul*, an art that can express what is inside, directly. What we *see* in such an art, it seems, *is* feeling.

To understand the extremes to which the rhetorically constructed music/visual arts affinity could be taken as modernist aestheticism rose to art world prominence, we can consider the case of Alfred Stieglitz's photographic theory. After abandoning the early, pictorialist phase of his photographic career, Stieglitz, who was responsible for the early New York gallery shows of Picasso, Matisse, and other key modern European artists, embraced rhetorics that were unabashedly modernist in their attempt to align the "true" art image with music. Of his well-known *Equivalents*, a series of cloud photographs that recall the cloud studies of Constable, Stieglitz delivers a statement that makes his modernist inclinations plain: "I wanted a series of photographs which when seen by Ernest Bloch . . . he would exclaim: Music! Music! Man, why that is music! How did you ever do that. And he would point to violins, and flutes, and oboes, and brass."[16] In responding to this passage, Allan Sekula writes: "The romantic artist's compulsion to achieve the 'condition of music' is a desire to abandon all contextual reference and to convey meaning by a virtue of metaphorical substitution. In photography this compulsion requires an incredible denial of the image's status as report."[17] The fact that photography, still more than painting, must by its very nature take a circuit through the external, material world remains a curiously small obstacle, easily denied, as Stieglitz promotes a photography of pure feeling, of music.

In various ways, the modern visual arts are thus established as existing "outside." If in Renaissance-based illusionist painting Clement Greenberg locates a parasitic dependence on the properties of the other arts (a dependence on the narrative inclination of literature, the three dimensionality of sculpture, etc.), he also insists that there is another possibility, a modern painting that refuses the narrative nature of literature, the three dimensionality of sculpture, a painting that, always negating, creates a space for itself outside of all that it is not. Further developing a vision of modern painting's *outsidedness*, Greenberg also establishes the place of modern painting as outside of popular culture.[18] It is as if Gustave Courbet's nineteenth-century efforts to break away and establish a salon independent from the official Universal Exposition—outside of the institution and the place of popular visual spectacle—became a defining reflex of the modernist movement. The more popular culture became a culture of spectacle, the more modernist aestheticism insisted upon an art outside of that—one that was autonomous and based not on spectacle, not on vision, but on feeling. Andreas Huyssen describes the modern artist as one "who tries to stake out his territory by fortifying the boundaries between genuine art and inauthentic mass culture."[19]

In so doing, that artist establishes mass culture as, in Huyssen's words, "modernism's Other."

Modern art is thus an art that came to be conceived as existing outside of the formal mandates associated with Renaissance-based institutions of art, as an art outside of popular culture, as an art beyond the reach of the other arts. The modern arts, at least as the rhetorics of modernist aestheticism insist, stand apart, refusing all that it is not. And by extension, so too does the modern artist stand apart, autonomous, and subject to no rules save those of his chosen medium. Thus lands the solitary romantic artist, with a twist, in the middle of the twentieth century. His is the protagonist and promoter in his own theater of purity.

The rhetorics of modernist aestheticism, absorbing elements from an earlier romanticism and reaching a culminating point in Clement Greenberg's writing, have done much to inform rock culture's formulation of authenticity, principally in passing on to rock culture the notion that art is an experience of outsidedness, and the true artist an outsider. An obsession with difference — "art is not that, art is outside of that" — is at the heart of modernism's efforts to describe innovation, and innovation is finally modernism's most crucial gesture. *Make it new!* Of course, this obsession with difference has been transplanted into rock culture to great effect. As Simon Frith argues: "The assumption is that rock music is good music only when it is not mass culture, when it is an art form or a folk sound."[20] The "not" in this statement becomes the sine qua non of a conception of the "good." As Frith's statement suggests, the assignment of value hinges on the declaration of difference — *this is good because it is not that*.

Pure abstraction, striving to escape reference, and by extension, language, striving for an unmediated and autonomous expression, requires *difference* in order to explain itself and, by extension, the place of art. That is, modernist aestheticism, while claiming to go beyond difference to discover purity, needs difference more than ever. Purity always needs its other. A statement by the modernist painter Ad Reinhardt makes the modernist position, or that need of art to say what it is not, quite clear: "The one thing to say about art is that it is one thing. Art is art-as-art and everything else is everything else. Art-as-art is nothing but art. Art is not what is not art. . . . The only way to say what abstract art or art-as-art is, is to say what it is not."[21]

Cervenka's description of the video problem — "we were all dragged kicking and screaming into it"—is merely one example of a position taken in which video functions as the object of difference, the object that serves to define relationally the *place* of punk authenticity. As mentioned above, the Replacements, long celebrated for their irreverence in the face of the music industry's dictates, initially refused to make videos at all, even as their one-time label Warner Brothers understood well the role video could play in breaking a band like the Replacements at a higher level. But in trying to get a band born of the underground and sworn to the underground to embrace video, Warner Brothers was butting up against a code that found its sturdy roots in art world rhetoric: the pop record album, a mass cultural form through which punk and post-punk bands generated their art, was adamantly differentiated from video, a mass cultural form understood to be intrinsically tainted. Music was not held to the same judgment as was a medium more inextricably bound to the visual register. Somehow, video was intrinsically *more* mass cultural, more mainstream (even more corporate) than recorded music. It was the differentiation of mediums as established by an inherited discursive logic. The fact that Warner Brothers was itself a corporate giant, situated in the heart of mainstream mass culture, was, true to the paradoxical nature of underground music culture's codes of authenticity, not the issue.

Mass culture has, since the nineteenth century, revolved around spectacle. Modernist aestheticism, both honoring and cultivating romantic conceptions of the artist and art as things apart, made crucial use of mass culture as the object of difference. There was no way to define artistic purity without the object of difference, without commercial culture, rooted in the spectacle, there as *other*. Thus the us/them structure of music culture romanticism, lifted from art world rhetorics, was for some time energized by the value systems that cast the visual spectacle of mass culture as art's other. The visual spectacle belongs on the side not of *us* but of *them*. And this historical "denigration of the image" hung over the medium of video. In this way, the punk ethos borrowed less from the moment of pop art than it did from the movement that pop disrupted, abstract expressionism.

The relationship between musical "artists" and video shifts and, of course, needs periodization. If among the underground in the eighties there was a relatively common and unabashed vilification of video, the situation has not remained static. There are several examples of present-day artists who have embraced video and done so without compromising their "purity." But, despite such examples, the visual remains a potentially troubled area, an anxious ground. Symptoms of the anxiety around the visual are today various. If artists such as Björk, Beck, Sonic Youth, the Beastie Boys, and the White Stripes are among those who have embraced video in the manner described, it is evident that the directors with whom these artists make videos are a notably select group. Elsewhere in this volume, Roger Beebe makes the point that rock video has transformed into something like an auteurist medium. The group of directors of whom I speak can certainly be considered in such terms. Importantly, with the auteur as leader (and, in the best case, as co-collaborator), musical artists can enter the troubled zone of video with far less threat to their authenticity. If the "denigration of the image" is a residue from the discourse of modern art, it is no surprise that another modernist residue, in the form of the auteur, arrives to balance out the scene. In popular music culture, modernist thought has found one of its most lasting homes. On some level, an affiliation with one of the established auteurs allows enough of an object of difference for the theater of purity to unfold. But, as video becomes less useful—in the wide sense—as an object of difference, it has made it more difficult for the underground to go through the process of self-definition. Something is lost. The underground relinquishes a tool with which it constructed its own identity. Even in the age of Clear Channel and alarming corporate mergers, without the "denigration of the image" underground self-definition is less obvious as a project.

THE LEGACY OF THE THEATER

The romantic fantasy of the underdog artist/outsider, at a remove from the "fake" mainstream, is worthy of study because it is this fantasy that sheds light on the question of how popular music and politics might mix. In many respects, the romanticism can become a blockade. If this romanticism, borrowed from art world discourses by various music world ideologies, pits the giant, decadent and immoral, against the underdog, lean and good, herein is a discourse that has generated a simplistic conception of antagonism. It flatters the "artist" as it glosses over what is really a complicated situation of alliances between the giant and his purported enemy.

In the worst case, the drama of giant-slaying proves a *distraction* from the political realities and possibilities of rock culture. The pose of resistance, common in the music culture, only rarely becomes more than a pose. In particular, myths of art's distance from commerce have resulted in a loftiness that often leaves little room for self-criticism among those who wield such myths—the underground David, making a great show of his interest in giant slaying, tends to pay little or no mind to the not-so-simple fact that he is often on the giant's payroll.

As has frequently been the case in popular music culture, the underground stance often conceals (though sometimes barely) a notable intimacy with the "machine" of the music business. We can rage, quite heroically, and still enjoy the fruits of commercial success as only the "machine" can provide them. Bands deeply engaged in corporate alliances can wave, righteously even, bold anticorporate flags. Herein lies one aspect of the disingenousness that underpins the rock stance and, finally, contributes to the clumsiness of the relationship between rock culture and politics. If we "turn off" when the music performer starts to speak of politics—and many fans do just this, much to the performers' consternation—is this simply the fans' impatience at work? Or is this "turning off" perhaps a reaction to the deep paradoxes behind the idealism and romanticism that structure the politics so often espoused by the rock and pop performer? For instance, who in the music industry is surprised by the tension between word and deed when a group known for publicly and very adamantly advocating free speech negotiates a gag order when a band member chooses to leave the band? Is it possible to take seriously the politics of such a band? In pop music culture, politics are sometimes crucial to the rock stance while remaining shot through with inconsistencies when viewed in relation to the artist's actual practices and alliances.

What the situation of 1980s video reveals is the manner in which music culture has played home to some alarming ideological paradoxes. From the art world, and particularly from modernist aestheticism, comes a romanticism that in music culture has helped to support a soft, ineffective politics. Perhaps after considering at greater length certain aspects of video's reception within music culture, we can look beyond the situation of video and understand more generally the manner in which music culture romanticism, thick with oversimplification and bombastic gestures meant to suggest "purity," has continued to trouble that culture's efforts to engage politics. A study of the place of the visual can help to demonstrate the fact that the theater of purity makes use of cheap sets.

Perhaps there is a way to move forward the project of underground self-definition—the moment calls for it—but to move it forward without generating systems of difference that are themselves built on weak foundations. As we can learn from the underground's use of video in the 1980s, a good object of difference can *make* the project of self-definition. But as we can also learn, one effect of overly simplistic, even archaic systems of difference (art vs. commerce, image vs. truth) is the erosion of credibility in the political arena. The "denigration of the image" in the theater of purity is there as a model and a cautionary tale both.

NOTES

1 I use the term "underground" to describe an oppositional musical culture that defines itself against the mainstream. Because the term was used with greater regularity in the 1980s, I use it now to evoke this period, which ultimately is my focus.

2 Cited in Charles Harrison and Paul Wood, eds., *Art in Theory* (Cambridge: Blackwell, 1992), 529–41.

3 Cited in Mark Spitz and Brendan Mullen, *We Got the Neutron Bomb: The Untold Story of L.A. Punk* (New York: Three Rivers Press, 2001), 276–77.

4 Robert Cantwell, *When We Were Good* (Cambridge, Mass.: Harvard University Press, 1996).

5 We learned that a number of bands and performers who would not do commercials in the United States were quick to do so in Europe, where audiences had a different relationship to the authenticity/advertising dilemma. It was a way to make the money without losing favor stateside.

6 See Simon Frith and Howard Horne, *Art into Pop* (London: Routledge and Kegan Paul, 1988); and Greil Marcus, *Lipstick Traces* (Cambridge, Mass.: Harvard University Press, 1989).

7 Simon Frith and Andrew Goodwin, eds., *On Record* (New York: Pantheon, 1990), 181.

8 Peter Burger, *Theory of the Avant-Garde* (Minneapolis: University of Minnesota Press, 1984), 22.

9 Roger Beebe, Denise Fulbrook, and Ben Saunders, eds., *Rock Over the Edge* (Durham, N.C.: Duke University Press, 2002), 3.

10 Richard Tansey and Horst de la Croix, *Gardner's Art through the Ages* (New York: Harcourt Brace, 1986), 1022.

11 Ibid.

12 Cited in Harrison and Wood, eds., *Art in Theory*, 755.

13 Cited in Albert Hofstadter and Richard Kuhns, eds., *Philosophies of Art and Beauty* (Chicago: University of Chicago Press, 1964), 39.

14 Ibid., 28.

15 Wassily Kandinsky, *Concerning the Spiritual in Art* (London: Constable and Co., 1914), 19.

16 Allan Sekula, "On the Invention of Photographic Meaning," in *Thinking Photography*, in Victor Burgin, ed. (London: Macmillan, 1982), 101.

17 Ibid.

18 See Clement Greenberg, "Avant-Garde and Kitsch," in *Pollock and After: The Critical Debate* (New York: Harper and Row, 1985).

19 Andreas Huyssen, *After the Great Divide* (Bloomington: Indiana University Press, 1986), 53.

20 Simon Frith, *Sound Effects* (New York: Pantheon, 1981), 41.

21 Reinhardt, cited in Harrison and Wood, *Art in Theory*, 806.

"I'M FROM RAGS TO RICHES": THE DEATH OF JAY-Z

Cynthia Fuchs

> In the struggles of urban youths for survival and pleasure
> inside capitalism, capitalism has become both their greatest friend
> and greatest foe.—ROBIN D. G. KELLEY,
> *Yo' Mama's Disfunktional!*

> Like the face of a Sprewell rim—which keeps spinning after
> the tire has stopped—best black MC Jay-Z has an out-of-sync rela-
> tionship with his surroundings.—NICK CATUCCI,
> *Village Voice*, January 2003

> *PLAYBOY*: Every time you say, "I'm from the hood," you screw up
> your face like a cartoon villain.
> JAY-Z: Because it's funny. "I'm from the hood." It's a joke. You can't
> take that seriously. Rappers, we ain't from the hood.
> We got nice homes and nice cars. We from the mansion.
> —ROB TANNENBAUM, *Playboy*, April 2003

On his retirement from The Game, Jay-Z started spending more time at Nets games. Like any other team owner or part owner, Shawn Carter appeared on the 2004 playoffs sidelines as a man with a stake in an enterprise and a manifestly mainstream future to build. No longer "just" a hip hop artist with his name attached to the requisite fashion line, Carter is now a corporate citizen, with his capacity to "give back" to the community quite exponentially increased.

Jay's new standing as a hustler of note is most visibly marked by his announcement that he's given up actual rapping. Roc-A-Fella continues, as do Rocawear, Armadale vodka, and his Reeboks kicks contract, but he's gone out of his way to display his new identity—a suit with New York baseball cap. Specifically, Shawn Carter's own tastes appear to reflect his shifting sense of responsibilities and effects. As Guy Trebay writes in the *New York Times*, "Last November when the *Black Album* by Jay-Z was released, the rapper made the point succinctly. 'And I don't wear jerseys, I'm 30-plus,' Jay-Z rapped. 'Give me a crisp pair of jeans . . . Button up.' As early as last August, he signaled a shift in his sartorial direction by wearing a jacket with well-defined shoulders and rear vents to the MTV Video Music Awards."[1]

This is not to say that Jay-Z, even as he first came on the music scene in 1995 with the influential underground single "In My Lifetime," was ever unaware of the power of his image. To the contrary, from his first music video, Abdul Malik Abbott's street-set "I Can't Get Wit That" (with a low budget of $5000), he showed an acute understanding of how image might shape reality, or at least contribute to that all-important hip hop asset, the illusion of "keeping it real." Jay-Z has used videos, like he has used his famously nuanced lyrics, to reveal and remember his past in Marcy Projects, to reimagine his life as a means to an end, to reshape his experiences to accommodate his ambition. The fact that his music videos frequently set him in the projects or 'round the Brooklyn way, as well as on the occasional big white yacht (as in Hype Williams's "Big Pimpin'" [2000]) is as much a function of self-performance as promoting product. In almost all of his video incarnations, Jay-Z recalls himself as hustler, not only the dealer he once was in Marcy, but also the storyteller and the self-promoter, the roles he continues to play.

Jay-Z's recent (as of 2006) adult incarnations—in designer suits and striped dress shirts, at fashion shows or ball games—led to reassertions, of his name, career options, and potential political functions. First, the incitement: He (or rather, the character named Jay-Z) is shot to death at the end of his reportedly last video, for "99 Problems." The Mark Romanek-directed clip thus incited a whole new round of MTV's claims to "controversy." Indeed, Jay tells *Rolling Stone*, "I feel like Madonna," recalling the flap over her video for "What It Feels Like for a Girl."[2] Directed by Madonna's husband Guy Ritchie, that video was also deemed "controversial" for its "excessive" and explicit violence. In 2001 it was aired just once by MTV, which then banned and resurrected it—one second of it, anyway, along with Prodigy's "Smack My Bitch Up"—in John Norris's somber introduction to "99 Problems" as a demonstration of the network's serious concerns with displays of gun violence. Given that Jay-Z's video went into more or less regular rotation on MTV Jams, MTV, and MTV2, these concerns appear to have dissipated. That is, the video hasn't particularly been censored, save for the nominal attachment of Norris's taped "warning label." The track also became intermittently anthemic during the 2004 NBA playoffs timeouts.

Asked to explain the video's gun violence and, specifically, its potential effects on "kids," Jay tells MTV's Sway that he approached the role as such: "Just like Denzel in *Training Day* or any other actor, I was acting out a part."[3] What Jay-Z overlooks here—with understandable political reason—is that hip hop artists are rarely granted such distance from the "roles" they play; rather, hip hop performances tend to be read as direct translations of the artists' experiences, beliefs, and self-understandings: if you act like a thug in a video, it's because you want to show that you are one. The role and the actor are interchangeable: just ask Ice T, who ran into a similar controversy with "Cop-Killer" back in 1992.

Further, and somewhat more complicated, Jay-Z insists that this particular performance is a rite of passage: "It's symbolic to the whole retirement thing," he says. "And putting the whole Jay-Z thing to rest."[4] The whole Jay-Z thing will never be put to rest, of course, but as Shawn Carter endeavors to move on, and to imagine himself as a "mature" individual and community representative, he might also imagine that he lives in a universe premised on faiths in free will and free markets. He identifies himself as a member of a particular class and generation, even asserting the identification as a choice. Still, it's not as if he doesn't understand the significance of this self-assessment: as he points out frequently, he has been able to make choices that are typically unavailable to his childhood peers in Marcy Projects, to which he returns for the "99 Problems" video shoot (or, as Norris calls it, "the streets of his beloved Brooklyn"), naming the location, for the cameras in MTV's *Making the Video*, "My home right there. I'm from the bottom."

Jay-Z has repeatedly made his home visible in lyrics and video imagery. Perhaps most famously, "Hard Knock Life" directed by Steve Carr and Jay-Z) returns the artist, at the moment of his mainstream crossover in 1998, to his old neighborhood as act and icon, a moment and place underscored by excess. The video shows "residents" ostensibly doing what they do: riding bikes, shooting craps, chatting on stoops, and posing on in the hood of Jigga-man's extremely fine ride. The track's celebrated use of the *Annie* anthem, with the video kids mouthing the Broadway kids' voices, sets him amid a fantasy of poverty and resilience. Jay enters the video by walking through a neighborhood convenience store, the aisles close as the camera peers up at him in motion, casual, neighborly. Stepping outside, he tips his hat, a gesture of respect as he comes onto the street proper, where folks reside. Jay-Z strolls, then pauses, leaning against an intensely red wall, at the back of the frame. The camera tracks past him, following a girl as she walks at ease in her space and cognizant of her 'hood. Such equanimity is indicative of the 'hood's resonance for Jay-Z: while it warranted notoriety as the site of gangster activity, hustling, and violence, it also comprised a community, a place where people knew each other and understood their shared lot. "Quite simply stated," writes Murray Forman in *The 'Hood Comes First: Race, Space, and Place in Rap and Hip-Hop*, "The 'hood exists as a 'home' environment."[5]

At the same time, as "Hard Knock Life" reveals, the 'hood is also a specific and imaginative construction, a means to designate place (in terms of class, gender, and race), as well as to assign and deflect identity. Unlike earlier "ghetto" videos such as Grandmaster Flash and the Furious Five's "The Message" (1982), Tupac's "Brenda's Got a Baby" (1992), or Nas's "Nas Is Like" (Nick Quested, 1994) that exposed street "realities" as such, "Hard Knock Life" is simultaneously diurnal and sensational, depressed and sanguine, a dramatization of the dreams ignited by such an environment even as it lays out geography and connectedness. When Jay-Z appears again, he describes his journey, his life story (and most marketable asset), the way he "stretched the game out, put Jigga on top." As he has moved on "from standing on the corners, boppin,'" now he says, "I flow for those droned out, / All my niggas locked down in the ten by four, controlling the house, / We live in hard knocks, we don't take over, we borrow blocks. / Burn 'em down and you can have 'em back, daddy, I'd rather that." In this keen breakdown of the projects' economic structure, residents don't own space.

Jay-Z's talent for "stretching out" analogies and analyses is well known and much revered. In "Do It Again," off the third volume, *Life and Times of S. Carter*, of his autobiographical series (the first of which is *In My Lifetime*, the second *Hard Knock Life*), Jay renegotiates hip-hop time with a gappy drum machine; this shufflelike beat controverted the common industry wisdom of the moment, as most rappers were intent on spitting fast, deft rhymes in 4–4 time. (Jay-Z's own "Nigga What, Nigga Who" and "Can I Get a . . . ," both from *Hard Knock Life* were among the speediest.) These performances proved the point: Jay-Z could do anything he put his mind to, and moreover, he could change the game, on his initiative. While Malik Sayeed's frankly stunning 1999 video for "Nigga What" is nearly science-fictional in its images of desolation and use of wind machines and backlighting, the video for "Can I Get a . . ." (Steve Carr, 2000), relocates Jay-Z again, this time in a club where he reigns supreme, even with backup dancers and even as the video also pimps Brett Ratner's movie *Rush Hour* (1998) and introduces the Tupac-wannabe Ja Rule to the MTV audience.

For the "Do It Again" video (Dave Meyers, 2000), Jay appears in the literal street, his Timberlands unlaced, his jeans crisp, as he raps for the camera, tugging on his collar. In the club, he enters with all kinds of attitude, respected as he mounts the stairs to the lounge, from which he surveys the dance floor. His rap describes his "typical" nights out now that he's a player, with his hustler image spread wide and powerfully: "Both arms are chunky, the sleeves on chill, / Any given times 100 Gs in your grill. / Don't talk to me about MC's got skills, / He's all right, but he's not real. / Jay-Z's that deal with seeds in the field." Affluent, changed, and self-conscious about such change, Jay here reshapes his environment to frame his status, his access and options. While he "digs out" his date for the night and sends her home before the night is over, Amil (then the designated "girl MC" for the Roc-A-Fella crew) holds her own, announcing that women might also enjoy one-night stands, gossip with their friends, and judge the men who attempt to play them. This inclusion of an alternative, if parallel, view of the club and street life makes the track and video for "Do It Again" doubled in plot as well as musical structure.

Identities and biographies rarely coincide precisely, as performative and generic demands impose expectations on artists and consumers. Jay-Z/Shawn Carter embodies the paradoxes that shape today's hip hop industry, the ways that it creates and also extracts from and reforms such identity. There are numerous ways that identity is vexed in celebrity culture and in hip hop especially, not the least of which has to do with the naming process. It's common practice for MCs to self-select names (or have names assigned by savvy marketers or childhood compatriots). Jay-Z's several names — Jigga, Hova, Izzo — connote a shifting designation and evolution, from youthful specificity to increasing reach. They allude to contexts as well: commercial and local, underground and mainstream. As Robin Kelley argues, rap expresses the fact that economic restructuring, and the resulting massive unemployment, "created criminals out of black youth."[6] For all of its emphasis on the accumulation of wealth that follows from successful commodification, hustler hip hop continues, in Jay's version, to address project conditions, class disparities, and racism. Kelley calls this the "politics of ghettocentricity," insisting on the ways that "the specific class, race, and gendered experiences in late-capitalist urban centers coalesce to create a new identity—'Nigga.'"[7]

For Jigga, whose own name conflates "nigga" with "Jay" (and thus challenges the very idea that names, even racist labels, can be definitive rather than contextual and relative), this identity is also a means to forge and acknowledge community. As he told *Blaze* in 1999, "I just want people to really see me as a regular nigga—'cause I'm their voice. I'm the nigga that speaks to what they go through, the things they feel. When I say it, it's like, 'Oh, you said what I felt.' Because I'm the same nigga."[8] Even as Jay asserts an identity that's ostensibly stable over time, a self that he can recognize in the mirror morning after morning, he also wields it as a performance, a shifty twisty act—whether in self-defense or self-expression hardly matters. He exploits its flexibility and reveals its artifice; in this expression of image "control" he also refashions the terms of "authenticity" so crucial in hip hop. And so his professed sameness is only partly true, in a traditional sense. "The same nigga" is myriad, a trickster perpetually transforming and transformative, a perennially variable function of location, affiliation, and aspiration. As Jay-Z reworks his own imaginative terrain, he also conjures new paradigms, stretches out new spaces, and resituates his persona. On the next album after "Can I Get a . . . ," Jay-Z also raps, on "There's Been a Murder," about the murder of Jay-Z and the return of Shawn Carter (anticipating his more spectacular self-disappearance in 2004): "Learn why we buck the guys that came up with us, / Ain't enough bucks for us to split in this shit. / Plus ain't nobody lovin' us, and with that said, / back to Shawn Carter the hustler, Jay-Z is dead." Such overhaul is not always neatly marked or wholly effective; as Elizabeth Mendez Berry writes, *Life and Times of S. Carter* "showcases Jay-Z at his most menacing. The gangsta may have retired, but for Jay, the drug-related metaphors will last forever."[9] As Jay-Z in this instance, back in 1999, is unable to kill off the rapper to get back to the hustler, so he absorbs the one into the other, an act of self-destruction turned self-creation, or at least self-iteration.

Moreover, change is not always a matter of will or even self-control. It's worth remembering that Jay-Z's own career endured two different and unpredictable events: the release of *The Blueprint* on September 11, 2001 (moved up a week because of bootlegs), and the release of *Best of Both Worlds*, his collaborative album with R. Kelly, as child abuse charges were made against the singer. These collisions of history and livelihood, morality and commercialism, illustrate the impossibility of control. In the face of such difficulty, one can only hustle. Throughout his brief and prolific career (nine albums), Jay-Z has repeatedly elaborated his self-perception as a hustler, a dealer who moves product even if that product appears to be "self." He recognized early on the usefulness of the hustle in boardrooms. As Kelefa Sanneh writes in the *New Yorker*, Jay-Z is a premier "corporate rapper."[10] He resonates not only in his "real" stories — rendered via intellectual lyrics and assured demeanor — but also, importantly, in his embrace of corporate structures and consumer culture.

As Jay-Z performs his experiences he reinterprets them and reshapes their meanings so that they become authentic in a fluid sense — celebratory and huge, abstract but recognizable. "Jay-Z," the performed identity, is incongruously ghetto and large, casually transgressive, and resiliently conformist. Using the stereotypes associated with his young black maleness as a threat and a challenge, he raps in "So Ghetto": "I'm so gangsta, prissy chicks don't wanna fuck with me / I'm so gutter, ghetto girls fall in love with me." Such lyrics recall a time when Jay wouldn't change his attire to suit his new status: he staunchly stuck to his hood wear, large jewelry that he never could have afforded in his prior "real" life, accessorizing with emblems of his aspirations and achievements: "So I'm cruisin' in the car with this boozy broad," he asserted, in "So Ghetto." "She said, 'Jigga-Man, you rich, take the doo-rag off' / Hit a U-turn; ma, I'm droppin you back off." Now, of course, he's got the button-down, striped shirts and suit jackets. He's accommodating a new sense of self, one that he's renaming, perhaps nostalgically, perhaps resonantly, Shawn Carter.

With the *Black Album*, he has once again changed everything. Or at least that's what he says. In part, this stated purpose is manifested in his decision to use a different producer for each track, so the album is all about seemingly ongoing transformation. As he describes himself in "Public Service Announcement," "I've got a hustler's spirit, nigga period." It's a summing up that's also a kind of resignation. Berry writes of this song — and more generally, of Jay-Z's ongoing effort to maintain a stable-seeming persona — "In hip-hop, a culture that confuses cleverness with wisdom, Jay-Z is certainly one of the best. But he's a hustler first, an artist second."[11] You can't knock it, but you have to distrust it, apparently by definition. In "Moment of Clarity," produced by Eminem, he recognizes the tradeoff he's made, without apologizing. Self-awareness and self-control: these are street lessons, useful in the corporate world as well. "Music business hate me cause the industry ain't make me. / Hustlers and boosters embrace me and the music I be makin,'" he raps, in a minor paean to those who would "know." "I dumbed down for my audience to double my dollars. / They criticized me for it, yet they all yell, 'Holla!'" Not that it's news, but still. Stating it outright doesn't make it okay, but it does preempt criticism, a masterful hustle in its own right.

Success, Jay asserts repeatedly, is a function of hustling, an incessant process that even self-declaration can't stop. Of the four videos that emerged from the *Black Album*, the first is the recording of a live performance of "Encore," framing Jay once more in his element, on stage and thronged by screaming fans, who, incidentally, know all of his lyrics long before the album has been released. "When you first come in the game, they try to play you, / Then you drop a couple of hits, look how they wave to you, / From Marcy to Madison Square." Now that he's "made," Jay-Z can call for all to scream "'til you lungs get sore," and on cue, you do. "Now look at me," he commands. "All star-studded. / Golfer above par like I putted, / All 'cause the shit I uttered, was utterly ridiculous. / How sick is this?" How can it matter, amid the adulation, that any of it was "utterly ridiculous"? Who would believe that? The fans push to the stage, the camera pans over a sea of thrilled faces and "diamonds in the air," that is, Roc-A-Fella signs thrown up to show loyalty and devotion.

The video for the seemingly trifling "Change Clothes," featuring producer Pharrell Williams (as well as cameos by Russell Simmons, Kathy Rippa, and Naomi Campbell), reshuffles the performance trappings along a high-fashion runway. It makes visible the exchanges of wealth, influence, and possibility in the form of smiling as well as scrapping models (a seeming "catfight" occurs backstage, silhouetted behind the curtains and exaggerated by spotlights—even models perform according to expectations). The setting makes literal Jay's claim to marketing his identity, a product for sale and subtext, an image open to appropriation and interrogation. Now an "elder" statesman of sorts, he's on his way out even as he announces, "The boy is back." His departure pose is composed and self-knowing. "I been through that, been shot at, shoot back. / Gotta keep a peace like a Buddhist," he raps. "I ain't a New Jack, nobody gon' Wesley Snipe me. / It's less than likely, move back. / Let I breathe, Jedi Knight. / The more space I get, the better I write." Expanding as if to fill this newly conceived space, Jay looks relaxed, and even smiles, in this video. No longer big pimping, he's observing and participating, an owner of his own fashion line. As hip hop is always a process of analysis and narration, "Change Clothes" ("and go," as the chorus exhorts), proposes new ways to consider inevitable progression. Rather than remain the same, or be "the same nigga," Jay-Z—whom Kris Ex of *XXL* calls "the Stephen King of hiphop . . . able to make the most of having the most marketed-to audience in his genre's history," has found his way to embrace change, to be other and same at once, comfortably.[12] Whether this new look denotes maturity, authority, or empathy, it serves as communication that questions at the same time that it pronounces. "You know I stay, fresh to death, a boy from the projects, / And I'ma take you to the top of the globe." The projects as a means to the "top of the globe." Jay remains that "same nigga," as he narrates and elevates hip hop's permeation of mainstream consumer culture, by way of production and profits.

In his last videos, Jay deploys hip hop—as a tool, as a politics—with increasing caginess and complexity. In bidding it farewell he pushes it forward, as a manifestly politicized instrument, an enterprise relentlessly self-deconstructing and reconstructing by definition. Subsumed by the need to support itself, to sell product—to make available what is familiar and readable—hip hop has turned, by Jay's own account, less interesting, more "been there, done that" than challenging or intriguing. And yet, hip hop's seemingly inevitable and over-already commodification need not be a one-way ticket to banality and languor. As Jay-Z illustrates in "Dirt Off Your Shoulder," ingeniously produced by Timbaland, the commercial process itself can also raise questions about meaning and expectation, as well as respect. "Your homey Hov in position, in the kitchen with soda," he raps. "I just whipped up a watch, tryin' to get me a Rover, / Tryin' to stretch out the coca, like a wrestler, yessir. / Keep the heckler close, you know them smokers'll test ya." Boastful, playful, and at ease. He knows who he is and how much he needs it. Or so it seems. "Even as he rhymes the male fantasy," writes Kris Ex, "he touches on complex emotions." Understanding the pose, cool and savvy, he delivers truth as performance, and vice versa. What makes him seem the same also renders him extraordinary: he connects.

The video illustrates connections among consumers and producers, hustlers and hustled. Cutting back and forth in time, it shows Jay literally "take over" a radio station (with a focus on his own designer kicks

CYNTHIA FUCHS

as he enters the room) as his words reach out to a range of folks in the community, including a couple of Latino kids stopped by the cops, girls in the beauty shop, a woman striding to her car. All "brush off" the dirt offered by others, to move forward, resilient (not destructive) in their self-knowledge. "I paid a grip for the jeans, plus the slippers is clean," observes Jay. "No chrome on the wheels, I'm a grown-up for real." He doesn't have to explain his identity in the way he once did; he knows who he is, and so does his public. Taking his injunction to "get that dirt off your shoulders," the community (or all the pretty girls in it) join him for a late-night block party: from his limo, he shuffles his deck of cards then snaps his fingers, so the city lights go out, allowing an infrared hallucinatory glow to ignite the partiers (who include Jermaine Dupri and ?uestlove of the Roots, with a brief cameo of Beyoncé's dazzling smile, when he introduces her as "the hottest chick in the game, wearin' my chain"). By the video's end the lights come back and Jay reenters his limo, tipping his hat as the sun comes up in the frame's deep background: the hero rides off, gracefully.

Presuming his power, Jay pledges to know his community, even if he's no longer "from the 'hood," as he tells Rob Tannenbaum of *Playboy*. Ever dissenting, ever testing, Jay turns his last video back to Marcy, circa 1994, where he reintroduces Shawn Carter, seated in his mother's apartment (or a reasonable facsimile), where patterned couch and rug crowd the room. He leans into the camera and points to his mind, where his ideas are born: "Rap mags try and use my black ass / So advertisers can give 'em more cash for ads, fuckers! / I don't know what you take me as, / Or understand the intelligence that Jay-Z has. / I'm from rags to riches, niggas, I ain't dumb."

Descending the stoop, he enters the 'hood, noting those ads on subway markers and elsewhere. At the same time, the video pauses on graffiti and mural work—Martin Luther King Jr. and Malcolm X—heroes whose images now sell something else, a sense of self and collectivity. Driving with the track's producer and Def Jam cofounder Rick Rubin (in his present form, huge, fur-coated, and bearded), Jay's pulled over by a pair of circa 1994 uniforms. "Son," asks one, leaning into the window and mouthing Jay's lyrics (as he raps, in his best "cop" voice), "Do you know why I'm stoppin' you for?" He slumps in his seat, peeps up from under his baseball cap: "Cause I'm young and I'm black, and my hat's real low?

/ Or do I look like a mind-reader, sir? I don't know." No matter how rich you are, you're black while you're driving. It's the gift and the curse, a perpetually antagonistic relationship with the state, embodied here by cops and prison guards, but extending as well to more abstract and grander displays of "authority."

Shot in black and white, the video makes clear the interrelations among moments in time, forms of cultural expression and consumption, self-making and self-effacing: Jay walks on Brooklyn Bridge and in a record store (Checking his own? Competition? What's new?), a location that gives way to street murals. A series of connections are established through images that appear in juxtaposition: a booty girl, complete with short shorts and a tee-shirt-wetting hose, an African tribal dancer deep in a subway station, a fraternity step troupe spread over the street, break dancers flipping over an abandoned mattress, bikers doing wheelies, Vincent Gallo (of all people) shuffling and rattling on a street corner, a puking addict and a corpse, neatly laid out in his coffin, mourned by his family and remembered by the choir. Such portraits, fleeting, poignant, and evocative, suggest the ways that a neighborhood might linger in memory, bits and pieces reassembled to make sense of a life and perhaps a death.

Invested in "the real," hip hop insists on its political and experiential projects. "And there I go, trapped in the Kit-Kat again," Jay-Z raps. "Back through the system with the riff-raff again, / Fiends on the floor, scratchin' again. Paparazzis with they cameras, snappin' them. / D.A. try to give a nigga shaft again. / Half a mill' for bail cause I'm African." The cameramen in this instance are shooting convicts for mug shots, the inmates' faces grim, number cards on their chests. Naked in their cells, observed and humiliated, the cons stride past the video's camera, puff up their bodies, tattooed and hardened by years of working out, emblems of their hard time spent on self-perpetuation.

As Jay notes here, his visible status as "African" makes him, again and at last, the "same nigga." And yet, he is not. Jay-Z's subsequent "death"—violent, slow motion, and sensational—is startling and potentially upsetting for viewers not paying attention. The death, however, is not final. Jay-Z walks again on Brooklyn Bridge, down the alley, and into the camera at Marcy. And so he is once more reframed, reappearing after the shooting. Looking at the camera, he smiles, released and renamed. He looks at the camera, persistent means of surveillance and performance, containment and independence, his vehicle to superstardom and self-exposure. And he hits it, sends the frame tumbling, as if the world within it is suddenly out of control. As Jeffrey Rotter describes it, the assault is "the most memorable—and instructive—moment of the video because it reminds us of what Jay-Z did best for nearly a decade: box us around until we saw things his way."[13] This is right, but also simplistic. Jay-Z has hustled his audience, but he has also, as he has said again and again, played the hand he was dealt. At the same time, "99 Problems" represents Shawn Carter's control as a means to redefine "authenticity." Of the streets and from the mansion, he's also entering another phase. While Jay-Z surely is a "corporate rapper," Shawn Carter is now emerging as a kind of "corporate citizen," retired from rapping in 2004 and unretired as of 2006 (with the album *Kingdom Come*). His work with the Nets and Def Jam, his support of Beyoncé and other artists (Lincoln Park, Kanye West), and efforts to "give back" to various communities, performing on behalf of disaster victims (for instance, at 2005's Live 8 concert) and through the U.N., with a focus on global water shortage, reveal his broadening sensibility and sense of responsibility. Back home again, he brings difference and his own "truth," reflected and inflected in his performance of the same.

NOTES

1 Guy Trebay, "Maturing Rappers Try on a New Uniform: Yo, a Suit!" *New York Times*, February 6, 2004, A1.

2 Austin Scaggs, "Jay-Z Has Big Problems," *Rolling Stone*, May 4, 2004.

3 Sway Calloway, "From 99 Problems to 100 Rumors," MTV.com. April 23, 2004.

4 Ibid.

5 Murray Forman, *The 'Hood Comes First: Race, Space, and Place in Rap and Hip-Hop* (Middletown, Conn.: Wesleyan University Press, 2002), xix.

6 Robin D. G. Kelley, "Kickin Reality, Kickin Ballistics: Gangsta Rap and Postindustrial Los Angeles" in *Droppin Science: Critical Essays on Rap Music and Hip Hop Culture*, ed. William Eric Perkins (Philadelphia: Temple University Press, 1996), 118.

7 Ibid., 137.

8 Darrell Dawsey, "You Can Knock the Hustle," *Blaze* (December/January 1999): 98.

9 Elizabeth Mendez Berry, "Jay-Z: *Reasonable Doubt*; *Vol. 3 . . . Life and Times of S. Carter*; *The Blueprint*," in *Classic Material: The Hip-Hop Album Guide*, ed. Oliver Wang (Toronto: ECW Press 2003), 94.

10 Kelefa Sanneh, "Getting' Paid," *New Yorker*, August 20 and 27, 2001, 60.
11 Elizabeth Mendez Berry, "The Last Hustle," *Village Voice*, November 26–December 2, 2003.
12 Kris Ex, "Cheers." *XXL*, December 2003.
13 Jeffrey Rotter, "Jay-Z Wants to Kill Himself," *New York Times*, May 9, 2004.

PARADOXES OF PASTICHE: SPIKE JONZE, HYPE WILLIAMS, AND THE RACE OF THE POSTMODERN AUTEUR

Roger Beebe

S ince the inception of MTV, certain key information has been burned into the image at the start and end of every music video: the artist's name, the song title, the album title, and the record label. This information remained untouched for the first decade of the channel's existence, but in the early 1990s one additional detail was added to the end of the list: the director's name. Following MTV's lead, all of the other music television channels (VH1, BET, CMT et al.) slowly started adding the director's names to their videos.[1]

What exactly happened in the early 1990s that prompted this small but significant addition to the way that music videos were presented? And what are the consequences of that addition? In this essay I explore a knot of issues involving the auteur, postmodernism, style, genre, and race as played out in this moment of transformation in music video, primarily by looking at how it played out on MTV. I will attempt to disentangle that knot of issues by looking at each thread sequentially. First, I explore the ostensible challenge to auteurism offered by the postmodern fragmentation of the subject (also sometimes termed the "death of the subject"); second, I document the paradoxical reinscription of auteurism in postmodern accounts of the outmoding of individual style (that hallmark of the modernist subject) and its replacement with generic pastiche, elaborating the theoretical consequences of this reinscription; third, I look at the reemergence of style (in a slightly altered form) in hip hop video; fourth, I look at the parallel reemergence of genre (as opposed to the metageneric practice of pastiche) in the hip hop video of the same period; and finally, I assess the theoretical repercussion of this return of style and genre for the theorization of postmodern media culture, focusing on the question of race.

At present there seem to be two general critiques of auteurism in academic circulation. The first, which is presented as part of almost every introductory film text (e.g., Bordwell and Thompson's widely used *Film Art: An Introduction*), is the critique of the false analogy between the author of a literary work and the auteur of a film, a critique based on the industrial and collaborative nature of film production.[2] The second critique of auteurism (which derives initially from poststructuralism,[3] and then was adopted and partly retheorized by postmodern theory) requires a more substantial rethinking of the very grounds upon which the notion of authorship (and auteurism by extension) was initially premised: namely, it challenges the fundamental integrity and depth of the subject that was the bedrock of the auteurist myth from the beginning. The postmodern revisions of this challenge insist on the historical component of this theoretical intervention by pointing to the outmoding of the modernist aesthetic valorization of "expression" (the exteriorization of a "deep" interior existence) and its replacement with a kind of surface play. While Bordwell and Thompson's critique holds out the possibility that we can discern (after a sufficient amount of scrutiny) multiple authorships and consequently multiple styles or signatures in any given film—that is, the various influences of the writer, cinematographer, art director, camera operator, actors, etc. in addition to the director—the poststructuralist/postmodern critique questions both the very consistency of those subjects who influence the final form of the film as well as the associated aesthetic criteria that direct our attention to those people in the first place. That is, this critique assumes a fragmentation of the subject that challenges the presupposition of a coherence of intent both at the moment of the given film's production and across the individual's body of work. In addition, the critique points to a new set of aesthetic codes that are no longer invested in the expressivity of a deep subject in any case.

In the following pages, I focus my inquiry on the latter half of this second critique (the more strictly "postmodern" rather than "poststructuralist" problematic). I do so partially to free my study from the literary model of poststructuralism (auteur in lieu of author, style in place of signature), which has historically been the source of a number of problems (not the least of which is the very notion of auteurism). Additionally, however, I choose to focus on the postmodern model to offer a more profoundly historicized context for the understanding of auteurism both as an aesthetic practice and as a part of the more general workings of a cultural logic in transformation.

Of the original postmodern theorists Fredric Jameson has been the most articulate about the transformation of cinematic practice, and it is thus not surprising that his work should also include the clearest elaboration of the nature of postmodern auteurism. Jameson's essay "Historicism in *The Shining*" opens with a passage that is overtly concerned with setting up the problematic of genre in postmodern film, to which the essay is devoted, but then it simultaneously sets up an auteurist approach to this question. As he writes, "The most interesting filmmakers today—Robert Altman, Roman Polanski, Nicholas Roeg, Stanley Kubrick—are all in their very different ways practitioners of *genre*, but in some historically new sense."[4] This is a deceptively complex sentence, and, upon closer inspection, many aspects of it may seem surprising. The sentence first requires a good deal of unpacking so that the stakes of my eventual interrogation of its contradictions are clearer.

The "historically new sense" in which these filmmakers marshal genre is characterized by a switching between genres, not, as Jameson writes, "as a matter of individual taste, but rather . . . [as] the result of objective constraints in the situation of cultural production today."[5] Jameson thus immediately unseats this genre-jumping from the realm of individual aesthetic choice (and from a subject-based approach) and instead contextualizes it as a symptom of greater cultural shifts. He further elaborates this historical argument through Adorno's notion of "pastiche." Pastiche is differentiated by Adorno (and consequently by Jameson) from parody: while parody "aims at ridiculing and discrediting styles which are still alive and influential," pastiche "is meant . . . to display the virtuosity of the practitioner rather than the absurdity of the object."[6] The aforementioned postmodern auteurs utilize genre in this pastiche mode rather than in the older modernist mode of parody. (Think here of Polanski or Altman's forays into film noir in *Chinatown* and *The Long Goodbye*, respectively. Clearly such a mobilization of pastiche, perhaps in even purer form, is still at work in the recent metageneric efforts of the Coen Brothers, Quentin Tarantino, Robert Rodriguez, and many others.) Jameson's analysis makes clear the connection between this pastiche mode and the challenge to the subject posed by postmodernism: "As individualism begins to atrophy in a post-industrial world, the quest for a uniquely distinctive style and the very category of 'style' come to seem old-fashioned."[7] Thus the challenge to subjectivism or individualism is imbricated with (in the consideration of cinema aesthetics) the upheaval of the traditional notion of style (where style is understood in the modernist sense of the unique and characteristic exteriorization [expression] of the subject's interiority). Three years later when Jameson writes his "Postmodernism" essay, this connection has become a given for him and a ground for the entire theoretical apparatus of postmodernism: "The disappearance of the individual subject, along with its formal consequence, the increasing unavailability of the personal style, engender the well-nigh universal practice today of . . . pastiche."[8]

It should strike us as strange or paradoxical that this postmodern challenge to individualism is articulated through the bodies of work of a handful of individual directors. What are we to make of the fact that some kind of subject persists in the era of postmodern pastiche, and, further, that the theory itself is most easily elaborated by looking at their oeuvres? We might at least provisionally note that Jameson does not mean to endorse these directors as great geniuses as, say, Andrew Sarris would have done for a previous generation of auteurs; it nevertheless remains somewhat of a surprise (and perhaps even a disappointment) that the auteur persists in even this weaker sense under postmodernism.

Since the directors that Jameson points to made their work in a moment of transition (both in the machinery of Hollywood filmmaking and in the cultural logic as the shift from an industrial to a service economy kicked into high gear), we might hypothesize that later forms would work out this contradiction and realize a "pure" pastiche form that is not seen to issue from an individual or group of individuals. The list of auteurs that Jameson enumerates could be taken, if it proves to be the case, as a vanguard of such a mass-cultural movement (with the persistence of the auteur in this first moment merely a residuum from high modernist aesthetics). This nonauteurist deployment of pastiche has not, however, arrived in cinema where the directors I name above (the Coen Brothers, Tarantino, et al.) are already entering a number of different film-historical canons. We can see this in a (semi-)popular canon, for example, with the inclusion of *Fargo* and *Pulp Fiction* on the American Film Institute's list of the 100 greatest American films. In an academic context, a 1998 volume titled *The New American Cinema* elevates Tarantino to equal status with Spielberg and Hitchcock in terms of the number of mentions each receives in the collection.[9]

Given this failure of cinema to rupture the auteur-pastiche nexus, it seems logical to think that television might be a more appropriate location to begin the search for nonauteurist pastiche since television has historically been taken to be profoundly antiauteurist. When the discourse of the auteur is marshaled in discussions of television, it is almost invariably through the figure of the producer and not the director that this unity is assumed (e.g., Stephen Bocchco, Aaron Spelling, Steven J. Cannell). The rare counterexamples (e.g., David Lynch's *Twin Peaks* [for which, interestingly, he wasn't even the sole director] or the Tarantino-directed episode of *E.R.*) simply prove the rule. Here I specifically want to look for the transformation of auteurism on MTV, supposedly one of the most postmodern of the televisual formats.[10]

If we look historically at MTV's origins, it would seem that the network was in its early years profoundly antiauteurist. While major directors frequently directed videos in the early days of MTV (Ridley Scott, Spike Lee, Herb Ritts, Martin Scorsese, et al.), their signatures were erased by the overwhelming focus on the musical performers themselves in a way that would not occur when such directors worked with Hollywood superstars (e.g., Ridley Scott's auteurial persona manages to survive Harrison Ford's presence in *Blade Runner*, and Martin Scorsese's signature can even coexist with Leonardo DiCaprio in *Gangs of New York* and *The Aviator*). As I mentioned at the start of this essay, in those early days of the cable network the directors' names were not even included in the clip identification information presented at the start and end of each video, thereby furthering the emphasis on the performer over the director and effectively erasing the question of individual directorial style.

However, while the director was missing in early MTV, so was the overwhelming presence of metageneric pastiche that has now become one of its trademarks. It is by now an academic commonplace to note the historical transformation in music video from a performance-driven medium (wherein shots of the musicians lip-synching predominate) to a more "narrative" (and, I would add, genre-driven) form. While I will not elaborate the entire parameters of the early MTV aesthetic, suffice it to say that while it had a recognizable style—all-white sets shot markedly overexposed and often with a good deal of fog, frontal shots of the performers in that proscenium space, frequent use of futuristic or vaguely science fictional elements in the mise-en-scène—this was certainly a far cry from the postmodern pastiche mode. (Interestingly, the Stone Temple Pilots's "Big Bang Baby" video [1995] is actually a pastiche of this early MTV-style, harkening back most directly to the clip for the J. Geils Band's single "Freeze Frame.")

However, as MTV "matured" and new narrative/generic forms emerged, we see a coincident emergence of both pastiche and the auteur on MTV, echoing the paradoxical auteurist origins of the notion of cinematic pastiche in Jameson's writings. While there is no radical moment of rupture, the late 1980s and early 1990s saw a major transformation of MTV on a number of fronts.[11] All of these related changes collectively represent an aesthetic (and ultimately theoretical) upheaval of the channel's format related to and bespeaking a coincident transformation in the cultural logic.

One of these many changes that came in the early 1990s was the inclusion of the names of the directors in the burns that frame every video. With the inclusion of this information that for so long had seemed inessential, MTV allowed for (or perhaps even called into being) the development of the music video as an auteurist medium. This auteurist tendency has continued to intensify, and not simply through the increasing name recognition prompted by repeated exposure to the information framing the video's presentation.[12] One typical high-profile celebration of the music video auteur came in 1995, as MTV's *The Week in Rock* ran a feature on the body of work by the professional skateboarder turned music video auteur Spike Jonze.[13] Jonze's video work includes Weezer's "Buddy Holly," which is made to look like an episode of *Happy Days* complete with recontextualized footage of the Fonz, Richie, and the gang; Elastica's "Car Song" as a futuristic thriller combining elements of *Blade Runner* and Japanese monster films; Beck's "Devil's Haircut," which cites the early 1970s detective film complete with zooms on grainy freeze frames of the star wandering through Chinatown (apparently) performed on that beloved film technology of the 1970s, the optical printer; Björk's "It's Oh So Quiet" as an elaborate homage to the Hollywood musical; and the Beastie Boys's "Sabotage," perhaps Jonze's best known and most circulated video, which is a dense collage of allusions to the 1970s rogue cop films and TV shows like *Bullitt*, *Starsky and Hutch*, *Kojak*, and *Dirty Harry*. (This list of pastiche videos helmed by one of MTV's pioneering auteurs

ROGER BEEBE

Stills from Spike Jonze's "Sabotage," "It's Oh So Quiet," and "Buddy Holly" videos. *(left to right, top to bottom)*

should already begin to suggest a strong link between the emergent auteurism and the pastiche mode on that channel.)

The directors also found a place in the MTV Music Video Awards as key categories were set up simply to celebrate their efforts (both in awards for individual videos and for their body of work), rather than simply the achievements of the musical performers. In fact, one of the most legendary moments from MTV Music Video Award history (which still gets reaired on MTV fairly frequently as part of the network's constant narration of its own history) occurred at the 1994 awards ceremony when Jake Scott, the director for R.E.M.'s video "Everybody Hurts," was awarded best director in a music video over Spike Jonze for "Sabotage." Beastie Boy Adam Yauch (a.k.a. MCA), clad as his alter-ego Nathaniel Hornblower, stormed the stage and took the mic to decry the travesty of not giving the award to Spike Jonze.[14]

Perhaps the crowning moment for MTV auteurism (or at least a pinnacle in the recognition of MTV as an auteurist medium) was MTV's Top 50 of All Time ("all time" being understood here with proper televisual myopia to include the less than two decades of MTV's existence at that point), which aired in November 1997. Not only did this historical narration allow MTV to correct its oversight by appending directors' names to a number of videos that had formerly not fallen under the rubric of the auteur (although some remained notably lacking, presumably because MTV was unable to retrieve that long-ignored information), but it additionally gave MTV the chance to highlight the great achievements of the music video form. One of the primary ways in which MTV bolstered the prestigious roll call of great music videos was by including interviews with the directors of the videos. The interviewees included Samuel Bayer (director of videos for Blind Melon's "No Rain" and Nirvana's "Smells like Teen Spirit"), Wayne Isham (director of clips for Bon Jovi's "Wanted Dead or Alive" and Def Leppard's "Pour Some Sugar on Me"), Mark Pellington (helmsman on Pearl Jam's "Jeremy" video), and, of course, Spike Jonze (whose "Sabotage" charted at number 31). Notably, this list includes no directors from early MTV, and only one (Isham) from the transitional period of the late 1980s and early 1990s. In fact, Isham was used in his interview to periodize MTV and to represent the passage (referred to in the course of the interview as the "middle period of MTV") to its third (read: mature, auteurist) period.[15]

Perhaps the greatest proof in this countdown that MTV has become a profoundly auteurist medium is that the video for the Whitney Houston song "I Will Always Love You" (the theme from the feature film *The Bodyguard*) is credited to Alan Smithee, the pseudonym that has traditionally served as refuge for directors wishing to disavow their work on feature films.[16] The fact that this nom de plume has finally found its way to music video suggests, first, the amount of attention called to the director (so that someone could be sufficiently defensive as to have recourse to that pseudonym), and, second, the *necessity* of the director's name in the medium (lest there be an obvious absence where the director's name would normally be). At present, the names of music video directors like Spike Jonze, Mark Romanek, Stephane Sednaoui, Roman Coppola, Jonathan Dayton, Valerie Faris, and others are, if not household names, at least widely circulated testaments to the newfound auteurist biases of the form.

The simultaneous emergence of pastiche (signaled above in the list of Spike Jonze's directorial credits) is equally remarkable. While the videos of MTV's early and middle periods first ignored and then struggled with narrative and generic forms, the videos of the third period have routinely

ROGER BEEBE

and deftly mobilized the metageneric play of pastiche. The so-called alternative music (which began to dominate the charts and the airwaves after 1991, the legendary "year that punk broke") was the music of choice for the emergent MTV pastiche mode.

The Top 10 of All Time alternative videos list from MTV's series that aired in late 1997 and was rebroadcast throughout the first half of 1998 bespeaks this connection between alternative music and the pastiche mode.[17] Here I will limit my comments to the top five videos, which should amply demonstrate this connection. Number five is the aforementioned Spike Jonze–helmed video for the Beastie Boys's "Sabotage" which is an homage to the tradition of *Dirty Harry* et al. Number four is the video for the Smashing Pumpkins's "Tonight, Tonight," a lush, almost shot-for-shot re-creation of Georges Melies's "Trip to the Moon" directed by Jonathan Dayton and Valerie Faris. Number three is the video for the Nine Inch Nails song "Closer" directed by Mark Romanek, one of the earliest MTV auteurs whose work won him a lifetime achievement award at the MTV music video awards in 1997. The video for "Closer" was instrumental in the resuscitation of the primitive cinema look with all of its material marks of age and of the very materiality of film (scratches, visible cuts, etc.), which has now become one of the primary markers of youth (cultural) marketing. This video is, though, a double or second-order pastiche (i.e., a pastiche of a pastiche); while its style harkens back to primitive cinema, it makes that return via the more immediate stylistic referent of the photography of Joel-Peter Witkin, an artist who became known in the 1980s for his (pastiche) re-creations of early medical photography, specifically the early photographic representation of aberrant bodies (midgets, hermaphrodites, amputees, etc.). Number two on the list is the video for "Under the Bridge" by the Red Hot Chili Peppers — a video that focuses primarily on the guitarist playing in a desert and the singer (Anthony Keidis) walking around Los Angeles while singing, but also includes a bizarre sequence of Keidis running in slow motion away from the distant mushroom cloud of a presumed nuclear explosion. At number one, of course, is Nirvana, the band that is generally credited with initiating the alternative revolution.[18] The video for their breakthrough single "Smells Like Teen Spirit" portrays a pep rally gone awry as the seemingly well-behaved boys and girls are roused into a frenzy of moshing by the end of the video. Of these top five, three are clear pastiches with definite historical/stylistic referents ("Sabotage," "Tonight,

Stills from Dayton and Faris's Melies-inspired "Tonight, Tonight" video and Mark Romanek's second-order pastiche, "Closer," two of MTV's Top 10 of All Time Alternative Videos.

Tonight," and "Closer"), while one ("Smells Like Teen Spirit") has elements of pastiche but is much less completely structured around them, and only one ("Under the Bridge") contains few moments that hint at a generic form. (It should also be noted that all five of these videos were directed by well-known music video auteurs.)[19]

These pastiches and the alternative subgenre with which they are most closely associated have assumed a place of preeminence in the canon of 1990s music video, thus echoing Jameson's enshrinement of cinematic pastiche. Alternative music has been canonized by MTV and various other rock(ist) institutions as *the* music of the early 1990s[20] (while, presumably, hip hop stands poised to be its successor in historical accounts of the late 1990s). This central import of alternative was marked by MTV when the network offered it as the final top 10 list on the weekend when all of the lists were first broadcast back to back. The top 10 alternative list thus plays (according to the countdown logic of the program) somewhat like the *top* top 10. Further highlighting MTV's valuation of alternative music video is the fate of such videos on the network's Top 50 of All Time, which included five such videos in the top twenty-five (including "Smells Like Teen Spirit" at number one, displacing "Thriller" after better than a decade of dominance).

Thus it would appear that at least on MTV not only does the emergence of a "well nigh universal" practice of pastiche coincide with a new type of auteurism (as it does in cinema), but that its emergence actually seems to play a crucial role in establishing the very existence of auteurism.[21] It is important to stress again that although these two tendencies (toward auteurism and toward pastiche) evolve contemporaneously, they are (at least in theory) antithetical, with the one marking the dispersal of the subject and the other celebrating its unity. If, contrary to this apparent contraction, however, these two practices are ultimately interrelated, it would seem to demand a reevaluation or supplementing of the discourse on the "death of the subject" that has dominated theory since the early poststructuralist critiques better than two decades ago.[22] Even if the subject is hollowed out under postmodernism, it doesn't simply go away — rather, it persists as an anchor for interpretation (even Jameson's own), as some kind of guarantor of coherence (even if merely the new kind of schizophrenic coherence suggested by pastiche's genre-jumping), and as a signifier in the marketplace (perhaps the greatest reason that it has not simply disappeared along with the other relics of modernist aesthetics). While this is not a devastating critique, we certainly need to offer a more nuanced accounting for the ways in which the auteur (or a kind of auteur) persists and, indeed, appears inextricably coupled with the practice of pastiche.

There is a second set of questions that I want to explore here, and this set might just be more critical than the first. From the pages above, it might seem that Jameson is right to point to the "well nigh universal" practice of pastiche, but that universality becomes less apparent when we expand our scope to include the work of other directors as well as videos in other musical genres. In light of this I want to retrace the trajectory above (first through Jameson, then through music video) to look at the logic of the object choices in that theorization and to look at what gets excluded in that first act of choosing. Asking these questions may prove to be not just a significant critique of postmodern theory, but also might give us some purchase on the future of the globalized U.S.-led cultural logic.

I want to return to the first sentence of Jameson's initial attempts to elaborate the notion of pastiche: "The most interesting filmmakers today — Robert Altman, Roman Polanski, Nicholas Roeg, Stanley Kubrick — are all in their very different ways practitioners of genre, but in some historically new sense." The main question I wish to raise is what subtends Jameson's assessment (in Kantian terms, his aesthetic judgment) that these four directors are in fact the "most interesting filmmakers." Given the now commonplace critiques of Kant whereby aesthetic judgments that pretend to universality rest ultimately on contingent grounds, such an aesthetic claim is both startling and untenable.[23] The point of this interrogation is not simply to take Jameson to task for his oversight or overvaluation of this or that director; the point, rather, is that the selection of any director as "most interesting" is far from neutral and has major repercussions for the theoretical framework that he develops. The problems of this contingent assertion are in turn reproduced in the writings of those (numerous) scholars who have relied on the postmodern notion of pastiche (e.g., Vivian Sobchack's final chapter in *Screening Space* or Anne Friedberg's *Window Shopping*).[24] Therefore, this critique is not a quarrel with an isolated moment in a specific text, but rather a necessary intervention in the entire discourse of postmodern visual culture.

We can begin in less theoretical terms to call Jameson's evaluation into question by noting that there is not even a consensus that the auteurs that he enumerates are the "most interesting." While Jameson's discussion of these postmodern auteurs has been widely influential, it certainly has not foreclosed the emergence of other lists (or canons). For example, in Kenneth von Gunden's book titled, appropriately enough, *Postmodern Auteurs*,[25] he designates the group of filmmakers (Francis Ford Coppola, Steven Spielberg, George Lucas, Martin Scorsese, Brian DePalma) who are often called the "film generation" or the "film brats" as the titular "postmodern auteurs." While von Gunden's notion of the postmodern (which appears to be synonymous with "the contemporary") may give us pause, his list still clearly amounts to an assessment that these are "the most interesting filmmakers today." This list of directors (which seems to have established itself more fully as the canon of New American Cinema in film studies discourse [as attested to by the sometimes troublingly auteurist collection, *The New American Cinema*[26]]) seems to tap more immediately into both the middle-brow industry prestige of Academy awardees and the breadwinning, mass-cultural auteurs whose names have become fodder for commercial strategies. Jameson himself offers no other "proof" or defense of the "interest" of the directors on his own list than the fact that they practice genre in some historically new sense.

So, what are the criteria that subtend his aesthetic judgment? It ultimately appears that the choice of his specific list of auteurs is in some profound sense circular or tautological; that is, his judgment proceeds from his then-unformulated postmodern theoretical agenda so that the films and directors that fit in with that emergent conceptual field are "the most interesting." In other words, what Jameson finds "interesting" in these directors is perhaps their confirmation of his theoretical impulses that would later be formulated as postmodernism. One question that then arises (a question that I will defer until the end of the chapter) is what greater cultural or social interests are served by this validation of pastiche. This question may also be posed as a hypothetical: What would the cultural logic look like if we took as our point of departure not these (still arguably high cultural) practitioners of pastiche, but rather, to choose a pointed example, the blaxploitation directors such as Gordon Parks and Melvin van Peebles? Certainly the work of the blaxploitation directors has had a major impact on the shape of American cinema in the 1990s and beyond, largely in the films of Quentin Tarantino and his bevy of imitators who explicitly draw on these films. Thus we might well argue that they are the "most interesting" directors of that period in the 1970s when Jameson was first articulating his theory of pastiche. Or, to take a slightly less loaded example, how might our vision of the cultural logic change if we started with two of the most commercially significant filmmakers of the past thirty years, Spielberg and Lucas, both of whom are mentioned in Jameson's writings but who do not occupy a central position in his theorization of pastiche?[27]

A similar set of problems and exclusion happens within the realm of music video. The enshrinement by MTV of pastiche videos seems to echo Jameson's own (and it is no more explicit about its reasons for doing so). While the now canonical alternative music movement was accompanied by the co-emergence of auteurism and pastiche on MTV, other musical genres have been much slower to follow in its footsteps (if they have followed at all).

One of MTV's desires is to erase the heterogeneity of its musical forms in order to offer (or to appear to offer) the greatest good to the greatest number, but in fact a remarkable elision takes place in its canonization of alternative video pastiche. Almost no other genre has devoted itself wholeheartedly to pastiche in the way that alternative has done (or did). One of the most notable exceptions to the purported hegemony of pastiche is found in hip hop music, which is the primary rival to alternative (or, if we dare say it, "postalternative") music for the limited airtime for

The origins of a style: stills from Hype Williams's groundbreaking videos for "Woo Ha (Got You All in Check)" and "The Rain (Supa Dupa Fly)."

videos on MTV.[28] These hip hop videos tend to be much less frequently pastiche driven than are their alternative counterparts. Interestingly, auteurism *has* emerged in the postalternative era in hip hop with such figures as Hype Williams, Paul Hunter, Lionel C. Martin, et al., but these auteurs have rarely had recourse to the pastiche mode. It is to the model presented by the work of some of these auteurs who don't rely on pastiche that I now turn.[29]

The aesthetic of hip hop video in the late 1990s was largely marked (almost to the point of caricature) by the productions of one of its most distinct stylists, Hype Williams (and I use "style" here pointedly to gesture to what appears at first glance to be a modernist type of aesthetic production that was assumed vanquished with the omnipresence of pastiche).[30] Williams's signature style was primarily introduced through two early videos (for Busta Rhymes's "Woo Ha [Got You All in Check]" and Missy "Misdemeanor" Elliot's "The Rain [Supa Dupa Fly]"). In 1997 and 1998 Williams's videos were almost inescapable. This aesthetic is primarily characterized by the use of extreme wide-angle and fish-eye lenses; highly reflective (metallic or wet) surfaces; luminous objects in the frame (neon, incandescent, and fluorescent bulbs); jerky, stop-and-start motion created by shooting at high frame rates with the actors moving slowly and accentuated by ramping up and down the speed of playback; symmetrical and/or circular sets; costume and set design in bold primary colors creating a number of specifically colored environments; and the intercutting among a series of these colored environments within a single video. While Williams's style of music video does partake of Jameson's "cult of the glossy image," which he identifies later in "Historicism in *The*

ROGER BEEBE

Nearly identical stills from Mase's "Feel So Good" and the (almost instantaneous) Monster Magnet pastiche—or is it vice versa?

Shining" as one of the other defining characteristics of postmodern visual production, clearly this form does not represent the epitome of pastiche that we saw in alternative music video.[31]

As a testament to the currency of this style (and to its status as a *style*), there are now videos that are not simply imitations but actual pastiches of the Hype Williams style. Notable in this regard is the video for the heavy metal band Monster Magnet's single "Space Lord." It begins as a pastiche of Metallica's "The Unforgiven" but after a minute it abruptly shifts modes and becomes a pastiche of the Hype Williams–helmed video for Mase's "Feel So Good." (The pastiche was so "successful" in re-creating the object that Monster Magnet's frontman confessed [on the MTV program *Artist's Cut*] that upon seeing the Mase video a friend mistakenly called him to let him know that his video was airing.) Similar although less sustained pastiches of his style have also appeared in commercials for Sprite, Nintendo, and Mountain Dew. This style has also been parodied in an Arizona Jeans commercial in which a group of teenagers dismiss the dominant modes (styles) of contemporary youth marketing (of which the Hype Williams style is one of three) by demanding that companies just "show us the jeans." The existence of such clear citations of the Hype Williams style bespeaks its availability as a distinct signature rather than simply another postmodern appropriation, and thus it makes clear its difference from the model of auteurist pastiche that is purportedly "universal" under postmodernism.

Perhaps the clearest illustration of this distinction between Williams's style and the alternative pastiches discussed above is the Spike Jonze–helmed video for "Sky's the Limit" by the Notorious B.I.G. That video,

Examples of the "Bad Boy" look from the Hype Williams–helmed "Mo' Money, Mo' Problems" and "Gettin' Jiggy with It" and the Spike Jonze pastiche of that look in "Sky's the Limit." *(left to right, top to bottom)*

produced posthumously for B.I.G. by Sean "Puffy" Combs who heads the Bad Boy label on which B.I.G.'s recordings appeared, is a full-blown pastiche of the Hype Williams signature. In the booklet that accompanies Jonze's Director's Series DVD, he explains that they even hired someone for the shoot to give it the "Bad Boy look," which he clarifies is "Money. Flash. . . . The shine."[32] This, of course, is shorthand for the signature style of Hype Williams, who directed the bulk of the videos for the Bad Boy label during the period when Jonze's video was made.

Unlike others who adapted the Williams style to make knock-off videos, Jonze is explicit about the metageneric status of his effort. The video features a pair of twelve-year-old look-alikes playing the roles of B.I.G. and Puffy. Jonze says in the same Director's Series interview that the concept for the video came from his then-wife Sofia Coppola. "Basically it's like *Bugsy Malone*, which was one of her favorite movies when she was a kid. It's all kids 12 and under, Scott Baio, and I think Jodie Foster, but it's a gangster movie from the 1930s." So Jonze unabashedly recognizes not only that the concept is borrowed from another film (*Bugsy*

ROGER BEEBE

Malone), but he also knows full well that that film itself is a pastiche of an earlier genre. While the "Sky's the Limit" video replaces the gangsters with gangstas, it is otherwise as pure a pastiche as any on the list enumerated above. And as if that second-order pastiche were not already enough, Jonze includes in the mise-en-scène of his video a television set on which a pastiche of Hype Williams's groundbreaking "Woo Ha (Got You All in Check)" is acted out by a diminutive Busta Rhymes doppelganger. Nothing could have provided a clearer illustration of the different modes in which Spike Jonze and Hype Williams have made their names than does this video.

We might well try imagining the reverse as a final proof of the fundamental difference between the work of these two directors: what would a pastiche of a Spike Jonze video look like? It might be possible to imagine a pastiche of a single video of his (just as he can imagine a pastiche of *Bugsy Malone*), but there is no unified style from video to video that would allow us to re-create the "Spike Jonze look" as he re-creates the "Bad Boy look" in the "Sky's the Limit" video. It thus seems clear that if Spike Jonze confirms Jameson's analysis of pastiche, Hype Williams demands a complication of it.

While it was momentarily useful to view the Williams signature as (modernist) style without further elaboration, that was merely a starting point. For while Williams does have a quotable look, this is surely far from the expressive style of Edvard Munch's *The Scream*, which Jameson uses as one of the emblems of modernist style. Here we are no longer in the world of the deep expressions of anomie that characterized the productions of modernism, but rather in some new form of postmodern style (a seemingly paradoxical term) where the individual persists as a surface look, available as a commodity more than as a worldview. So this returns us closer to pastiche, where the auteur paradoxically persists largely as a way to differentiate products. And while the "aesthetic exhaustion" that characterizes pastiche seems not to plague Hype Williams, he certainly revels in the glossiness of his images as much as the most ironic of the alternative auteurs. Thus in the text above I seek not to jettison postmodern theory as an attempt to understand hip hop video, but rather I aim to suggest supplements and footnotes to that theory reflecting the unforeseen mutations within postmodernism that hip hop effects. In short, style (in the historically new form we see in the Hype Williams videos) appears not to be antithetical to postmodernism after all, but neither is it fully explained by the extant texts of postmodern theory.

Lest we reduce hip hop video to the work of Hype Williams, we should also note that there are some hip hop videos that do appear (again, at least at first glance) to mobilize the pastiche mode. But even when they do offer something that might be loosely considered pastiche, there are remarkable differences between them and the alternative pastiches discussed above. For example, when hip hop video has assumed this general mode of pastiche, the stylistic referent is more likely to be a recent popular form than the more rarefied, often high-cultural allusions cited above in alternative videos.[33] The privileged referent for hip hop video of late is the 1980s action blockbuster. This aesthetic is summoned by any number of videos, many of which rank among MTV's pantheon of the hip hop genre. To offer only a few examples of hip hop video's approach to this form of appropriation, the video for the Notorious B.I.G.'s "Hypnotize" centers on two high-speed chases in the Florida Keys that seem to echo *Miami Vice* (the first is comprised of a number of helicopters chasing a yacht, and the second includes motorcycles and a humvee pursuing B.I.G. and Puffy in a convertible); the Fugees's "Ready or Not" includes similar chases on jet skis, in a submarine, and on motorcycles through a jungle terrain; and Puff Daddy's "Been around the World" (in which Puffy plays an international playboy/secret agent á la James Bond) adds a desert chase sequence.[34] I should also point out that the allusion is performed not merely in the recitation of the plot but also is summoned through a number of other stylistic techniques. For example, with the exception of "Dangerous" all of the above videos are letterboxed, thereby connoting the widescreen theatrical experience. Frequently these videos also feature momentary suspensions of the song as certain elements of their narratives play out. For example, in "Hypnotize" the song stops for forty-five seconds as the scene shifts from sea to land and a new chase begins. (Interestingly, in this last sequence when B.I.G.'s song drops out a more generically theatrical instrumental score kicks in—one that is not featured on the CD version of the track.) This practice of suspending the song for a more narrative or cinematic moment has quickly become somewhat of a cliché itself.

As the Hype Williams videos seem to point to a certain resilience of style in hip hop video, the presence of these hip hop imitations of

The persistence of genre in videos for the Notorious B.I.G.'s "Hypnotize" video and Puff Daddy's "Victory."

the Hollywood blockbuster may be pointing to the persistence of genre (rather than "metagenre") as an active category. In other words, these videos position themselves not so much as allusions or recapitulations but as new additions to the blockbuster cycle.[35] Their transformations of the generic codes can be seen primarily in the recasting of the leads with black heroes (something that would have never happened in the 1980s films where the black buddy was either killed off, contained, or effectively domesticated).[36] Instead of "celebrating the virtuosity of the practitioner," these videos seem to be celebrating the merits of the genre: that is, the "coolness" of the blockbuster as a visual form. So this reinvigoration of genre seems to be more about how great the actual form of the blockbuster is and about (re)creating the actual affect of the original than either the ironic homage of the Beastie Boys's "Sabotage" or of the virtuoso and aestheticizing re-creations of "Closer" or "Tonight, Tonight."

Finally I want to turn my attention here to what, precisely, is at stake in this difference between the form of alternative pastiche videos and of these divergent forms of hip hop videos that I have outlined above. Basically the stakes are these: pastiche (in its pure [read: white cultural] form) appears to be profoundly premised upon the mastery and manipulation of what has, following the work of Pierre Bourdieu, come to be known as cultural capital.[37] While the music video may be a popular form, the kinds of aesthetic allusion made in the alternative pastiches are frequently far from it; the intimate knowledge of the style of primitive cinema, of Melies's shorts, or of Witkin's photographs clearly bespeak a certain position within a cultural elite and an inculcation in a certain type of knowledge culture. As noted above, when hip hop has approached the pastiche mode, the stylistic referent is more likely a recent popular form such as the 1980s action blockbuster. So if the mastery of a rarefied cultural capital ultimately subtends the valuation of the pastiche mode (both in music video and in cinematic auteurism [where the recent films of the latest wave of auteurs including the Coen Brothers et al. seem to confirm this hypothesis]), then this begins to throw into question the cultural politics of theories of the postmodern since such mastery is deeply linked to class (which itself, especially in the United States, is profoundly linked to race). The "most interesting" directors today turn out to be (not surprisingly) well-educated, middle- or upper-class white males who come equipped with a familiarity with historical forms bespeaking that class and educational status.[38] At one level, Jameson's diagnosis of a cultural dominant derived from the aesthetic production of a white cultural elite was bound to be "accurate": despite the increasing presence of other voices in culture, there is still clearly a (residual?) hegemony enjoyed by the white middle and upper classes. But this again approaches tautology — these people are the privileged symptoms of the cultural dominant because they are in a position to dominate the evaluation of culture. Staying within the confines of such a theory or (worse yet) beginning to celebrate the cultural production of those privileged classes ultimately plays a part in reinforcing that hegemony by mobilizing the theorist's own cultural capital and position of cultural authority to draw attention to and to canonize such works without examining the reasons that subtend such an evaluation.[39]

As I cautioned in my remarks on Hype Williams above, I do not want this critique to be taken as a call to abandon the understanding of the globalized U.S. cultural dominant gained through postmodern theory. On the contrary, what seems necessary (and I recognize that this represents nothing more than a first gesture in that direction, which must be played out more fully elsewhere) is a theory that presents an exploration of multiple cultural logics that is not simply derived from the aesthetic production of a white cultural elite. Such an exploration would provide a necessary supplement to Jameson's useful diagnosis of the state of the cultural dominant. Developing the models embodied by the reinvigoration of style in Hype Williams's videos and of genre in other hip hop videos is one possible avenue for the exploration of such alternative cultural logics. And as we develop these other logics we will no doubt be

ROGER BEEBE

forced to reconsider further our decades of trumpeting the "death of the author" and of our general theoretical understanding of a postmodern model developed without considering these other forms of contemporary cultural production.

NOTES

1 Director's names are now only missing for those rare repeated videos from the 1980s for which presumably no record exists of who directed the clips. As of 2004 the relatively new Fuse channel (formerly MuchMusic USA) was the only major music video channel in the United States that did not include the director's name. On CMT the director's name is offered at the start of the video and then is replaced with the songwriter's name at the end. This substitution of one "author" for another is incredibly suggestive. To fully tease out the meaning of that substitution would require, however, a much more extended analysis of the "force field" of country music than I have space for here.

2 See David Bordwell and Kristin Thompson, *Film Art: An Introduction*, 5th ed. (New York: McGraw-Hill, 1997), especially chapter 1.

3 The *loci classici* for the poststructuralist critique of authorship are Roland Barthes's challenge to the mythologization of the author in "The Death of the Author," in *Image, Music, Text* (New York: Hill and Wang, 1977); and Michel Foucault's analysis of the "author-function" in "What Is an Author?" in *Textual Strategies: Perspectives in Post-Structuralist Criticism*, ed. Josué V. Harrari (Ithaca, N.Y.: Cornell University Press, 1979).

4 Fredric Jameson, "Historicism in *The Shining*," in *Signatures of the Visible* (New York: Routledge, 1992), 82 (emphasis in original).

5 Ibid.

6 Ibid.

7 Ibid. Note that the term "post-industrial" is one that Jameson abandons in favor of "global" or "multinational" as he develops his theory of postmodernism.

8 Fredric Jameson, *Postmodernism, or, The Cultural Logic of Late Capitalism* (Durham, N.C.: Duke University Press, 1991), 16.

9 Jon Lewis, *The New American Cinema* (Durham, N.C.: Duke University Press, 1998).

10 Of course, the "postmodernism" of MTV has also been challenged, most notably in Andrew Goodwin's *Dancing in the Distraction Factory* (Minneapolis: University of Minnesota Press, 1992). While Goodwin's objections are often important in reining in the hyperbolic excesses of some postmodern writings on the cable network, even he ultimately concedes that there is much about MTV that is postmodern.

11 This period also, and I would argue not unrelatedly, saw the meteoric rise

(and, shortly thereafter, the fall) of the so-called alternative music of R.E.M., Nirvana, et al.

12 A connection could be made between MTV auteurism and the emergence of the *politique des auteurs* where each medium (film, music video) strives for respectability (despite its commercial and industrial nature) by aspiring to the higher status of an established cultural form. In fact, the gesture on the part of MTV was no doubt meant to latch onto not the prestigious notion of the literary author, but to the now-institutionalized notion of the auteur of the feature film.

13 It is of special significance here that Jonze, unlike the cinematic auteurs who tried their hands at music video in the 1980s (Scorsese, Ridley Scott, et al.), made his name primarily through directing videos. Thus MTV's celebration of his career is in many ways a celebration of its own place in the fostering and promoting of that new art form.

14 Nathaniel Hornblower, in addition to being the persona adopted for this "anonymous" prank, is also, suggestively, the pseudonym under which Yauch directs some of the Beastie Boys's videos. The footage of this stunt has now even made it onto his Director's Label DVD, *The Work of Director Spike Jonze* (2003). This DVD series, created by Jonze and fellow video directors Michel Gondry and Chris Cunningham, is a testimony to the continued importance of the auteur in music video years after its emergence, which I outline above.

15 This enshrinement of directors is no quirk of just this one countdown. Two years later when MTV unveils yet another iteration of their Top 100 videos (of all time — this time apparently closing out the millennium), the program includes interstitial segments highlighting the work of a number of music video auteurs: Spike Jonze, Mark Romanek, Wayne Isham, Hype Williams, David Fincher, and the husband-and-wife team of Jonathan Dayton and Valerie Faris.

16 It is unclear at what point this video was attributed to Alan Smithee, since, as I pointed out, MTV has frequently gone back to correct their earlier failure to include director's names. In any case, it is clear that by the time this countdown aired, the director's name had become de rigueur.

17 Since this alternative movement has now been more or less officially declared to be over, this canon of alternative videos — now safely tucked away as a historical movement — should prove to be a relatively stable indicator of the fate of those videos for the ages. That said, many of these videos have slipped further down MTV's more recent countdowns as the station and its viewers have become less immediately enchanted with the alternative music revolution.

18 The awarding of the top spot to "Smells Like Teen Spirit" should serve as a salutary reminder that these are *music* videos. While my focus here has been on the visual aspect (i.e., the "video"), this appears to be a case where the musico-historical import of the song is as significant as (if not more

significant than) the accompanying visual presentation in the assessment of its merits. While this video is certainly memorable, it isn't quite the tour de force that some of the other clips on the countdown are. In other words, this video had to be number one on the countdown because of the place of the song in the history of alternative music, rather than (as is largely the case with the other videos) as a reflection of an act of aesthetic judgment about the *video* per se.

19 Although the "Under the Bridge" video is not a pastiche, it is most assuredly still auteurist since it was directed by the indie cinema auteur Gus Van Sant. Indeed, we might argue that it is his external credibility as a director that allows him to eschew the dominant pastiche form, or that his preexisting cinematic style determines the form of this video more than does the music televisual context in which it is placed.

20 Cf. the decade-ending tributes to Nirvana on the covers of both *Spin* and *Rolling Stone*.

21 We might well trace the ways that pastiche and auteurism have played out on other music television channels such as VH1, BET, CMT, and MTV2 as well as on Internet sites like MTV.com and Launch.com. While these other sites have followed MTV's lead in crediting the music video directors, they have not followed the movement to pastiche with equal zeal. I address this issue in further detail below.

22 The language of the "death of the subject" has found new life lately as one of the catchphrases of the emergent discourse of the posthuman.

23 For one exploration of this "contingency of value," see the work of Jameson's colleague Barbara Herrnstein Smith in her *Contingencies of Value: Alternative Perspectives for Critical Theory* (Cambridge, Mass.: Harvard University Press, 1988).

24 Vivian Sobchack, *Screening Space: The American Science Fiction Film* (New Brunswick, N.J.: Rutgers University Press, 1997); Anne Friedberg, *Window Shopping: Cinema and the Postmodern* (Berkeley: University of California Press, 1993). These are just two of innumerable examples of texts that rely on Jameson's elaboration of the notion of pastiche.

25 Kenneth von Gunden, *Postmodern Auteurs* (Jefferson, N.C.: McFarland, 1991).

26 Jon Lewis, *The New American Cinema* (Durham, N.C.: Duke University Press, 1998).

27 Only Lucas's early *American Grafitti* (1973) is mentioned in conjunction with the notion of pastiche. Spielberg is altogether absent. Certainly some of their work would merely confirm his observations (e.g., the Spielberg/Lucas collaborations on the Indiana Jones films that draw heavily upon 1930s serials), but others have a more obscure connection to it (e.g., *Jaws*). Since Jameson has marked the importance of this last film through his lengthy reading of it elsewhere (namely in "Reification and Utopia in Mass Culture" in *Signatures of the Visible*), its absence here is especially interesting.

28 We might equally point to country music video as a genre with incredible popularity and little use of pastiche. Mark Fenster's essay "Genre and Form" starts to lay the groundwork for this, but we would certainly want also to look closely at CMT and the discourse surrounding these videos. See Fenster, "Genre and Form: The Development of the Country Music Video," in *Sound and Vision: The Music Video Reader*, ed. Simon Frith, Andrew Goodwin, and Lawrence Grossberg (New York: Routledge, 1993).

29 Note that this also represents a shift in my focus from MTV as a specific set of discourses surrounding music videos to the music videos themselves.

30 Later I problematize the simple assertion that this reemergence of style is *just* a return of the modernist model. However, at this point I wish only to unsettle the postmodern problematic.

31 Jameson, "Historicism," 85.

32 Interview by Mark Lewman in *The Work of Director Spike Jonze*. We might note quickly here the resonance between Jonze's language in describing the Williams/Bad Boy look and Jameson's phrase "the cult of the glossy image."

33 Hype Williams has also directed videos that are more simply pastiche videos (e.g., Missy Elliot's "Sock It 2 Me," the follow up to "The Rain," which is a Japanimation-influenced space saga, and Dr. Dre and 2Pac Shakur's "California Love," which directly echoes *Mad Max: Beyond Thunderdome*). However, Williams's name is more immediately identified with the other style I described above that became such a marker of hip hop video in the second half of the 1990s.

34 Interestingly, this form of hip hop video with a revitalized interest in genre is, at least in its first period, allied with a single auteur—namely, Paul Hunter. This connection between auteur and genre, though, is a more familiar paradox that dates back to the emergence of the politique des auteurs. The difference here is that rather than expressing himself *through* genre, Paul Hunter's signature *is* genre.

35 Of course, as I preliminarily suggested in an earlier footnote, none of these binary classifications should be taken as rigid or absolute. Hip hop has certainly seen some videos that are more referential and/or ironic in their mobilization of the 1980s blockbuster: e.g., the video for "Dangerous" by Busta Rhymes casts him as the crazy white cop in a buddy flick (after Riggs from the *Lethal Weapon* movies) and also includes a brief sequence with Busta playing the karate master from *The Last Dragon*. Some have also had referents that are as "high cultural" as their alternative counterparts: for example, Stanley Kubrick is alluded to both in the video for Usher's "My Way" (derived from the opening sequences of *A Clockwork Orange*) and that for Mystikal's "Shake Ya Ass" (which cites the party scene in *Eyes Wide Shut*).

36 Cf. Ed Guerrero, "The Black Image in Protective Custody: Hollywood's Biracial Buddy Films of the Eighties," in *Black American Cinema*, ed. Manthia Diawara (New York: Routledge, 1993).

37 Pierre Bourdieu, *Distinction: A Social Critique of the Judgement of Taste* (Cambridge, Mass.: Harvard University Press, 1984).

38 There are exceptions to these class identifications: for example, the oft-told stories about Quentin Tarantino's past as a video clerk seem to place him in a much more working-class context. Nevertheless, the image of the downwardly mobile slacker (especially the video clerk slacker and the attendant culture of cinematic autodidacticism, of which this is just one of hundreds of remarkable examples) is clearly implicated in the same racial and class structures that I discuss above.

39 This may be perhaps the secret motivation behind Jameson's most recent book of writings on film, *The Geopolitical Aesthetic* (Bloomington: Indiana University Press, 1992), which is concerned with non-U.S. film.

Alasuutari, Pertti, and Petri Ruuska. *Post-Patria? Globalisaation kulttuuri Suomessa*. Tampere: Vastapaino, 1999.

Allen, Robert C. *Channels of Discourse: Television and Contemporary Criticism*. Chapel Hill: University of North Carolina Press, 1987.

Altman, Rick. "Afterword: A Baker's Dozen Terms for Sound Analysis." In *Sound Theory / Sound Practice*, ed. Rick Altman. New York: Routledge, 1992.

——. "Television/Sound." In *Studies in Entertainment: Critical Approaches to Mass Culture*, ed. Tania Modleski. Bloomington: Indiana University Press, 1986.

Amanda, Dana, and Friis-Hansen Cruz. *Takashi Murakami: The Meaning of the Nonsense of the Meaning*. New York: Harry N. Abrams, 2000.

Anderson, Benedict. *Imagined Communities: Reflections on the Origin and Spread of Nationalism*. London: Verso, 1983.

Ang, Ien. *Living Room Wars: Rethinking Media Audiences for a Postmodern World*. London: Routledge, 1996.

Arnheim, Rudolph. *The Power of the Center*. Berkeley: University of California Press, 1988.

Back, Les. *New Ethnicities and Urban Culture. Racisms and Multiculture in Young Lives*. London: UCL Press, 1996.

Baker, David J. "*Ea* and Knowing in Hawai'i." *Critical Inquiry* (spring 1997): 645.

Banks, Jack. *Monopoly Television: MTV's Quest to Control the Music*. Boulder, Colo.: Westview Press, 1996.

Barthes, Roland. "The Death of the Author." In *Image, Music, Text*. New York: Hill and Wang, 1977.

Bazin, André. *What Is Cinema?* Berkeley: University of California Press, 1971.

Beebe, Roger, Denise Fulbrook, and Ben Saunders, eds. *Rock Over the Edge: Transformations in Popular Music Culture*. Durham, N.C.: Duke University Press, 2002.

Bergstrom, Janet. *Endless Night: Cinema and Psychoanalysis — Parallel Histories*. Berkeley: University of California Press, 1999.

Berland, Jody. "Sound, Image and Social Space: Music Video and Media Reconstruction." In *Sound and Vision: The Music Video Reader*, ed. Simon Frith, Andrew Goodwin, and Lawrence Grossberg. New York: Routledge, 1993.

———. "Space at the Margins: Colonial Spaciality and Critical Theory After Innis." *Topia* 1 (1997): 55–82.

Berry, Elizabeth Mendez. "Jay-Z: *Reasonable Doubt. Volume 3: Life and Times of S. Carter: The Blueprint.*" In *Classic Material: The Hip-Hop Album Guide*, ed. Oliver Wang. Toronto: ECW Press, 2003.

Björnberg, Alf. "Sign of the Times? Om musikvideo och populärmusikens semiotik." In *Svensk tidskrift för musikforskning*, Årgang/volume 72. Göteborg: Svenska samfundet för musikforskning, 1990.

———. Björnberg, Alf. "Structural Relationships of Music and Images in Music Video." *Popular Music* 13.1 (1994): 51–74.

Boddy, William. *Fifties Television: The Industry and Its Critics*. Urbana: University of Illinois Press, 1993.

Boggs, Joseph. *The Art of Watching Films*, 3rd ed. London: Addison-Wesley, 1991.

Bordwell, David, Janet Staiger, and Kristin Thompson. *Classical Hollywood Cinema*. New York: Columbia University Press, 1985.

Bordwell, David, and Kristin Thompson. *Film Art: An Introduction*. New York: McGraw-Hill, 1997.

Bourdieu, Pierre. *Distinction: A Social Critique of the Judgement of Taste*. Cambridge, Mass.: Harvard University Press, 1984.

Brackett, David. "(In Search of) Musical Meaning: Genres, Categories and Crossover." In *Popular Music Studies*, ed. David Hesmondhalgh and Keith Negus. London: Arnold, 2002.

Branigan, Edward. "Sound and Epistemology in Film." *Journal of Aesthetics and Art Criticism* 47 (1989): 312–24.

Burger, Peter. *Theory of the Avant-Garde*. Minneapolis: University of Minnesota Press, 1984.

Byrne, David. *E.E.E.I.: Envisioning Emotional Epistemological Information*. New York: Steidl, 2003.

———. "Learning to Love Powerpoint," *Wired* 11.9 (September 2003): 12–15.

Cantwell, Robert. *When We Were Good*. Cambridge, Mass.: Harvard University Press, 1996.

Carroll, Noël. "Notes on the Sight Gag." In *Comedy/Cinema/Theory*, ed. Andrew Horton. Berkeley: University of California Press, 1991.

Cavell, Stanley. *The World Viewed*. Cambridge, Mass.: Harvard University Press, 1979.

Chion, Michel. *Audio-Vision: Sound on Screen*, ed. and trans. Claudia Gorbman. New York: Columbia University Press, 1994.

———. *Le son au cinema*. Paris: Cahiers du Cinema / Editions de l'Etoile, 1985.

———. *The Voice in Cinema*, trans. Claudia Gorbman. New York: Columbia University Press, 1999.

Cleto, Fabio, ed. *Camp: Queer Aesthetics and the Performing Subject, a Reader*. Ann Arbor: University of Michigan Press, 1999.

Cook, Nicholas. *Analysing Musical Multimedia*. Oxford: Clarendon Press, 1998.

Dancyger, Ken. *The Technique of Film and Video Editing*. Boston: Focal Press, 1996.

Danziger, Kurt. *Interpersonal Communication*. New York: Pergamon Press, 1976.

Deleuze, Gilles, and Félix Guattari. "1837: Of the Refrain." In *A Thousand Plateaus: Capitalism and Schizophrenia*, trans. Brian Massumi. London: Athlone Press, 1996.

DeWitt, Howard A. *Elvis: The Sun Years*. Ann Arbor: Popular Culture Ink., 1993.

Doherty, Thomas. *Teenagers and Teenpics: The Juvenalization of American Movies in the 1950s*. Boston: Unwin Hyman, 1988.

Ehrnrooth, Jari. "Mentality." In *Finland: A Cultural Encyclopedia*, ed. Olli Alho, Hildi Hawkins, and Päivi Vallisaari. Helsinki: Finnish Literature Society, 1997.

Fenster, Mark. "Genre and Form: The Development of the Country Music Video." In *Sound and Vision: The Music Video Reader*, ed. Simon Frith, Andrew Goodwin, and Lawrence Grossberg. New York: Routledge, 1993.

Fish, Mick, and Dave Halberry. *Cabaret Voltaire: The Art of the Sixth Sense*. London: Serious Art Forms Publishing, 1985.

————. *Industrial Evolution: Through the 80s with Cabaret Voltaire*. London: Serious Art Forms Publishing, 2002.

Fiske, John. *Reading the Popular*. Cambridge: Cambridge University Press, 1989.

Forman, Murray. *The 'Hood Comes First: Race, Space, and Place in Rap and Hip-Hop*. Middletown, Conn.: Wesleyan University Press, 2002.

Foucault, Michel. "What Is an Author?" In *Textual Strategies: Perspectives in Post-Structuralist Criticism*, ed. Josué V. Harrari. Ithaca, N.Y.: Cornell University Press, 1979.

Friedberg, Anne. *Window Shopping: Cinema and the Postmodern*. Berkeley: University of California Press, 1993.

Frith, Simon. *Music for Pleasure: Essays on the Sociology of Pop*. Cambridge: Polity Press, 1988.

————. *Performing Rites: On the Value of Popular Music*. Oxford: Oxford University Press, 1996.

————. *Sound Effects*. New York: Pantheon, 1981.

Frith, Simon, and Andrew Goodwin, eds. *On Record*. New York: Pantheon, 1990.

Frith, Simon, Andrew Goodwin, and Lawrence Grossberg, eds. *Sound and Vision: The Music Video Reader*. New York: Routledge, 1993.

Frith, Simon, and Howard Horne. *Art into Pop*. London: Routledge and Kegan Paul, 1988.

Gabbard, Krin. *Jammin' at the Margins: Jazz and the American Cinema*. Chicago: University of Chicago Press, 1996.

Gee, Anne. "Contact, Change, and the Church." Dissertation, University of New England.

Gillet, Charlie. *The Sound of the City: The Rise of Rock and Roll*. New York: Pantheon, 1970.

Goffman, Erving. *The Presentation of Self in Everyday Life*. Garden City, N.Y.: Doubleday, 1959.

Goldenson, Leonard H., with Marvin J. Wolf. In *Beating the Odds: The Untold Story behind the Rise of ABC: The Stars, Struggles, and Egos that Transformed Network Television by the Man Who Made It Happen*. New York: Charles Scribner's Sons, 1991.

Goodman, Fred. *The Mansion on the Hill: Dylan, Young, Geffen, Springsteen, and the Head-On Collision of Rock and Commerce*. New York: Times Books, 1997.

Goodwin, Andrew. *Dancing in the Distraction Factory*. Minneapolis: University of Minnesota Press, 1992.

Gorbman, Claudia. *Unheard Melodies: Narrative Film Music*. Bloomington: Indiana University Press, 1987.

Greenberg, Clement. "Avant-Garde and Kitsch." In *Pollock and After: The Critical Debate*. New York: Harper and Row, 1985.

Grossberg, Lawrence. *We Gotta Get Out of This Place: Popular Conservatism and Postmodern Culture*. New York: Routledge, 1992.

Grossberg, Lawrence, Wartella, Ellen, and Whitney, D. Charles. *Mediamaking: Mass Media in a Popular Culture*. Thousand Oaks, Calif.: Sage, 1998.

Guerrero, Ed. "The Black Image in Protective Custody: Hollywood's Biracial Buddy Films of the Eighties." In *Black American Cinema*, ed. Manthia Diawara. New York: Routledge, 1993.

Guralnick, Peter. *Careless Love: The Unmaking of Elvis Presley*. Boston: Little, Brown, 1999.

———. *Last Train to Memphis: The Rise of Elvis Presley*. Boston: Little, Brown, 1994.

Halberstam, David. *The Fifties*. New York: Fawcett Columbine, 1993.

Hall, Stuart. "The Question of Cultural Identity." In *Modernity and Its Futures*, ed. Stuart Hall, David Held, and Tony McGrew. Cambridge: Polity Press, 1992.

Hanke, Robert. "'Yo Quiero Mi MTV!' Making Music Television for Latin America." In *Mapping the Beat: Popular Music and Contemporary Theory*, ed. Thomas Swiss, John Sloop, and Andrew Herman. Malden, Mass.: Blackwell, 1998.

Harbinson, W. A. *The Illustrated Elvis*. New York: Grossett and Dunlap, 1976.

Harrison, Charles, and Paul Wood, eds. *Art in Theory*. Cambridge: Blackwell, 1992.

Hayward, Philip. "A New Tradition: Titus Tilly and the Development of Music Video in Papua New Guinea." In *Sound Alliances: Indigenous People, Cultural Politics and Popular Music in the Pacific*, ed. Philip Hayward. London: Cassell, 1998.

———. "Industrial Light and Magic: Style, Technology and Special Effects in Music Video and Music Television." In *Culture, Technology and Creativity*, ed. Philip Hayward. London: John Libbey Press/Arts Council of Great Britain, 1990.

———. "Safe, Exotic and Somewhere Else: Yothu Yindi, 'Treaty' and the Mediation of Aboriginality." In *Sound Alliances: Indigenous People, Cultural Politics and Popular Music in the Pacific*, ed. Philip Hayward. London: Cassell, 1998.

Heiniö, Mikko. *Karvalakki kansakunnan kaapin päällä: Kansalliset attribuutit Joonas Kokkosen ja Aulis Sallisen ooperoiden julkisuuskuvassa, 1975–1985.* Helsinki: Suomalaisen Kirjallisuuden Seura, 1999.

———. "The Main Trends in Finnish Music in the 1970s and 1980s and the Problem of 'Finnishness.'" In *Music and Nationalism in Twentieth-Century Great Britain and Finland*, ed. Tomi Mäkelä. Hamburg: von Bockel Verlag, 1997.

Henriksson, Juha, and Risto Kukkonen. *Toivo Kärjen musiikillinen tyyli.* Helsinki: Suomen Jazz and Pop Arkisto, 2001.

Hill, Trent. "The Enemy Within: Censorship in Rock Music in the 1950s." In *Present Tense: Rock & Roll and Culture*, ed. Anthony DeCurtis. Durham, N.C.: Duke University Press, 1992.

Hofstadter, Albert, and Richard Kuhns, eds. *Philosophies of Art and Beauty.* Chicago: University of Chicago Press, 1964.

Huyssen, Andreas. *After the Great Divide.* Bloomington: Indiana University Press, 1986.

Innis, Harold. *The Bias of Communication.* Toronto: University of Toronto Press, 1951.

Jackson, John A. *American Bandstand: Dick Clark and the Making of a Rock 'n' Roll Empire.* New York: Oxford University Press, 1997.

———. *Big Beat Heat: Alan Freed and the Early Years of Rock and Roll.* New York: Schirmer Books, 1991.

Jakobson, Roman. "On Realism in Art." In *Readings in Russian Poetics*, ed. Ladislav Matejka and Krystyna Pomorska. Cambridge, Mass.: MIT Press, 1971.

Jalkanen, Pekka. "Popular Music." In *Finnish Music*, ed. Kalevi Aho, Pekka Jalkanen, Erkki Salmenhaara and Keijo Virtamo; trans. Timothy Binham and Philip Binham. Helsinki: Otava, 1996.

Jalkanen, Pekka, and Vesa Kurkela. "Populaarimusiikki ja historia." *Musiikki* 1 (1995): 13–28.

Jameson, Fredric. *The Geopolitical Aesthetic.* Bloomington: Indiana University Press, 1992.

———. "Historicism in *The Shining*." In *Signatures of the Visible*. New York: Routledge, 1992.

———. *Postmodernism, or, The Cultural Logic of Late Capitalism.* Durham, N.C.: Duke University Press, 1991.

———. "Reification and Utopia in Mass Culture." In *Signatures of the Visible*. New York: Routledge, 1992.

Jones, Peter. *Elvis.* London: Octopus Books, 1976.

Kalinak, Kathryn. *Settling the Score: Music and the Classical Hollywood Film.* Madison: University of Wisconsin Press, 1992.

Kallioniemi, Kari. "Onko sijaa ylväälle dandylle Suomenmaassa? Englantilaisuuden vaikutuksia suomalaisessa popmusiikissa ja siitä käydyssä keskustelussa." In *Pohjan tähteet: Populaarikulttuurin kuva suomalaisuudesta*, ed. Hannu Salmi and Kari Kallioniemi. Helsinki: BTJ Kirjastopalvelu Oy, 2000.

Kanahele, George S., ed. *Hawaiian Music and Musicians: An Illustrated History*, Honolulu: University of Hawaii Press, 1979.

Kandinsky, Wassily. *Concerning the Spiritual in Art*. London: Constable and Co., 1914.

Kaplan, E. Ann. *Rocking around the Clock: Music, Television and Consumer Culture*. New York: Methuen, 1987.

Kelley, Robin D. G. "Kickin Reality, Kickin Ballistics: Gangsta Rap and Postindustrial Los Angeles." In *Droppin Science: Critical Essays on Rap Music and Hip Hop Culture*, ed. William Eric Perkins. Philadelphia: Temple University Press, 1996.

Kinder, Marsha. "Music Video and the Spectator: Television, Ideology and Dream." *Film Quarterly* 38.1 (1984): 2–15.

Kleiler, David, and Robert Moses. *You Stand There: Making Music Video*. New York: Three Rivers Press, 1997.

Kurkela, Vesa. "Bulgarian tshalgavideot, poliittisuus ja orientalismi." In *Etnomusikologian vuosikirja*, volume 13, ed. Jarkko Niemi. Helsinki: Suomen etnomusikologinen seura, 2001.

Langer, John. "Television's Personality System." *Media, Culture and Society* 4 (1981): 351–65.

Lavin, Maud. *Cut with the Kitchen Knife: The Weimar Photomontages of Hannah Hoch*. New Haven, Conn.: Yale University Press, 1994.

Leonard, John. "Ed Sullivan Died for Our Sins." In *Smoke and Mirrors: Violence, Television, and Other American Cultures*. New York: New Press, 1997.

Lewis, George H. "Storm Blowing from Paradise: Oppositional Ideology in Popular Hawaiian Music." *Popular Music* 10.1 (1991): 53–68.

Lewis, Jon. *The New American Cinema*. Durham, N.C.: Duke University Press, 1998.

Lewis, Lisa. *Gender Politics and MTV*. Philadelphia: Temple University Press, 1990.

Lilliestam, Lars. *Svensk rock: Musik, lyrik, historik*. Göteborg: Bo Ejeby Förlag, 1998.

Lukow, Gregory. "The Antecedents of MTV: Soundies, Scopitones and Snaders, and the History of an Ahistorical Form." In *The Art of Music Video: Ten Years After*, ed. Michael Nash. Long Beach, Calif.: Long Beach Museum of Art, 1991.

Lynch, Joan D. "Music Videos: From Performance to Dada-Surrealism." *Journal of Popular Culture* 18.1 (summer 1984): 53–57.

Mäkelä, Janne. "Ismo: Suomalaisen rock-auteurismin jäljillä." In *Pohjan tähteet: Populaarikulttuurin kuva suomalaisuudesta*, ed. Hannu Salmi and Kari Kallioniemi. Helsinki: BTJ Kirjastopalvelu Oy, 2000.

———. "Yhteinen sävel vai riitasointu? Globaalin ja lokaalin suhteista populaarimusiikissa." In *Muuttuvat asemat: Kompassi integraation arkeen*, ed. Maija Mäkikalli and Katriina Siivonen. Turku: Kirja-Aurora, 2000.

Marcus, Greil. *Lipstick Traces*. Cambridge, Mass.: Harvard University Press, 1989.

Marks, Lawrence. "Bright Sneezes and Dark Coughs, Loud Sunlight and Soft

Moonlight." *Journal of Experimental Psychology: Human Perception and Performance* 8.2 (1982): 177–93.

———. "On Cross-Modal Similarity: Audio-Visual Interactions in Speeded Discriminations." *Journal of Experimental Psychology: Human Perception and Performance* 13.3 (1987): 384–94.

———. *The Unity of the Senses: Interrelations among the Modalities*. New York: Academic Press, 1978.

Marshall, P. David. *Celebrity and Power: Fame in Contemporary Culture*. Minneapolis: University of Minnesota Press, 1997.

Marx, Karl. "Private Property and Communism. Various Stages of Development of Communist Views: Crude, Equalitarian Communism and Communism as Socialism Coinciding with Humaneness." In *Economic and Philosophic Manuscripts of 1844*, trans. Martin Milligan. New York: International Publishers, 1971.

McCarthy, Anna. *Ambient Television: Visual Culture and Public Space*. Durham, N.C.: Duke University Press, 2001.

McCloud, Scott. *Understanding Comics*. Northampton, Mass.: Kitchen Sink Press, 1994.

McLafferty, Gerry. *Elvis Presley in Hollywood: Celluloid Sell-Out*. London: Robert Hale, 1989.

McLean, Albert F. Jr. *American Vaudeville as Ritual*. Lexington: University of Kentucky Press, 1965.

Meyer, Moe, ed. *The Politics and Poetics of Camp*. New York: Routledge, 1994.

Meyrowitz, Joshua. *No Sense of Place: The Impact of Electronic Media on Social Behaviour*. New York: Oxford University Press, 1985.

Millerson, Gerald. *Television Production*. Boston: Focal Press, 1999.

Mundy, John. *Popular Music on Screen: From Hollywood Musical to Music Video*. Manchester: Manchester University Press, 1999.

Murakami, Takashi. *SUPER FLAT*. San Francisco: Last Gasp Press, 2003.

Naremore, James. *Acting in the Cinema*. Berkeley: University of California Press, 1990.

Negus, Keith. *Popular Music in Theory: An Introduction*. Hanover, N.H.: University Press of New England, 1996.

Newitz, Annalee. "What Makes Things Cheesy? Satire, Multinationalism, and B-Movies." *Social Text* 63, vol. 18.2 (summer 2000): 59–82.

Nietzsche, Friedrich. "On Truth and Falsity in Their Ultramoral Sense." In *The Complete Works of Friedrich Nietzsche*, volume 2, ed. Oscar Levy; trans. Maximilian Mugge. London: George Allen and Unwin, 1924.

Ong, Walter. *Orality and Literacy: The Technology of the Word*. London: Methuen, 1985.

Oramo, Ilkka. "Beyond Nationalism." In *Music and Nationalism in Twentieth-Century Great Britain and Finland*, ed. Tomi Mäkelä. Hamburg: von Bockel Verlag, 1997.

Parks, Lisa. "Satellite Rhythms: Channel V, Asian Music Video, and Transnational Gender." In *Rock Over the Edge: Transformations in Popular Music Culture*, ed. Roger Beebe, Denise Fulbrook, and Ben Saunders. Durham, N.C.: Duke University Press, 2002.

Pegley, Karen. "'Simple Economics'? Images of Gender and Nationality on Much-Music (Canada) and MTV (US)." *Women and Music: A Journal of Gender and Culture* 4 (2000): 1–17.

Philpott, Malcolm. "Developments in Papua New Guinea's Popular Music Industry." *Perfect Beat: The Pacific Journal of Research Into Contemporary Music and Popular Culture* 2.3 (1994): 98–114.

Pit, Kenneth. *Bowie: The Pitt Report*. London: Omnibus Press, 1985.

Pomorska, Lataslav Matjeka Krystyna, ed. *Readings in Russian Poetics*. Cambridge, Mass.: MIT Press, 1971.

Press, Joy. "Reality Killed the Video Star: The Music TV Wars." *Village Voice*, July 23–29, 2003, 52.

Rantanen, Päivi. "Hevosenkaltainen kansa—suomalaisuus topeliaanisessa diskurssissa." In *Me ja muut: Kulttuuri, identiteetti, toiseus*, ed. Marjo Kylmänen. Tampere: Vastapaino, 1994.

Reisz, Karel. *The Technique of Film Editing*. Boston: Focal Press, 1988.

Ricoeur, Paul. "The Metaphorical Process as Cognition, Imagination and Feeling." In *Philosophical Perspectives on Metaphor*, ed. Mark Johnson. Ann Arbor, Mich.: University Microfilms International, 1994.

———. *The Rule of Metaphor: Multi-Disciplinary Studies of the Creation of Meaning in Language*, trans. Robert Czerny. Toronto: University of Toronto Press, 1977.

Rodman, Gilbert B. *Elvis after Elvis: The Posthumous Career of a Living Legend*. New York: Routledge, 1996.

Román-Velazquez, Patria. "Locating Salsa." In *Popular Music Studies*, ed. David Hesmondhalgh and Keith Negus. London: Arnold, 2002.

Rorty, Richard. *Objectivity, Relativism and Truth: Philosophical Papers*, volume 1. Cambridge: Cambridge University Press, 1991.

Rothman, William, and Marian Keane. *Reading Cavell's* The World Viewed: *A Philosophical Perspective on Film*. Detroit: Wayne State University Press, 2000.

Saito, Ayako. "Hitchcock's Trilogy: A Logic of Mise en Scène." In *Endless Night: Cinema and Psychoanalysis—Parallel Histories*, ed. Janet Bergstrom. Berkeley: University of California Press, 1999.

Salmenhaara, Erkki. "Birth of a National and Musical Culture in Finland." In *Finnish Music*, ed. Kalevi Aho, Pekka Jalkanen, Erkki Salmenhaara and Keijo Virtamo; trans. Timothy Binham and Philip Binham. Helsinki: Otava, 1996.

Salmi, Hannu, and Kallioniemi, Kari. "Pohjan tähteiden tuolla puolen: Suomalaisuuden strategioita populaarikulttuurissa." In *Pohjan tähteet: Populaarikulttuurin kuva suomalaisuudesta*, ed. Hannu Salmi and Kari Kallioniemi. Helsinki: BTJ Kirjastopalvelu Oy, 2000.

Sanjek, Russell. *American Popular Music and Its Business: The First 400 Years*. New York: Oxford University Press, 1988.

Sawchuck, Kim. "An Index of Power: Innis, Aesthetics, and Technology." In *Harold*

Innis in the New Century: Reflections and Refractions, ed. C. Acland and W. Buxton. Montreal: McGill-Queens University Press, 1999.

Sebree, Shirley. *Pele's Tears: Reclaiming the Lost Gems of Hawaiian Music in Western Music Styles*. New York: Vantage Press, 1994.

Sekula, Allan. "On the Invention of Photographic Meaning." In *Thinking Photography*, ed. Victor Burgin. London: Macmillan, 1982.

Shaviro, Steven. "The Erotic Life of Machines." *Parallax* 8.4 (October/December 2002): 21–31.

Shaw, Greg. "The Teen Idols." In *The Rolling Stone Illustrated History of Rock and Roll*. New York: Rolling Stone Press, 1980.

Shumway, David. "Rock and Roll as a Cultural Practice." In *Present Tense: Rock & Roll and Culture*, ed. Anthony DeCurtis. Durham, N.C.: Duke University Press, 1992.

————. "Watching Elvis: The Male Rock Star as Object of the Gaze." In *The Other Fifties: Interrogating Midcentury American Icons*, ed. Joel Foreman. Urbana: University of Illinois Press, 1997.

Siikala, Anna-Leena. "Suomalaisuuden tulkintoja." In *Olkaamme siis suomalaisia*, ed. Pekka Laaksonen and Sirkka-Liisa Mettomäki. Helsinki: Suomalaisen kirjallisuuden seura, 1996.

Smith, Barbara Herrnstein. *Contingencies of Value: Alternative Perspectives for Critical Theory*. Cambridge, Mass.: Harvard University Press, 1988.

Smith, Jeff. "Popular Songs and Comic Allusion in Contemporary Cinema." In *Soundtrack Available: Essays on Film and Popular Music*, ed. Pamela Robertson Wojcik and Arthur Knight. Durham, N.C.: Duke University Press, 2001.

————. *The Sounds of Commerce: Marketing Popular Film Music*. New York: Columbia University Press, 1998.

Sobchack, Vivian. *Screening Space: The American Science Fiction Film*. New Brunswick, N.J.: Rutgers University Press, 1997.

Sontag, Susan. "Notes on 'Camp.'" In *Against Interpretation and Other Essays*. New York: Farrar, Straus and Giroux, 1966.

Spitz, Mark, and Brendan Mullen. *We Got the Neutron Bomb: The UNtold Story of L. A. Punk*. New York: Three Rivers Press, 2001.

Still, Judith, and Worton, Michael. "Introduction." In *Intertextuality: Theories and Practices*, ed. Judith Still and Michael Worton. Manchester: Manchester University Press, 1990.

Stockbridge, Sally. "Intertextuality: Video Music Clips and Historical Film." In *History on/and/in Film*, ed. T. O'Regan and B. Shoesmith. Perth: History and Film Association of Australia, 1987.

Stratemann, Klaus. *Duke Ellington Day by Day and Film by Film*. Copenhagen: Jazz Media, 1992.

Straw, Will. "Popular Music and Post-Modernism in the 1980s." In *Sound and Vision: The Music Video Reader*, ed. Simon Frith, Andrew Goodwin, and Lawrence Grossberg. New York: Routledge, 1993.

Street, John. *Politics and Popular Culture*. Cambridge: Polity Press, 1997.

Sullivan, Nancy. "Film and Television Production in Papua New Guinea: How the Medium Became the Message." *Public Culture* 11 (1993): 533–46.

Sussman, Warren I. *Culture as History: The Transformation of American Society in the Twentieth Century*. New York: Pantheon Books, 1984.

Tansey, Richard, and Horst de la Croix. *Gardner's Art through the Ages*. New York: Harcourt Brace, 1986.

Tatar, Elizabeth. *Strains of Change: The Impact of Tourism on Hawaiian Music*. Honolulu: Bishop Museum Press, 1987.

Tate, Joseph. "Radiohead's Antivideos: Works of Art in the Age of Electronic Reproduction." *Postmodern Culture: An Electronic Journal of Interdisciplinary Criticism* 12.3 (May 2002).

Terenzio, Maurice, Scott MacGillivray, and Ted Okuda. *The Soundies Distributing Corporation of America: A History and Filmography*. Jefferson, N.C.: McFarland, 1991.

Tobenkin, David. "The All-Music Channels." *Broadcasting and Cable* 126/127 (1996): 38–44.

Topelius, Z. *Maamme kirja: Lukukirja Suomen alimmille opilaitoksille*. Köping: Bokförlaget Oden, 1980.

Toynbee, Jason. "Mainstreaming, from Hegemonic Centre to Global Networks." In *Popular Music Studies*, ed. David Hesmondhalgh and Keith Negus. London: Arnold, 2002.

Trimillos, Richard. *Musics of Hawai'i*. Honolulu: State Foundation on Culture and the Arts/Fold Arts Program, 1994.

Tzara, Tristan. "Dada Manifesto." In *Dada Painters and Poets*, ed. Robert Motherwell. Cambridge, Mass.: The Belknap Press of Harvard University Press, 1951.

Vernallis, Carol. "The Aesthetics of Music Video: An Analysis of Madonna's 'Cherish.'" *Popular Music* 17.2 (1998): 153–85.

———. *Experiencing Music Video: Aesthetics in Cultural Context*. New York: Columbia University Press, 2004.

Von Gunden, Kenneth. *Postmodern Auteurs*. Jefferson, N.C.: McFarland, 1991.

Walker, Robert Matthew. *Elvis Presley: A Study in Music*. Tunbridge Wells, U.K.: Midas Books, 1982.

Walser, Robert. *Running with the Devil*. Hanover, N.H.: University Press of New England, 1993.

Ward, Brian. *Just My Soul Responding: Rhythm and Blues, Black Consciousness, and Race Relations*. Berkeley: University of California Press, 1998.

Webb, Michael. *Lokal Musik: Lingua Franca Song and Identity in Papua New Guinea*. Boroko, PNG: National Research Institute, 1993.

Weingarten, Marc. *Station to Station: The History of Rock 'n' Roll on Television*. New York: Pocket Books, 2000.

Whittall, Arnold. "Personal Style, Impersonal Structure? Music Analysis and Nationality." In *Music and Nationalism in Twentieth-Century Great Britain and Finland*, ed. Tomi Mäkelä. Hamburg: von Bockel Verlag, 1997.

William, Joseph. "Synaesthetic Adjectives: A Possible Law of Semantic Change." *Language* 52 (1976): 461.

Williams, Alan. "Pierrot in Context(s)." In *Jean-Luc Godard's Pierrot Le Fou*, ed. David Wills. Cambridge: Cambridge University Press, 2000.

Williams, Raymond. *Technology and Cultural Form*. New York: Schocken Books, 1974.

Wilson, Rob. "*Goodbye Paradise*: Global/Localism in the American Pacific." In *Global/Local: Cultural Production and the Transnational Imaginary*, ed. Rob Wilson and Wimal Dissanayake. Durham, N.C.: Duke University Press, 1996.

The Work of Director Spike Jonze. New York: Metropolis DVD, 2003.

Wurtzler, Steve. "'She Sang Live, But the Microphone Was Turned Off': The Live, the Recorded and the *Subject* of Representation." In *Sound Theory / Sound Practice*, ed. Rick Altman. New York: Routledge, 1992.

Zeidner, Lisa. "No Mo Po Mo, Or: I Had a Dream." *Tin House* (summer 2001): 75–79.

Zettl, Herbert. *Sight, Sound, Motion: Applied Media Aesthetics*. San Francisco: Wadsworth, 1998.

ROGER BEEBE is an associate professor of film and media studies in the English Department at the University of Florida. He is the coeditor of a volume on popular music, *Rock Over the Edge* (published by Duke University Press), as well as the author of essays on *Terminator 2*, Kurt Cobain and Tupac Shakur, and other products of mass culture. In addition to his scholarship he is also an award-winning experimental filmmaker and an active film programmer, currently as director of FLEX, the Florida Experimental Film/Video Festival.

NORMA COATES is an assistant professor in the Don Wright Faculty of Music and the Faculty of Information and Media Studies at the University of Western Ontario. Her essays on gender and popular music are published in several anthologies and journals. She is currently writing for Duke University Press a cultural history of popular music—from Elvis Presley to MTV—on American network television.

KAY DICKINSON lectures in the Media and Communications Department of Goldsmiths College, University of London. She has published on the interaction of music and the moving image and is the editor of *Movie Music, The Film Reader*, and (with Glyn Davis) *Teen TV: Genre, Consumption and Identity*. She is currently working on a manuscript titled *Off Key: Film, Music and the Politics of the Mismatch*.

CYNTHIA FUCHS is the director of George Mason University's film and media studies program, as well as one of the film-TV-DVD editors for PopMatters .com and film reviewer for *Common Sense Media* and *Philadelphia Citypaper*. She has published essays on hip hop, Prince, Michael Jackson, the Spice Girls, queer punks, *Taxi Driver, Bully,* and *George Washington*, and media coverage of the war against Iraq. She is the editor of *Spike Lee: Interviews* and coeditor of *Between the Sheets, In the Streets: Queer, Lesbian, and Gay Documentary*. She has a forthcoming book on Eminem, as well as essays on *Buffy*, Shakira, Brad Pitt, and Gollum.

PHILIP HAYWARD is a research team leader in the Department of Contemporary Music Studies at Macquarie University in Sydney, and the network convenor of the Small Island Cultures Research Initiative. He is currently researching the nature and operation of the Melanesian Music Industries.

AMY HERZOG is an assistant professor of media studies at Queens College, City University of New York, where she teaches courses on film, critical theory, and popular music. She has contributed to an edited volume on film adaptations of Carmen, as well as a forthcoming collection on Deleuze and cinema. Her current research explores the intersections of Deleuzian philosophy and questions of temporality, history, and embodiment in musical film.

ANTTI-VILLE KÄRJÄ works currently as a lecturer in musicology at the University of Turku in Finland. For his 2005 doctoral degree at the University of Helsinki he analyzed the relationship between national identity and popular musical performances in the feature films made in Finland between 1957 and 1966. His research interests include the relationship between music and audiovisual media, especially Finnish music videos, popular music historiography, and music and cultural theory.

MELISSA MCCARTNEY graduated with degrees in film studies and English from the University of California, Santa Barbara. She currently works as a freelance writer for the American Association of Zookeepers.

JASON MIDDLETON is a visiting assistant professor of film and media studies in the English Department at the University of Rochester. He has published essays on film, television, and popular music in collections from Duke University Press and in journals including *The Velvet Light Trap* and *Popular Music*. For *Polygraph: An International Journal of Culture and Politics* he has edited and coedited two special issues: "Margins of Global Culture" and "Film and Postmodern Theory." He is completing a book titled *Documentary/Genre*, on the intersections of documentary film with narrative fiction genres, including comedy, horror, and pornography. He is also an award-winning experimental filmmaker.

LISA PARKS is an associate professor of film and media studies at the University of California, Santa Barbara. She is the author of *Cultures in Orbit: Satellites and the Televisual* (published by Duke University Press) and coeditor of *Planet TV: A Global Television Studies Reader*. She has published essays in numerous books and in journals such as *Screen*, *Television and New Media*, *Convergence*, *Ecumene*, and *Social Identities*. Currently she is working on a new book called *Mixed Signals: Media Technologies and Cultural Geography*.

KIP PEGLEY is an associate professor of music at Queen's University in Kingston, Ontario. Her book *Coming to You Wherever You Are: MuchMusic, MTV and the*

Construction of Youth Identities is forthcoming. Her most recent work explores nationhood, gender, and race in post-9/11 mass-mediated benefit concerts.

MAUREEN TURIM is a professor of English and film studies at the University of Florida. She is author of *Abstraction in Avant-Garde Films, Flashbacks in Film: Memory and History*, and *The Films of Oshima Nagisa: Images of a Japanese Iconoclast*. She has also published over eighty essays in anthologies and journals on a wide range of theoretical, historical, and aesthetic issues in cinema and video, art, cultural studies, feminist and psychoanalytic theory, and comparative literature. Her new book project, *Desire and Its Ends: The Driving Forces of Recent Cinema, Literature, and Art*, examines the different ways that desire structures narratives and images in various cultural traditions, and the way that our very notion of desire may be shaped by these representations.

CAROL VERNALLIS is an associate professor in the Media Arts and Studies Division of the Department of Communication at Wayne State University, where she teaches film and video theory and production. Her first book is titled *Experiencing Music Video: Aesthetics and Cultural Context*, and her forthcoming book, *The Art and Industry of Music Video: Conversations and Essays*, contains interviews with music video directors, musicians, and others in the industry, as well as an account of the production, postproduction, and distribution of music videos. Her essays on music video have appeared in *Screen, American Music, Popular Music*, and *The Journal of Popular Music Studies*. She is also a videomaker whose works have been screened at festivals in the United States and in Europe.

WARREN ZANES is a vice president at the Rock and Roll Hall of Fame and Museum and a visiting professor at Case Western Reserve University. He is the author of *Dusty in Memphis* and has just released his second solo recording, *People That I'm Wrong For*, on Dualtone.

189–90, music video production in, 174–76; popular culture exportation and, 194; popular music in, 184–86, 190

Freed, Alan, 238–39, 244

French Kiss, 204

Frith, Simon, 183, 188, 276–77, 284

Froos, Sylvia: "The Wise Old Owl," 38

Fuentes, Diego, 213–14

Fugees, the: "Ready or Not," 320

Galama, Ronnie: *Goruna*, 163–66; *Rinunu*, 161–66; *Uana*, 164. *See also* Tilly, Titus

Gaye, Marvin: "I Heard It Through the Grapevine," 61

Gee, Anne, 162

Gender, 226–29, 232–36, 243, 246

Gillett, Charlie, 226

Goffman, Erving, 214

Gogol Bordello, 85–86

Gondry, Michel, 105–6. *See also* Bjork

Goodwin, Andrew, 1, 13–15, 18–19, 60–61, 81, 180–82, 208, 210, 277, 323 n.10

Gorbman, Claudia, 39

Gore, Lesley: "Wonder Boy," 50

Gould, Jack, 237–38

Greenberg, Clement, 270, 277, 280–83

Grossberg, Lawrence, 5, 276

Guattari, Félix, 18–19

Guralnick, Peter, 245

Hall, Stuart, 177, 179, 189

Hanke, Robert, 191–92

Havana Black: "East Is Red," 182–83

Hawaii: cultural expression and, 261; tourism and, 253, 260–61; United States and, 254, 262

Hawaiian music: as commodity, 261; hapa haole, 252–54; history and traditions of, 252–54, 260

Heiniö, Mikko, 178, 184

Henriksson, Juha, 190

HIM, 175, 189; "Pretending," 176

Hip hop: auteurism and, 316; authenticity and, 295, 301; commodification of, 298–99; identity and, 294–98; music video style, 320, neighborhood and, 293, 299–300; pastiche and, 316–17, 320; performance and, 292; politics and, 298–300; postmodern theory and, 319

"Hits, The," 87

Ho, Don: "Tiny Bubbles," 252

Höch, Hannah, 92

Homoeroticism, 50

Horn, Bob, 240

Hornblower, Nathaniel. *See* Beastie Boys; Yauch, Adam

Houston, Whitney: "I Will Always Love You," 310

Hunter, Paul, 316, 326 n.34

Incubus: "Drive," 100

Innis, Harold, 221–22

Internet, the, 3, 88, 270

Intonation theory, 184

Ishioka, Eiko, 107

Iskelmä, 183, 187–88

Jackson, Janet: "Anytime, Anyplace," 117, 138

Jackson, Michael: "Man in the Mirror," 60; "Thriller," 121

Jalkanen, Pekka, 184–85, 193

Jameson, Fredric, 84, 88, 305–6, 313–15, 322

Jarmusch, Jim, 104

Jay-Z, 290–301; *Black Album*, 296–97; "Can I Get a . . . ," 293–94; "Change Clothes," 297–98; "Dirt Off Your Shoulder," 298–99; "Do It Again," 293–94; "Encore," 297; "Hard Knock Life," 292–93; "Moment of Clarity," 296–97; "Nigga What, Nigga Who," 293; "99 Problems," 291–92, 299–301; "Public Service Announcement," 296; "So Ghetto," 296; "There's Been a Murder," 295

Jones, Spike: "Clink! Clink! Another Drink," 35–36

Jonze, Spike, 89, 98, 106, 308–10, 317–19. *See also* Beastie Boys; Beck; Bjork; Daft Punk; Elastica; Fatboy Slim; Notorious B.I.G.; Weezer

Jukebox films: audience and, 52–54, 36–37; as camp, 44–45, 51; literal representation and, 40–42; music industry and, 47–49; race and, 34–35; sexuality and, 49–51; television and, 43–44, 47

Jyrki, 174–75, 194

Kalinak, Kathryn, 65
Kallioniemi, Kari, 177, 190, 192
Kandinsky, Wassily, 282
Kansa, Tapani: "Salaisuudessain," 186
Kaplan, E. Ann, 4, 6, 13, 111
Kärki, Toivo, 190
Kid Rock: "American Badass," 131
Kirk, Richard H. *See* Cabaret Voltaire
Kelly, R., 295; "Down Low," 139
Kelly, Robin, 294
Klee, Paul, 105
Kleiler, David, 88–89
Kukkonen, Risto, 190
Kuleshov, Lev, 130

Lambert, Mary, 88
Langer, John, 210–11
Lansing, Joi: "Web of Love," 51
Lilliestam, Lars, 178, 182
Live Aid, 262–64
Lordi: "Would You Love a Monster-man?" 188
Lynch, Joan, 93

Madonna: "Frozen," 99; "Material Girl," 88; "Take a Bow," 118–19, 138. *See also* Cunningham, Chris
Maea, Hollie: *Kerama*, 159–60. *See also* Tilly, Titus
Mäkelä, Janne, 185–86, 188, 194
Manson, Marilyn: "Tourniquet," 94

Marcus, Greil, 90, 277
Marshall, David, 215
Martin, Lionel C. 316
Masculinity, 226–27, 232, 234, 243, 247
Mase: "Feels So Good," 317
Mattila, Anne: "Valokuva," 188
McCarthy, Anna, 43–44
McCloud, Scott, 129
McLean, Albert F., Jr., 230
Mercer, Johnny: "The Biggest Aspidistra in the World," 38
Merchant, Natalie: "Wonder," 138
Meyrowitz, Joshua, 214–15
Middleton, Richard, 142
Miller, Jody, "The Race Is On," 44
Mills Brothers, "Paper Doll," 40–42
Mimesis, 281–82
Modern art, 279–84
Modernist aestheticism, 276–87
Mondino, Jean Baptiste, 107. *See also* Bjork
Monster Magnet: "Space Lord," 317
Morissette, Alanis: "You Oughta Know," 123–24
Moses, Robert, 88–89
MTV, 1–3, 8; African Americans and, 21; alternative music and, 312, 315; auteurism and, 307–10; Canada and, 200; celebrities and, 208, 215–17; commercials, 219–20; controversy and, 291; globalization and, 192, 265; hierarchical structures of, 214–15, 222; household flow and, 205–9; influence of, 190–91; media bias and, 221–22; music video directors and, 304, 307–8; pastiche and, 308–10, 312; postmodernism and, 307; programming on, 203–5; repertoire and, 212, 217–19; viewing community of, 201–2, 205, 217; VJs, 211–17
MTV2, 1–2, 87–88
Much Music, 2, 174; celebrities and, 208, 215–17; hierarchical structures

and, 214–15, 222; household flow
and, 205–9; media bias and, 222;
programming on, 204–5; repertoire
and, 217–19; station commercials,
219–20; viewing community, 201–2,
205, 217; VJs, 212–17
Muller, Sophie, 89, 106. *See also* Bjork
Murakami, Takashi, 84–85
Musical Festival 70, 256–57
Music video, 1–3; advertising and,
274–76; appropriation and, 88–89;
alternative music and, 76, 89; audience and, 53–54, 165–66; auteurist
medium as, 286, 303; avant-garde
and, 85–86, 89; characters in, 120,
138–44; commodity as 25–26, 92–93;
319; country music and, 323 n.13,
326 n.28; cultural identity and, 155,
159–60, 186–88; Dada and, 90–93;
editing and, 125–36; genre and,
88–89, 166–68, 183, 188, 321–22;
hip hop and, 292–93, 316, 320–22;
historical transformations of, 154,
307–8; human body and, 15, 16, 23–
24, 27, 98–100, 133, 140; lyrics and,
60–65, 69–70, 76–80, 124; mass culture and, 275, 285; meaning and, 75–
76, 79, 129–31; narrative and, 76–80,
89, 113–24; objects in, 136–38; performance art and, 100–102; Russian film and, 130–31; scholarship,
3–6, 32; sexuality and, 25, 49–50, 87,
96–97; sound-image relationships
and, 30–33, 36–41, 60–66, 70–79,
131–35; surrealism and, 93–102, 106;
synaesthesia and, 14–27, 180–82,
186; the underground and, 270–76,
285–86

Naremore, James, 137
Nightwish: "Over the Hills and Far
Away," 186–87
Nine Inch Nails: "Closer," 138, 311, 321.
See also Romanek, Mark

Nirvana: "Smells Like Teen Spirit,"
140, 310–11
"No Mo Po Mo, Or: I Had a Dream"
(Zeidner), 95
"Notes on Camp" (Sontag), 44–45
Notorious B.I.G.: "Hypnotize," 320;
"Sky's the Limit," 317. *See also*
Jonze, Spike
Nylon Beat: "Syytön," 186

Oramo, Ilkka, 178
O-Shen, 170–71
"Over the Rainbow," 74–75

Panoram Soundie, 31–42
Pan Sonic, 192
Papua New Guinea: dance, 162; impact
of television in, 152–54; influence of
Polynesian music in, 169–71; influence of Western popular music in,
152, 156; music industry in, 154–55,
171; music video production in,
155–59, 167–68; traditional music
of, 156–57, 160
Parker, Colonel Tom, 246–47
Pastiche: alternative music and, 311–
12, auteurism and, 312–15; cultural
politics and, 321–22; defined, 84,
305; film and, 305–6; hip hop and,
316–22; MTV and, 308–10, 312, 315
Payola, 244
Pearl Jam: "Jeremy," 310
Pellington, Mark, 310
Permian Strata (Conner), 62–66
Petty, Tom, and the Heartbreak-
ers: "Don't Come Around Here
No More," 96; "Mary Jane's Last
Dance," 97; "Runnin Down a
Dream," 97
Philpott, Malcolm, 153–54
Photography, 283
Pietiläinen, Tommi, 194
Pink Floyd: "Brain Damage," 69;
"Breathe," 80; *Dark Side of the Moon*,

Pink Floyd (*continued*)
66, 74; "Great Gig in the Sky, The,"
70–73, 75; "Money," 73–75
Plato, 281–82
Polynesian music, 169–71
Popular Music: authenticity and, 273–
79, 284–85; avant-garde and, 83–86;
industry, 269–72, 287; modernist
aestheticism and, 276–86; race and,
20; romanticism in, 277–79, 286–87;
youth and, 245
Postmodernism: auteurism and, 304–
6, 313–14; cultural politics and, 321–
23; genre and, 88, hip hop and, 319;
MTV and, 307; surrealism and, 95
Presley, Elvis, 226, 229, 231–32, 236–
38, 246–47, American nationalism
and, 259–60; Hawaii and, 252–58,
261–62
Prodigy: "Smack My Bitch Up," 116–
17, 291
Puff Daddy, "Been Around the World,"
320
Punk, 90–91, 272–73, 277–78, 285

Queen, "Bohemian Rhapsody," 157

Race: jukebox films and, 34–35; popu-
lar music and, 20; rock and roll
and, 235, 243; television and, 20–21,
239–40, 243
Radiohead, 86, 92–93; "Karma Police,"
77–78, 80
Rage Against the Machine: "Bulls on
Parade," 122–23
R.E.M.: "Everybody Hurts," 309
Replacements, the, 273–74, 285
Rhymes, Busta: "Dangerous," 326 n.35;
"Gimme Some Mo," 21–25; "Woo Ha
(Got You All In Check)," 316, 319.
See also Williams, Hype
Ricour, Paul, 17–18
Riffaterre, Michael, 182
Rock and Roll: authenticity and, 243,
284; consumerism and, 235–36, 242;

criticism and scholarship, 226, 234;
gender and, 226–28, 232–34, 236,
243, 246–47; mass culture and, 226,
243–47; music industry and, 245;
race and, 235, 243; television and,
226–29, 231–40; youth and, 234–37,
245–47
Romanek, Mark, 310–11. *See also* Nine
Inch Nails
Rorty, Richard, 17
Ruoska, 189
Ruuska, Petri, 177–78

Salmi, Hannu, 177, 190, 192
Sanguma, 156
Scopitone, 31–33, 44–53
Scott, Jake, 309
Shaviro, Steven, 107
Shumway, David, 227
Sigismondi, Floria, 94, 100, 107
Siikala, Anna-Leena, 177–78
Sinclair, Charlie, 238–39
Smashing Pumpkins: "Tonight, To-
night," 88, 311, 321. *See also* Dayton,
Jonathan; Faris, Valerie
Smith, Jeff, 61, 63, 65
Sontag, Susan: "Notes on Camp,"
44–45
Starr, Kay: "Wheel of Fortune," 49–50
Stein, Jeff, 96
Street, John, 176
Sullivan, Ed, 230–32, 235, 246
Surrealism, 93–106
Stieglitz, Alfred, 282–83
Stone Temple Pilots: "Big Bang Baby,"
308
Suburban Legend (Becker), 66–67
Sullivan, Nancy, 154
Synaesthesia, 14–16, 181–82, 186;
African American performers and,
21, 23–24; capitalism and, 25–26;
defined, 14–15; 180–81, metaphor,
and 16–19, 26–27
Synchronicity, 68, 78–79, 80–81, 158

ROGER BEEBE is an associate professor of film and media studies in the English Department at the University of Florida.

JASON MIDDLETON is a visiting assistant professor of film and media studies in the English Department at the University of Rochester.

Library of Congress Cataloging-in-Publication Data

Beebe, Roger, 1971–
Medium cool : music videos from soundies to cellphones / Roger Beebe and Jason Middleton, editors.
p. cm.
Includes bibliographical references and index.
ISBN-13: 978-0-8223-4139-0 (cloth : alk. paper)
ISBN-13: 978-0-8223-4162-8 (pbk. : alk. paper)
1. Music videos—History and criticism. I. Middleton, Jason, 1971- II. Title.
PN1992.8.M87B44 2007
780.26´7—dc22   2007009341